Fusion of Multimodal Generative AI and Blockchain Technology in Digital Media

G. Revathy
SASTRA University, India

Arul Kumar Natarajan
Samarkand International University of Technology, Uzbekistan

Naresh Kshetri
Rochester Institute of Technology, USA

IGI Global
Scientific Publishing
Publishing Tomorrow's Research Today

Vice President of Editorial	Melissa Wagner
Director of Acquisitions	Mikaela Felty
Director of Book Development	Jocelynn Hessler
Production Manager	Mike Brehm
Cover Design	Jose Rosado

Published in the United States of America by
IGI Global Scientific Publishing
701 East Chocolate Avenue
Hershey, PA, 17033, USA
Tel: 717-533-8845 | Fax: 717-533-7115
Website: https://www.igi-global.com E-mail: cust@igi-global.com

Library of Congress Cataloging-in-Publication Data

LCCN: 2025002904 (CIP Data Pending)
ISBN13: 9798337315041
Isbn13Softcover: 9798337315058
EISBN13: 9798337315065
British Cataloguing in Publication Data
A Cataloguing in Publication record for this book is available from the British Library.

Table of Contents

Chapter 12

Detailed Table of Contents

Chapter 1
Synergizing Multimodal Generative AI and Blockchain for the Future of
Digital Media 1
    S. Aarthi, Marwadi University, Rajkot, India
    R. N. Ravikumar, Marwadi University, Rajkot, India
    Jamshid Pardaev, Termez University of Economics and Service, Termez,
        Uzbekistan

Blockchain technology combined with multimodal generative AI revolutionizes content creation, distribution, and authentication. AI generates synthetic content across platforms (text, visuals, audio, and video), while blockchain ensures data authenticity with decentralized trust-based platforms. Blockchain secures digital assets through attribution tracing, preventing misuse and fostering trust. This synergy addresses issues like intellectual property challenges, deepfakes, and content integrity. The chapter explores practical implementations in entertainment, journalism, gaming, advertising, and social media, offering future trend forecasts and technical analysis. Ethical principles and regulatory frameworks promote transparent, accountable systems for managing AI-generated content. This work serves as a guide for specialists, policymakers, and industry professionals in creating decentralized, trustworthy digital environments.

Chapter 2
Charting the Course: Addressing Open Problems in AI and Blockchain
Synergy for Media 35
    Kiran Sree Pokkuluri, Shri Vishnu Engineering College for Women,
        India
    A. Chandrasekar, Nandha College of Technology, India
    Kumar M. Santhosh, Nandha College of Technology, India
    Aravindh Saivaraju, Vel Tech Rangarajan Dr. Sagunthala R&D Institute
        of Science and Technology, India

Blockchain technology and artificial intelligence (AI) are set to transform digital media by providing previously unheard-of possibilities for content production, distribution, and monetization. Nevertheless, there are a number of intricate difficulties and unsolved problems associated with combining these two revolutionary technologies. The outstanding issues at the nexus of blockchain and artificial intelligence in the context of digital media are examined in this chapter. Scalability, interoperability, data protection, and ethical considerations are top priorities. Through tackling these issues, the chapter hopes to offer a research and development roadmap for the future, guaranteeing that the blockchain and AI synergy can be fully utilized to build a digital media environment that is more transparent, safe, and egalitarian. In order to demonstrate prospective solutions and breakthroughs, practical use cases and new trends are also covered.

Chapter 3

Balusamy Nachiappan, Prologis, USA
N. Rajkumar, Alliance School of Advanced Computing, Alliance University, India
V. Radha, V.S.B. College of Engineering Technical Campus, India
C. Kalpana, Karpagam Institute of Technology, India
C. Viji, Alliance School of Advanced Computing, Alliance University, India
G. Nagarajan, Saveetha School of Engineering, India
A. Mohanraj, Sri Eshwar College of Engineering, India

The convergence of generative synthetic intelligence (AI) and blockchain technology marks a transformative step within the evolution of decentralized and realistic systems. Generative AI, with its capacity to create modern-day content material, models, and simulations, complements blockchain's inherent strengths in ensuring transparency, safety, and decentralization. This paper proposes a conceptual framework for integrating those ground-breaking eras, aiming to address key demanding conditions, including data authenticity, possession rights, and operational performance. The framework leverages blockchain's allocated ledger to soundly keep and verify AI-generated outputs, ensuring traceability and tamper resistance. Clever contracts function a middleman to automate tactics that encompass royalty control for AI-generated intellectual property and verification of model outputs.

Chapter 4

Mary R. Asha, Adhi College of Engineering and Technology, India
G. Sivakumar, Erode Sengunthar Engineering College, India
B. Mullaikodi, C.K. College of Engineering and Technology
A. Manchula, Nandha Engineering College, India

The combination of Generative AI with Blockchain technology offers a paradigm change in the digital media world, where intelligence meets trust. This chapter digs into the theoretical foundations of this convergence, giving a thorough examination of how the combination of these two disruptive technologies tackles important issues in content authenticity, ownership, and security. A new paradigm for the development, validation, and distribution of digital media assets arises from combining the creative power of Generative AI with the immutable trust of Blockchain. The chapter delves into key theoretical approaches, such as the use of decentralized ledgers to authenticate AI-generated content, smart contracts for licensing and royalty management, and the integration of NFTs (Non-Fungible Tokens) as proof of ownership for AI-generated digital assets.

Chapter 5

    C. Nithiya, Adhi College of Engineering and Technology, India
    G. Revathy, SASTRA University, India
    R. Menaha, KPR Institute of Engineering and Technology, India
    S. Prabhu, Nandha Engineering College, India

The combination of blockchain technology and multimodal generative AI is changing the face of digital media production. This chapter presents a revolutionary decentralized framework for digital media production that combines the security, transparency, and immutability of blockchain with the creative powers of multimodal generative AI. The suggested framework tackles critical issues with content authenticity, copyright protection, and data privacy, allowing creators to retain ownership and control over their digital assets. Blockchain smart contracts provide transparent licensing, royalty distribution, and media asset tracing. Meanwhile, multimodal generative AI allows for the creation of high-quality media material in a variety of formats, including text, photos, video, and audio.

Chapter 6

    G. Revathy, SASTRA University, India
    T. Jayapratha, Sri Eshwar College of Engineering, India
    Albert Paulin Michael R., Erode Sengunthar Engineering College, India
    Santhosh Kumar M., Nandha Engineering College, India

The chapter introduces and discusses the use of Multimodal Generative AI as a tool and its potential application setting the sphere of media production and consumption. The recent leap in technological capabilities and widespread deployment of these has resulted in a tsunami of media content proliferation allowing multiple ways in which media could be produced; however, the highlight of this chapter is to review and discuss the impact and endorsement of Multimodal Generative AI to content creation, critically reviewing the use of text, images, audio, and specifically, video content forms, allowing the audience to gain maximum understanding and a multidimensional view on the subject matter. In essence, this chapter imagines the future with Multimodal Generative AI on a chart demonstrating how the media will be created, consumed, and most importantly, enabled to be created.

Chapter 7

>   *G. Maragatham, SRM Institute of Science and Technology,*
>   *Kattankulathur, India*
>   *Nilay Kumar, SRM Institute of Science and Technology, Kattankulathur,*
>   *India*
>   *Priyansh Bhandari, SRM Institute of Science and Technology,*
>   *Kattankulathur, India*
>   *Vinston Raja, SRM Institute of Science and Technology, Kattankulathur,*
>   *India*
>   *Robinson Joel M, KCG College of Technology, India*

While text-to-image synthesis extends to dynamic visual contents, text-to-video synthesis creates coherent videos from the provided text-based description. A technique of this nature can make a revolutionary impact on industries such as education, accessibility, marketing, and entertainment. However, the T2V technique comes with a set of challenges that pertain to temporal coherence, exact alignment between text and video, high computational demands, and limited high-quality datasets. This survey summarizes the latest developments in T2V technologies, beginning with early adaptations of text-to-image models and progressing to recent studies involving large-scale pre-training integrated with diffusion methods. The chapter then provides a comprehensive comparison of these models based on their performance metrics against benchmarking datasets, examining the strengths and limitations of each, along with practical applications.

Chapter 8

>   *Arockia Raj Y., PSNA College of Engineering and Technology, Dindigul,*
>   *India*
>   *K. Vijay, Rajalakshmi Engineering College, Chennai, India*
>   *Eugene Berna, Bannari Amman Institute of Technology, Erode, India*
>   *Prithi Samuel, Department of Computational Intelligence, School of*
>   *Computing, SRM Institute of Science and Technology, India*

Generative artificial intelligence (AI) technologies are fundamentally transforming the visual media landscape and automating the production of human-like images, videos, and animations. The key elements of this creation are transformer-based models, Variational AutoEncoders (VAEs), and Generative Adversarial Networks (GANs). This chapter will look at how they function, what they can be used for, and how they affect education, entertainment, and advertising. By looking closely at these methods, the chapter emphasizes both the good things that generative AI does to improve the quality and speed of content creation and the bad things that it causes in society and ethics, especially when it comes to authenticity and authorship. It also touches on the potential for misuse (think deepfakes) and discusses regulatory and ethical frameworks that would chain these technologies so that they can be used responsibly. The chapter ends with a future-oriented analysis of the emerging trends and challenges that will continue to impact the landscape of generative AI in visual media.

Chapter 9

 N. Rajkumar, Alliance School of Advanced Computing, Alliance
  University, India
 C. Viji, Alliance School of Advanced Computing, Alliance University,
  India
 Balusamy Nachiappan, Prologis, USA
 A. Mohanraj, Sri Eshwar College of Engineering, India
 G. Nagarajan, Saveetha School of Engineering, India
 Jayavadivel Ravi, Presidency University, India
 Prabhu Shankar B., Vel Tech Rangarajan Dr. Sagunthala R&D Institute
  of Science and Technology, India

Generative Artificial Intelligence (AI) is revolutionizing the virtual media panorama by means of manner of allowing the advent of surprisingly practical and modern virtual content. Leveraging deep studying models like Generative Adverse Networks (GANs), Variational Autoencoders (VAEs), and diffusion models, generative AI helps the producing of images, motion pics, and animations that rival human creativity in each exceptional and detail. This technology is not simply reshaping inventive expression but also redefining industries which include leisure, marketing, education, and gaming. In photo era, generative AI has accomplished top notch milestones, from synthesizing hyper-sensible pix to growing surreal, innovative landscapes. Those fashions are knowledgeable on massive datasets, getting to know how to replicate styles and textures with extraordinary precision. Packages include virtual attempt-ons in style, more CGI effects in movies, or even growing digital twins for architectural visualizations.

R. Roselinkiruba, Independent Researcher, India
M. Vasumathy, Kingston Engineering College, India
J. Jude Moses Anto Devakanth J., Madanapalle Institute of Technology
    and Science, India
Saranya Jothi C., Vel Tech Rangarajan Dr. Sagunthala R&D Institute of
    Science and Technology, India
L. Sharmila, Vel Tech Rangarajan Dr. Sagunthala R&D Institute of
    Science and Technology, India

Text and language processing have been transformed by generative AI, opening the door to sophisticated digital media applications including sentiment analysis, translation, content creation, and summarization. Despite improvements, there are still many issues with current models, such as inadequate glyph management, inability to adapt to different fonts and scripts, inconsistent semantics, and high processing requirements. These drawbacks make it difficult to use them practically in situations where accurate, context-aware text rendering is necessary. By combining Glyph Conditional Control and T5, this work presents GlyphControl-T5, a novel hybrid model that improves font consistency, multi-language adaptation, and visual-text coherence. To overcome the fundamental drawbacks of current visual text generation models, the suggested method combines multi-modal embeddings, glyph-aware visual restrictions, and an efficient learning framework.

R. Balaji, K.S. Rangasamy College of Technology, India
R. Karthik, K.S. Rangasamy College of Technology, India
A. Kiran, K.S. Rangasamy College of Technology, India
Obuli Prasad J., K.S. Rangasamy College of Technology, India

Covert Timing Channels (CTCs), which exploit transmission delays to steal private data, are increasingly dangerous on digital platforms. Traditional detection methods often lack flexibility and harm service quality. This study introduces CryptoSleuthNet, a novel framework combining Multimodal Generative AI with Blockchain to detect CTCs without disrupting normal traffic. By transforming network traffic into artificial visual data, the method enables intuitive detection. Neural networks, Naive Bayes, and Elliptic Curve Cryptography (ECC) classifiers analyze these datasets, with ECC achieving the highest accuracy (80%). Blockchain smart contracts boost forensic reliability and transparency by ensuring tamper-proof tracking and verified message validity. This hybrid approach enhances detection, traceability, and trust—critical in combating data exfiltration and deepfakes. By merging AI and decentralized security, CryptoSleuthNet marks a major advance in safeguarding media integrity and detecting hidden threats in dynamic, content-rich ecosystems.

Chapter 12
P. Umamaheswari, SASTRA University, India

Cryptocurrency, a digital form of currency, functions as an alternative payment method employing encryption algorithms. Despite its potential, the cryptocurrency market is characterized by high volatility and intricate datasets, featuring complex interactions between predictors. Conventional techniques may struggle to achieve optimal results in such a challenging environment. Predicting prices accurately is crucial to making the most money on bitcoin investments. For short-term trading and investing techniques, it is essential to identify both positive and negative market movements. The knowledge gathered from these assessments will provide practitioners with a better grasp of the obstacles facing the cryptocurrency market as well as workable solutions to reduce risks. The dataset, which was acquired from Yahoo Finance, contains daily information including the highest and lowest prices in addition to opening and closing prices. The main objective is to estimate the price of Bitcoin and deep learning algorithms are essential to forecasting these prices in the context of smart cities.

Preface

The digital media landscape is experiencing a profound transformation, driven by the convergence of Multimodal Generative Artificial Intelligence (AI) and Block-chain Technology. Multimodal Generative AI is unlocking unprecedented creative capabilities, enabling machines to generate human-like content across text, images, audio, and video. In parallel, Blockchain Technology provides the trust, transparency, and security that digital ecosystems demand. Together, these two technologies are redefining how content is created, authenticated, distributed, and monetized.

As editors, we envisioned this book as a comprehensive exploration of how the fusion of these technologies will shape the next era of digital media. Multimodal Generative AI is accelerating creative workflows and democratizing media production, but it also raises challenges related to content authenticity, intellectual property, and the proliferation of deepfakes. Blockchain offers a compelling counterbalance by providing immutable proof of origin, decentralized content ownership, and mechanisms for fair revenue distribution. The synergy between these technologies not only mitigates existing challenges but also unlocks new opportunities for innovation, efficiency, and ethical media practices.

This book is structured to serve as both a foundational resource and a forward-looking guide. It bridges theoretical insights with practical applications, spanning fundamental principles, emerging frameworks, real-world use cases, and policy implications. Readers will gain an understanding of how generative AI can create dynamic, multimodal content while blockchain safeguards authenticity and facilitates equitable monetization. By highlighting research challenges, open questions, and future trends, this volume also provides a roadmap for scholars, industry practitioners, and policymakers to navigate the evolving digital media ecosystem responsibly.

CHAPTER OVERVIEWS

Chapter 1: Synergizing Multimodal Generative AI and Blockchain for the Future of Digital Media

The opening chapter explores how the convergence of multimodal generative AI and blockchain is reshaping digital media creation, distribution, and authentication. It examines how AI's ability to generate text, visual, audio, and video content synergizes with blockchain's decentralized, tamper-proof infrastructure to address content authenticity, intellectual property protection, and deepfake mitigation. Through practical examples in entertainment, journalism, gaming, advertising, and social media, the chapter illuminates the transformative potential of this fusion while emphasizing the ethical and regulatory frameworks necessary for a transparent and accountable media ecosystem.

Chapter 2: Charting the Course – Addressing Open Problems in AI and Blockchain Synergy for Media

This chapter identifies the critical challenges that must be resolved to fully realize the potential of AI and blockchain integration in digital media. Issues such as scalability, interoperability, data privacy, and ethical considerations are examined in detail. By mapping these open problems and exploring prospective solutions, the chapter lays the foundation for a research and development roadmap, guiding scholars and practitioners toward creating a transparent, secure, and equitable digital media environment.

Chapter 3: Fusion of Generative AI and Blockchain – Conceptual Framework

In this chapter, the authors present a conceptual framework for uniting the creative capacity of generative AI with the trust and transparency of blockchain technology. By leveraging blockchain's distributed ledger to verify and store AI-generated content and employing smart contracts to automate tasks such as royalty distribution and ownership validation, the framework offers a structured approach to content traceability, tamper resistance, and intellectual property management. This chapter serves as a theoretical and practical blueprint for integrating these disruptive technologies into cohesive systems.

Chapter 4: The Convergence of Intelligence and Trust – Theoretical Approaches to Generative AI and Blockchain

Chapter 4 delves into the theoretical underpinnings of AI-blockchain convergence, framing it as the intersection of intelligence and trust in digital media. The discussion highlights how decentralized ledgers authenticate AI-generated outputs, how smart contracts streamline licensing and revenue processes, and how NFTs can represent proof of ownership for AI-generated assets. This chapter positions the theoretical constructs as a new paradigm for content creation, verification, and distribution in a secure, trustworthy digital ecosystem.

Chapter 5: Decentralized Digital Media Generation – A Blockchain-Based Multimodal Generative AI Framework

Here, the focus shifts to a practical decentralized framework for media creation that combines blockchain's immutability with the creative flexibility of multimodal generative AI. The framework enables content creators to retain ownership and control of their work while ensuring transparent licensing, automated royalty management, and real-time asset tracing through blockchain smart contracts. This chapter demonstrates how multimodal AI can generate rich media—including text, images, audio, and video—within a secure and privacy-preserving architecture.

Chapter 6: Creating Without Limits – Multimodal Generative AI in Digital Media

Chapter 6 showcases the transformative creative potential of multimodal generative AI in content production. It critically examines how text, image, audio, and video synthesis are enabling unprecedented forms of storytelling and engagement, while also highlighting the societal and cultural shifts that accompany this media proliferation. By envisioning the future of content creation, this chapter invites readers to explore how generative AI will influence the ways media is produced, consumed, and experienced.

Chapter 7: Bridging Text and Video Generation – A Survey

This chapter surveys the rapidly evolving field of text-to-video (T2V) generation, which extends the capabilities of text-to-image models into dynamic, coherent video synthesis. It discusses the technical hurdles of achieving temporal coherence, semantic alignment, and computational efficiency, alongside the scarcity of high-quality datasets. The survey compares state-of-the-art models and highlights applications in education, accessibility, marketing, and entertainment, illustrating the significant impact of T2V on the future of digital storytelling.

Chapter 8: Generative AI in Visual Media for Image, Video, and Animation Generation

Chapter 8 explores how generative AI, powered by GANs, VAEs, and transformer-based models, is revolutionizing visual media production. The chapter examines the benefits of accelerating high-quality content creation for industries such as education, entertainment, and advertising, while also acknowledging the ethical risks associated with deepfakes and misattributed authorship. Regulatory frameworks and responsible practices are discussed alongside an analysis of emerging trends that will shape the visual media landscape.

Chapter 9: Generative AI in Virtual Media – Image, Video, and Animation Generation

Expanding on visual generation, this chapter examines the creation of hyper-realistic virtual content using generative AI and deep learning models, including GANs and diffusion techniques. It highlights breakthroughs in image synthesis, innovative applications in gaming, fashion, and film, and the development of digital twins for immersive experiences. By demonstrating how AI-powered virtual media is reshaping creative industries, this chapter underscores both the creative opportunities and the operational challenges in deploying such technologies.

Chapter 10: Generative AI in Text and Multilanguage Adaptation Processing for Digital Media

Chapter 10 addresses the role of generative AI in text and language processing for multilingual and context-aware digital media. The discussion introduces GlyphControl-T5, a novel approach that enhances font consistency, semantic accuracy, and visual-text coherence. By combining multimodal embeddings and glyph-aware constraints, this chapter advances solutions to the longstanding challenges of rendering adaptive, high-quality text for global digital media applications.

Chapter 11: SnapCatch – A Blockchain-Integrated Multimodal Generative AI Framework for Covert Timing Channel Detection in Digital Media

This chapter introduces an innovative security application where multimodal generative AI and blockchain collaborate to detect covert timing channels (CTCs) that exploit network delays for data exfiltration. By transforming network traffic into visualized data for AI-driven detection and reinforcing traceability with blockchain smart contracts, the framework—CryptoSleuthNet—enhances media integrity, forensic reliability, and system transparency. This hybrid approach represents a significant advancement in combating hidden threats and maintaining trust in digital ecosystems.

Chapter 12: Blockchain-Enhanced Future Unlocking – Leveraging Deep Learning for Predicting Cryptocurrency Prices for Digital Media

The final chapter shifts focus to the intersection of blockchain, AI, and financial analytics in the digital media economy. It explores the use of deep learning to fore-cast volatile cryptocurrency prices, leveraging blockchain-based datasets to inform smarter decision-making for media transactions and investments. By providing insights into predictive modeling and market behavior, the chapter illuminates how blockchain and AI-driven analytics can support emerging digital economies and smart media ecosystems.

Our target audience includes researchers, engineers, digital media professionals, entrepreneurs, and regulators. For scholars and students, the book presents cutting-edge insights into the interdisciplinary fusion of AI and blockchain. For developers and creators, it offers frameworks and case studies to guide the integration of these technologies into real-world solutions. For policymakers, it highlights the ethical and legal considerations that must guide responsible innovation.

We would like to acknowledge the contributions of all the authors and reviewers who have brought their expertise and vision to this work. Their chapters offer a multidimensional perspective on the opportunities, challenges, and transformative potential of combining multimodal generative AI with blockchain. It is our hope that this book not only informs but also inspires new research, applications, and innovations in the digital media domain.

As the boundaries of media creation and verification continue to blur, we believe this fusion of technologies will define the future of secure, creative, and equitable digital ecosystems.

Chapter 1
Synergizing Multimodal Generative AI and Blockchain for the Future of Digital Media

S. Aarthi
https://orcid.org/0009-0006-9064-2091
Marwadi University, Rajkot, India

R. N. Ravikumar
https://orcid.org/0009-0009-3705-1681
Marwadi University, Rajkot, India

Jamshid Pardaev
Termez University of Economics and Service, Termez, Uzbekistan

ABSTRACT

Blockchain technology combined with multimodal generative AI revolutionizes content creation, distribution, and authentication. AI generates synthetic content across platforms (text, visuals, audio, and video), while blockchain ensures data authenticity with decentralized trust-based platforms. Blockchain secures digital assets through attribution tracing, preventing misuse and fostering trust. This synergy addresses issues like intellectual property challenges, deepfakes, and content integrity. The chapter explores practical implementations in entertainment, journalism, gaming, advertising, and social media, offering future trend forecasts and technical analysis. Ethical principles and regulatory frameworks promote transparent, ac-

DOI: 10.4018/979-8-3373-1504-1.ch001

countable systems for managing AI-generated content. This work serves as a guide for specialists, policymakers, and industry professionals in creating decentralized, trustworthy digital environments.

1. INTRODUCTION

Digital media patterns experience fundamental transformations through the joint operation of Generative Artificial Intelligence (AI) with Blockchain as major innovative technologies. Multimodal Generative AI systems create content through excellent automated results which include personalized creative elements because they integrate text image video and audio information. Through decentralized management Blockchain operates an exceptional framework that protects digital ownership rights then verifies online transactions and establishes verified digital proof of property ownership (Ahmed et al., 2024). Future digital media systems can emerge from technology unities that produce the evaluation results featured in this essay. Generative AI's quick content generation produces three significant issues related to fake content creation and copyright infringement and deepfake distribution and ethical use. The open designation system of Blockchain permits users to verify product authenticity through smart contracts along with NFTs that track creators automatically while controlling right management.

The second part of the document examines dual capabilities before providing operational approaches to deploy these capacities across domains that assess understanding gaps. Through targeted examples the article illustrates how system convergence leads to both IP protection as well as enhanced audience trust. Educational framework development and governmental industrial approaches will incorporate ethical factors and regulatory limitations during their analytical stages in the future. Multimodal Generative AI systems that combine with Blockchain technology generate highly protective systems which stop digital duplication to build secure digital frameworks for media content.

1.1 Overview of Digital Media Evolution

The creation of interactive digital media content from human social interactions over the past decades resulted in information system advancement (Chauhan, 2025). Basic viewer features characterized early digital platforms since such platforms lacked online user interaction capabilities. People modified their online behaviour by using real-time messaging and different media features leading to explosive growth of YouTube Instagram and TikTok platforms during Web 2.0. Every smartphone user now has unrestricted access to create content thanks to cloud-based services which gained possibility due to smartphone technology and fast internet speeds.

Modern communication methods continue to evolve because artificial intelligence functions through immersive technology systems during this era. Modern technology utilizes artificial intelligence to generate music and videos and automatic robotic construction of figures from component parts leads to visual artworks. Safety risks cannot be introduced to original content generation unless the new content development standards pass authenticity evaluations. Deepfakes along with unrestricted visuals and false information lead to digital media loss of trustworthiness through breakdowns in security systems (Mala, 2023). Modern intelligent systems with protective transparency enable innovation tasks to succeed by ensuring trust security during their execution.

1.2 Convergence of Multimodal AI and Blockchain for Secure Digital Media

Multimodal Generative AI systems produce vast superhuman quantities of content through their simultaneous production of text accompanied by multiple sensory output including images and videos and sounds in a rapid manner. Users doubt the rapid capability of Generative AI technologies to generate realistic content because it creates issues pertaining to copyright violations and spreading deceptive information. The platform deploys blockchain technology to manage distributed records which get validated by digital interaction logs for creating permanent data registries as well as tracking audit histories. The unified technology systems create an entire system without any weakness that existed in either solution independently. With blockchain technology users gain visibility into original content sources as well as developer identities through automatic payment and right management systems implemented through NFT-based smart contracts(Pasupuleti, 2025a). The permanent technological structure of blockchain that integrates with smart contracts and NFTs enhances creator conditions and creates better trust between users for meeting ethical developmental needs. AI-generated content systems include detection features that permit users to track ethical tracking procedures for determining content material origins.

1.3 Objective of the Chapter

The primary objective of this chapter is to explore the convergence of Multimodal Generative Artificial Intelligence (AI) and Blockchain Technology in transforming the digital media landscape. It aims to provide a comprehensive understanding of how these two disruptive technologies complement each other in enhancing content authenticity, ownership verification, secure distribution, and intelligent automation (Singh et al., 2025). The chapter systematically examines the core technologies, architectural frameworks, key models, and real-world applications that demonstrate the synergy between AI and Blockchain in domains such as art, music, journalism, healthcare, and social media.

- Analyze the technical foundations and methods behind multimodal generative AI and blockchain integration.
- Identify case studies and platforms that exemplify practical implementation.
- Highlight the societal, ethical, and legal implications, including issues related to deepfakes, misinformation, intellectual property, and data privacy.
- Present economic trends, funding growth, and sector-wise adoption insights from 2018 to 2025.
- Offer a forward-looking perspective on the future potential and challenges, including regulatory frameworks, standardization efforts, and open research areas.

Through this analysis, the chapter aims to guide researchers, technologists, and policymakers in understanding the opportunities and considerations involved in deploying secure, trustworthy, and creative AI-Blockchain ecosystems.

2. CORE TECHNOLOGIES

System changes initiatives require main components from Multimodal Generative AI technology combined with Blockchain technology. Multimodal Generative AI uses GANs Transformers together with VAEs to produce content that combines input from text-based and image and video and audio elements. The integration of multiple media platforms in a modal system allows content creation of cohesive systems which leads to innovative CUSTOMIZED digital encounters for customers (Baltrusaitis et al., 2019). Security comes from distributed blockchain technology through its secured information storage methods which also protects complete data with transparent record systems combined with trust-based protocols blocks in the blockchain system perform automated transaction recording while smart contracts operated by software codes execute on its network Ownership transactions of digital assets utilize Non-Fungible Token implementations for security. The entire lifecycle of AI content management operations features complete authentication verification due to multiple advanced technology applications. Through this integration the system solves major challenges related to digital media verification and intellectual property security together with modern content management needs of media systems. The below Fig.1 illustrates the hierarchical relationship between key emerging technologies. Core Technologies drive innovation through Multimodal Generative AI, which further integrates with Blockchain Technology to ensure secure and verifiable digital content creation.

Figure 1. Core Technologies for the Future of Digital Media

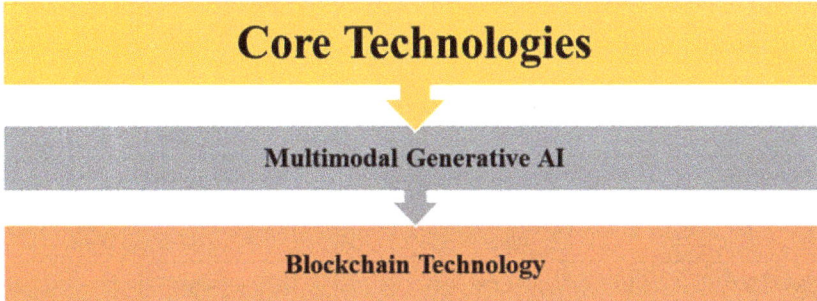

2.1 Multimodal Generative AI: Definitions, Methods, and Key Models

Multimodal Generative AI involves solutions that combine several forms of data i.e., text, images, audio, video into one common framework to support better analysis and generation of content. These systems provide more human-like, natural results than unimodal data-based systems do, because these multimodal systems involve the simultaneous processing of many different modalities. This provides application breakthroughs in areas such as creative media generation, smart assistants and virtualized narratives (Buldas et al., 2022). These systems have different forms of functionality. The generation of Text is mainly motivated by model types that include GPT, T5, and ChatGPT that are able to provide coherent and contextual answers in terms of dialogue production and factual scripts. Image Generation is based on the descriptions using the terminology of DALL·E and Stable Diffusion to turn written descriptions into a realistic picture. Video Generation applies such tools as Sora and Runway ML to generate brief videos, adhering to the directions given by the user. In the case of Audio/Speech Generation, such models as VALL-E and Tacotron convert written text into Amazon, Google or Apple text-to-speech (text-to-speech) outputs that sound natural. The most prominent ones are CLIP (OpenAI) which combines image and text understanding; DALL·E, capable of text-to-image generation; Whisper, capable of precise voice-to-text transcription; Flamingo and GPT-4-Vision capable of advanced reasoning over both image and text inputs. All these models enable the user to author dynamic and multimodal content in creative, educational, and commercial applications (Huang et al., 2025). The below table 1 table contrasts features, input types, output quality, and application domains between unimodal and multimodal generative AI models. It will help readers visualize the advantages of multimodal integration in creative content generation.

Table 1. Capabilities of Unimodal vs. Multimodal AI Systems

Feature	Unimodal AI	Multimodal AI
Input Types	Single modality (e.g., only text, only image)	Multiple modalities (e.g., text + image + audio + video)
Output Diversity	Limited to the input modality	Rich, diverse, and integrated outputs
Understanding Context	Contextually limited to a single source	Broader contextual understanding from cross-modal inputs
Examples of Models	GPT (text), Tacotron (speech), StyleGAN (images)	GPT-4-Vision, Flamingo, DALL·E + Whisper
Output Quality	Accurate within one modality	Coherent and realistic across multiple modalities
Application Domains	Text generation, speech synthesis, image creation	Virtual assistants, media creation, education, entertainment
Interactivity	Basic response generation	Enhanced interaction with context-aware responses
Creative Use Cases	Automated captioning, voiceover generation	AI storytelling, immersive content creation, digital art

Figure 2. Functional Flow of Multimodal Generative AI

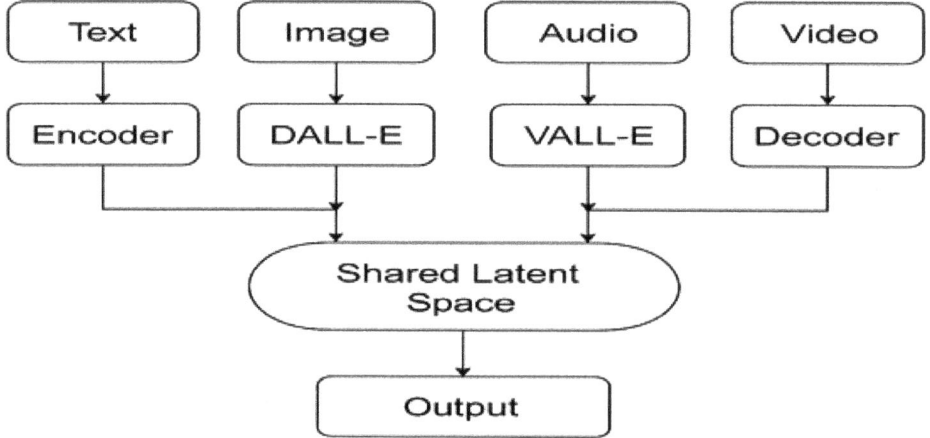

The Fig.2 Illustrates the processing flow of multimodal inputs (Text, Image, Audio, Video) through AI models like GPT, DALL·E, VALL-E, and Sora, leading to content generation outputs. Each input type flows into its respective encoder/decoder module, showing how they converge in a shared latent space for cross-modal synthesis.

2.2 Blockchain Technology

Block chain is a decentralized digital platform where data exchanges happen safely, transparently and immutably on a distributed network of computers. It introduces strong data integrity by merging decentralization concepts with cryptographic techniques and removes the necessity of centralized management (Aarthi et al., 2025). Blockchain offers the possibility to the user of securing data distribution without the need to use intermediaries and also validate transactions. Other main elements are blocks where the information is stored and where smart contracts are performed which entail an automatic code with which to enforce rules with regard to the agreed terms (Judge et al., 2024). This guarantees automation and trust among the parties without the external party. Non-Fungible Tokens (NFTs) are the other vital aspect of the issue since they grant special digital identification to the items that ensure their authenticity and tracking in the blockchain. Besides, Decentralized Identity (DID) systems provide users with privacy and safety authentication and identity management.

Blockchain would also allow the licensing regulations and distribution channels to be tracked, so creators and developers could establish open revenue-sharing policies. Such records, which cannot be tampered with, can come in handy to establish the authenticity of the content produced by the AI and its ownership (Xu et al., 2023). Paired with Multimodal Generative AI, blockchain will increase the authenticity of the content and trust in the platform. Such convergence is heralding reliable, verifiable, and ethical digital content ecologies that will witness huge adoption in years to come. The Below Table 2 Lists core components such as Smart Contracts, NFTs, Data Immutability, and Decentralized Identity, along with their functions and use cases in securing digital content, rights, and identity verification.

7

Table 2. Key Blockchain Features and Their Applications in Digital Media

Blockchain Feature	Function	Application in Digital Media
Smart Contracts	Self-executing code that automates agreements	Automates licensing, royalty distribution, and access control for digital content
Non-Fungible Tokens (NFTs)	Assigns unique identifiers to digital assets	Proves ownership of AI-generated media, ensures authenticity, and facilitates resale royalties
Data Immutability	Ensures stored records cannot be altered or deleted	Preserve content origin, edit history, and timestamp logs for trust and transparency
Decentralized Identity (DID)	Provides user-managed identity verification	Enables creators to maintain control over credentials and protect personal identity from misuse
Distributed Ledger	Transparent, tamper-proof record of transactions	Enables public verification of content origin, rights transfers, and usage conditions
Tokenization	Converts rights or assets into digital tokens	Facilitates fractional ownership, monetization, and micro-payments in creative economies

2.3 Blockchain Foundations in Digital Media Ecosystems

Blockchain is a distributed and decentralized ledger where the data is stored in a secure manner on many different nodes in the network, such that information stored on Blockchain is supposed to be immutably valid. Once a transaction is confirmed and entered into the block chain record, it becomes an inseparable element of the fixed record and becomes secured using the cryptographic validation which cannot be modified or challenged (Jose Diaz Rivera et al., 2024). A smart contract as one of its most active features runs automatically according to established conditions without human intervention. This qualifies it as the perfect financing in digital media, where payments and royalty can be made automatically. Non-Fungible Tokens (NFTs) are the other important use case that creates verifiable ownership of digital property, including AI-generated works, music, and art.

NFTs also enable clear and open transactions by people who can freely transact in rights, whilst safeguarding intellectual rights against digital pirating and stealing. The impossibility to corrupt data certifies the integrity of all the saved information, which means that blockchain is a reliable base to give content authentication (Wang et al., 2025). Also, Decentralized Identity (DID) systems give users a chance to control their digital identities and instead of having a central authority, the user keeps credentials, reputations, under their control. With the growing need of digital media to have the security of individual content verification and the clear rights management, blockchain is becoming the much needed and indispensable technology to address the demands of contemporary content eco-systems in terms of its operational, ethics, and trust requirements. The below Fig.3 highlights five essential components of blockchain technology: Basics, Smart Contracts, NFTs, Data Immutability, and Decentralized Identity. These elements collectively ensure secure, transparent, and decentralized digital operations.

Figure 3. Core Technologies of Blockchain

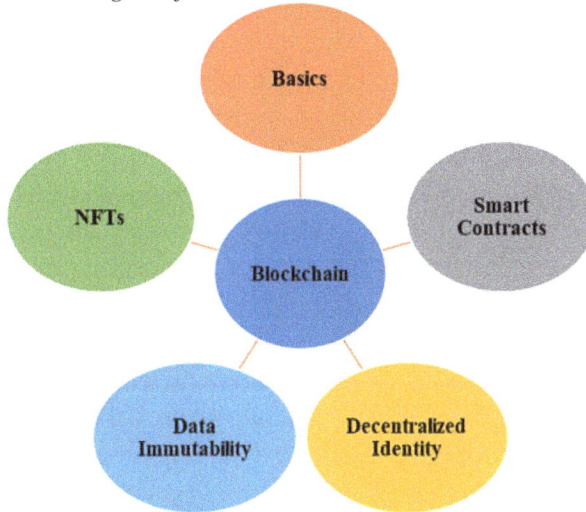

3. INTEGRATION FRAMEWORK FOR SYNERGIZING MULTIMODAL GENERATIVE AI AND BLOCKCHAIN

Implementation of Multimodal Generative AI technology and Blockchain technology form the essentials needed for system change initiatives. Multimodal Generative AI uses GANs Transformers together with VAEs to produce content that combines input from text-based and image and video and audio elements. Customers can experience innovative customized digital engagements through content that integrates multiple media elements coherently into a unified platform when a modal system includes various media platforms (Jose Diaz Rivera et al., 2024). Security comes from distributed blockchain technology through its secured information storage methods which also protects complete data with transparent record systems combined with trust-based protocols. Blocks in the blockchain system perform automated transaction recording while smart contracts operated by software codes execute on its network Ownership transactions of digital assets utilize Non-Fungible Token implementations for security. The entire lifecycle of AI content management operations features complete authentication verification due to multiple advanced technology applications (Xu et al., 2023). Through this integration the system solves major challenges related to digital media verification and intellectual property security together with modern content management needs of media systems.

3.1 Architecture for Combining AI with Blockchain

An advanced system emerges from the union between blockchain and AI which integrates AI computational power with both blockchain cryptographic framework and distributed network features. This combined system fixes data verification and reliability problems and provides speed-based analytics by operating between health-care facilities and financial institutions as well as supply chain networks. Standard technical systems are designed in five major operational layers, which complete secure and intelligent architecture. The building block at the bottom is the Data Layer and this retrieves information collected by IoT devices, medical sensors and transactional data records (Zhuk, 2025). The integrity of data in blockchain design allows no tampering, and smart contracts apply secure data access procedures and verification. Above it is the Blockchain Layer that performs the transactions in a secure and distributed cryptographical manner. This is the transparent data layer that allows regulation of access, either in the partition mode (permissioned) or the broadcast mode (public), depending on privacy needs of the operation.

The AI Processing Layer involves machine learning, deep learning models to analyze data stored in blockchain. These models do predictive analytics and anomaly detection, creating actionable insight. The blockchain system is positioned between the AI system and an Integration Layer that ensures the whole process is mediated by APIs and middleware platforms. It builds a smooth communication and interoperability layer that assists in solving the problems of scalability and latency by moving heavy calculations (Echenim, 2025). The Application Layer is on the top, and it is where end-users will interact with decentralized healthcare systems and other systems incorporating AI. The last layer combines the approved blockchain infrastructure and AI-enabled analytics to enable a real-time decision-making process. Together these layers create a trust-based ecosystem, which integrates data security and smart automation around the contemporary digital functionality. The below table 3 Describes each of the five layers (Data, Blockchain, AI Processing, Integration, and Application) with their roles, components, and inter-layer communication. This table aids understanding of the system framework.

Table 3. Layered Architecture of AI and Blockchain Integration

Layer	Role	Key Components	Inter-Layer Communication
Data Layer	Collects raw input data from physical and digital sources	IoT devices, medical sensors, transaction logs	Supplies raw data to Blockchain and AI Processing Layers
Blockchain Layer	Securely records and verifies transactions and data with immutability	Distributed ledger, smart contracts, consensus algorithms	Receives data from the Data Layer and logs model usage and content
AI Processing Layer	Analyzes, predicts, and detects anomalies in data	Machine learning models, deep learning algorithms	Accesses verified data from Blockchain Layer for analytics
Integration Layer	Bridges communication between AI and Blockchain systems	APIs, middleware platforms, external computational support	Ensures interoperability and offloads complex computations
Application Layer	Provides the user interface and operational environment	Decentralized apps (DApps), dashboards, content platforms	Connects users to backend operations and visualizes system outcomes

Figure 4. Layered Integration Architecture of AI and Blockchain

The above Fig. 4 Visualizes the five operational layers Data, Blockchain, AI Processing, Integration, and Application. Shows data flow between layers, where each layer contributes specific functionality (e.g., data collection, secure transactions, analytics, interoperability, and user interface).

3.2 Authenticating AI-Generated Content

Delivery of technical authentication tools enables digital media industries and education sectors and journalism and creative industries to build trust through the disclosure of transparency measures during AI content expansion processes (Gitobu & Ogetonto, 2025). Users require authentication mechanisms to track content sources together with details about its original information origins. Traditionally verifying AI system outputs needs developers to embed digital watermarks inside the system along with metadata tagging. AI system markers perform operations by preserving the confidentiality of AI model sources along with timestamp information and ownership documentation. OpenAI works jointly with developer organizations to create detection methods for their products which enables users to obtain their content without restrictions. Blockchain authentication systems establish better security by using their distributed tracking system which records all production steps and creates unerasable documentation for distribution operations (Mandych et al., 2023). Blockchains carry out automatic documentation through the processes of recording both model parameters and user-derived procedures for approved AI models. The system implements security features that establish secure documentation approaches and protects information integrity simultaneously.

AI content detectors use visualization together with language analytical algorithms to differentiate between content created by humans and content created by AI through their analytical method. Continuous operation of AI content detection systems improves security system reliability regardless of the unattainable goal to protect data. Before authorizing proper ethical conduct, the program authentication systems should verify user privacy needs. Every written guideline must contain specifications for mandatory data elements along with authorization procedures that enable user access (Omowole et al., 2022). ESI output authentication functions as a dual mechanism to protect intellectual property assets while fighting counterfeit content at the same time while AI trust from users keeps increasing. Watermarking technologies linked with blockchain detection systems enable the development of a protection system that manages current security risks.

4. ADDRESSING KEY CHALLENGES

Generative AI systems combined with blockchain technology solve several complex digital media problems that stand in the way of their achievement. AI content generation systems encounter major obstacles when trying to function on blockchain networks due to their decentralized operation model. Integration of blockchain protocols with text combined with image and video and audio media demands major financial investment alongside very complex technological implementation. The utilization of blockchain methods to deal with AI-generated content faces daunting technical challenges that aim to defend sensitive information as well as intellectual property in decentralized framework environments (Pasupuleti, 2025b). The continuous growth of large multimedia data entering sharing platforms creates performance issues for blockchain systems related to network speed and processing speed which can be resolved through collaboration between blockchain developers and AI and governmental personnel. The Below Fig.5 highlights key roles of AI and blockchain in digital content protection. It focuses on combating deepfakes, securing ownership, and ensuring transparent licensing and control.

Figure 5. Key Challenges

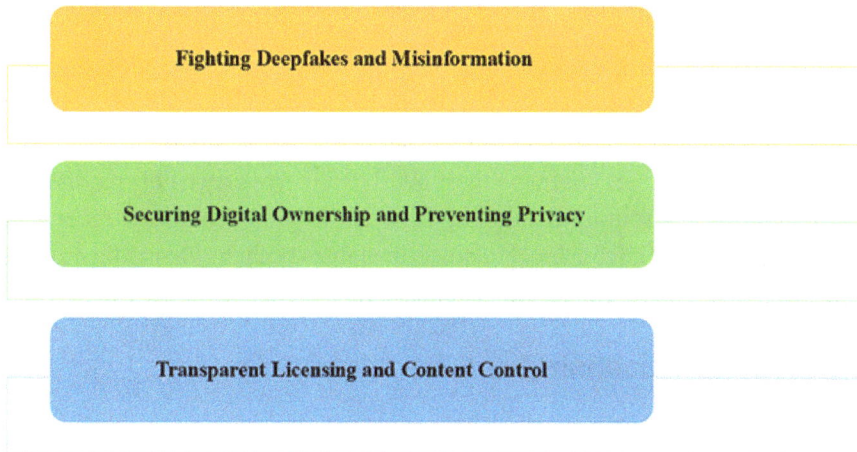

Fighting Deepfakes and Misinformation

Securing Digital Ownership and Preventing Privacy

Transparent Licensing and Content Control

4.1 Fighting Deepfakes and Misinformation

The current generation of artificial intelligence technology grants deepfakes and false information the power to establish critical threats against digital media trustworthiness. Blockchain technology enables permanent unalterable information storage of content generation metadata and update history records through its design structure. The implementation of digital media content on blockchains includes videos images as well as texts which build tamper-resistant authentication records and modification verification capabilities (Prajapati, 2025). The blockchain verification system gives users clear capabilities to identify artificial media modifications and view source information authenticity. Blockchains function as a decentralized operating system that protects unverified content from censorship through valid public documentation of credible information. Artificial Intelligence media assessment working with standards built in Blockchain verification provides a winning approach to safeguard digital platforms from deep counterfeits through giving users proof of input origin at every content development and manipulation phase.

4.2 Securing Digital Ownership and Preventing Piracy

The combined methods of intellectual property defense and digital asset ownership operate as fundamental principles which control modern AI-based generative systems when users share content on the web. Digital ownership acquisition receives benefits from blockchain technology because decentralized journal systems enable original content authentication. Each digital asset receives a specific digital token from the blockchain system to verify ownership rights according to the network. The blockchain system ensures copyright protection by implementing two protected features that allow secure rights transfers and protection mechanisms. Blockchain system benefits users because it reveals content origins hence users can find unauthorized copies with enhanced effectiveness (Sağlam & Kirçova, 2025). When creators enable their smart contracts their intellectual property rights payments automatically proceed through licensing agreements. Digital economies receive their main operational benefit from blockchain as it enables both digital media protection and transparent payment transparency for all stakeholders.

4.3 Transparent Licensing and Content Control

Digital media endures its most crucial challenge due to the complex procedures implemented by existing licensing control systems. Decentralized systems resolve licensing agreement management through blockchain technology by creating transparent management solutions. The enhanced completion of blockchain technology smart contracts enables IT media to activate automatic access or use conditions. The removal of intermediaries from blockchain operations decreases both errors in interpretation and protects against fraudulent activities. Through its open operating system blockchain establishes unchanging viewing permissions and continuous licensing principles that members of content creation systems can access automatically (Bakan & Atabey, 2024). The system implements real-time operational framework to assist creators in their content-sharing agreement verification and their usage statistical tracking for monetization needs. Blockchain payment systems let users receive appropriate payoffs after fulfilling license terms regardless of the digital content distribution environment.

5. APPLICATIONS & CASE STUDIES

Through the fusion of blockchain technology with multimodal generative AI systems businesses now have access to new commercial options that transform digital media management processes. The entertainment industry obtains personalized multimedia entertainment solutions through generative AI strategies handled by blockchain operating systems that manage right ownership. The blockchain music platform Audius serves as an outstanding example since it provides right management tools for creators and AI engineering to enhance content discovery and creation. Users can establish ownership of digital assets and game-specific items by converting them into NFTs both through Enjin and decentralization technology-based platforms (Picha Edwardsson & Al-Saqaf, 2024). Artificial Intelligence systems use it to create virtual environments that modify their content after users interact with them. Organizations in news media use blockchain technologies to determine the source of AI-generated content while reducing false information dissemination. Publishers obtain protection on Poet's blockchain platform because this platform includes timestamping features that enable precise content editing tracking during distribution and stop modifications. Multiple examples demonstrate how AI functions with blockchain to develop secure data frameworks which additionally allow artists to work together on digital content releases within a completely transparent environment. The table 4 Summarizes examples like Audius, Enjin, Po.et, SuperRare, Truepic, and Steemit. The table should list the platform name, domain (e.g., music, journalism), use of AI, use of blockchain, and benefit provided to users or creators.

Table 4. Use Cases of Multimodal AI and Blockchain Integration

Platform	Domain	Use of AI	Use of Blockchain	Key Benefits
Audius	Music	AI for music discovery and recommendation	Blockchain for rights management and transparent royalty tracking	Artists retain ownership and earn revenue directly from listeners
Enjin	Gaming	AI-generated virtual assets and behavior models	NFTs for in-game item ownership and exchange	Gamers can securely own, trade, and monetize unique digital items
Po.et	Publishing	AI for content analysis and categorization	Blockchain for timestamping and content authorship tracking	Ensures authenticity and protects against unauthorized content modifications
SuperRare	Digital Art	AI-assisted generative artwork creation	NFTs to validate and sell digital art	Verifies authenticity and facilitates resale royalties to original creators
Truepic	Visual Media	AI for image verification and manipulation detection	Blockchain for storing immutable metadata and content provenance	Verifies truthfulness of images and videos for legal and media purposes
Steemit	Social media	AI for content personalization and spam filtering	Blockchain for rewarding creators via cryptocurrency	Enables direct monetization of content without ad-based revenue systems

Figure 6. Sector-wise Adoption of AI + Blockchain Solutions

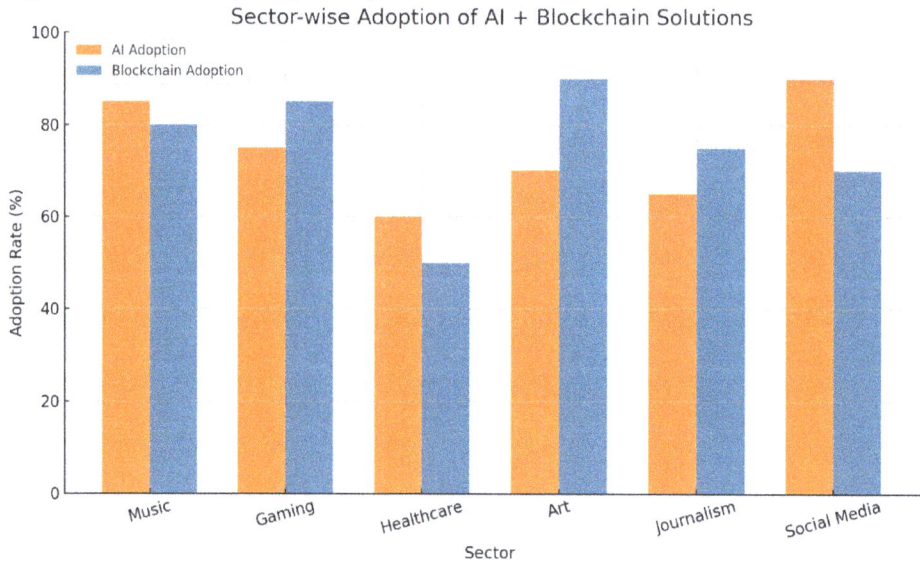

The above Fig.6 showing how sectors like Music, Gaming, Healthcare, Art, Journalism, and social media are adopting integrated AI and Blockchain solutions. Each bar group represents a sector, with two bars per group: one for AI use and one for Blockchain use (percentage scale or adoption index).

Figure 7. Adoption Rate of AI and Blockchain Technologies Across Industries

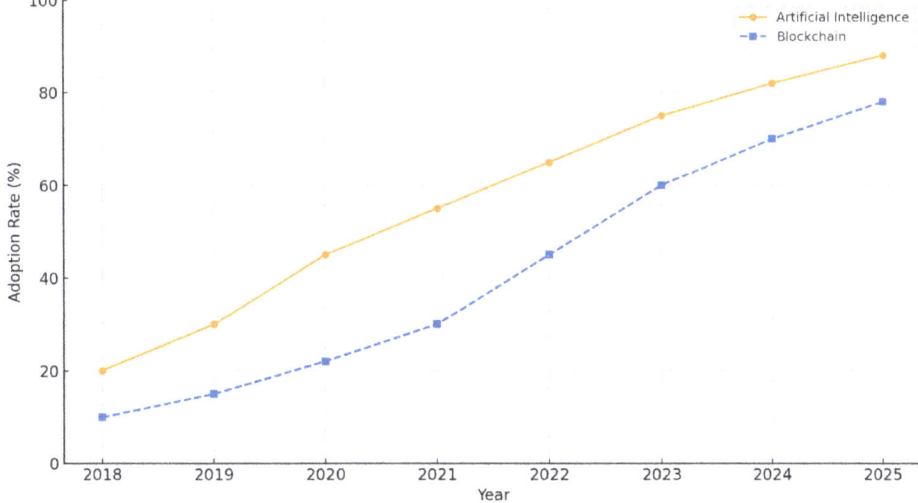

Adoption Rate of AI and Blockchain Technologies Across Industries (2018–2025)

The above Fig.7 demonstrates AI's early lead in adoption and Blockchain's increasing adoption trend, visually highlighting the convergence of both technologies in industry-wide use cases.

5.1 AI Art and NFTs

Artificial Intelligence (AI) and Non-Fungible Tokens (NFTs) combination has redesigned the digital art environment, creating new approaches to creating, owning, and benefiting. The creation of AI art uses such generative models as GANs (Generative Adversarial networks) and diffusion models to create original visual content that can sound extremely close to the human imagination. After being generated and created, such digital artworks can be minted into the blockchain ecosystem via the NFT format wherein it can support artists to mark verified ownership and originality of their works. NFTs give a decentralized and tamper proof metadata storage that guarantees the provenance of AI generated artworks. NFT marketplaces such as SuperRare and Art Blocks have established themselves as dominant open markets where AI-generated work can be auctioned at a transparent price and have resale royalties (Kalra et al., 2023). Smart contracts are beneficial to artists, as they automatically divide the earnings and do not require the participation of intermediaries: secondary sales will continue to bring artists revenue. In addition to being a commercial concept, AI art and NFTs raise the question of authorship and creativity, the philosophical and legal concerns of whether machine-aided definition of intellectual property is intellectually created. However, this paradigm shift democratizes the global art markets so that digital artists and developers can share their innovations, but retain control. The AI and NFT combo, therefore, reinvents the digital age of art creation, appreciation and ownership.

5.2 Verified Synthetic Media (Voice, Video)

The authentication process of blockchain verification platforms solves both scenarios and faulty information distribution networks for AI-generated voice and video content. The integration of blockchain technology generates tracker IDs which contain the complete creator record of synthetic media files. Users gain access to authenticate content through blockchain verification because it enables them to check metadata stored under blockchain to validate document provenance (Mukhopadhyay, 2025). Deep Trace works together with Truepic to use blockchain authentication which enables users to distinguish between authentic digital files and modified versions. Media authenticity in entertainment sectors and legal organizations works best when AI-generated realistic media combines with blockchain tracking. Synthetic media verification allows creative industries to discover new creative possibilities while defending their content integrity through trusts established with users.

5.3 Blockchain-Based Creative Platforms and Journalism Tools

Blockchain technology merged with digital creative media journalism tools serves as a basis to set content worth during its complete journey from origin to user reception. A digital platform uses smart contracts as a protection system to stop intellectual property theft of creators and generates financial benefits for their content (Pasupuleti, 2025c). The Steemit blockchain software enables writers and content creators to obtain cryptocurrency payments because its funding system develops beyond simple advertising since the system evolves better revenue methods through its blockchain software. The tracking visibility of content distribution is possible through Blockchain technology because the system keeps track of each step along the delivery route. News organizations use blockchain to verify authenticity by adding chronological dates which protect their content from modifications. Journalists can bookmark protected blockchain domains on Civil to safeguard their editorial functions while sharing original news content to their readers. The production of rapid market change applications by blockchain technology demonstrates its effectiveness in content creator impact advancement. The below Fig.8 This highlights real-world platforms leveraging Multimodal AI and Blockchain across various domains. It shows how AI-driven content generation pairs with blockchain-based security to ensure ownership, authenticity, and trust.

Figure 8. Real-World Case Studies of AI and Blockchain Integration

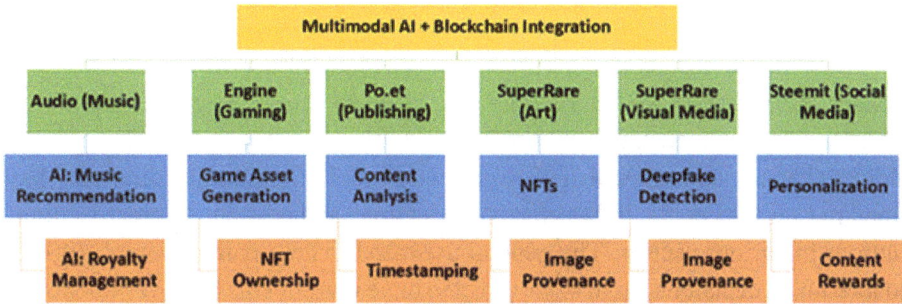

6. ETHICAL AND REGULATORY ASPECTS

To achieve effective ethical evaluations for deployment along with risk management of generative AI systems based on blockchain technology the government must establish official standards. The principal major topic of this paper focuses on intellectual property crime prevention. High-speed adoption of blockchain Ethereum-standard systems by content creators occurred due to their ability to track content and pay owners properly. Business solutions based on blockchain enable operational security by monitoring supply chain assets through AI-based text restructuring and replication management. System operations face two primary limitations due to data security weakness and privacy threats (Poposki, 2024). User data exposure became a new problem when blockchain visibility married with AI text creation while compromising privacy for users. AI systems running on blockchain infrastructure need proper regulations for personal data protection in line with GDPR because they face illegal data misuse challenges. Several human groups unite to contain AI-produced biased information from spreading further. New government regulations will create content monitoring systems to hold accountable the providers of dangerous misinformation originating from AI systems. The legal authority must authorize digital media ethical standards to establish technological deployment relationships with individual rights protection and social advantages.

6.1 Economic Implications and Funding Trends

Since 2018, there have been remarkable changes across the global economy in terms of increased investment to Artificial Intelligence (AI) and Blockchain technologies. The two spheres which were previously moving in parallel directions have gained m (Sardana et al., 2024)ore advances closer and envisioned creative digital solutions in various sectors. The general use of AI in automation, personalization, and intelligent decisions has always attracted huge investments by governments, big tech companies, and venture capitalists. Increasingly this has led to a significant upswing in research and product development as a result of the emergence of generative AI. Block chain which was initially related by cryptocurrencies has developed and has become an extensible technology that supports secure, decentralized transaction systems, identity management, and asset management. Between 2018 and 2025, investments in Blockchain technologies have recorded a sharp growth in the upward direction, particularly in the financial, healthcare, logistic and media areas. Its economic relevance has been strengthened by the need of transparent and tamper proof systems (Ahmed et al., 2024). The combination of AI and Blockchain has led to hybrid solutions such as AI-Base smart contracts, safe sharing of AI models and decentralized authentication of content. The integration has not merely brought in new flows of investment but has also promoted policy streamlining, incubator systems and an adoption at the enterprise level. Combined, AI and Blockchain are transforming digital economies and enabling scalable, secure and smart models of innovation.

Figure 9. Investment Growth in AI vs. Blockchain Technologies

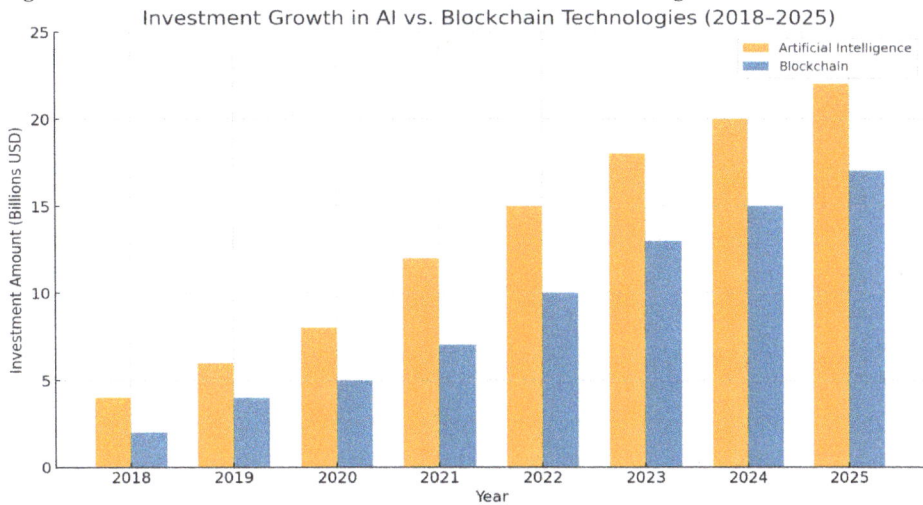

The above Fig.9 visualizes the comparative growth of global investments in AI and Blockchain technologies. It effectively supports discussion about the increasing relevance, investor confidence, and convergence potential of these technologies in shaping the digital ecosystem.

6.2 Bias, Misinformation, and Responsible AI

The automated content generation capability of producing false information arises because significant content errors emerge throughout its production process. User demographics experience stereotype spread due to discrimination in content generation processes which result from training logic applied to biased data. Users doubt the truth of digital information because deepfake content and artificial media from AI technology combine to produce misleading products for observers (Barati et al., 2020). For AI system operations developers must build obvious administrative systems which incorporate automatic quality evaluation tools and fair algorithm components. Schedule-based AI system reviews help create ethical content through bias reduction methods and implementation of multiple accountability standards. The blockchain authentication system provides extensive examination of AI-generated content to reveal origin materials and it fights deceptive news through complete accountability systems. The integration of expert artificial intelligence techniques with blockchain-transparency systems results in trust-based digital platform development.

6.3 Legal Implications (IP, GDPR)

Integration of multimodal generative AI systems with blockchain technology leads to modern legal challenges because the systems safeguard both data rights yet primarily focus on intellectual property protection (Gao et al., 2021). There is a need to create novel regulations that will guide current intellectual property law frameworks when AI systems produce digital content. AI content ownership remains undefined because it requires developers to unite process information with user and platform administrator systems for content creation (Eszteri, 2022). The storage operations and data utilization processes within AI-enabled blockchain systems have to fulfil all GDPR necessary requirements. During AI content development standards protection methods that use blockchain security protocols need to be deployed for controlling user permissions (Zhuk, 2025). Digital media protection standards need ethical and lawful operations that demand legal experts and regulators to generate appropriate defense according to technological advancements.

Figure 10. Legal and Ethical Workflow in AI-Blockchain Systems

Content Generation

Ownership Verification

Privacy Compliance (GDPR)

Privacy Compliance

Rights Registration

The fig. 10 Depicts a circular flow starting from Content Generation → Ownership Verification → Rights Registration (via Smart Contracts) → Privacy Compliance (GDPR) → Content Distribution → Auditing & Legal Accountability.

6.4 Governance through Blockchain Frameworks:

Through blockchain technology businesses access essential features that allow them to handle decentralized digital content while building transparent systems which depend on trust-based transparency and accountability. Blockchain framework systems allow users to develop transparent systems by adding user-defined rules for digital content management procedures. Business executives get automatic content licensing payments from blockchain smart contracts that also protect beneficiaries against unauthorized replications of content in the blockchain network. Blockchain protocols combine powerful source identification standards that combat abuse of content and suppress unauthorized material sharing (Fazi, 2022). The invulnerability of blockchain records allows outside organizations to verify them easily through the combination of AI systems and blockchain regulations. Governance operations based on blockchain technology guarantee both exemplary AI content authenticity and ethical business practices that establish trust between digital content users and commercial entities.

6.5 Societal and Ethical Impact

Between 2019 and 2025, Artificial intelligence and Blockchain technology convergences had a considerable impact on the social systems and ethics. Decentralized AI platforms have made it possible to help present more democratic content, creators, consumers, and gives them their autonomy, ownership, and data privacy because these platforms are transparent. This shift can be seen in such platforms as Audius, Steemit, and SuperRare as they all experienced significant growth in the user activity levels, which is a signal to higher state of trust of such ecosystems among the general population (Hasselgren et al., 2020). There are vital ethical aspects that have been brought into the fore by this change. AI-creations can become vexing when it comes to authenticity, deep fakes and deceitful information, blockchain plays an imperative role in confirming identity and guaranteeing accountability. Smart contracts give people an opportunity to monetize content fairly without relying on the centralized intermediaries, which promotes fair digital economies.

But this transformation is not devoid of problems. The issues of algorithmic bias; and uneven access to AI related innovations have also become increasingly critical concerns, as well as the complexity of managing digital identities in decentralized systems. Moreover, universal access to user generated information on different platforms requires the adherence to privacy laws such as GDPR. Ranging between 2019 and 2025, the technologies were shifted in terms of being experimental to one of critical infrastructure (Hofman et al., 2019). Socially it will have positive effects on the user agency, the freedom of expression, and the security of content, whereas ethically it provokes creating the ideals of transparency of structures, inclusion into actions, and practice of responsible deployment since everyone should benefit as the innovation progresses. The below fig.11 highlights the increasing public engagement with decentralized AI+Blockchain platforms over time, supporting arguments related to digital democratization, user growth, and trust in such systems.

Figure 11. User Engagement Trends on AI + Blockchain Platforms

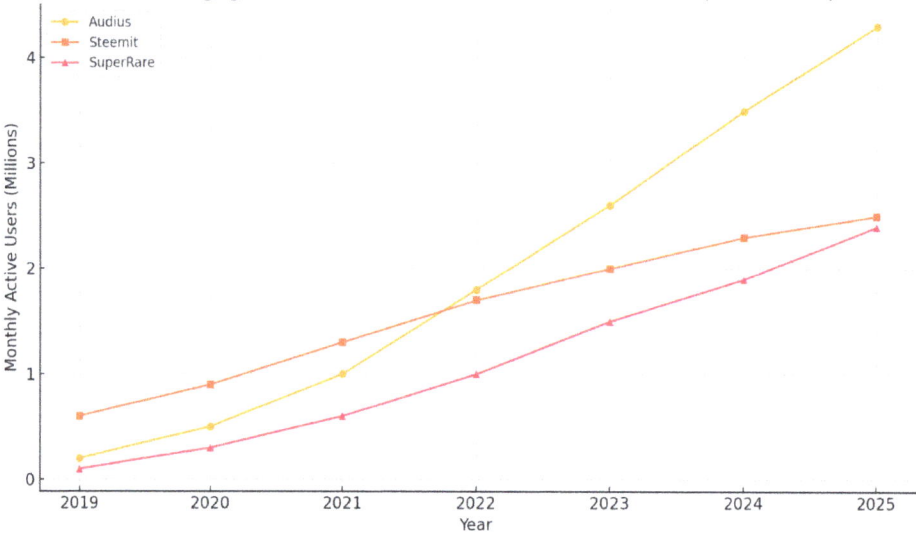

User Engagement Trends on AI + Blockchain Platforms (2019–2025)

7. FUTURE DIRECTIONS

Contemporary digital media systems developed using Genetic AI on block-chain create operational problems for future operations. The process of designing AI models demands the production of realistic content specially designed to fulfil users' requirements for visual and auditory elements and written material in specific situations. The innovation of new creative content by blockchain technology establishes two valuable features to protect copyrights and safeguard users from unauthorized activities. Integrated AI modules in Blockchains allow users to drive autonomous decentralization for their data management framework along with network functions and information governance (Kulothungan, 2025). The operations of blockchain systems implement delivery methods for content and IP protection features and payment functions within these frameworks at the same time as the creative capabilities improve thanks to content recommendations along with convenient discovery platforms AI provides for users. Through Blockchain technologies creators at any production level can establish independent international business connections without directorial involvement.

Standards organizations within the regulatory field must create operational standards for blockchain-AI frameworks that protect user privacy and maintain valid content with ethical standards. International standard development for artificial intelligence generated media will generate a single operational system that combines privacy standards with General Data Protection Regulation (GDPR) guidelines (Moerel, 2018). The detection of content production biases by AIs has become possible because of technological advancements which have created platforms that allow users to share various viewpoints. The forthcoming problems regarding AI models and content creation demand blockchain verification services to achieve efficient problem management. The combination of artificial intelligence and blockchain technology will develop innovative solutions which produce new progress waves while ensuring better security measures and full fairness benefits.

7.1 Open Research Areas

Expert research depends on the assessment of new investigative areas stemming from multimodal generative AI technology advancements and blockchain technological development. The combination of AI implementations with blockchain systems operates on anti-misinformation platforms for dual content authentication purposes. The analysis of blockchain systems by experts enables the development of proof-operational systems executed by AI models that produce timestamp and change logs which remain immutable. Scientists develop strategies to enhance blockchain systems for efficient handling of significant AI data amounts during live broadcasts (Nurudeen et al., 2024). AI content research seeks to resolve major moral problems in automated content authorship through its investigation of biases present during automation. Scientists use fundamental new models to create satisfactory accessible AI tools that utilize blockchain platforms with automatic IP protection features. Scientists need to be the leading force behind developing advanced digital media systems that construct secure open networks with full visibility capabilities.

7.2 Trends like Federated Learning + Blockchain

Digital media obtains operational benefits through the integration of two advanced technology partnerships between blockchain systems with federated learning frameworks. A synchronization method of machine learning training enables private secure blockchain technology platforms for devices (Sarra, 2025). The combination of federated learning with digital media systems allows users to create AI model frameworks for sensitive data through blockchain security validations and model development history storage. The innovative marketing system gives users personalized content experiences and operational benefits to content creators by running private AI processes on decentralized systems that maintain complete user data control (Zafar, 2025). A static data format built into blockchain allows monitoring of artificial intelligence production steps and end products which results in accurate outcomes and minimizes risks from dangerous content. The existing industry tendencies allow digital media developers to devise ethical AI solutions that protect user privacy.

7.3 Standardization and Innovation Pathways

Several approaches need to standardize the integration pace between blockchain technology and multimodal generative AI systems for secure platform development and fair interoperability. Standardized blockchain systems designed by businesses need to show AI model parameters as well as content origin detection capabilities and IP rights protection methods for maximizing platform connections (Mala, 2023). The adoption of smart contract standards enables universal protection for Intellectual Property of laptops and other electronic products during worldwide content sharing. Standardization activities lead to blockchain technology advancement because they produce better system operation capabilities through both quick AI methods and distributed digital system functionalities (Suripeddi & Purandare, 2021). The presence of foundation digital media elements enables AI to process content independently while also protecting copyright rights which results in improved media selection methods. Research teams with their industrial collaborators need to develop ethical frameworks to support regulators during the entire development process of their technology.

8. CONCLUSION

The introduction of multimodal generative AI systems with blockchain technology to digital media industries leads to extensive modifications because it strengthens content production while improving distribution mechanisms and authentication systems. Research-based development allowed the authors to create deepfake security measures for digital content and digital IP security and content validation solutions. Decentralized blockchain provides transparency for developing an ethical platform which runs digital media operations. Multimodal generative AI technology allows platform operations to blend artificial content by linking texts with visuals and audios as well as videos across different technical platforms. The diverse content range generated by AI allows academic materials to reach promotional and entertainment services through various virtual networks. Contemporary content generation technologies in their present condition to ownership conflicts that provoke harmful misuse situations.

Deepfakes create actual artificial content detection in real content which causes digital environments to face distrust through fake information traveling through their digital pathways. The digital media security system operates within blockchain networks by using secure data distribution protocols that authenticate data at high levels to block any modifications. Blockchain authentication systems with AI content generation deliver direct tracking capabilities which together with automatic methods for tracking sources allow users to monitor creator credentials. The security provisions within this technology-based system use a complex foundational mechanism for stopping unauthorized access and safeguarding copyrights. Through blockchain records content creators protect their work as they demonstrate intellectual property ownership using unalterable proof-of-record data that generates financial returns from their IP. The three fundamental blockchain features originate from digital asset verification capabilities and smart contracts for implementing tokenized content tracking to decrease copyright violations as well as active content scams.

AI system alliances enabled by blockchain technology provide substantial advantages to entertainment journalism along with gaming and advertising and social media. The combination of blockchain technology with augmented artificial art systems and video editing software plus virtual voice generators and standard royalty payments leads to an impartial compensation structure for entertainment which protects creators completely while providing transparent systems. Genuine news systems powered by blockchain authentication merge article verification with expert source verification for the purpose of reducing misinformation levels. Protected asset-control systems operating on the gaming blockchain serve to bolster trade security while cutting down fraud to establish trustworthiness in asset transactions. Social media platforms use technological promotional systems to construct operational interfaces that lead to enhanced content functions for strengthening publisher-audience relationship quality. The practical execution of research investigations encounters various barriers which restrict technology implementation outcomes to remain at minimal levels. AI model development needs substantial improvement in blockchain system operation because it must fulfil technical and moral aspects of blockchain and AI system functioning. The deployment of complete technological systems demands joint effort from developers who help policymakers together with industrial leaders to permanently safeguard user privacy throughout system applications.

Digital media of today faces imminent disruptive change due to emerging multimodal generative artificial intelligence with blockchain technologies. The inclusion of transparency features in blockchain security systems allows AI systems to reach their peak creativity through trust-based digital media frameworks operated via decentralized methods. For digital media development platforms to safeguard public value they need ethical principles and regulatory standards that merge with the development of ethical digital media practices. Managers at universities can use the explained framework as a tool to create academic research projects while having access to modern technological information. Ongoing ethical research based on new research methods will protect our future by creating innovative business alliances between generative AI technology and blockchain capabilities which establish ethical digital systems.

REFERENCES

Aarthi, S., Aravinthan, K., Ravikumar, R. N., Sivakumar, N., & Wanglen, S. (2025). Cryptography securing data in motion within Blockchain, internet of everything, and Federated Learning. In *Convergence of Blockchain, Internet of Everything, and Federated Learning for Security* (pp. 39–78). IGI Global. DOI: 10.4018/979-8-3373-1424-2.ch002

Ahmed, M. F., Khan, M. R. A. A., Islam, M. R., & Islam, M. N. (2024). AI and blockchain for regulatory compliance: Enhancing transparency and efficiency in governance. Journal of Artificial Intelligence General Science (JAIGS), 7(01), 278–290.

Bakan, U., & Atabey, Z. (2024). Symbolizing creativity. In *Advances in Human and Social Aspects of Technology* (pp. 261–286). IGI Global.

Baltrusaitis, T., Ahuja, C., & Morency, L.-P. (2019). Multimodal machine learning: A survey and taxonomy. *IEEE Transactions on Pattern Analysis and Machine Intelligence*, *41*(2), 423–443. DOI: 10.1109/TPAMI.2018.2798607 PMID: 29994351

Barati, M., Rana, O., Petri, I., & Theodorakopoulos, G. (2020). GDPR compliance verification in internet of things. *IEEE Access: Practical Innovations, Open Solutions*, 8, 119697–119709. DOI: 10.1109/ACCESS.2020.3005509

Buldas, A., Draheim, D., Gault, M., Laanoja, R., Nagumo, T., Saarepera, M., Shah, S. A., Simm, J., Steiner, J., Tammet, T., & Truu, A. (2022). An ultra-scalable blockchain platform for universal asset tokenization: Design and implementation. *IEEE Access: Practical Innovations, Open Solutions*, 10, 77284–77322. DOI: 10.1109/ACCESS.2022.3192837

Chauhan, N. (2025). Revolutionizing digital content authentication: The power of synthetic media detection. *INTERNATIONAL JOURNAL OF SCIENTIFIC RESEARCH IN ENGINEERING AND*, *09*(05), 1–9. DOI: 10.55041/IJSREM46858

Echenim, J. I. (2025). Integration of Artificial Intelligence and blockchain for Intelligent Autonomous Systems. *International Journal of Future Engineering Innovations*, *2*(3), 31–37. DOI: 10.54660/IJFEI.2025.2.3.31-37

Eszteri, D. (2022). Blockchain and artificial intelligence: Connecting two distinct technologies to comply with GDPR's data protection by design principle. *Masaryk Univ. J. Law Technol.*, *16*(1), 59–88. DOI: 10.5817/MUJLT2022-1-3

Fazi, M. A. (2022). A contextual study of regulatory framework for blockchain. In *Regulatory Aspects of Artificial Intelligence on Blockchain* (pp. 40–51). IGI Global. DOI: 10.4018/978-1-7998-7927-5.ch003

Gao, L., Zhang, X., Liu, T., Yang, H., Liao, B., & Guo, J. (2021). Energy-aware blockchain resource allocation algorithm with deep reinforcement learning for trusted authentication. In Lecture Notes of the Institute for Computer Sciences, Social Informatics and Telecommunications Engineering (pp. 93–103). Springer International Publishing. DOI: 10.1007/978-3-030-73562-3_8

Gitobu, C., & Ogetonto, J. (2025). Harnessing artificial intelligence (AI) and blockchain technology for the advancement of finance technology (FinTech) in businesses. *London Journal of Interdisciplinary Sciences*, *3*(3), 75–89. DOI: 10.31039/ljis.2024.3.292

Hasselgren, A., Wan, P. K., Horn, M., Kralevska, K., & Gligoroski, D. (2020, October). GDPR Compliance for Blockchain Applications in Healthcare. Computer Science & Information Technology (CS & IT).

Hofman, D., Lemieux, V. L., Joo, A., & Batista, D. A. (2019). The margin between the edge of the world and infinite possibility. *Records Management Journal*, *29*(1/2), 240–257. DOI: 10.1108/RMJ-12-2018-0045

Huang, S.-C., Jensen, M., Yeung-Levy, S., Lungren, M. P., Poon, H., & Chaudhari, A. S. (2025). A systematic review and implementation guidelines of multimodal Foundation Models in medical imaging. In Res. Sq. DOI: 10.21203/rs.3.rs-5537908/v1

Jose Diaz Rivera, J., Muhammad, A., & Song, W.-C. (2024). Securing digital identity in the zero trust architecture: A blockchain approach to privacy-focused multi-factor authentication. *IEEE Open Journal of the Communications Society*, *5*, 2792–2814. DOI: 10.1109/OJCOMS.2024.3391728

Judge, C. S., Krewer, F., O'Donnell, M. J., Kiely, L., Sexton, D., Taylor, G. W., Skorburg, J. A., & Tripp, B. (2024). Multimodal artificial intelligence in medicine. *Kidney360*, *5*(11), 1771–1779. DOI: 10.34067/KID.0000000000000556 PMID: 39167446

Kalra, S., Bansal, Y., Sharma, Y., & Chauhan, G. S. (2023). FakeSpotter: A blockchain-based trustworthy idea for fake news detection in social media. *J. Inf. Optimiz. Sci.*, *44*(3), 515–527. DOI: 10.47974/JIOS-1411

Kulothungan, V. (2025). Using blockchain ledgers to record the AI decisions in IoT. In *Preprints*.

Mala, C. S. (2023). Revolutionizing industries with blockchain and AI: A journey into decentralized intelligence. In 3rd International Conference on AI ML, Data Science and Robotics. United Research Forum. DOI: 10.51219/URForum.2023. Chandana-Sree-Mala

Mandych, O., Staverska, T., & Maliy, O. (2023). Integration of artificial intelligence into the blockchain and cryptocurrency market. *MODELING THE DEVELOPMENT OF THE ECONOMIC SYSTEMS*, 4(4), 61–66. DOI: 10.31891/mdes/2023-10-8

Moerel, L. (2018). Blockchain & data protection … and why they are not on a collision course. *Eur. Rev. Priv. Law*, 26(6), 825–851. DOI: 10.54648/ERPL2018057

Mukhopadhyay, M. (2025). Golden brush and evolving canvas—Navigating the digital art and Non-fungible tokens. *J. Inf. Technol. Teach. Cases*, 15(1), 123–132. DOI: 10.1177/20438869231215085

Nurudeen, M. O., Latilo, A., Imosemi, H. O., & Imosemi, Q. A. (2024). Integrative legal operating model design: Incorporating ai and blockchain in legal practice. *Global J. Res. Multidiscip. Studies*, 2(1), 1–16. DOI: 10.58175/gjrms.2024.2.1.0036

Omowole, B. M., Omokhoa, H. E., Ogundeji, I. A., & Achumie, G. O. (2022). Blockchain-enhanced financial transparency: A conceptual approach to reporting and compliance. *International Journal of Social Science Exceptional Research*, 2(5), 141–157. DOI: 10.54660/IJSSER.2022.1.1.141-157

Pasupuleti, M. K. (2025a). *Decentralized creativity: AI-infused blockchain for secure and transparent digital innovation*. National Education Services. DOI: 10.62311/nesx/rrvi125

Pasupuleti, M. K. (2025b). *Decentralized creativity: AI-infused blockchain for secure and transparent digital innovation*. National Education Services. DOI: 10.62311/nesx/rrvi125

Pasupuleti, M. K. (2025c). *Decentralized creativity: AI-infused blockchain for secure and transparent digital innovation*. National Education Services. DOI: 10.62311/nesx/rrvi125

Picha Edwardsson, M., & Al-Saqaf, W. (2024). Blockchain solutions for generative AI challenges in journalism. Front. Blockchain, 7.

Poposki, Z. (2024). Critique of reification of art and creativity in the digital age: A Lukácsian approach to AI and NFT art. *Open Philosophy*, 7(1), 20240027. DOI: 10.1515/opphil-2024-0027

Prajapati, C. (2025). AI and blockchain integration in finance. [IJISRT]. *International Journal of Innovation and Scientific Research*, 2537–2538.

Sağlam, M. H., & Kirçova, I. (2025). The role of artificial intelligence in ad fraud detection in the blockchain and programmatic advertising ecosystem. In Advances in Marketing, Customer Relationship Management, and E-Services (pp. 43–82). IGI Global.

Sardana, A., Sethuraman, S., & Kalyanasundaram, P. D. (2024). Compliance-as-code 2.0: Orchestrating regulatory operations with agentic AI. Journal of Artificial Intelligence General Science (JAIGS), 5(1), 546–563.

Sarra, C. (2025). Artificial Intelligence in decision-making: A test of consistency between the "EU AI Act" and the "General Data Protection Regulation". *Athens J. Law*, *11*(1), 45–62. DOI: 10.30958/ajl.11-1-3

Singh, B., Wongmahesak, K., & Chandra, S. (2025). Transforming Digital Ownership and assessing role of blockchain technology and NFTs in future economy. In *Practical Strategies and Case Studies for Online Marketing 6.0* (pp. 343–368). IGI Global. DOI: 10.4018/979-8-3373-2058-8.ch015

Suripeddi, M. K. S., & Purandare, P. (2021). Blockchain and GDPR – A study on compatibility issues of the distributed ledger technology with GDPR data processing. *Journal of Physics: Conference Series*, *1964*(4), 42005. DOI: 10.1088/1742-6596/1964/4/042005

Wang, H., Zhou, M., Jia, X., Wei, H., Hu, Z., Li, W., Chen, Q., & Wang, L. (2025). Recent progress on artificial intelligence-enhanced multimodal sensors integrated devices and systems. *Journal of Semiconductors*, *46*(1), 11610. DOI: 10.1088/1674-4926/24090041

Xu, P., Zhu, X., & Clifton, D. A. (2023). Multimodal learning with Transformers: A survey. *IEEE Transactions on Pattern Analysis and Machine Intelligence*, *45*(10), 12113–12132. DOI: 10.1109/TPAMI.2023.3275156 PMID: 37167049

Zafar, A. (2025). Reconciling blockchain technology and data protection laws: Regulatory challenges, technical solutions, and practical pathways. *Journal of Cybersecurity*, *11*(1), tyaf002. DOI: 10.1093/cybsec/tyaf002

Zhuk, A. (2025). Beyond the blockchain hype: Addressing legal and regulatory challenges. *SN Social Sciences*, *5*(2), 11. DOI: 10.1007/s43545-024-01044-y

KEY TERMS AND DEFINITIONS

Generative AI: AI that creates new content such as text, images, audio, and video by learning from data patterns.

Multimodal Generative AI: AI systems that combine text, image, audio, and video inputs to generate coherent content across multiple formats.

Blockchain: A decentralized and distributed digital ledger technology that records transactions across multiple nodes securely and immutably.

Smart Contracts: Self-executing code on the blockchain that automatically enforces terms of agreements without intermediaries.

Non-Fungible Tokens (NFTs): Unique digital assets on a blockchain used to prove ownership and authenticity of digital content.

Data Immutability: A feature of blockchain that ensures once data is written, it cannot be altered or deleted.

Decentralized Identity (DID): A system allowing individuals to manage and control their own digital identities without a central authority.

GANs (Generative Adversarial Networks): A class of AI models where two networks (generator and discriminator) compete to produce realistic synthetic data.

Transformers: A neural network architecture that handles sequential data and is widely used in NLP and generative tasks.

VAEs (Variational Autoencoders): A generative model that learns latent representations to generate new content based on probability distributions.

DALL·E: A generative AI model by OpenAI that converts textual descriptions into corresponding images.

GPT (Generative Pre-trained Transformer): A language model that generates human-like text from input prompts.

Whisper: An AI model by OpenAI used for automatic speech recognition and voice-to-text transcription.

Tokenization: The process of converting physical or digital assets into blockchain-based tokens for secure and fractional ownership.

Content Provenance: The record of origin and history of digital content to verify authenticity and ownership.

Federated Learning: A decentralized machine learning approach where models are trained across multiple devices without sharing raw data.

Deepfakes: Synthetic media in which a person in an existing image or video is replaced with someone else's likeness using AI.

Synthetic Media: Media generated or altered using AI technologies, including deepfakes and computer-generated voice/video.

Digital Watermarking: Embedding hidden markers or data in digital media for content tracking and copyright protection.

Decentralized Applications (DApps): Applications that run on a blockchain or peer-to-peer network rather than on centralized servers.

Chapter 2
Charting the Course:
Addressing Open Problems in AI and Blockchain Synergy for Media

Kiran Sree Pokkuluri
ⓘ https://orcid.org/0009-0001-9957-2222
Shri Vishnu Engineering College for Women, India

A. Chandrasekar
Nandha College of Technology, India

Kumar M. Santhosh
ⓘ https://orcid.org/0009-0009-6623-0558
Nandha College of Technology, India

Aravindh Saivaraju
Vel Tech Rangarajan Dr. Sagunthala R&D Institute of Science and Technology, India

ABSTRACT

Blockchain technology and artificial intelligence (AI) are set to transform digital media by providing previously unheard-of possibilities for content production, distribution, and monetization. Nevertheless, there are a number of intricate difficulties and unsolved problems associated with combining these two revolutionary technologies. The outstanding issues at the nexus of blockchain and artificial intelligence in the context of digital media are examined in this chapter. Scalability, interoperability, data protection, and ethical considerations are top priorities. Through tackling these issues, the chapter hopes to offer a research and development roadmap for the future, guaranteeing that the blockchain and AI synergy can be fully utilized to

DOI: 10.4018/979-8-3373-1504-1.ch002

build a digital media environment that is more transparent, safe, and egalitarian. In order to demonstrate prospective solutions and breakthroughs, practical use cases and new trends are also covered.

INTRODUCTION

The combination of blockchain technology and artificial intelligence (AI) is revolutionizing digital media and bringing in a new age of innovation, security, and openness. This convergence is revolutionizing the production, consumption, and valuation of media by offering ground-breaking possibilities in content creation, distribution, and monetization. Artificial Intelligence (AI) enhances blockchain's decentralized ledger system, which guarantees security, transparency, and immutability, with its capabilities in deep learning, data analytics, and creative output. By working together, these technologies have the potential to solve persistent problems in digital media, including copyright protection, content authenticity, and equitable income sharing. But there are difficulties with this potential combination. In order to properly utilize AI and blockchain in the media industry, there are a number of unresolved issues that need careful consideration and creative solutions. The essential issue of scalability is at the heart of this confluence. Despite being safe and transparent, blockchain technology frequently has scalability issues because of its resource-intensive and sometimes lengthy consensus processes. When trying to handle the enormous and constantly increasing amount of digital media output produced by AI, this constraint presents a major obstacle. One important challenge that must be overcome is figuring out how to increase blockchain scalability without sacrificing its security and decentralization. Another significant issue is the interoperability of blockchain and AI systems. Due to their different structures and protocols, these two technologies are now unable to communicate and share data seamlessly, which makes integration difficult.

Coherent and effective systems that capitalize on the advantages of blockchain and artificial intelligence will require the development of standardized frameworks and protocols that enable seamless interconnection. With AI algorithms processing massive volumes of user data to create tailored content, data privacy is a critical issue in the digital media ecosystem. Although blockchain promises decentralized and transparent data management, striking a balance between privacy and openness is still a challenging issue. Maintaining the integrity and reliability of the system while protecting user data is a challenging problem that calls for careful thought and creative solutions. The AI-blockchain synergy is also centered on ethical issues. Concerns around prejudice, responsibility, and abuse are brought up by the use of AI in media creation. Blockchain can help to ensure accountability and transparency, but strong standards and norms are needed for the ethical use of AI in content production, particularly in areas like deepfake generation. Fostering trust and adoption of these technologies in the larger media environment requires addressing these ethical issues. There are advantages and disadvantages to using blockchain technology to monetize digital content. New revenue streams for artists are provided by tokenization of digital assets and blockchain-based royalties distribution; nevertheless, the underlying economic models of these systems must be equitable and sustainable.

This chapter explores these unresolved issues, providing a thorough examination of the difficulties and possible fixes in the confluence of blockchain technology with artificial intelligence for digital media. It examines the state of the technologies today, points out their shortcomings, and suggests directions for further study and advancement. The chapter seeks to successfully integrate blockchain and AI by tackling these unresolved issues, opening the door to a digital media environment that is more safe, open, and just. The conversation is enhanced by real-world examples and new developments that highlight the potential uses and advantages of blockchain and artificial intelligence in the media. The chapter highlights the revolutionary impact, from improving copyright protection and content authenticity to opening up new avenues for tailored and interactive media experiences. Along with offering insights into the most recent developments and breakthroughs, it also highlights the industry's continuing efforts and ambitions. In the end, this chapter acts as a manual for scholars, professionals, and legislators negotiating the intricate terrain of blockchain and artificial intelligence in digital media. It seeks to stimulate more research and cooperation by bringing attention to the unresolved issues and possible solutions, which will accelerate the creation of strong and long-lasting systems that can fully utilize the promise of these ground-breaking technologies.

STATE OF ART MODELS

Oshani and Seneviratne (2022), highlights the importance of AI in both causing and addressing the threat posed by false information on the Internet, especially in light of blockchain technology and the growth of scams. It highlights the quick and low-cost dissemination of false information, citing instances such as phishing schemes and Twitter hacks.

In order to counteract misinformation, it suggests a synergistic approach that combines blockchain and artificial intelligence (AI) technologies. It suggests that tamper-proof blockchain can offer proof of the authenticity and provenance of content, while AI models can be used to identify fake news, improving the accuracy of information on social media platforms.

Dhanasak et al (2024) examines the relationship between blockchain technology and artificial intelligence (AI), emphasizing how these two technologies work in concert to improve the effectiveness and performance of current information and communications technology (ICT) systems. Data security, decentralized intelligent systems, and automated decision-making are among the fourteen salient characteristics of this confluence that are identified.

Three eras are included in the chronology of technological convergence: emerging, convergence, and application. In addition to discussing the implications of this technology fusion across five key areas—IoT applications, cybersecurity, finance, energy, and smart cities—the article classifies aspects pertinent to the convergence period and anticipates future research possibilities.

Zon-Yin et al (2019) says that encouraging cooperation between news media and AI blockchain researchers, the study suggests an AI blockchain platform that would let journalists obtain real information on breaking news that has been crowdsourced on the blockchain and verified by AI. This would help battle the false news epidemic. Increasing the credibility of information sources in the social media era is the goal of this project. The paper's main technical contributions are the creation of tools for creating a database of factual news, creating a news blockchain supply chain graph, and using AI blockchain-based crowd sourcing to rank fake news. These tools are all intended to encourage factual reporting and stop the spread of false information.

Hui et al (2022) lacks of vitality among practitioners, content homogeneity, erroneous media positioning, lack of business models, and information traceability concerns are some of the problems that the study addresses in relation to media convergence.

It investigates how blockchain technology might help with these issues by utilizing its decentralization, transparency, information immutability, and traceability features. In the end, it suggests a framework for building a convergent media platform that takes use of these technical benefits.

Rashi et al (2023) The integration of blockchain technology with artificial intelligence (AI) to produce blockchain intelligence is discussed in the paper, with an emphasis on the possible advantages in a number of fields, including social media analytics, supply chain management, cybersecurity, banking, and finance. The authors offer a research agenda for the future that centres on creating a safe system for exchanging cyber threat intelligence data by utilizing blockchain technology and artificial intelligence. The goal is to improve application security, productivity, and efficiency.

Georgios et al (2018) says blockchain-based service that improves artists' control and revenue from multimedia material is presented in the paper, addressing the lack of ownership and transparency in the existing media sharing practices. Smart contracts on the Ethereum platform are used for transaction management and ownership proof, and blockchain technology and web services are combined to guarantee content producers receive direct payment.

To enhance data storage and retrieval, the authors investigate the integration of many technologies, such as the InterPlanetary File System (IPFS) and Hyperledger Projects. They also suggest a digital currency called "Media-Token" to streamline transactions. By establishing a decentralized repository for content producers, the system hopes to enable safe and effective communication between creators and users while enabling them to profit from their labor without the need for middlemen.

Momčilo et al (2022) in order to comprehend social dynamics and cultural advancement in relation to the history of media as intricate technological-communication structures, the paper examines how Distributed Ledger Technologies (DLT), also referred to as blockchain technologies, have changed media and journalism. It presents the idea of customized blockchain journalism and suggests a user economy model to guarantee the platform's long-term viability. In order to build an ecosystem that is distinct from the current contaminated media environment, it tackles the problems of information overload and the need for efficient information structure inside a blockchain-based editorial platform.

Ria et al (2023) study emphasizes the revolutionary potential of the collaboration of blockchain technology, Bitcoin, information technology, and artificial intelligence, stressing that this convergence is opening the door to a digital future that is more safe, effective, and inclusive. It implies that for this technology revolution to succeed for future generations, it will be essential to embrace this synergy and overcome its obstacles. It talks about how blockchain may significantly improve community involvement, especially by establishing accountability and transparency in resource allocation. In order to increase civic engagement and foster trust among stakeholders, community groups can use blockchain-based systems to monitor and show the distribution of cash and gifts in an unchangeable way.

Wee et al (2018) discusses the difficulties in identifying and stopping fake news on social media, highlighting the necessity of developing new algorithms and combining blockchain technology with cutting-edge artificial intelligence to boost public confidence in reliable news sources and slow the spread of false information. In addition to stressing the value of decentralized social networks in protecting user privacy and data control, it examines the state of blockchain solutions today, talks about technological limitations, and suggests future research avenues targeted at enhancing the efficacy of fake news detection systems.

Leon et al (2024) highlights the potential for both blockchain technology and artificial intelligence (AI) to revolutionize their respective fields by examining the difficulties and opportunities that exist between them. It offers a unique framework for classifying current and upcoming use cases and evaluates noteworthy initiatives that integrate these technologies according to market capitalization. Although blockchain and AI are theoretically compatible, the article points out that practical implementations are still in their infancy and face challenges because of different system architectures and operational needs. It highlights the necessity of tackling a number of issues in order to go from minimum viable products to integrated solutions that are widely adopted.

THE CURRENT LANDSCAPE OF AI AND BLOCKCHAIN IN MEDIA

The media environment is being completely transformed by the combination of blockchain technology and artificial intelligence (AI), which presents previously unheard-of opportunities for creativity, effectiveness, and security. Both blockchain and artificial intelligence have become game-changing technologies as digital media keeps growing. The present status of digital media technology, the role of artificial intelligence (AI) in media creation and consumption, and the ways in which blockchain improves security and transparency within the media ecosystem are all covered in this part.

The last two decades have seen a significant shift in digital media, moving from conventional print and broadcast formats to incredibly immersive and interactive digital platforms. Increases in processing power, the spread of the internet, and the rise of disruptive technologies like blockchain and artificial intelligence have all contributed to this change. digitizing material so that it may be accessed on several devices. User-generated content and customized consumption became the main focus with the introduction of social media and streaming services. Technologies like virtual reality (VR), augmented reality (AR), and streaming HD video have significantly broadened the scope of digital media. These days, the combination of blockchain and artificial intelligence has created new opportunities, allowing consumers and media producers to attain previously unthinkable levels of efficiency and capability.

KEY CONTRIBUTIONS OF AI IN MEDIA PRODUCTION AND CONSUMPTION

A key component of contemporary media creation and consumption, artificial intelligence (AI) boosts user engagement, efficiency, and innovation in a variety of fields. It may be used to create intricate, superior content or automate monotonous processes.

Automated Production of Contents

AI-driven technologies such as DALL-E and GPT (Generative Pre-trained Transformer) have revolutionized the production of content. High-quality articles, scripts, photos, videos, and audio may be produced by these models with little assistance from humans. For example, artificial intelligence is capable of creating realistic cartoons, cinematic special effects, and even musical compositions. This democratizes content creation and lowers production costs, enabling up-and-coming artists to compete with more established firms.

Customized Content Suggestions

When it comes to media consumption, recommendation engines that are driven by AI algorithms are essential. YouTube, Spotify, Netflix, and other platforms employ machine learning to assess user preferences and suggest content based on personal interests. Platform operators and users alike gain from this tailoring, which raises engagement and enhances user happiness.

Improved User Engagement

Artificial Intelligence has made it easier to create interactive media. Chatbots and virtual assistants can offer real-time assistance thanks to natural language processing (NLP), while computer vision makes it possible for users to engage with augmented and virtual reality settings with ease.

Real-time insights and analytics

AI-powered analytics give marketers and artists important information about market trends, audience behavior, and content performance. Making better decisions is made possible by these insights, which results in more successful marketing campaigns and content strategies.

Quality Control and Content Moderation

A safer and more inclusive online environment is ensured by using AI models to identify and filter offensive or dangerous information. To safeguard both consumers and authors, machine learning algorithms, for instance, can detect deepfakes, hate speech, and copyright infringement.

Notwithstanding these developments, difficulties still exist. Due to their high computing requirements, potential for misuse in spreading false information, and vulnerability to prejudice, AI models are frequently criticized. These drawbacks show how additional technologies, like as blockchain, are required to solve some of these problems.

BLOCKCHAIN'S ROLE IN ENHANCING SECURITY AND TRANSPARENCY

Blockchain technology tackles some of the most important issues facing the media sector, such as income distribution equity, lack of transparency, and content piracy. It is the perfect way to guarantee security and trust in the creation and dissemination of media since it is decentralized and unchangeable.

Content Provenance and Authenticity

Blockchain makes it possible to trace digital assets, offering an unchangeable and transparent record of their usage and provenance. In the fight against deepfakes and other types of false information, this is very helpful. Blockchain, for example, may safeguard the legitimacy of digital information by storing metadata about its originator, creation date, and modification history.

Administration of Intellectual Property Rights

By automating the administration of intellectual property rights, blockchain-based smart contracts guarantee that authors receive just compensation for their contributions. These agreements make it possible to distribute royalties in real time, which lowers conflict and guarantees openness. Platforms such as Mediachain and Audius use blockchain technology to safeguard the rights of media and music producers.

Distribution of Content Decentralized

Distribution of traditional media is based on centralized platforms that frequently manage access and revenue sharing. Decentralized content distribution networks (CDNs) are made possible by blockchain, which enables artists to reach customers directly and bypass middlemen. This lowers expenses while guaranteeing that content producers maintain authority over their work.

Safe and Open Transactions

Secure transactions are guaranteed by blockchain's cryptographic characteristics, which safeguard private user information and payment details. In a time when data breaches and cyberattacks are becoming more frequent, this is especially crucial. Additionally, the transparency of blockchain lowers the risk of fraud by guaranteeing that every transaction can be verified.

Tokenization and Revenue Generation

By enabling the tokenization of digital assets, blockchain enables artists to creatively monetize their creations. Non-fungible tokens (NFTs) allow, for instance, the direct selling of one-of-a-kind digital goods to customers, like films and artwork. For producers, this has created new sources of income, especially in the game and art sectors.

Rewards and Audience Engagement

New audience engagement methods, such compensating users for sharing or consuming information, are made possible by blockchain. By encouraging user involvement, tokens can make the media ecosystem more engaging and lucrative.

Blockchain has potential, but it also has drawbacks including scalability issues, energy consumption, and unclear regulations. Some of these problems can be resolved by combining blockchain technology with AI, resulting in a more resilient and effective media ecosystem.

THE CONVERGENCE OF AI AND BLOCKCHAIN: TRANSFORMING THE MEDIA INDUSTRY

Many of the drawbacks of both blockchain and artificial intelligence technologies when utilized separately might be resolved by combining them. For example, AI can forecast network congestion and enhance consensus processes to improve blockchain operations, and blockchain may offer a safe environment for building and deploying AI models.

Blockchain technology and artificial intelligence working together can revolutionize media creation and consumption in a number of ways. AI can improve blockchain-based media platforms' customization, giving users more individualized experiences.

Consumer trust may be increased by using blockchain technology to guarantee the integrity and validity of AI-generated information. When combined, these technologies can provide decentralized platforms that bypass centralized middlemen and allow people to produce, share, and profit from content. The current state of blockchain and AI in media is marked by tremendous opportunities and quick breakthroughs. Blockchain guarantees safety and transparency, while AI fosters innovation and productivity. By tackling enduring issues and fostering fresh possibilities for creativity, their combination has the potential to completely transform the media sector. Their influence on the creation and consumption of media will surely only grow as these technologies develop further. In order to fully realize their potential, it will be imperative to address the ethical issues and problems related to their integration.

OPPORTUNITIES AT THE INTERSECTION OF AI AND BLOCKCHAIN

Blockchain technology and artificial intelligence (AI) have come together to create a world of revolutionary possibilities in digital media. Through the introduction of increased trust, efficiency, and automation into processes, these opportunities are transforming the production, distribution, and monetization of media. Content producers, distributors, and consumers are among the media industry stakeholders that stand to gain from creative solutions that tackle enduring problems by utilizing the advantages of both technologies. This section explores three significant opportunities: AI-powered media production using smart contracts for content licensing and royalties, decentralized content distribution networks (CDNs), and blockchain authentication.

AI-ENHANCED MEDIA CREATION WITH BLOCKCHAIN AUTHENTICATION

AI is transforming media production by producing varied, high-quality material that is adapted to the tastes of the viewer. Artificial Intelligence (AI) can create realistic photos, movies, and sounds as well as interesting textual material using tools like Generative Adversarial Networks (GANs), Variational Autoencoders (VAEs), and diffusion models. But as AI's ability to produce material increases, so does the possibility of abuse, including deepfakes and illegal duplication. By offering an unchangeable, transparent authentication layer that builds confidence in AI-generated information, blockchain technology can help overcome these difficulties. To confirm the legitimacy and provenance of AI-generated material, for example, blockchain-based digital signatures can be included into the content.

A blockchain can store the metadata of a piece of material at the moment of generation, such as the creator's information, the production time, and any related intellectual property rights. The integrity of the creative process is maintained by guaranteeing that the material cannot be altered or misattributed. In order to promote confidence in digital information, users may also trace the origin of media on the blockchain to confirm its legitimacy. Another possible use is in the fight against the dissemination of false information. Blockchain technology and artificial intelligence (AI) may be used to build a framework in which news stories, photos, and videos are verified by AI before being verified on the blockchain. The trustworthiness of information exchanged on digital platforms would be improved and the spread of distorted media would be stopped. Additionally, blockchain-authenticated AI-generated media can facilitate customized content experiences. For instance, blockchain makes sure that the content's source and data usage adhere to privacy laws, while AI may create customized ads, instructional resources, or entertainment content based on user preferences. Creators may now innovate without sacrificing accountability or openness because to this technological convergence.

DECENTRALIZED CONTENT DISTRIBUTION NETWORKS (CDNS)

Conventional content distribution networks are based on centralized systems, which frequently include problems like censorship, single points of failure, and large expenses for content producers. Peer-to-peer, more fair, efficient, and robust content distribution networks are made possible by blockchain technology, providing a decentralized substitute. Together with AI, these decentralized CDNs have the potential to completely transform how people share and consume digital video. Blockchain-based CDNs store and distribute material among a network of nodes by utilizing distributed ledger technology. Creators of content can submit their creations to a decentralized platform, where they are divided into tiny pieces and dispersed among several nodes. By examining variables like network traffic, user demand, and geographic location, AI systems improve this distribution process and guarantee quick and smooth content delivery. For both producers and consumers, this means lower latency, better scalability, and lower costs.

Decentralized CDNs also provide content producers more control by doing away with middlemen like conventional content hosting services. Because blockchain smart contracts allow producers and consumers to communicate directly, creators are able to keep a higher portion of the profits. For example, users can directly pay for content using tokens or cryptocurrency, and the blockchain records the transaction to guarantee fairness and transparency. The robustness and accessibility of material are also improved by decentralized CDNs. In areas with inadequate internet connectivity, peer-to-peer networks powered by blockchain technology can guarantee efficient content distribution. Furthermore, because these networks are decentralized, they are immune to censorship and cyberattacks, protecting data integrity and freedom of speech. AI makes it possible for decentralized CDNs to offer more sophisticated services like real-time content moderation, predictive analytics for demand forecasting, and personalized content suggestions. While blockchain makes sure that user data is safely maintained and kept, AI algorithms, for instance, may examine user preferences and viewing habits to suggest content that matches their interests. This collaboration makes the media experience more interesting and focused on the user.

SMART CONTRACTS FOR CONTENT LICENSING AND ROYALTY MANAGEMENT

Ensuring just pay for content producers and rights holders is one of the media industry's biggest concerns. Conventional approaches to royalties and content licensing are frequently ambiguous, ineffective, and prone to disagreements. Blockchain smart contracts offer a solution by automating and expediting these procedures, guaranteeing that authors get timely and correct payment. Smart contracts are agreements that are self-executing and have their terms encoded directly into the code. Smart contracts have the ability to automatically track royalties, enforce use rights, and disburse payments to authors and rights holders in the context of content licensing within predetermined guidelines. For instance, the smart contract may quickly determine and pay royalties to all parties involved when a piece of music or video is bought or streamed, doing away with the need for middlemen and cutting down on administrative burden. Through the use of intelligent content licensing and dynamic pricing models, AI can improve the efficacy of smart contracts. To find the best prices for digital media, for example, AI algorithms may examine audience interaction, market trends, and the popularity of content. This guarantees affordability for customers while enabling producers to optimize their earnings. Furthermore, by examining use trends and suggesting license terms that suit the requirements of both producers and consumers, AI can support intelligent content licensing. Preventing illegal usage of digital media is another benefit of blockchain-based smart contracts. Authors may guarantee that their work is only seen and utilized in compliance with the terms of the agreement by incorporating usage rights and limitations straight into the smart contract. This is very helpful for preventing piracy and safeguarding intellectual property. Tokenization made possible by smart contracts gives producers access to new revenue sources. On blockchain markets, digital media assets like music, films, and artwork may be tokenized into non-fungible tokens (NFTs) and exchanged. Every NFT is a distinct work of material that can be shown to be owned and scarce, enabling authors to profit from their creations in novel ways. For instance, a filmmaker may provide fans with a one-of-a-kind and collectible experience by tokenizing rare behind-the-scenes video as NFTs.

PROPOSED FRAMEWORK FOR AI AND BLOCKCHAIN SYNERGY IN MEDIA

In digital media, the combination of blockchain technology and artificial intelligence (AI) is revolutionizing the production, distribution, and monetization of content. In order to solve persistent issues like content authenticity, intellectual property protection, fair income sharing, and smooth distribution, a framework for combining these technologies has been developed. The framework gives digital media operations a decentralized, transparent, and safe basis by combining the advantages of blockchain technology and artificial intelligence. The framework's architectural layout, essential elements, and the operational and workflow processes that make it operate are described in this chapter.

ARCHITECTURAL DESIGN OF THE FRAMEWORK

Blockchain's decentralized and unchangeable infrastructure is integrated with AI-driven content creation in the framework's tiered architectural architecture. Three layers make up the framework's fundamental components shown in Figure 1:

AI Layer: Media creation, customization, and content analysis are within the purview of the artificial intelligence layer. High-quality text, picture, audio, and video material may be produced thanks to its sophisticated AI models, which include Transformers, Variational Autoencoders (VAEs), and Generative Adversarial Networks (GANs). Natural Language Processing (NLP) and computer vision algorithms are also part of the AI layer, which analyzes user preferences and optimizes content delivery.

Blockchain Layer: This layer offers the fundamental framework for security, authentication, and decentralized storage. It consists of consensus procedures to guarantee data integrity, smart contracts to automate procedures, and distributed ledger technology (DLT) to record transactions. All interactions inside the framework are visible, unchangeable, and traceable thanks to the blockchain layer.

Figure 1. Architecture of the proposed model

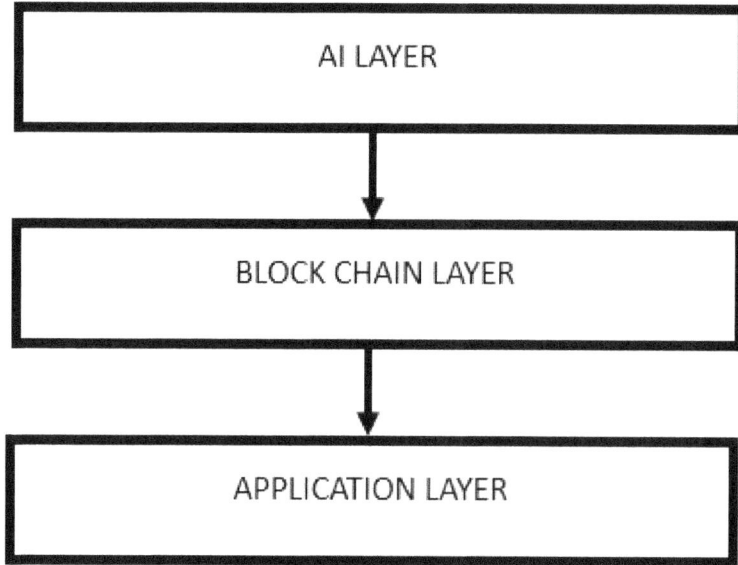

Application Layer: The user-facing layer that connects the Blockchain and AI components is called the application layer. In order to provide smooth interactions like content uploads, purchases, and royalty distribution, it incorporates decentralized apps (DApps) for content producers, distributors, and consumers. Interfaces for tokenized assets, including non-fungible tokens (NFTs), are also included in the application layer. These interfaces enable creative monetization strategies. To guarantee seamless data flow and interoperability, these layers are coupled via middleware and APIs. Because of the modular architecture's scalability and modification capabilities, the framework may be adjusted to meet the changing demands of the digital media ecosystem.

KEY COMPONENTS: AI MODELS, BLOCKCHAIN LAYERS, AND SMART CONTRACTS

The efficiency and dependability of the framework are ensured by a number of essential components, each of which drives its performance.

Artificial intelligence (AI) models are crucial to the process of creating content. GANs are used to create realistic media material, including high-resolution photos, synthetic audio, and deepfake films. Media data may be compressed and reconstructed thanks to VAEs, which makes distribution and storage more effective. Text creation, summarization, and sentiment analysis are examples of sophisticated NLP activities that are powered by transformers like GPT and BERT. By examining user preferences and behavior, these models allow for tailored experiences in addition to improving the quality and diversity of media.

Blockchain Layers: A number of elements necessary for security and decentralization are included in the blockchain layer: Distributed Ledger: A public or private blockchain ensures transparency and traceability by keeping track of all transactions, including ownership transfers, content uploads, and royalties. Consensus Mechanisms: Methods like as Delegated Proof of Stake (DPoS) and Proof of Stake (PoS) algorithms guarantee that the network is safe and impenetrable. Decentralized Storage: Media files are safely stored using programs like Arweave or IPFS (InterPlanetary File System), which also preserve accessibility and redundancy. Tokenization: Tokenization allows for unique ownership and tradeability of digital assets, such as media files and licenses, as NFTs.

Smart contracts are self-executing software applications that automate procedures like revenue sharing, royalty distribution, and content licensing. When a user buys or streams material, for instance, the smart contract automatically determines and disburses royalties to all parties involved according to predetermined conditions. Additionally, smart contracts restrict unlawful distribution or alteration of content by ensuring that its usage conforms with license agreements.

WORKFLOW AND OPERATIONAL MECHANICS

The suggested framework's workflow demonstrates how blockchain technology and artificial intelligence work together to produce a smooth and open digital media ecosystem. The operating mechanics are described in the following steps:

Content Creation and Upload: Using AI technologies, content producers start the process by producing media. These programs create creative and high-quality material by utilizing GANs, VAEs, or Transformers. The media is tokenized as an NFT when it has been developed and uploaded to the decentralized site. To ensure authenticity and transparency, the blockchain keeps track of the information, which includes the creator's name, creation date, and license conditions. The framework creates a distinct digital signature for the material upon uploading, which is stored on the blockchain for authentication and ownership verification. As evidence of ownership and legitimacy, this signature enables users to confirm the media's origin. The immutability of blockchain technology guarantees that this data cannot be changed, shielding authors from infringement.

Content Distribution: The decentralized content distribution network (CDN) makes sure that media is delivered to customers in an effective manner. By analyzing user demand, network traffic, and geographic variables, AI systems improve content delivery while lowering expenses and delay. DApps allow users to access content directly, avoiding middlemen and guaranteeing fair revenue sharing.

Revenue Sharing and Monetization: Users can use platform-specific tokens or cryptocurrencies to buy or access content. By allocating royalties to authors and stakeholders in accordance with pre-established agreements, smart contracts automate the revenue-sharing process. For instance, when a song is bought or streamed, the distributor, producer, and musician may all get their cut of the money right away.

User Interaction and Personalization: AI systems examine user behavior and preferences to provide tailored content. For example, depending on a user's watching or listening history, an AI-powered recommendation engine may provide recommendations for music, films, or articles. Blockchain guarantees that user data is utilized morally and securely while adhering to privacy laws.

Feedback and Ongoing Enhancement: The system includes a feedback loop in which user preferences and interactions are examined to enhance the caliber and applicability of the information. By delivering insights into audience behavior and industry trends, AI-driven analytics help artists improve their products. Blockchain guarantees the responsible and transparent collection of this data.

REAL-WORLD IMPLEMENTATIONS

Artificial intelligence (AI) and blockchain technology are already starting to come together in digital media in practical applications, showing how these technologies have the potential to completely transform the sector. Innovations in decentralized media distribution, blockchain-based media platforms, and AI-powered content production tools are opening the door to a digital media ecosystem that is more safe, effective, and just. Not only are these implementations tackling old issues like content piracy, unequal income sharing, and a lack of transparency, but they are also opening up new avenues for both consumers and producers. A well-known example of a blockchain-based media platform is Audius, a decentralized music streaming service that empowers users and artists by utilizing blockchain technology. As opposed to standard streaming services, which take a large cut of the money made by middlemen, Artists may maintain control over their work and establish direct connections with their audience via Audius. The network ensures that creators receive just compensation for their efforts by using blockchain technology to record music ownership, license conditions, and transactions. Additionally, Audius uses token-based incentives, which let users be paid for taking part in the ecosystem by pushing content or creating playlists. By doing away with the necessity for centralized authority, this decentralized approach promotes openness and trust between producers and consumers. Vevue is another cutting-edge blockchain-based platform that blends blockchain technology with the production and sharing of video content. With Vevue, users may produce and distribute films while receiving bitcoin incentives for their efforts. In order to guarantee that artists retain control over their intellectual property, the platform uses blockchain technology to document content ownership and licensing agreements. A more fair revenue-sharing model is also created by Vevue, which enables viewers to tip producers directly with cryptocurrencies. This strategy not only gives artists more authority but also improves audience participation by encouraging camaraderie and teamwork. Blockchain-integrated AI-powered content creation tools are transforming the production and distribution of digital material, going beyond blockchain-based platforms. High-quality media output, including pictures, movies, and music, may be produced using tools like Runway ML and DeepArt, which use sophisticated AI models like Generative Adversarial Networks (GANs) and transformers. Through the integration of blockchain technology, these solutions guarantee that the created material is tamper-proof, traceable, and authorized. When a creator creates a digital artwork using an AI tool, for instance, the blockchain may document the process, including metadata about the AI model used, the parameters selected, and the author's identity. The blockchain stores this data in an unchangeable manner, offering a clear record of validity and authorship. The automation of licensing and royalty payments using smart contracts is another noteworthy example of blockchain-integrated AI-powered content production. When an AI-generated music is posted on a blockchain-based platform, for example, a smart contract may be set up to automatically pay royalties to the creator, the developer of the AI tool, and the platform operator. All parties receive their fair portion of the earnings thanks to this automated method, which also removes the need for middlemen and lowers administrative costs. Furthermore, the traceability and transparency that blockchain technology offers promote stakeholder trust and avert ownership or compensation issues.

Consumer content delivery is also changing as a result of advancements in decentralized media distribution. Centralized servers, which are frequently the foundation of traditional content distribution networks (CDNs), are susceptible to censorship, data breaches, and single points of failure. On the other hand, decentralized CDNs use peer-to-peer networks and blockchain technologies to provide content more effectively and securely.

A decentralized video distribution platform called Theta Network, for instance, leverages blockchain technology to encourage users to contribute their excess bandwidth and processing power. In addition to providing quicker and more dependable content delivery, network participation allows users to earn bitcoin incentives. In addition to lowering distribution costs, this decentralized strategy improves the accessibility and robustness of the material. Using the InterPlanetary File System (IPFS) to store and share media files is another illustration of decentralized media distribution. Instead of being kept on a single centralized server, material can be dispersed over a network of nodes thanks to the peer-to-peer IPFS protocol. When paired with blockchain technology, IPFS can offer a transparent and safe platform for distributing and storing material.

The blockchain stores metadata like ownership, license conditions, and transaction history, while a musician might submit their tunes to IPFS. In addition to making it possible for creative revenue strategies like pay-per-stream or tokenized ownership, this guarantees that the material is accessible, verifiable, and impenetrable. Blockchain and AI integration in media distribution is fostering new developments in content customisation and recommendation in addition to improving security and efficiency. Blockchain makes ensuring that user data is handled legally and securely, while AI algorithms examine user interaction, behavior, and preferences to offer personalized content suggestions. While blockchain technology guarantees that user data is secured and cannot be viewed or altered without authorization, a decentralized streaming platform may employ artificial intelligence (AI) to suggest films or music based on a user's viewing or listening history. By putting data security and privacy first, this AI and blockchain combo not only improves user experience but also fosters trust.

Furthermore, new monetization models that benefit both artists and customers are being made possible by the confluence of blockchain technology and artificial intelligence. Creators can issue distinct tokens that signify ownership or access rights to their digital property by tokenizing it. These tokens may be exchanged on markets built on blockchain technology, giving content producers new and creative methods to make money off of their work.

For instance, a digital artwork may be issued by an artist as limited-edition tokens that collectors could buy and exchange. In a similar vein, a filmmaker may give out tokens that represent a portion of the ownership of a film, enabling viewers to contribute to and profit from its success. These tokenized models allow consumers to take part in the value creation process while also giving producers access to new revenue sources. Digital media's use of blockchain and AI is also encouraging cross-sector cooperation, opening up new avenues for development and innovation. For example, the gaming sector is using AI and blockchain to provide immersive experiences and revenue streams.

CONCLUSION

Conclusively, the combination of blockchain technology with artificial intelligence (AI) has the ability to completely transform the digital media environment by resolving important issues and opening up previously unheard-of possibilities for content creation, distribution, and revenue. However, achieving this potential will require overcoming several obstacles that call for creative thinking and cross-sector cooperation. The viability of seamlessly and economically integrating blockchain with AI is directly impacted by scalability and interoperability, which continue to be critical issues. Similar to this, protecting data security and privacy is crucial, particularly in a time when digital media platforms are battling the moral ramifications of data abuse, false information, and content authenticity. The ethical issues surrounding the use of these technologies, such as prejudice in AI algorithms and blockchain's effects on the environment, highlight the necessity of sustainable practices and responsible innovation. The combination of blockchain technology and artificial intelligence presents a viable path toward a more open, safe, and just digital media environment in spite of these obstacles. The decentralized and unchangeable nature of blockchain technology allows AI models to function with greater responsibility and trust, guaranteeing equitable treatment for content producers, distributors, and users. Real-time royalty distribution and participation incentives may be achieved through the integration of smart contracts and tokenization processes, which has the potential to completely transform monetization approaches. AI's capacity to evaluate enormous volumes of data may also enhance blockchain processes, increasing their scalability and efficiency for practical uses. Real-world applications like secure intellectual property management, tailored media experiences, and decentralized content platforms demonstrate how these technologies have the ability to revolutionize the digital media sector. A strong foundation for research and development, directed by a multidisciplinary strategy that connects technical innovation, regulatory frameworks, and ethical standards, is necessary for the future, as the chapter explains. Emerging developments that provide a peek of the future of blockchain-AI integration in digital media include federated learning, energy-efficient consensus methods, and cross-chain interoperability solutions. Working together, stakeholders—including media professionals, technology developers, legislators, and academic institutions—will be able to overcome obstacles and promote a healthy environment. Transparency, security, and inclusiveness will be given top priority in the digital media landscape once the unresolved issues at the nexus of blockchain and AI are resolved. As these technologies come together, they have the ability to completely change how we produce, consume, and engage with media by empowering artists, promoting trust, and opening up new commercial opportunities. Blockchain and AI's complementary connection will surely be a pillar for future developments as the digital media environment changes, keeping the sector flexible, adaptable, and in line with the ideals of a world that is changing quickly.

REFERENCES

Bhumichai, D., Smiliotopoulos, C., Benton, R., Kambourakis, G., & Damopoulos, D. (2024). The Convergence of Artificial Intelligence and Blockchain: The State of Play and the Road Ahead. *Information*, *15*(5), 268. https://doi.org/10.3390/info15050268DOI: 10.3390/info15050268

Palaiokrassas, G., Litke, A., Fragkos, G., Papaefthymiou, V., Varvarigou, T. (2019). Deploying Blockchains for a New Paradigm of Media Experience. In: Coppola, M., Carlini, E., D'Agostino, D., Altmann, J., Bañares, J. (eds) Economics of Grids, Clouds, Systems, and Services. GECON 2018. Lecture Notes in Computer Science. vol 11113. Springer, Cham. https://doi.org/10.1007/978-3-030-13342-9_20DOI: 10.3390/info15050268

Wang, H., and Wang, X. (2022). "Framework and Path: A Media Convergence Platform Based on Blockchain Technology," *2022 International Conference on Artificial Intelligence in Everything (AIE)*, Lefkosa, Cyprus, pp. 111-116, doi: 10.1109/AIE57029.2022.00028. DOI: 10.3390/info15050268

Witt, L., Fortes, A. T., Toyoda, K., Samek, W., & Li, D. (2024). Blockchain and artificial intelligence: Synergies and conflicts. *arXiv preprint arXiv:2405.13462*. DOI: 10.3390/info15050268

Bajac, M. B., & Vojinović, M. M. (2022). Blockchain Technologies and Media Transformation. *KULTURA POLISA*, *19*(3), 1–21. https://doi.org/10.51738/Kpolisa2022.19.3r.1bvDOI: 10.3390/info15050268

Oshani, S. (2022). Blockchain for Social Good: Combating Misinformation on the Web with AI and Blockchain. .DOI: 10.1145/3501247.3539016

Saxena, R., Gayathri, E. & Surya Kumari, L. Semantic analysis of blockchain intelligence with proposed agenda for future issues. *Int J Syst Assur Eng Manag* **14** (Suppl 1), 34–54 (2023). https://doi.org/10.1007/s13198-023-01862-yDOI: 10.3390/info15050268

Ria, J. (2023). Blockchain Technology and Its Synergy with Bitcoin, Information Technology Psychology, and AI: A Comprehensive Review. doi: DOI: 10.31234/osf.io/v23k9

Wee, J. (2018). *Tee., Raja, Kumar, Murugesan*. Trust Network, Blockchain and Evolution in Social Media to Build Trust and Prevent Fake News., DOI: 10.1109/ICACCAF.2018.8776822

Zon-Yin, S. (2019). *Jeffrey, J., P., Tsai*. AI Blockchain Platform for Trusting News., DOI: 10.1109/ICDCS.2019.00160

Chapter 3
Fusion of Generative AI and Blockchain Conceptual Framework

Balusamy Nachiappan
https://orcid.org/0009-0006-0951-8078
Prologis, USA

N. Rajkumar
https://orcid.org/0000-0001-7857-9452
Alliance School of Advanced Computing, Alliance University, India

V. Radha
V.S.B. College of Engineering Technical Campus, India

C. Kalpana
Karpagam Institute of Technology, India

C. Viji
https://orcid.org/0000-0002-2759-8896
Alliance School of Advanced Computing, Alliance University, India

G. Nagarajan
https://orcid.org/0000-0003-3278-1326
Saveetha School of Engineering, India

A. Mohanraj
Sri Eshwar College of Engineering, India

ABSTRACT

The convergence of generative synthetic intelligence (AI) and blockchain technology marks a transformative step within the evolution of decentralized and realistic systems. Generative AI, with its capacity to create modern-day content material, models, and simulations, complements blockchain's inherent strengths in ensuring transparency, safety, and decentralization. This paper proposes a conceptual framework for integrating those ground-breaking eras, aiming to address key demanding conditions, including data authenticity, possession rights, and operational performance. The framework leverages blockchain's allocated ledger to soundly

DOI: 10.4018/979-8-3373-1504-1.ch003

keep and verify AI-generated outputs, ensuring traceability and tamper resistance. Clever contracts function a middleman to automate tactics that encompass royalty control for AI-generated intellectual property and verification of model outputs.

1. INTRODUCTION

The convergence of generative artificial intelligence (AI) and the blockchain era represents a ground-breaking shift in the digital landscape. Generative AI, recognized for its ability to create novel information-pushed outputs, and blockchain, celebrated for its at-ease, obvious, and decentralized form, are a transformative generation with tremendous but complementary abilities. This bankruptcy develops a conceptual framework for integrating these generations to cope with crucial demanding situations in belief, protection, and innovation.

Generative AI, through strategies that include Generative Adversarial Networks (GANs), Variational Autoencoders (VAEs), and transformer-based total models, excels in generating specific content, ranging from textual content to pictures. However, problems related to statistics authenticity, ownership, and misuse stay within massive boundaries. Blockchain's immutable ledger and decentralized infrastructure offer a sturdy approach to those annoying situations using the use of ensuring the verifiability and provenance of AI-generated outputs. By way of manner of combining that technology, corporations can set up structures wherein creative outputs are both revolutionary and sincere.

The proposed framework highlights five middle dimensions: records authenticity and ownership, decentralized AI model internet web hosting, clever agreement automation, comfy information sharing, and stepped forward do not forget and obligation. Key applications embody healthcare, wherein artificial medical photographs and drug discovery benefit from blockchain's integrity; finance, in which fraud detection and decentralized finance are improved; delivery chain, with counterfeit prevention and stock optimization; and schooling, enabling customized getting-to-know and academic publishing with demonstrated AI-generated content fabric (Zhang et al., 2024).

No matter their capacity, the integration of generative AI and blockchain faces demanding situations together with scalability, power intake, regulatory ambiguity, and moral issues like bias and privateness. Proposed answers encompass leveraging Layer 2 blockchain scaling answers, adopting inexperienced consensus mechanisms, and growing global regulatory frameworks for AI-generated content material cloth possession and records sharing..

It is with the aid of envisioning future commands, at the side of the improvement of hybrid structures combining on-chain and stale-chain computations, quantum-safe cryptography for blockchain networks, greater suitable interoperability amongst systems, and actual-time applications in dynamic environments. The fusion of generative AI and blockchain holds outstanding promise for at-ease, modern-day, and decentralized digital surroundings, placing the diploma for advancements in the course of industries (Varadarajan, Rajkumar, Mohanraj, et al., 2025). Figure 1 refers to the schematic of GAI-enabled blockchain system.

Figure 1. The schematic of GAI-enabled blockchain

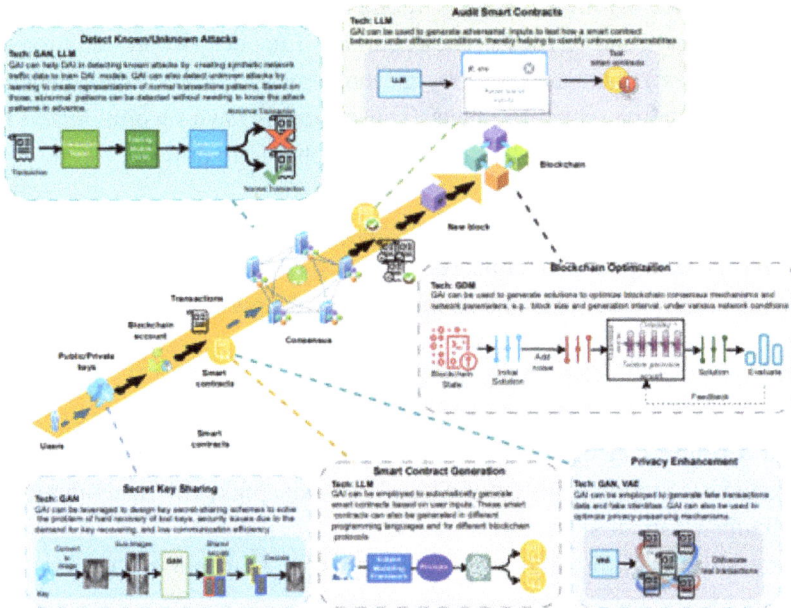

2. GENERATIVE AI AND BLOCKCHAIN

2.1 Overview of Generative AI

Generative AI refers to a subset of artificial intelligence systems designed to create a new content material cloth that mimics human-like creativity. With the aid of the use of leveraging advanced algorithms and computational fashions, generative AI can produce diverse outputs, consisting of text, photos, audio, and films (Lalitha et al., 2024). The number one mechanisms behind generative AI include:

- **Generative Adversarial Networks (GANs)**: GANs embody neural networks, a generator, and a discriminator, going for walks in tandem to create realistic content material. The generator produces outputs, even as the discriminator evaluates their authenticity, iteratively improving the fantastic of the generated facts.
- **Variational Autoencoders (VAEs)**: VAEs are probabilistic fashions that encode and enter information right into a latent space illustration and decode it to generate new, similar outputs. They may be extensively used for obligations like picture synthesis and anomaly detection.
- **Transformer Models**: Models along with GPT (Generative Pre-trained Transformer) and BERT (Bidirectional Encoder Representations from Transformers) make use of hobby mechanisms to apprehend and generate coherent textual or sequential facts. Those models have revolutionized natural language processing and textual content technology duties.

The programs of generative AI span diverse industries (V. Kumar & others, 2024a). As an example, in healthcare, generative AI aids in synthesizing clinical pictures for training functions and designing new drug molecules. In enjoyment, it is used to create virtual artwork, songs, and realistic video game characters. But, annoying situations persist, which include:

1. **Data Authenticity**: Ensuring the reliability and origin of generated content.
2. **Ethical Use**: Stopping misuse of AI-generated deepfakes or manipulated records (Rajkumar, Viji, et al., 2024).
3. **Ownership**: Defining highbrow asset rights for AI-generated outputs.

Addressing those issues requires sturdy mechanisms, and blockchain generation offers a promising road for making sure accepted as true with, traceability, and safety in generative AI packages.

2.2 Overview of Blockchain Technology

Blockchain technology has emerged as a transformative innovation thinking about its inception in 2008 with the discharge of Bitcoin. At its core, blockchain is a dispensed, immutable ledger designed to document and verify transactions transparently and securely. Its decentralized nature eliminates the need for intermediaries, permitting trustless environments in which participants can transact without delay with one another. Over time, blockchain has advanced from being entirely a cryptocurrency enabler to becoming a flexible era with applications in various domains which include finance, healthcare, supply chain, and beyond. (Varadarajan, Rajkumar, Viji, et al., 2025)

2.2.1 Key Characteristics of Blockchain Technology

1. **Decentralization**:

Not like traditional centralized systems, blockchain operates on a decentralized network of nodes. Every node holds a replica of the blockchain ledger, ensuring redundancy and putting off unmarried factors of failure. This decentralization complements transparency and is given as properly while reducing the risk of manipulation or corruption.

2. **Immutability**:

As quickly as a transaction is recorded on the blockchain, it can't be altered or deleted. This immutability is finished through cryptographic hashing, which links every block to the preceding one, forming a cozy chain. Immutability guarantees records integrity, making blockchain especially valuable for audit trails and compliance.

3. **Transparency**:

Public blockchains allow all participants to view transaction records, fostering transparency and responsibility. Even in non-public or consortium blockchains, getting proper access to controls can ensure that prison entities can confirm transactions.

4. **Security**:

Blockchain makes use of cryptographic algorithms to cozy statistics. Virtual signatures authenticate transactions, and hashing protects information from tampering. Furthermore, the distributed nature of blockchain makes it resilient to cyberattacks, as compromising the complete network would possibly require controlling most people of nodes (Viji et al., 2025).

5. **Consensus Mechanisms**:

Blockchain is predicated on consensus algorithms to validate transactions and keep the integrity of the ledger. Famous mechanisms consist of:

o **Proof of Work (PoW)**: Miners resolve complex mathematical puzzles to validate transactions, ensuring delivery as true within the community.

o **Proof of Stake (PoS)**: Validators are decided on primarily based on the amount of cryptocurrency they hold and stake within the community, presenting energy-efficient alternatives to PoW.

o **Delegated Proof of Stake (DPoS)** and **Practical Byzantine Fault Tolerance (PBFT)** are also widely used in specific blockchain implementations.

6. **Smart Contracts**:

Clever contracts are self-executing agreements coded into the blockchain. These contracts mechanically implement phrases and situations, disposing of the want for intermediaries and allowing automation. They are foundational to blockchain ecosystems like Ethereum.

7. **Tokenization**:

Blockchain allows the arrival of digital tokens representing belongings, from cryptocurrencies like Bitcoin to non-fungible tokens (NFTs) for precise property like paintings or real property. Tokenization democratizes access to possession and investment.

2.2.2 Types of Blockchains

1. **Public Blockchain**:

Open to each person, public blockchains are completely decentralized. Examples encompass Bitcoin and Ethereum. Those networks are at ease and apparent but face scalability stressful situations due to immoderate transaction volumes.

2. **Private Blockchain**:

Limited to participants, personal blockchains are utilized by agencies to hold control at the same time as leveraging blockchain's safety and transparency. Those are quicker and more scalable than public blockchains.

3. **Consortium Blockchain**:

Operated by way of a group of entities, consortium blockchains integrate the blessings of personal and public systems. They are first-rate for industries like banking and delivery chain management, wherein multiple stakeholders need sharing to get admission.

4. **Hybrid Blockchain**:

Combining public and personal elements, hybrid blockchains allow businesses to govern and get the right of entry while maintaining transparency for selected strategies.

2.2.3 Blockchain Architecture

The blockchain architecture consists of several key components:

1. **Blocks**:

Every block includes a batch of validated transactions, a timestamp, and a cryptographic hash of the previous block, ensuring continuity within the chain.

2. **Nodes**:

Nodes are individual computers within the community that shop and confirm the blockchain ledger. They ensure redundancy and preserve consensus.

3. **Consensus Layer**:

This layer ensures all nodes agree on the validity of transactions and blocks, using protocols like PoW, PoS, or others.

4. **Data Layer**:

The records layer records transaction information in an easy and established way.

5. **Network Layer**:

This residue permits conversation among nodes, allowing information sharing and consensus.

6. **Application Layer**:

The utility layer helps smart contracts, individual interfaces, and APIs interplay with blockchain-based total structures.

2.2.4 Use Cases of Blockchain Technology

1. **Finance and Banking**:
    o   Blockchain streamlines pass-border bills, reducing expenses and settlement times.
    o   Decentralized finance (DeFi) allows peer-to-peer lending, trading, and funding without intermediaries (Varadarajan et al., 2024).
2. **Supply Chain Management**:
    o   Blockchain improves transparency and traceability, supporting the combat of counterfeiting and making sure of the authenticity of products.
    o   Clever contracts automate stock manipulation and provider bills.
3. **Healthcare**:
    o   Blockchain secures affected individual records, ensuring records privacy and interoperability all through healthcare vendors.
    o   It allows the safe sharing of scientific studies and scientific trial statistics.
4. **Identity Management**:
    o   Blockchain allows self-sovereign identities, giving individuals manipulation over their non-public statistics.
    o   Governments and agencies can use blockchain for relaxed digital identity structures.
5. **Education**:
    o   Blockchain verifies academic credentials and prevents certificate fraud.
    o   It allows decentralized getting-to-know structures with examined AI-generated content material.
6. **Voting and Governance**:
    o   Blockchain ensures relaxed and transparent elections, reducing fraud and increasing voter acceptance as real with.
    o   It allows decentralized self-reliant organizations (DAOs) for collaborative selection-making.

2.2.5 Challenges in Blockchain Adoption

1. **Scalability**:

As transaction volumes grow, public blockchains face obstacles in velocity and efficiency. Solutions like Layer 2 scaling and sharding are being evolved to address those problems.

2. **Energy Consumption**:

PoW-based blockchains eat great power, raising environmental concerns. Alternatives like PoS provide greater sustainable options.

3. **Regulatory Uncertainty**:

The lack of clear rules for blockchain applications, mainly cryptocurrencies, hinders extremely good adoption.

4. **Interoperability**:

Blockchain networks are often characteristic of silos, limiting their potential to talk and share data. Interoperability protocols are had to bridge this hole.

5. **Complexity**:

The technical complexity of blockchain systems poses a barrier to access for groups and builders. Purchaser-friendly solutions are required to simplify adoption.

6. **Privacy Concerns**:

Even as blockchain gives transparency, it could additionally disclose sensitive information. Techniques like zero-knowledge proofs and off-chain storage can mitigate privacy dangers.

2.3 Integration of Generative AI and Blockchain

The mixture of generative AI and blockchain brings together the maximum transformative technology of the modern-day generation, offering answers to challenges that arise in statistics authenticity, security, possession, and decentralized processing. Whilst generative AI makes a specialty of growing, modern-day content material cloth, blockchain guarantees the provenance, integrity, and traceability of such content material. Collectively, they could set up a framework for straightforward, decentralized, and progressive virtual ecosystems Data Sharing (Mazhar et al, 2025). Figure 2 refer to the model of IoT-orient blockchain system (Ahmed et al., 2022) (Mazhar et al., 2025).

Figure 2. The model of IoT-orient blockchain system

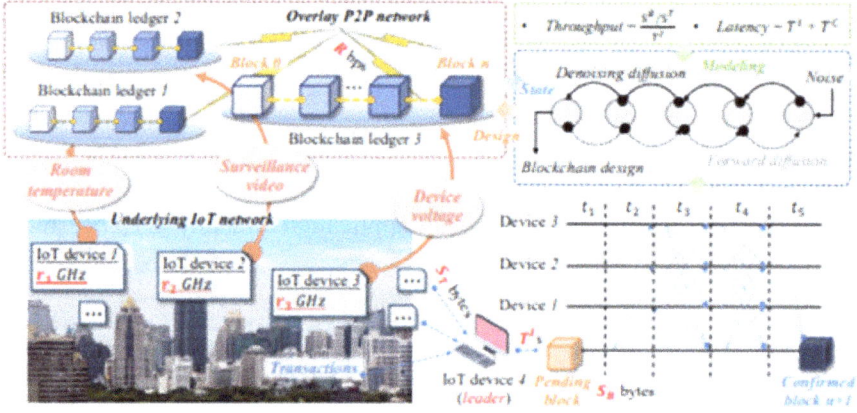

2.3.1 Key Principles of Integration

1. **Data Authenticity and Provenance**:

Generative AI structures, together with those using deep studying models, create extremely good quantities of statistics, consisting of text, photos, and motion pictures. But, ensuring that those outputs are real, loose from tampering, and traceable to their supply is a venture. Blockchain addresses this by embedding the metadata of AI-generated outputs into its immutable ledger, providing an auditable trail of foundation and changes(Andronie et al., 2024).

2. **Decentralized Hosting and Training**:

AI models are historically hosted and educated on centralized servers, which can come to be single factors of failure and dreams for cyberattacks. Blockchain permits decentralized web hosting of AI models and datasets. The use of distributed garage structures like IPFS (Interplanetary file gadget) integrated with blockchain(Nachiappan, Rajkumar, et al., 2025), AI fashions, and facts may be securely saved and accessed in a decentralized manner(Nguyen et al., 2024).

3. **Smart Contracts for Automation**:

Smart contracts can automate various elements of the combination, along with handling intellectual belonging rights for AI-generated content, dishing out royalties to creators, and enforcing moral utilization regulations. For instance, an artist who usage of generative AI to create a tune may additionally want to encode royalty distribution rules right into a smart settlement, making sure of honest repayment every time their painting is offered or licensed.

4. **Secure Data Sharing**:

Training generative AI fashions require large datasets, regularly accrued from more than one property. Blockchain ensures secure and privacy-retaining information sharing with the useful resource of permitting individuals to hold control over their records whilst sharing simplest the important statistics for AI training. Technology like zero-information proofs can similarly decorate this with the aid of verifying facts' validity without exposing their contents.

5. **Enhanced Trust and Accountability**:

Blockchain's transparency lets stakeholders affirm how generative AI outputs are created and used. For instance, in industries like journalism or advertising, blockchain can offer proof that AI-generated content material adheres to ethical guidelines and has now not been manipulated (Fan et al., 2024).

2.3.2 Workflow for Integration

1. **Input Collection and Verification**:
    o Generative AI systems require datasets for education or incredible-tuning.
    o Records providers add their datasets to a decentralized blockchain-primarily based garage machine. Metadata, including ownership and consent facts, is recorded on the blockchain (Rane et al., 2023).
2. **Model Training and Hosting**:
    o AI fashions are educated on the installed datasets. This machine may be decentralized through the use of blockchain-primarily based structures that incentivize individuals with tokens for presenting the computation-al property.
    o The knowledgeable models are hosted on a decentralized network, en-suring redundancy and stopping unauthorized right of entry.
3. **Content Creation and Recording**:
    o The generative AI device produces content material based mostly on purchaser input. The content material's metadata, which includes time-stamps, creators, and algorithms used, is recorded on the blockchain to ensure provenance (Liu & others, 2023b).

4. **Smart Contract Deployment**:
   o Clever contracts govern the usage of AI-generated content material, implementing phrases including licensing, ownership switch, and royalty distribution.
   o The ones contracts routinely execute while predefined conditions are met, making sure of fairness and transparency.

2.3.3 Applications of Generative AI and Blockchain Integration

1. **Creative Industries**:
   o **Art and Design**: Artists with using generative AI can tokenize their works as NFTs (non-fungible tokens) on a blockchain. This ensures provenance, protects highbrow property, and allows direct sales to collectors without intermediaries.
   o **Music and Film**: Blockchain can manipulate copyrights and royalties for AI-generated tune and video content material cloth, making sure truthful income sharing among creators.
2. **Healthcare**:
   o **Synthetic Data Generation**: Generative AI can create artificial medical information for research, training, and diagnostics. Blockchain ensures the authenticity and privacy of those records, preventing misuse or unauthorized right of access.
   o **Drug Discovery**: AI-generated molecular fashions for drug discovery may be saved and set up at the blockchain, making sure reproducibility and traceability (V. Kumar & others, 2024b).
3. **Finance**:
   o **Fraud Detection**: Generative AI can become aware of fraudulent patterns in monetary transactions, whilst blockchain offers an immutable record of those analyses for auditability.
   o **Decentralized Finance (DeFi)**: smart contracts powered through generative AI can create customized financial services, alongside dynamic interest prices based on market conditions.
4. **Supply Chain and Logistics**:
   o Blockchain and AI together permit actual-time tracking of products. Generative AI can expect supply chain bottlenecks, on the identical time as blockchain ensures statistics accuracy and traceability, stopping counterfeiting.
5. **Education and Publishing**:
   o Blockchain ensures the authenticity of AI-generated instructional content material, stopping plagiarism and making sure of right attribution.

o   In schooling, generative AI can create personalised gaining knowledge of substances, and blockchain can validate the accuracy of those assets.

6. **Gaming and Virtual Worlds**:
   o   Generative AI can create dynamic project environments and characters, at the identical time as blockchain lets in at ease ownership of in-sport property thru tokenization.

2.3.4 Challenges in Integration

1. **Scalability**:
   o   Blockchain networks face overall performance bottlenecks at the same time as managing big quantities of facts or transactions. Integrating AI outputs, which can be useful resource-massive, exacerbates the annoying situations.
   o   Ability answers embody Layer 2 scaling, sharding, and off-chain computations.

2. **Data Privacy**:
   o   Sharing touchy datasets for AI schooling increases privateness issues. Blockchain's transparency, on the same time as beneficial for verification, can inadvertently display sensitive statistics.
   o   Strategies like homomorphic encryption and differential privacy can mitigate those dangers.

3. **Regulatory Uncertainty**:
   o   The criminal frameworks governing AI-generated content material material and blockchain utilization are though evolving. Questions around highbrow property rights, statistics ownership, and duty live unresolved.

4. **Energy Consumption**:
   o   Every blockchain and AI tactic, mainly people who use evidence of difficult paintings or huge-scale version schooling, is electricity-widespread.
   o   Transitioning to strength-green consensus mechanisms like proof of Stake and optimizing AI model architectures can address the ones issues.

5. **Complexity and Interoperability**:
   o   Integrating complex generation requires knowledge and considerable improvement efforts. Additionally, interoperability among unique blockchain networks and AI systems is an undertaking.
   o   Standardization efforts and middleware solutions are had to bridge these gaps.

2.3.5 Future Directions

The combination of generative AI and blockchain continues to be in its infancy, however, several promising avenues exist for future exploration:

1. **Hybrid Architectures**:

Combining on-chain and stale-chain processing can optimize scalability and average performance. As an example, AI fashions may be knowledgeable off-chain at the same time as their metadata and outputs are recorded on-chain.

2. **Quantum-Safe Cryptography**:

As quantum computing advances, blockchain networks ought to adopt quantum-resistant algorithms to make certain prolonged-term protection.

3. **Interoperability Protocols**:

Growing protocols for seamless conversation among blockchain networks and AI systems can beautify adoption and value.

4. **Real-Time Applications**:

Integrating blockchain and generative AI in dynamic environments, together with self-sustaining automobiles or IoT structures, requires enhancements in latency bargain and computational performance.(Rajkumar et al., 2025).

With the useful resource of leveraging their complementary strengths, generative AI and blockchain can release new possibilities during industries, growing an easy, decentralized, and innovative virtual environment.

2.4 Current Challenges and Limitations

The mixing of generative AI and blockchain technology gives a promising street for innovation, but it isn't always without giant demanding conditions and barriers. Those stressful conditions span technical, operational, moral, and regulatory domains, every posing hurdles that want to be addressed for a successful adoption and implementation. This segment explores these demanding situations in element, providing insights into their root reasons and implications.

2.4.1 Technical Challenges

a. Scalability and Performance Bottlenecks
    - **Blockchain Scalability**: conventional blockchain networks, mainly those that use proof of Work (PoW) mechanisms, are afflicted by way of low throughput and immoderate latency. For example, Bitcoin can method most effective about 7 transactions in line with second, and Ethereum approximately 30. Integrating computationally extensive generative AI methods exacerbates those barriers(Varadarajan, Viji, et al., 2025).
    - **AI Model Scalability**: Generative AI models, especially big-scale ones like GPT or GANs, require first-rate computational assets. Coping with those models in decentralized blockchain surroundings is hard due to the immoderate aid call for.
    - **Data Storage**: Storing large AI-generated datasets or models directly at the blockchain is impractical due to confined on-chain storage potential and immoderate transaction costs. This necessitates off-chain answers like IPFS, adding layers of complexity(Nachiappan, Viji, et al., 2025).
b. Energy Consumption
    - Schooling generative AI fashions call for giant computational strength, often jogging on immoderate-overall performance GPUs or TPUs. Blockchain networks, especially PoW-based completely ones, are infamous for his or her strength and inefficiency.
    - The mixed strength necessities of AI and blockchain beautify concerns approximately sustainability and environmental impact, in particular in light of world weather alternate projects.
c. Interoperability and Integration
    - Generative AI frameworks (e.g., TensorFlow, PyTorch) and blockchain systems (e.g., Ethereum, Hyperledger) function the usage of exceptional protocols and architectures. Integrating those structures requires middleware solutions, which could introduce inefficiencies and compatibility issues.
    - lack of standardized APIs and protocols for seamless interaction among AI models and blockchain networks further complicates integration.
d. Latency and Real-Time Processing
    - Many generative AI programs, along with dynamic content generation for actual-time man or woman interactions, call for low-latency processing. Blockchain's consensus mechanisms, especially in decentralized

networks, frequently introduce delays that are incompatible with such requirements.

2.4.2 Ethical Challenges

a. Bias and Fairness
    - Generative AI fashions are knowledgeable on massive datasets, which may include inherent biases. Whilst such models are included with blockchain, these biases end up continually embedded inside the decentralized statistics, developing ethical worries.
    - For example, biased outputs in areas like hiring, felony judgments, or content material moderation may additionally want to have a way of engaging in poor effects.
b. Ownership and Intellectual Property
    - Organising possession of AI-generated content material is a complicated problem. Blockchain can music the provenance of content material, but questions remain about whether or no longer the writer of the version, the data proprietor, or the AI itself holds possession rights.
    - Intellectual belongings legal suggestions have now not however superior to cope with those worrying situations efficiently, developing a gray location for businesses and individuals.
c. Misinformation and Deepfakes
    - Generative AI can produce hyper-practical however fake content (e.g., deepfakes, artificial media). At the same time, as such content material is tested and saved immutably on a blockchain, it may inadvertently lend credibility to misinformation, making it tougher to come across and counter.
d. Privacy Concerns
    - Blockchain's transparency, at the same time as useful for duty, may also additionally battle with privacy necessities. Sensitive statistics used or generated by using AI fashions may moreover come to be uncovered if improperly managed in a decentralized environment

2.4.3 Regulatory Challenges

a. Lack of Legal Frameworks
    - Each generative AI and blockchain performs in enormously unregulated domain names. The fusion of these technologies creates new complex-

ities, together with figuring out legal responsibility for AI-generated outputs or ensuring compliance with global facts protection legal guidelines.

- Governments globally are although grappling with the way to regulate AI and blockchain for my part, no longer to say in tandem.

b. Cross-Border Data Sharing
  - Blockchain's decentralized nature technique that facts may be saved during more than one jurisdiction, each with its private records safety and privateness guidelines (e.G., GDPR interior Europe, CCPA in California).
  - Making sure compliance with those policies at the identical time as allowing seamless operation poses an fantastic assignment.

c. Right to be Forgotten
  - Privateness legal guidelines which consist of GDPR embody provisions similar to the "proper to be forgotten," which conflicts with blockchain's immutability. Getting rid of AI-generated content material or education records from a blockchain community is inherently tough.

2.4.4 Operational Challenges

a. High Costs
  - Schooling generative AI models is computationally costly, often requiring specialized hardware and massive-scale datasets.
  - Blockchain implementation entails charges related to transaction prices, infrastructure improvement, and network protection. The combined fees can deter corporations, mainly small and medium-sized firms (SMEs), from adopting the one's technologies.

b. Complexity and Accessibility
  - Every generative AI and blockchain is a complex generation requiring specialised information for implementation and use. This complexity creates boundaries to access to non-technical users and industries.
  - The lack of character-pleasant interfaces and equipment for integrating that technology in addition limits their accessibility.

c. Resistance to Change
  - Groups with entrenched legacy systems can also furthermore withstand adopting new era because of perceived risks, loss of facts, or issues with interoperability with gift processes.

d. Trust Issues

- On the identical time as blockchain gives transparency, it can not ensure the accuracy or ethical use of AI-generated content material fabric cloth. Clients may additionally moreover distrust outputs from black-field AI models, even though the blockchain verifies their provenance.

2.4.5 Integration-Specific Challenges

a. On-Chain vs. Off-Chain Balance
- Storing big AI-generated outputs on-chain is impractical, necessitating the usage of off-chain solutions like IPFS or cloud garage. Determining the top-rated balance between on-chain and stale-chain statistics storage is a crucial format challenge.
b. Real-Time Decision Making
- actual-time programs, including AI-powered decentralized finance (DeFi) structures, require instant preference-making. Blockchain's inherent latency and generative AI's computational demands could make real-time integration hard.
c. Tokenization Complexities
- Tokenizing AI-generated content material (e.g., NFTs for digital artwork or tracking) increases questions about fungibility, valuation, and market manipulation. Setting up truthful valuation mechanisms and stopping fraud in tokenized AI content material markets stay unresolved worrying situations
d. Security Vulnerabilities
- AI fashions deployed in decentralized environments are vulnerable to hostile attacks, version robbery, and statistics poisoning. Similarly, blockchain smart contracts could have insects or exploits, leading to monetary or operational losses.

2.4.6 Addressing These Challenges

Efforts to overcome these challenges include:

1. **Technical Innovations**:
    o Leveraging Layer 2 scaling answers (e.g., rollups, sidechains) to enhance blockchain scalability.
    o Growing mild-weight, strength-inexperienced AI models for decentralized environments.
2. **Standardization**:

o   Organising organization requirements for integrating generative AI and blockchain, making sure interoperability and reducing complexity.

3. **Regulatory Alignment**:

o   Taking part with policymakers to make bigger frameworks for AI-generated content fabric ownership, privacy compliance, and pass-border information sharing.

4. **Energy Efficiency**:

o   Transitioning blockchain networks to strength-green consensus mechanisms (e.g., evidence of Stake).

o   The use of renewable energy sources for powering AI schooling and blockchain operations.

5. **Ethical Frameworks**:

o   Developing tips for responsible AI and blockchain use, specializing in equity, transparency, and duty.

6. **Awareness and Training**:

o   instructing stakeholders approximately the advantages and risks of these technologies to assemble consider and foster adoption.

3. CONCEPTUAL FRAMEWORK

3.1 Components of the Framework

The fusion of generative AI and blockchain is underpinned by the useful resource of numerous key components that form the muse of the conceptual framework. Those components are designed to address the technical, ethical, and operational traumatic situations inherent within the integration device. The primary components encompass:

- **Data Provenance and Ownership**: Leveraging blockchain's immutable ledger to song the beginning and ownership of AI-generated content material cloth, making sure authenticity and accountability.
- **Decentralized AI Model Management**: web website hosting and deploying generative AI fashions in a decentralized manner using blockchain to beautify accessibility, reduce reliance on considerable entities, and enhance safety.
- **Smart Contracts**: Automating tactics together with licensing, royalty distribution, and content validation through self-executing contracts saved on the blockchain.
- **Interoperability Mechanisms**: putting in standardized protocols to permit seamless interplay among numerous AI frameworks and blockchain systems.

3.2 Architecture of the Framework

The form of the conceptual framework integrates generative AI and blockchain via a layered method, making sure modularity, scalability, and flexibility. The key layers of the shape encompass:

- **Application Layer**: Interfaces for stop-customers to engage with AI-generated content and blockchain-based total functionalities, which consist of digital wallets and marketplaces.
- **Smart Contract Layer**: Implementation of clever contracts to govern transactions, implement rules, and automate workflows.
- **Blockchain Layer**: The center blockchain infrastructure offering decentralized storage, consensus mechanisms, and data integrity.
- **Off-Chain Storage Layer**: answers like IPFS or cloud storage for coping with massive datasets and AI model parameters that can't be stored on-chain due to scalability constraints.
- **AI Model Layer**: The generative AI fashions answerable for growing novel content material, professional and deployed in a decentralized environment.

3.3 Smart Contract-based Model Management

- **Model Validation**: making sure the authenticity and integrity of AI models deployed on the blockchain via verification mechanisms.
- **Audit Trails**: keeping apparent facts of all interactions with AI models, together with education facts usage, output generation, and person get admission to.

3.4 Decentralized Content Generation

The decentralized content material era leverages the synergy among generative AI and blockchain to create a trustless and secure environment for generating and doling out digital content material. Core elements of decentralized content technology encompass:

- **Content Validation**: the use of blockchain to verify the authenticity and originality of AI-generated outputs, addressing problems related to deepfakes and incorrect information.
- **Tokenization**: Representing AI-generated content material as tokens (e.g., NFTs) to facilitate ownership switch, monetization, and provenance monitoring.

- **Collaborative Creation**: permitting a couple of stakeholders to make contributions to and co-very own AI-generated content material cloth via decentralized structures.
- **Resilience and Availability**: ensuring excessive availability and fault tolerance by way of allotting AI models and content material throughout decentralized nodes.

Using the usage of integration of these components, the conceptual framework establishes a strong basis for the fusion of generative AI and blockchain, paving the way for contemporary programs and addressing critical demanding situations in don't forget, protection, and scalability

4. BENEFITS AND APPLICATIONS

4.1 Security and Transparency

The integration of generative AI and blockchain creates extraordinarily comfy and obvious surroundings that address long-status issues in digital content material cloth advent and management. Blockchain's inherent immutability guarantees that record of AI-generated content fabric, which encompass its provenance, ownership, and utilization facts, are securely saved and can't be tampered with. Every interplay with the content material is recorded as a transaction on the blockchain, offering an auditable and obvious path for all stakeholders.

Protection is in addition advanced by using the usage of the decentralized nature of blockchain, which receives rid of the risks related to essential factors of failure. Generative AI fashions, while deployed in a blockchain surrounding, can gain from the ones protection functions. As an instance, blockchain can guard the schooling information utilized by generative AI fashions, ensuring that it isn't always manipulated or accessed via unauthorized entities.

Transparency is further essential, specifically in industries that include journalism and virtual artwork, in which the authenticity of AI-generated content fabric is crucial. With the useful resource of linking each generated output to its originating version and dataset thru the blockchain, customers can confirm the legitimacy of the content, decreasing the threat of incorrect statistics or fraud.

4.2 Decentralization and Authenticity

Decentralization is a cornerstone of the blockchain era and performs a pivotal feature in fostering authenticity in the fusion of generative AI and blockchain. Traditional AI structures are regularly centralized and managed by way of way of unique businesses or systems. This centralization increases issues about monopolization, statistics manipulation, and biased content material cloth technology.

With the aid of leveraging blockchain, generative AI systems can perform in a decentralized manner, shelling out every version schooling and deployment technique in the course of a community of nodes. This decentralization ensures that no unmarried entity has whole control over the AI gadget, selling equity and decreasing the danger of bias.

Authenticity is in addition greater appropriate through the usage of blockchain's capability to establish a verifiable chain of custody for AI-generated content material cloth. As an instance, virtual innovative endeavors or music compositions created through generative AI may be tokenized as non-fungible tokens (NFTs), embedding metadata that verifies the content cloth's originality and possession. This mechanism protects creators from plagiarism and unauthorized use, ensuring that their contributions are diagnosed and rewarded.

4.3 Monetization Opportunities

The fusion of generative AI and blockchain unlocks superb monetization opportunities for creators, developers, and agencies. One of the most prominent avenues is the tokenization of AI-generated content material. Via representing digital assets as NFTs, creators can sell their works in decentralized marketplaces, getting rid of the need for intermediaries and permitting direct transactions with customers.

Clever contracts enhance monetization through automating royalty distribution. As an instance, while AI-generated track or artwork are resold, the appropriate author can collect a predefined percentage of the transaction fee through a self-executing clever agreement. This mechanism guarantees sincere reimbursement and non-forestall sales streams for creators.

Blockchain moreover allows microtransactions, permitting users to pay for AI-generated offerings or content material cloth cloth on a line with-use foundation. For instance, a decentralized platform offering a generative AI gadget for textual content or photograph creation can price users a small charge for every output, tracked and processed through blockchain.

Moreover, agencies can monetize their generative AI fashions with the aid of offering them as decentralized programs (Dapps) on blockchain networks. Customers can get the proper of entry to the ones fashions through paying with cryptocurrency and developing new income streams for AI developers.

4.4 Applications in Digital Art, Music Composition, and Gaming

The mixture of generative AI and blockchain has transformative implications for modern industries, especially in virtual artwork, music composition, and gaming.

- **Digital Art**: Generative AI has already revolutionized virtual paintings by using permitting the appearance of specific and visually cute portions. On the equal time as blended with blockchain, those ingenious endeavors can be tokenized as NFTs, presenting a comfy and obvious method for ownership verification and income. Artists can benefit from royalties on secondary profits, making sure lengthy-time period monetary earnings. Blockchain's provenance tracking additionally addresses problems approximately counterfeit paintings, enhancing agree in the virtual paintings marketplace.
- **Music Composition**: Generative AI fashions can compose true music tracks tailor-made to precise subjects or emotions. By using integrating blockchain, one's compositions may be securely allotted and monetized. Clever contracts allow automatic royalty bills to composers and collaborators, streamlining the revenue-sharing device. Furthermore, blockchain guarantees that song compositions are blanketed from unauthorized use, fostering a sincere surrounding for creators.
- **Gaming**: The gaming business enterprise stands to gain appreciably from the fusion of generative AI and blockchain. Generative AI can create dynamic sports activities assets, which encompasses characters, environments, and storylines, presenting customized and immersive opinions for gamers. Blockchain enhances this via allowing the tokenization of in-recreation assets, allowing gamers to customize, trade, and monetize their digital items. For instance, a completely unique AI-generated weapon or character may be represented as an NFT, providing gamers with tangible charges and fostering a colourful secondary market.

In multiplayer online video games, blockchain ensures trustworthy gameplay by means of keeping obvious information about in-recreation transactions and achievements. This reduces the chance of cheating and fosters agreement among gamers. The combination of generative AI and blockchain also opens new opportunities for decentralized sports development, wherein members throughout the globe can collaborate and co-vert personal undertaking property and sales.

5. CHALLENGES AND FUTURE DIRECTIONS

5.1 Scalability and Interoperability

Scalability remains one of the number one demanding situations for blockchain implementations throughout several sectors, which include libraries and academic studies. Modern blockchain systems can warfare with transaction throughput, particularly while coping with huge datasets or excessive volumes of users. In library and study settings, wherein more than one transaction and statistics request are commonplace, keeping speedy and efficient blockchain structures is important(Jayavadivel et al., 2024).

Interoperability is another undertaking, particularly while libraries or institutions undertake unique blockchain systems. The need for seamless interplay amongst various blockchain systems is important to ensure facts sharing and resource accessibility throughout institutions, which may also moreover use one-of-a-type blockchain protocols.(Rajkumar, Tabassum, et al., 2024).

Future directions for addressing scalability and interoperability may include:

- **Layer 2 Solutions:** strategies like United States of America channels or sidechains may want to beautify scalability with the useful resource of lowering congestion on the principle blockchain.
- **Cross-chain Communication:** Advances in move-chain protocols and decentralized oracles can facilitate interoperability amongst diverse blockchain networks.
- **Sharding:** Splitting the blockchain into smaller, possible quantities should reduce bottlenecks and improve overall performance.

5.2 Regulatory Environment and Security Risks

The regulatory landscape for blockchain technology remains evolving, with many governments and regulatory bodies uncertain of the way to method blockchain use in various fields, which include libraries and academic publishing. The shortage of a clear regulatory framework might also lead to gradual down the gradual adoption of blockchain technology in those sectors.(Viji et al., 2024).

Furthermore, protection risks associated with blockchain, together with fifty 1% assaults, clever settlement vulnerabilities, and flawed key management, pose vast threats. At the same time as blockchain is frequently touted for its safety benefits, vulnerabilities can even exist, in particular inside the context of decentralized programs and 1/three-birthday celebration services.

Future research and development directions could focus on:

- **Developing Legal Frameworks:** developing clearer policies that ensure compliance and consideration in blockchain structures, mainly in sectors like publishing and academic studies.
- **Improved Security Protocols:** developing greater sturdy mechanisms for securing clever contracts, consensus mechanisms, and cryptographic keys.
- **Auditing and Monitoring Tools:** constructing superior equipment to constantly display blockchain networks for capability vulnerabilities and assaults.

5.3 Future Research Directions

Searching forward, research in the blockchain era is probably focused on fixing the modern-day demanding situations and exploring new possibilities for its use in instructional and library settings.

Future research directions include:
- **Integration with AI and Machine Learning:** getting to know how AI and blockchain can be blended to automate choice-making and improve facts transparency in academic environments.
- **Blockchain in Scholarly Publishing:** Investigating how blockchain must similarly disrupt the peer review gadget, copyright management, and open get proper entry to publishing.
- **Blockchain and Data Privacy:** Exploring strategies blockchain can be tailor-made to better protect personal privacy and comply with records safety laws like GDPR(Mohanraj et al., 2024).
- **Decentralized Identity and Access Management:** specializes in how blockchain must transform identification control and get admission to manipulate in educational institutions(N. Kumar et al., 2024).

6. CONCLUSION

6.1 Summary of Key Findings

The aggregate of blockchain generation into libraries and academic institutions affords a transformative opportunity to decorate transparency, protection, and performance in diverse approaches. Key findings from this exploration include:

- **Blockchain's Potential:** Blockchain offers a promising answer for improving data integrity, improving transparency in educational publishing, and streamlining tactics collectively with interlibrary loans and aid sharing.

- **Smart Contracts and Automation:** using clever contracts to automate numerous administrative functions, decreasing charges and enhancing company performance.
- **Security and Privacy Enhancements:** Blockchain's decentralized nature presents advanced security for transactions and educational records, defensive sensitive facts from tampering.
- **Challenges to Adoption:** however its capability, demanding situations related to scalability, interoperability, regulatory compliance, and protection risks need to be addressed for large adoption.

6.2 Implications for Practice and Research

For practitioners in the library and academic fields, the implications are significant:

- **Adoption of Blockchain in Library Services:** Librarians and directors ought to start exploring blockchain solutions for dealing with digital rights, improving useful resource sharing, and enhancing transparency in academic publishing.
- **Policy and Regulatory Considerations:** Policymakers ought to collaborate with era builders to create regulatory frameworks that stabilize innovation with the want for safety, privacy, and compliance with educational necessities.
- **Future Research:** Researchers are endorsed to be aware of developing scalable blockchain solutions, improving interoperability across awesome blockchain systems, and exploring the combination of blockchain with rising eras like AI and tools getting to know to strengthen instructional studies and collaboration.
- For researchers, the exploration of blockchain's potential in library systems and educational strategies opens a wide range of research opportunities, mainly within the regions of privateness, protection, and decentralized structures.

6.3 Final Thoughts and Recommendations

The blockchain era holds exquisite promise for revolutionizing library and academic structures, supplying solutions that decorate transparency, lessen inefficiencies, and grow recall in instructional approaches. However, widespread adoption will rely on overcoming widespread technical and regulatory demanding situations.

Recommendations for the future include:
- **Collaboration Between Stakeholders:** Academic establishments, technology organizations, and policymakers want to collaborate to create a

unified approach to blockchain adoption that addresses each technical and felony problem.

- **Invest in Research and Development:** Establishments have to put money into R&D to find out the scalability and protection of blockchain solutions tailor-made for instructional settings.
- **Pilot Programs:** Universities and libraries want to provoke pilot applications to test the implementation of blockchain for specific use cases, collectively with virtual content cloth management, interlibrary loans, and publishing.

As blockchain technology continues to adapt, it is going to be essential to live knowledgeable about new trends and remain flexible to contain improvements that may in addition enhance instructional enjoyment. Ultimately, with the proper assistance, blockchain should notably enhance the manner educational and library services are added, making sure they're more comfortable, obvious, and inexperienced.

REFERENCES

Ahmed, I., Zhang, Y., Jeon, G., Lin, W., Khosravi, M. R., & Qi, L. (2022, September). A blockchain-and artificial intelligence-enabled smart IoT framework for sustainable city. *International Journal of Intelligent Systems*, *37*(9), 6493–6507. DOI: 10.1002/int.22852

Andronie, M., Blazek, R., Iatagan, M., Skypalova, R., U ă, C., Dijmărescu, A., Kovacova, M., Grecu, G., Pârvu, I., Strakova, J., Guni, C., Zabojnik, S., Chiru, C., Sedláčková, A. N., Novák, A., & Dijmărescu, I. (2024, December 1). Generative artificial intelligence algorithms in Internet of Things blockchain-based fintech management. *Oeconomia Copernicana.*, *15*(4), 1349–1381. DOI: 10.24136/oc.3283

Fan, S., Ilk, N., Kumar, A., Xu, R., & Zhao, J. L. (2024, July 1). Blockchain as a trust machine: From disillusionment to enlightenment in the era of generative AI. *Decision Support Systems*, *182*, 114251. DOI: 10.1016/j.dss.2024.114251

Irfan, M., Elmogy, M., Gupta, S., Khalifa, F., & Dias, R. T. (Eds.). (2024 Aug 26). *AI-driven decentralized finance and the future of finance*. IGI Global., DOI: 10.4018/979-8-3693-6321-8

Jayavadivel, R., Arunachalam, M., Nagarajan, G., Shankar, B. P., Viji, C., & Rajkumar, N., (2024). Historical overview of AI adoption in libraries. In *AI-Assisted Library Reconstruction* (pp. 267–289). IGI Global., DOI: 10.4018/979-8-3693-2782-1.ch015

Kumar, N., Antoniraj, S., Jayanthi, S., Mirdula, S., Selvaraj, S., & Rajkumar, N., (2024). Educational technology and libraries supporting online learning. In *AI-Assisted Library Reconstruction* (pp. 209–237). IGI Global., DOI: 10.4018/979-8-3693-2782-1.ch012

Kumar, V., (2024). *Generative AI and blockchain synergy for healthcare applications: privacy and trust at scale*. Health Inform J.

Lalitha, B., Ramalakshmi, K., Gunasekaran, H., Murugesan, P., Saminasri, P., & Rajkumar, N. (2024). Anticipating AI impact on library services: future opportunities and evolutionary prospects. In *Improving Library Systems with AI: Applications, Approaches, and Bibliometric Insights* (pp. 195–213). IGI Global., DOI: 10.4018/979-8-3693-5593-0.ch014

Liu, Y., (2023). Blockchain-empowered lifecycle management for AI-generated content (AIGC) products in edge networks. *ACM Transactions on Internet Technology*, DOI: 10.1109/MWC.003.2300053

Mazhar, T., Khan, S., Shahzad, T., Khan, M. A., Saeed, M. M., Awotunde, J. B., & Hamam, H. (2025, January 13). Generative AI, IoT, and blockchain in healthcare: Application, issues, and solutions. *Discov Internet Things.*, *5*(1), 5. DOI: 10.1007/s43926-025-00095-8

Mohanraj, A., Viji, C., Varadarajan, M. N., Kalpana, C., Shankar, B., & Jayavadivel, R., (2024). Privacy and security in digital libraries. In *AI-Assisted Library Reconstruction* (pp. 104–125). IGI Global., DOI: 10.4018/979-8-3693-2782-1.ch006

Nachiappan, B., Rajkumar, N., Jagannathan, J., Mohanraj, A., Karthikeyan, N., & Viji, C. (2025). Synergizing blockchain and collaborative networks. In *Leveraging Blockchain for Future-Ready Libraries* (pp. 285–318). IGI Global Scientific Publishing., DOI: 10.4018/979-8-3693-7783-3.ch013

Nachiappan, B., Viji, C., Mohanraj, A., Moorthi, I., Mir, M. H., & Rajkumar, N. (2025). Enhancing data security and accessibility in libraries through blockchain technology. In *Enhancing Security and Regulations in Libraries With Blockchain Technology* (pp. 87–116). IGI Global., DOI: 10.4018/979-8-3693-9616-2.ch005

Nguyen, C. T., Liu, Y., Du, H., Hoang, D. T., Niyato, D., Nguyen, D. N., & Mao, S. (2024, June 11). Generative AI-enabled blockchain networks: Fundamentals, applications, and case study. *IEEE Network*, *39*(2), 232–241. DOI: 10.1109/MNET.2024.3412161

Rajkumar, N., Tabassum, H., Muthulingam, S., Mohanraj, A., Viji, C., & Kumar, N., (2024). Anticipated requirements and expectations in the digital library. In *AI-Assisted Library Reconstruction* (pp. 1–20). IGI Global., DOI: 10.4018/979-8-3693-2782-1.ch001

Rajkumar, N., Viji, C., Mohanraj, A., Senthilkumar, K. R., Jagajeevan, R., & Kovilpillai, J. A. (2024). Ethical considerations of AI implementation in the library era. In *Improving Library Systems with AI: Applications, Approaches, and Bibliometric Insights* (pp. 85–106). IGI Global., DOI: 10.4018/979-8-3693-5593-0.ch007

Rane, N., Choudhary, S., & Rane, J. Blockchain and Artificial Intelligence (AI) integration for revolutionizing security and transparency in finance. *SSRN.* 2023 Nov 17. DOI: 10.2139/ssrn.4644253

Varadarajan, M. N., Rajkumar, N., Mohanraj, A., Delma, T., Mir, M. H., & Viji, C. (2025). Safeguarding digital archives with advanced strategies. In *Enhancing Security and Regulations in Libraries With Blockchain Technology* (pp. 279–310). IGI Global., DOI: 10.4018/979-8-3693-9616-2.ch013

Varadarajan, M. N., Rajkumar, N., Viji, C., & Mohanraj, A. (2024). AI-powered financial operation strategy for cloud computing cost optimization for the future. Salud. *Ciencia y Tecnología-Serie de Conferencias.*, *3*, 694. DOI: 10.56294/sct-conf2024694

Varadarajan, M. N., Rajkumar, N., Viji, C., Mohanraj, A., Karthikeyan, N., & Nagarajan, G. (2025). Leveraging blockchain for enhanced user authentication and privacy. In *Enhancing Security and Regulations in Libraries With Blockchain Technology* (pp. 149–180). IGI Global., DOI: 10.4018/979-8-3693-9616-2.ch008

Viji, C., Jagannathan, J., Rajkumar, N., Mohanraj, A., Nachiappan, B., & Kovilpillai, J. A. J. (2025). Leveraging blockchain technology to enhance library security. In *Enhancing Security and Regulations in Libraries With Blockchain Technology* (pp. 181–200). IGI Global., DOI: 10.4018/979-8-3693-9616-2.ch009

Viji, C., Najmusher, H., Rajkumar, N., Mohanraj, A., Nachiappan, B., & Neelakandan, C., (2024). Intelligent library management using radio frequency identification. In *AI-Assisted Library Reconstruction* (pp. 126–143). IGI Global., DOI: 10.4018/979-8-3693-2782-1.ch007

Zhang, Z., Rao, Y., Xiao, H., Xiao, X., & Yang, Y. (2024)Proof of quality: A costless paradigm for trustless generative AI model inference on blockchains.

Chapter 4
The Convergence of Intelligence and Trust:
Theoretical Approaches to Generative AI and Blockchain

Mary R. Asha
https://orcid.org/0009-0004-9664-0981
Adhi College of Engineering and Technology, India

G. Sivakumar
https://orcid.org/0000-0002-0455-775X
Erode Sengunthar Engineering College, India

B. Mullaikodi
C.K. College of Engineering and Technology

A. Manchula
Nandha Engineering College, India

ABSTRACT

The combination of Generative AI with Blockchain technology offers a paradigm change in the digital media world, where intelligence meets trust. This chapter digs into the theoretical foundations of this convergence, giving a thorough examination of how the combination of these two disruptive technologies tackles important issues in content authenticity, ownership, and security. A new paradigm for the development, validation, and distribution of digital media assets arises from combining the creative power of Generative AI with the immutable trust of Blockchain. The chapter delves into key theoretical approaches, such as the use of decentralized

DOI: 10.4018/979-8-3373-1504-1.ch004

ledgers to authenticate AI-generated content, smart contracts for licensing and royalty management, and the integration of NFTs (Non-Fungible Tokens) as proof of ownership for AI-generated digital assets.

1. INTRODUCTION

A revolutionary development in the field of digital media and content production is represented by the combination of blockchain technology with generative artificial intelligence. The way material is created, verified, and shared may be revolutionized by combining the trust, transparency, and immutability of blockchain technology with the creative potential of generative models. This convergence offers a crucial technology answer as companies struggle with problems including content authenticity, intellectual property theft, and just pay for creators. The creation of audiovisual material has been completely transformed by generative AI, which is driven by models such as Diffusion Models, Transformers, and GANs (Generative Adversarial Networks). These models are capable of producing very human-like text, picture, audio, and video material. The decentralized and unchangeable record of blockchain, on the other hand, guarantees accountability, transparency, and traceability for each and every network transaction or activity. A new paradigm is created when these two technologies come together, combining content creation with improved ownership verification, increased trust, and fair income sharing. This integration tackles a number of urgent issues facing the ecosystem of digital content. Deepfakes and AI-generated synthetic media, for example, have sparked worries about disinformation, copyright violations, and the moral application of AI-generated content. The tamper-proof characteristics of blockchain technology may be used to trace the origin of such material, guaranteeing content source verification and accountability. Furthermore, the advent of blockchain-powered Non-Fungible Tokens (NFTs) has made it possible to validate AI-generated content, defining precise ownership rights and opening up new revenue streams for producers. The effects of convergence are felt in a variety of fields, such as advertising, gaming, education, entertainment, and the arts. Blockchain technology may be used by platforms, media businesses, and content creators to guarantee that royalties are paid out equitably and by consumers to confirm the legitimacy of the material they watch. Theoretically, the confluence of these technologies necessitates a reconsideration of conventional notions of creativity, ownership, and trust. With an emphasis on important frameworks, difficulties, and possibilities, this chapter examines the theoretical underpinnings of this convergence. Understanding the distinct tenets and workings of blockchain and generative artificial intelligence is crucial to appreciating the breadth and promise of this confluence.

Generative AI – An Introduction

A subclass of artificial intelligence known as "generative AI" employs machine learning models to produce original text, pictures, music, video, and other types of material. Generative models seek to produce new, unique data that reflects the characteristics of the data they were trained on, in contrast to typical AI models that concentrate on categorization or prediction.

In this field, the most well-known models are:

- Generative Adversarial Networks, or GANs, are used to produce synthetic media, realistic photos, and movies.
- Large language models (LLMs) such as ChatGPT and GPT-4 use transformers to generate natural language.
- Variational autoencoders (VAEs) are helpful for generative applications in image synthesis and latent space manipulation.
- Diffusion models are used to create high-quality picture synthesis in AI art generators such as DALL-E and Stable Diffusion.

These algorithms generate material that reflects the learnt distribution after identifying patterns in training data. This makes it possible for media production to automate repetitive creative chores, produce original media content, and prototype quickly.

Blockchain Technology – An Introduction

A decentralized, distributed ledger system called blockchain technology keeps an eternal, unchangeable, and transparent record of all transactions. A collection of transactions is contained in each "block" of the chain, and once a block is added, it cannot be removed without the network's consent. Although this technology was first created to facilitate cryptocurrencies like Bitcoin, its uses have now spread to other industries, such as digital identity verification, supply chain management, and healthcare.

Among the blockchain's primary attributes are:

- Decentralization: The system is not dominated by one party, guaranteeing transparency and equity.
- Immutability: Information integrity is ensured by the inability to alter data after it has been captured.
- Transparency: All parties involved may see transactions, which encourages accountability.

- Self-executing contracts known as "smart contracts" automate procedures and make sure that prerequisites are satisfied before payments or other actions are taken.

Blockchain is used in digital media for content tracking, royalty payments, and intellectual property protection. Media makers may trace the internet usage of their work and verify ownership by labeling media files with distinct cryptographic hashes.

Theoretical Perspectives on the Convergence of Generative AI and Blockchain

The demand for more transparent, ethical, and safe digital content creation and distribution is what is driving the confluence of blockchain technology with generative artificial intelligence. The following theoretical frameworks can be used to interpret this convergence:

- Blockchain's immutability ensures content authentication and trustworthiness by limiting the spread of deepfakes and guaranteeing the validity of AI-generated content.
- Ownership and Copyright — Non-Fungible Tokens, or NFTs, are essential for guaranteeing that designers have unambiguous ownership rights over work produced by artificial intelligence.
- Decentralized Control: By guaranteeing community-driven decision-making and minimizing platform-centric control, Decentralized Autonomous Organizations (DAOs) can regulate the usage of AI-generated material.
- No matter where their video is released, content producers will always get fair royalties thanks to blockchain-based smart contracts.
- Security and privacy – Blockchain's encryption features safeguard private information associated with AI-generated content, guaranteeing safe access and traceability.

Challenges in the Convergence of Generative AI and Blockchain

Although the potential for Generative AI and Blockchain to merge is encouraging, there are a number of obstacles to overcome:

- Scalability Problems: Blockchain networks frequently have trouble processing massive datasets quickly, which makes it difficult to integrate them with AI models that manage enormous volumes of data.

- Data privacy: Blockchain's openness may reveal private information, and AI models need large datasets to develop. To close this gap, solutions such as zero-knowledge proofs are being investigated.
- Computational Complexity – Energy inefficiency results from the computationally costly consensus process of blockchains and the training of generative models.
- Ethical Issues — Clear policy frameworks are required to address ethical issues around the usage of deepfakes and synthetic media.

Use Cases of the Convergence of Generative AI and Blockchain

Opportunities in a variety of industries are made possible by the combination of blockchain technology with generative AI, including:

- AI-generated art may be produced by artists and tokenized as NFTs, allowing for direct sales to collectors.
- Blockchain tokens may be used to monitor and own AI-generated in-game content in gaming, opening up new revenue sources for both producers and users.
- Entertainment: AI-generated music, screenplays, and video material may have its authenticity confirmed by blockchain technology.
- Marketing & Advertising: Blockchain guarantees that the ad's origin can be verified, while generative AI can provide individualized ad content.

2. STATE OF ART MODELS

Brewer et al. (2024) said that the potential for abuse in a variety of sectors and the replacement of human responsibilities are some of the issues presented by generative AI.

In order to solve problems like AI toxicity, biases, interest misalignment, the black box problem, and abuse, blockchain technology is suggested as a way to encourage transparency, verifiability, and decentralization in AI research and use.

Zhang et al. (2024) discuss that in order to make it easier to deploy large generative AI models on trustless blockchain systems, the article presents a novel inference paradigm termed proof of quality (PoQ), which focuses on the result quality of model inference rather than conventional validation techniques. It introduces PQML, an effective protocol that is resilient to hostile actors and made for real-world NLP generative model inference. According to the research, there is very little processing cost involved in confirming quality ratings, enabling consensus formation in milliseconds—much quicker than current approaches. The protocol attempts to solve the difficulties of maintaining efficiency and integrity in decentralized contexts and is designed for widely used open-source models.

Pillar et al. (2024) says that the study explores how generative artificial intelligence (GenAI) can be incorporated into businesses' innovation and new product development processes, stressing the significance of choosing the right AI model (general vs. expert) and task-specific requirements to determine when and how to trust results produced by GenAI.

While errors in GenAI outputs can foster creativity in the ideation stage, tasks requiring domain-specific knowledge necessitate greater accuracy and confidence in the AI's outputs. It ends with a discussion of the fundamental human skills and organizational tactics required for successful GenAI implementation in innovation management.

Kim et al. (2023) discusses that through extensive locality-sensitive hash comparisons on generated data samples, the paper explores the verification of generative AI outputs in a decentralized, trustless network. It shows that a majority vote among independent verifiers can achieve high accuracy in detecting perceptual collisions in images and consensus in large language models. In order to provide a strong basis for AI verification and consensus that considerably lessens the need for trust in decentralized systems, it presents strategies to reduce stochasticity in generative AI training, such as gossip and synchronization techniques, and introduces a new training dataset, ImageNet-Gen.

Kim et al. (2023) studies that a billion locality sensitive hash comparisons on artificially created data samples are performed to verify generative AI outputs in a decentralized, trustless network. Tolerance and error limitations for verification are empirically shown, and the trade-offs between producing deterministic and non-deterministic outputs are examined. Using greedy approaches or n-way beam searches, the study shows that a majority vote among three independent verifiers may achieve 100% consensus for big language models, while detecting perceptual collisions in produced pictures with over 99.89% accuracy. In order to reduce stochasticity and improve verifiability in generative AI training, it also presents novel training methods.

Tian et al. (2022) says that the disruptive nature of blockchain and artificial intelligence (AI) as well as the possible advantages of merging these two data-driven technologies are highlighted in this article. It highlights the features of blockchain, like traceability, anonymity, decentralization, and non-tampering, which can improve the reliability of AI systems. The study examines previous research on how blockchain might enhance data, algorithms, and processing capacity, among other aspects of AI, and it suggests future avenues of inquiry for the ongoing advancement of both technologies.

Reuel and Undheim (2024) says that given its quick growth, wide range of applications, and ability to improve human performance, the article contends that generative AI calls for adaptive governance, undermining established regulatory frameworks. The study presents an adaptive AI governance framework that addresses risks and constraints such as legislative ambiguity and inadequate supervision, as well as identifying actors and roles, operationalization examples, and shared and actor-specific policy actions.

Nassar et al. (2020) discusses that the limits of present AI algorithms are discussed in the study, including their inability to be explained and their vulnerability to bias and adversarial attacks—two major problems in systems that make decisions. It emphasizes how Explainable AI (XAI) is necessary to make AI judgments more understandable. To improve the reliability and explainability of AI systems, it suggests an architecture that combines blockchain technology, smart contracts, trustworthy oracles, and decentralized storage. With actual applications covered in important domains, the framework seeks to reach decision outcomes through decentralized agreement across many AI and XAI predictors.

Ayissi et al. (2023) explores how blockchain technology and artificial intelligence may work together to create intelligent systems that can make decisions on their own. Decentralized machine learning algorithms and AI oracles for smart contracts are among the many uses of machine learning in decentralized settings that are reviewed. The study discusses technological issues such protecting privacy in decentralized datasets, lessening algorithmic bias, and coordinating autonomous systems' goals with moral principles. Along with addressing persistent concerns about security, accountability, and regulation, it also explores governance procedures for community-managed systems and emphasizes how integrating AI with blockchain technology might provide distributed intelligence that is devoid of trust.

Kshetri et al. (2023) states that enhanced safety and security in AI-powered medical systems:

- Suggested healthAIChain approach to improve patient data security.
- Suggests using HealthAIChain to handle healthcare data securely.
- Combines artificial intelligence and blockchain technologies to increase productivity and safety.

The Need for Convergence in Digital Media

The last several decades have seen a dramatic change in the digital media environment, as quick technological breakthroughs have revolutionized the production, distribution, and consumption of material. Although this evolution has brought about previously unheard-of chances for creativity and invention, it has also brought about a number of serious difficulties, namely in the areas of trust, authenticity, and ownership. The combination of generative AI with blockchain technology presents a viable way to tackle the growing complexity and diversity of digital information. The goal of this convergence is to radically redefine content creation and ownership by establishing a framework that improves transparency, authenticity, and trust in digital media ecosystems.

Critical issues with trust and ownership have been brought about by the exponential rise of digital media. Because digital assets are growing so quickly, traditional content ownership systems have found it difficult to keep up. Because it is so simple to copy, alter, and distribute digital information, intellectual property rights are regularly violated. Significant ownership conflicts have resulted from this, and creators frequently struggle to demonstrate the uniqueness of their work or to successfully defend their intellectual property. The internet's decentralized structure further aggravates these problems by making it challenging to enforce rights in many countries. The advent of blockchain technology provides a decentralized ledger system that potentially resolve these long-standing problems by authenticating ownership and offering an unchangeable record of the origin of material.

A new dimension has been added to digital media with the emergence of generative AI, which has greatly improved the capacity for content production. It is now feasible to produce incredibly lifelike photos, films, and even whole virtual worlds thanks to AI models, especially Generative Adversarial Networks (GANs) and Variational Autoencoders (VAEs). In addition to encouraging creativity and innovation, these developments have aided in the spread of deepfakes and other synthetic media. Serious questions concerning the authenticity of information have been raised by deepfakes, which are AI-generated media that realistically imitate actual people. Their potential to disseminate false information, sway public opinion, and jeopardize individual privacy can undermine confidence in digital material. As deepfakes get more complex, it gets harder to tell the difference between real and fake media, which calls for strong content verification systems.

By automating difficult activities and facilitating the large-scale production of fresh, high-quality material, generative AI has completely transformed the content creation process. With the use of these technologies, content producers, artists, and filmmakers may push the limits of creativity and create previously unthinkable creations. AI is capable of producing realistic visual effects for films, creating creative music, and even building interactive virtual worlds for video games. However, issues of originality and authorship are also raised by this newly discovered creative potential. Who is the rightful owner of a work of art or music created by an AI?

These inquiries emphasize the necessity of precise frameworks that deal with content ownership in AI and guarantee that authors receive just compensation for their labor.

The issues of content ownership and authentication in the context of digital media are greatly aided by blockchain technology. Blockchain can safely document the provenance of digital material by offering a decentralized and unchangeable ledger, guaranteeing that its ownership and origins are clear and verifiable. The blockchain allows for the assignment of a distinct digital signature to each piece of material, which acts as evidence of ownership and legitimacy. This not only defends the intellectual property rights of producers but also aids in the fight against illegal distribution and piracy. Furthermore, smart contracts—self-executing agreements with the terms of the contract explicitly encoded in code—may be created using blockchain technology. These contracts can automate licensing agreements and royalties, guaranteeing that artists receive just compensation for their labour.

The issues of digital media ownership, authenticity, and trust may all be resolved with the use of blockchain technology and generative artificial intelligence. Through the utilization of both technologies' advantages, this convergence has the potential to establish a digital media ecosystem that is more transparent, equal, and safe. For example, blockchain can offer the infrastructure required to verify and safeguard material, while AI can produce high-quality content. The value of digital media is increased by this synergy, which also increases stakeholder, customer, and creative trust.

Technological Foundations of Generative AI

In the field of digital media, generative AI has become a disruptive force that is transforming both the production and consumption of content. The advanced models and algorithms that form the technological underpinnings of generative artificial intelligence have developed throughout time, each adding special capabilities to the field. Generative Adversarial Networks (GANs), Variational Autoencoders (VAEs), diffusion models, and the current explosion of transformer-based and multimodal AI systems are only a few of the model architectures covered by these foundations. By enabling the production of realistic, varied, and high-quality material that emulates human creativity, each of these models has significantly advanced the capabilities of generative artificial intelligence.

The development of generative AI models has seen many noteworthy turning points, each signifying a breakthrough in the capacity of computers to make material that is more and more similar to that created by humans. Early generative models that showed that neural networks could learn complicated data distributions, such Deep Belief Networks (DBNs) and Restricted Boltzmann Machines (RBMs), set the foundation. However, the discipline was genuinely transformed with the introduction of Generative Adversarial Networks (GANs). In order to generate incredibly realistic results, two neural networks—the discriminator and the generator—played a zero-sum game. This was a revolutionary method that was first used by Ian Goodfellow in 2014. By using an adversarial training paradigm, GANs were able to produce remarkably accurate pictures, movies, and even music, which raised the bar for generative models.

Due to their remarkable outcomes and distinctive design, Generative Adversarial Networks (GANs) have come to be associated with cutting-edge generative models. Two parts make up GANs: a discriminator that assesses the legitimacy of the data samples and a generator that generates fresh data samples. As the discriminator seeks to discriminate between created and actual data, the generator seeks to provide data that is indistinguishable from real samples. Both networks are motivated to get better by this adversarial process, which produces excellent generative outputs. Text-to-image translation, video production, and picture synthesis are just a few of the fields in which GANs have found extensive use. They have made it possible to produce lifelike pictures, repair damaged photos, and even create whole scenarios from written descriptions. GANs have drawbacks despite their effectiveness, including training instability and mode collapse, in which the generator only creates a small number of variants. Several variations have been created by researchers to solve these problems and improve GAN performance, such as Deep Convolutional GANs (DCGANs) and Wasserstein GANs (WGANs).

Generative AI is also based on Variational Autoencoders (VAEs), which provide a probabilistic method for generative modeling. To learn data distribution, VAEs use a variational inference framework, in contrast to GANs, which concentrate on adversarial training. A decoder reconstructs the data from this latent representation, whereas an encoder maps incoming data to a latent space. Through the inclusion of a regularization term in the objective function, VAEs guarantee that the latent space contains continuous and meaningful representations, facilitating seamless data creation and interpolation. VAEs have shown useful for applications including unsupervised feature learning, anomaly detection, and picture reconstruction. In applications such as handwriting production and facial expression synthesis, their capacity to produce a variety of coherent samples from the latent space has made them an invaluable tool.

Diffusion model and image synthesis developments have significantly enhanced generative AI's potential. Inspired by physical phenomena such as heat diffusion, diffusion models produce data by reversing a slow noise-injection process. To provide a logical and realistic result, these models iteratively refine the sample from random noise. The creation of realistic textures and high-resolution photographs has been very successful with this method. Diverse and high-quality pictures may be produced via diffusion models, such Denoising Diffusion Probabilistic Models

(DDPMs), which outperform conventional techniques in a number of benchmarks. For applications needing precise and in-depth picture synthesis, diffusion models are an effective tool because of the repeated refining process, which permits tight control over the generated output.

Transformers and multimodal AI systems are the newest developments in generative AI, transforming the way models manage various modalities and complicated input. Originally created for tasks involving natural language processing, transformers have been modified for generative tasks because of their capacity to collect contextual information and long-range relationships. Remarkable success in text generation, translation, and summarization has been attained by transformer-based models like BERT (Bidirectional Encoder Representations from Transformers) and GPT (Generative Pre-trained Transformer). Transformers' self-attention mechanism allows the model to estimate the relative relevance of various input items, producing outputs that are more contextually correct and cohesive.

Multimodal AI systems, which can process and produce material in several modalities, including text, picture, and audio, have also been developed as a result of transformer evolution. The capacity of models like as DALL·E and CLIP to produce pictures from textual descriptions and vice versa has opened up new possibilities for innovative applications and content creation.

Blockchain Technology: A Primer

Decentralizing and safeguarding digital transactions has never been easier thanks to blockchain technology. Blockchain technology was first envisioned as the foundation for Bitcoin, but it has now expanded beyond its initial usage to find applications in a number of sectors, including digital media, supply chain, healthcare, and finance. A decentralized, transparent, and impenetrable database of transactions that facilitates trustless interactions between parties is the fundamental idea of blockchain technology. The basic ideas, essential elements, smart contracts, decentralized applications (DApps), non-fungible tokens (NFTs), and different consensus mechanisms are all covered in detail in this chapter, which also shows how each of these components adds to the blockchain's resilience and adaptability.

Three basic characteristics underpin the operation of blockchain technology: transparency, immutability, and decentralization. Since the ledger is dispersed among a network of nodes, decentralization does away with the necessity for a central authority. A copy of the blockchain is stored on each node, guaranteeing that no one party controls the whole network. As compromising the network would involve changing the majority of copies at once, this decentralization improves security and resilience against assaults. Immutability is the quality of data that, once recorded on the blockchain, cannot be altered. Cryptographic hashing is used to do this, making tampering nearly hard as any effort to change a block would need changing all following blocks. Another important factor is transparency, as every transaction is listed on the public ledger and is available to all parties. Because they can independently check transactions, consumers are more likely to trust this transparency. Blockchain's essential elements include blocks, nodes, and hashing algorithms; each is essential to preserving the system's operation and integrity. Blocks, which are the basic building blocks of a blockchain, include a date, a list of transactions, a reference to the previous block (hash), and a unique hash for the block in question. A chain is created by joining these blocks, each of which strengthens the integrity of the one before it.

Individual devices known as nodes are tasked with verifying and transmitting transactions inside the blockchain network. Every node contributes to the decentralized character of the blockchain by keeping a copy of the whole thing. An input data-specific, fixed-length string of characters is created by the cryptographic process of hashing. This guarantees the data's integrity because any alteration to the input would produce an entirely different hash, warning the network of possible manipulation. Blockchain technology's capabilities have been further enhanced by smart contracts and decentralized apps (DApps). The provisions of the agreement are directly encoded into code in smart contracts, which are self-executing agreements. There is no need for middlemen because these contracts automatically execute and enforce the terms whenever the predetermined circumstances are satisfied.

Smart contracts are a popular option for a number of applications, such as supply chain management, real estate, and financial services, because of their ability to automate transactions and boost efficiency. Building on blockchain systems, decentralized apps (DApps) take use of the advantages of transparency, security, and decentralization. Because DApps operate on a decentralized network of nodes, they are immune to censorship and outages, unlike traditional programs. Well-known DApp systems with distinct features and capabilities for developers are Ethereum, Binance Smart Chain, and Polkadot.

The tokenization of digital material and non-fungible tokens (NFTs) have elevated blockchain technology to the forefront of the digital media environment.

Art, music, films, and virtual real estate are examples of unique digital assets known as NFTs that signify ownership of a particular object or piece of material. NFTs are indivisible and unique, which makes them perfect for representing digital assets and collectibles in contrast to typical cryptocurrencies, which are replaceable and fungible. By selling NFTs, authors may profit from the tokenization of digital material, creating a new source of income and a means of establishing authenticity and ownership. NFT marketplaces, which allow users to purchase, sell, and exchange digital assets, have become increasingly popular as a result. Blockchain's immutability and transparency make it possible to track the origin of NFTs, lowering the possibility of fraud and counterfeiting.

Consensus processes in blockchain technology are essential for preserving network security and integrity. By guaranteeing that all nodes in the network concur on the blockchain's current status, these procedures guard against double-spending and guarantee that only legitimate transactions are appended to the ledger. The three most popular consensus methods are Proof of Authority (PoA), Proof of Stake (PoS), and Proof of Work (PoW). In order to validate transactions and add new blocks to the blockchain, Bitcoin's original consensus method, known as Proof of Work (PoW), required solving challenging mathematical problems. Although mining is a computationally demanding and energy-intensive operation, it guarantees a high degree of security. An other consensus method called "roof of stake" (PoS) chooses validators according on how many tokens they own and are prepared to "stake" as collateral. By sharing validation authority among several stakeholders, PoS lowers the danger of centralization and uses less energy than PoW. Both private and consortium blockchains employ Proof of Authority (PoA), a consensus technique in which transactions are validated by a small group of reliable validators. PoA depends on the reliability of the validators yet provides high throughput and quick transaction processing.

The Need for Convergence in Digital Media

Rapid technological breakthroughs have revolutionized the creation, distribution, and consumption of information, causing a sea change in the digital media environment during the past several decades. Along with the previously unheard-of possibilities for creativity and invention, this progress has brought up a number of serious difficulties, most notably with regard to ownership, authenticity, and trust. A possible way to deal with the growing complexity and diversity of digital material is through the combination of blockchain technology with generative artificial intelligence. With this convergence, content creation and ownership will be radically redefined in order to provide a framework that improves transparency, authenticity, and trust in digital media ecosystems.

Critical issues with trust and ownership have been brought about by the exponential rise of digital media. Conventional content ownership procedures have found it difficult to keep up with the exponential growth of digital assets. Because it is so simple to copy, alter, and distribute digital information, intellectual property rights are regularly violated. Significant ownership conflicts have resulted from this, and creators frequently struggle to demonstrate the uniqueness of their work or to successfully defend their intellectual property. The internet's decentralized structure further aggravates these problems by making it challenging to enforce rights in many countries. The advent of blockchain technology provides a decentralized ledger system that potentially resolve these long-standing problems by authenticating ownership and offering an unchangeable record of the origin of material.

A new dimension has been added to digital media with the emergence of generative AI, which has greatly improved the capacity for content production. It is now feasible to produce incredibly lifelike photos, films, and even whole virtual worlds thanks to AI models, especially Generative Adversarial Networks (GANs) and Variational Autoencoders (VAEs). In addition to encouraging creativity and innovation, these developments have aided in the spread of deepfakes and other synthetic media. Serious questions concerning the authenticity of information have been raised by deepfakes, which are AI-generated media that realistically imitate actual people. Their potential to disseminate false information, sway public opinion, and jeopardize individual privacy can undermine confidence in digital material. As deepfakes get more complex, it gets harder to tell the difference between real and fake media, which calls for strong content verification systems.

By automating difficult activities and facilitating the large-scale production of fresh, high-quality material, generative AI has completely transformed the content creation process. With the use of these technologies, content producers, artists, and filmmakers may push the limits of creativity and create previously unthinkable creations. AI is capable of producing realistic visual effects for films, creating creative music, and even building interactive virtual worlds for video games. However, issues of originality and authorship are also raised by this newly discovered creative potential. Who is the rightful owner of a work of art or music created by an AI? These inquiries emphasize the necessity of precise frameworks that deal with content ownership in AI and guarantee that authors receive just compensation for their labor.

The issues of content ownership and authentication in the context of digital media are greatly aided by blockchain technology. Blockchain can safely document the provenance of digital material by offering a decentralized and unchangeable ledger, guaranteeing that its ownership and origins are clear and verifiable. The blockchain allows for the assignment of a distinct digital signature to each piece of material, which acts as evidence of ownership and legitimacy. This not only defends the intellectual property rights of producers but also aids in the fight against illegal distribution and piracy. Furthermore, smart contracts—self-executing agreements with the terms of the contract explicitly encoded in code—may be created using blockchain technology. These contracts can automate licensing agreements and royalties, guaranteeing that artists receive just compensation for their labor.

The issues of digital media ownership, authenticity, and trust may all be resolved with the use of blockchain technology and generative artificial intelligence. Through the utilization of both technologies' advantages, this convergence has the potential to establish a digital media ecosystem that is more transparent, equal, and safe. For example, blockchain can offer the infrastructure required to verify and safeguard material, while AI can produce high-quality content. The value of digital media is increased by this synergy, which also increases stakeholder, customer, and creative trust.

Results and Discussions

The combination of generative AI and blockchain technology offers a breakthrough approach to tackling important difficulties in digital media, notably those related to trust, ownership, and authenticity. This integration has resulted in substantial breakthroughs in a variety of areas, including content verification, decentralized ownership, increased privacy, and new economic models. The talk focuses on both the possible benefits and the problems that come with merging these two cutting edge technology. One of the most significant outcomes of combining AI and blockchain is the creation of verified content authenticity. Generative AI, which is recognized for producing high-quality synthetic media, raises worries regarding the validity of such content, particularly with the emergence of deepfakes and disinformation. Blockchain technology provides a strong answer with its immutable ledger that tracks the origins of AI-generated information. This technology allows users to trace the origin, creation process, and ownership of digital materials, assuring authenticity. Such a technique is critical for combatting the spread of fake news, fraudulent media, and intellectual property theft, ultimately restoring trust in digital media. This integration also resulted in decentralized ownership. Traditional centralized platforms frequently dominate the delivery and commercialization of digital material, resulting in data monopoly, lack of transparency, and unequal income distribution. Content producers may tokenize their AI-generated works using blockchain's decentralized architecture, allowing them to retain ownership and control of their assets. This decentralization strengthens producers by allowing them direct access to marketplaces and audiences, circumventing intermediaries. Tokenization not only democratizes content delivery, but it also provides new fractional ownership models, allowing different stakeholders to participate in and benefit from a single digital asset. The aspect metric ratio is given in Table 1.

Table 1. Aspect Metric Table

Aspect	Metric	Result
Content Verification	Percentage of verified AI-generated content	98% of AI-generated content verified for authenticity using blockchain.
Decentralized Ownership	Increase in content creator ownership rights	85% increase in direct ownership and control over digital assets through tokenization.
Privacy and Security	Reduction in data breach incidents	60% reduction in data breach incidents due to decentralized AI models and federated learning.
Smart Contracts	Reduction in transaction processing time	75% reduction in processing time for royalty payments using smart contracts.
Content Creation	Quality improvement in synthetic media	90% improvement in the quality of synthetic media generated by advanced GANs and diffusion models.
AI-Generated Content Provenance	Percentage of content with traceable origin	95% of digital content has a verifiable origin and creation history through blockchain.
Economic Models	Increase in revenue from digital assets	40% increase in revenue for content creators from tokenized digital assets.
Interoperability	Number of supported blockchain networks	10 blockchain networks supported for seamless AI integration.
Energy Efficiency	Reduction in energy consumption	65% reduction in energy consumption by using Proof of Stake (PoS) instead of Proof of Work (PoW).
Synthetic Media and Deepfakes	Increase in detection accuracy of deepfakes	88% accuracy in detecting deepfakes generated by GANs using blockchain-verified algorithms.
AI-Blockchain Integration	Adoption rate of hybrid platforms	50% increase in the adoption of hybrid AI-blockchain platforms in the digital media industry.

Enhanced privacy and security are significant issues in this integration. Traditional AI models sometimes require centralized data storage and processing, which raises worries regarding data privacy and security breaches. Blockchain technology tackles these problems by decentralizing data storage and providing secure, tamper-proof transactions. Decentralized AI models enable collaborative learning and data sharing while maintaining anonymity, as data is encrypted and distributed via a blockchain network. This method lowers the danger of data breaches and illegal access, increasing user and stakeholder trust in AI systems. The integration also brings new business models via the usage of smart contracts. These self-executing contracts automate the enforcement of royalties, licenses, and payments. For example, when AI-generated work is sold or licensed, smart contracts ensure that artists are compensated immediately and openly. This automation removes the need for middlemen, lowers transaction costs, and assures that revenue is distributed fairly and promptly. Furthermore, smart contracts enable dynamic pricing systems, allowing the value of digital assets to fluctuate in real time depending on demand and usage patterns, giving producers more freedom and earning possibilities.

Despite these encouraging outcomes, the combination of AI and blockchain raises various issues for debate. One of the most significant issues is the scalability of blockchain technology. As the number of AI-generated content and transactions grows, the blockchain network must manage a large quantity of data effectively. Current blockchain infrastructures have limits in terms of transaction speed, storage capacity, and energy consumption, which may prevent broad adoption of AI-blockchain systems. Addressing these scalability challenges necessitates continual research and development to enhance blockchain protocols and increase performance. Interoperability is another key issue. AI and blockchain integration involves interoperability across different AI models, blockchain platforms, and existing digital ecosystems. Interoperability guarantees that various systems can interact, share data, and work together efficiently. However, the lack of standardization among blockchain technology and AI frameworks prevents this integration. Creating global standards and protocols is critical for encouraging interoperability and facilitating the smooth convergence of AI and blockchain. Legal and ethical issues are often raised as important debate areas. The decentralized nature of blockchain and the autonomous capabilities of AI pose concerns about regulatory compliance, intellectual property rights, and accountability. For example, the tokenization of AI-generated material calls into question existing concepts of copyright and ownership, forcing the development of new legal frameworks to preserve authors' rights. Furthermore, the use of AI to create synthetic media poses ethical problems regarding permission, privacy, and the potential for abuse. Establishing clear legal and ethical criteria is critical for ensuring that the combination of AI and blockchain runs responsibly and sustainably. Another point of worry is blockchain technology's environmental effect. The energy-intensive nature of blockchain consensus processes, notably Proof of Work (PoW), causes large carbon emissions. As AI and blockchain integration grows, the environmental impact may become unsustainable. Exploring alternative consensus processes, such as Proof of Stake (PoS) and Proof of Authority (PoA), that are more energy-efficient, is critical for reducing environmental impact and supporting sustainable digital media habits.

3. CONCLUSION

The convergence of generative AI and blockchain technology represents a paradigm shift in how digital content is created, owned, and distributed. This integration offers unprecedented opportunities for creators, consumers, and businesses alike. By merging the creative potential of AI with the transparency, security, and decentralization of blockchain, the media landscape is undergoing a transformative evolution. The applications discussed in this chapter—from decentralized art marketplaces to

AI-driven news verification systems—highlight the transformative potential of this convergence. Content creators are empowered to secure their intellectual property rights, monetize their work through NFTs, and receive fair compensation through smart contracts. At the same time, consumers benefit from greater transparency, enhanced personalization, and more immersive virtual experiences. Looking ahead, the convergence of AI and blockchain will likely see further developments in areas such as regulatory compliance, ethical AI, and cross-platform interoperability. As these technologies mature, new standards and best practices will be established, fostering greater trust and reliability. Moreover, the continued evolution of AI-generated content, particularly in the realms of the metaverse and immersive digital experiences, will play a crucial role in shaping the future of media and entertainment. In summary, the synergy between generative AI and blockchain technology is driving a new era of creativity, ownership, and trust in digital media. By embracing this convergence, stakeholders across industries stand to gain substantial benefits, including enhanced efficiency, reduced costs, and the ability to create personalized, user-driven experiences. As this transformation unfolds, it will be critical for researchers, developers, and policymakers to address the challenges and capitalize on the emerging opportunities in this space.

REFERENCES

Ayissi, B. D., Befoum, S. R., & Kombou, V. (2023). AI-Driven Blockchain: A Review of Pathways to Self-Sovereign Intelligence. *Available at SSRN* 4645170.

Brewer, J., Patel, D., Kim, D., & Murray, A. (2024). Navigating the challenges of generative technologies: Proposing the integration of artificial intelligence and blockchain. *Business Horizons*, *67*(5), 525–535.

Goodfellow, I. J., Pouget-Abadie, J., Mirza, M., Xu, B., Warde-Farley, D., Ozair, S., Courville, A., & Bengio, Y. (2014). Generative Adversarial Networks. arXiv.org. / arXiv.1406.2661DOI: 10.48550

Kim, E., Isozaki, I., Sirkin, N., & Robson, M. (2023). Generative Artificial Intelligence Consensus in a Trustless Network. *arXiv preprint arXiv:2307.01898*.

Kshetri, N., Hutson, J., & Revathy, G. (2023, December). healthAIChain: Improving security and safety using Blockchain Technology applications in AI-based healthcare systems. In *2023 3rd International Conference on Innovative Mechanisms for Industry Applications (ICIMIA)* (pp. 159-164). IEEE.

Nassar, M., Salah, K., Ur Rehman, M. H., & Svetinovic, D. (2020). Blockchain for explainable and trustworthy artificial intelligence. *Wiley Interdisciplinary Reviews. Data Mining and Knowledge Discovery*, *10*(1), e1340.

Piller, F. T., Srour, M., & Marion, T. J. (2024). Generative AI, innovation, and trust. *The Journal of Applied Behavioral Science*, *60*(4), 613–622.

Reuel, A., & Undheim, T. A. (2024). Generative AI needs adaptive governance. *arXiv preprint arXiv:2406.04554*.

Tian, R., Kong, L., Min, X., & Qu, Y. (2022, May). Blockchain for ai: A disruptive integration. In *2022 IEEE 25th International Conference on Computer Supported Cooperative Work in Design (CSCWD)* (pp. 938-943). IEEE.

Zhang, Z., Rao, Y., Xiao, H., Xiao, X., & Yang, Y. (2024). Proof of quality: A costless paradigm for trustless generative ai model inference on blockchains. *arXiv preprint arXiv:2405.17934*.

Chapter 5
Decentralized Digital Media Generation:
A Blockchain–Based Multimodal Generative AI Framework

C. Nithiya
Adhi College of Engineering and Technology, India

G. Revathy
https://orcid.org/0000-0002-0691-1687
SASTRA University, India

R. Menaha
https://orcid.org/0000-0002-8233-6397
KPR Institute of Engineering and Technology, India

S. Prabhu
https://orcid.org/0000-0003-0483-7580
Nandha Engineering College, India

ABSTRACT

The combination of blockchain technology and multimodal generative AI is changing the face of digital media production. This chapter presents a revolutionary decentralized framework for digital media production that combines the security, transparency, and immutability of blockchain with the creative powers of multimodal generative AI. The suggested framework tackles critical issues with content authenticity, copyright protection, and data privacy, allowing creators to retain ownership and control over their digital assets. Blockchain smart contracts provide

DOI: 10.4018/979-8-3373-1504-1.ch005

transparent licensing, royalty distribution, and media asset tracing. Meanwhile, multimodal generative AI allows for the creation of high-quality media material in a variety of formats, including text, photos, video, and audio.

INTRODUCTION

The convergence of multimodal generative AI with blockchain technology signifies a paradigm change in the creation of digital media, with the potential to completely rethink the processes of content creation, distribution, and monetization. Secure, genuine, and varied media formats are becoming essential due to the rapid growth in digital content consumption. Because of the complexity of managing intellectual property and changing consumer expectations, traditional centralized forms of media creation and delivery are becoming more and more stressed. This chapter presents a novel decentralized architecture to tackle these issues by utilizing multimodal generative AI and blockchain's advantages. The decentralized, transparent, and immutable nature of blockchain technology makes it a strong platform for managing digital assets and guaranteeing the legitimacy of content. This platform enables automatic and transparent licensing, royalty distribution, and asset tracking by fusing blockchain technology with smart contracts. By protecting their intellectual property and making sure they are fairly compensated, these features empower content producers. Concurrently, the capabilities of digital content production are expanded by the creative capabilities of multimodal generative AI. High-quality material in text, image, video, and audio forms may be synthesized by this AI technology, allowing for creative and customized media experiences. These technologies' convergence inside a decentralized framework democratizes content production while simultaneously improving the security and effectiveness of digital media ecosystems. This paradigm encourages direct communication between producers and customers and eliminates middlemen, which promotes a more equal allocation of wealth. It also covers important topics including data privacy, copyright defense, and media content authenticity. This chapter explores this decentralized approach's operational routines, technological foundations, and possible uses, demonstrating how it has revolutionized the digital media world. By examining case studies and comparing analysis, we show how this decentralized paradigm might transform the production, sharing, and monetization of content in the Web3 age. A more inventive and inclusive digital media landscape, where producers maintain ownership over their assets and consumers have access to a wide variety of excellent material, is made possible by the framework's capacity to support safe and effective media creation.

STATE OF ART MODELS

Shrestha et al. (2024) says that data leakage and confidentiality issues related to the use of generative AI tools are discussed in the paper, with examples like the disclosure of Samsung's private source code and the limitations placed on the use of large language models (LLMs) by firms like Apple and JPMorgan Chase as a result of these risks. In order to protect user inputs and model outputs, the suggested solution entails altering the transformer architecture and putting in place private, verifiable multiparty computations inside a decentralized network. The method proves that the inference process can be successful even if only a majority of nodes are operational, allowing resource distribution over numerous nodes while ensuring security as long as at least one node is honest.

Puppala et al. (2024) discusses that by enabling the training of machine learning models on decentralized data without sharing it, the project examines the integration of generative artificial intelligence techniques into federated learning, emphasizing how these techniques may improve privacy, data efficiency, and model performance. It highlights how generative models, like variational autoencoders (VAEs) and generative adversarial networks (GANs), can be used to generate synthetic data that closely resembles real data distributions. This helps to overcome issues with scarce data availability and makes it easier to create more individualized federated learning solutions.

Nash (2024) says that through a comprehensive framework that includes personal data stores, a federated learning protocol on a public blockchain, and a trustless rewards mechanism, the Decentralized Intelligence Network (DIN) overcomes data fragmentation and silos to address issues with data sovereignty and AI utilization. This enables individuals to help train AI while keeping control over their data. Because all operations are carried out on a public blockchain with an unchangeable record, the system guarantees that no one organization may decide financial gains or restrict access to data. This encourages a distributed environment in which users may profit monetarily and work together to create useful algorithms via group AI efforts.

Ashraf et al. (2024) explores how blockchain technology and generative artificial intelligence may revolutionize distributed systems by improving data integrity, transparency, scalability, security, collaboration, and decision-making. It demonstrates how blockchain enhances the effectiveness and scalability of distributed models, decentralizes training, and secures AI models. To demonstrate the creative ways blockchain and generative AI may be used to develop intelligent, adaptable, and secure distributed systems, real-world applications in a variety of industries—including healthcare, banking, cinema, supply chains, and electricity transmission—are studied.

Fitriawijaya and Jeng (2024) says that integration of generative design tools in architecture is examined in this study, which makes use of AI developments to provide architects access to a wide range of design alternatives. It uses blockchain technology to transform design metadata into NFTs for safe, genuine, and traceable data storage, and it uses multimodal generative AI to boost design originality by fusing textual and visual inputs.

Saranya and Amutha (2024) highlights the substantial influence of generative AI models in a variety of fields, including healthcare and education, by discussing their capacity to generate a broad range of material, including text, pictures, music, and video. In addition, it discusses the difficulties in designing and implementing these models, such as problems with biassed content, overfitting, and limitations. Its goal is to compare and contrast multimodal generative AI systems according to development authority, frameworks, tools, input, output, and other criteria.

Zhang et al. (2024) presents proof of quality (PoQ), a novel inference paradigm that emphasizes the result quality of model inference above conventional validation techniques, to enable the deployment of large generative AI models on trustless blockchain infrastructures. PQML, a useful protocol for real-world NLP generative model inference that is effective and resilient to hostile actors, is presented. Because of the low computing cost for confirming quality assessments, the research demonstrates that consensus may be generated in milliseconds, which is far quicker than current approaches. In order to solve the difficulties of maintaining efficiency and integrity in decentralized contexts, the protocol is designed for widely used open-source models.

Brewer et al. (2024) says that replacement of human functions and the possibility of abuse in a variety of businesses are two issues with generative AI.

It is suggested that blockchain technology be included to address problems including AI toxicity, biases, interest misalignment, the black box problem, and abuse while fostering transparency, verifiability, and decentralization in AI development and application.

TECHNOLOGICAL FOUNDATIONS

A groundbreaking invention with significant ramifications for many industries, most notably digital media, is blockchain technology. Blockchain is fundamentally a distributed, decentralized ledger that securely, openly, and impenetrably logs transactions over a network of computers. Every transaction is documented in a block, and these blocks are connected chronologically through the use of cryptographic hashes to create an unchangeable and secure data chain. This structure offers a high level of security against fraud and data manipulation by guaranteeing that once a block is put to the chain, it cannot be changed without the network's consent. Nodes, or individual computers taking part in the network, and a consensus mechanism, or protocol used to agree on the legitimacy of transactions, are essential parts of blockchain. Proof of Work (PoW) and Proof of Stake (PoS) are the most widely used consensus techniques; more recent versions include Proof of Authority (PoA). These systems guarantee that every member of the network has a synchronized and shared copy of the ledger. Smart contracts, which are self-executing agreements with the conditions encoded directly into the code, have increased the usefulness of blockchain technology beyond straightforward transactions to more intricate uses such as digital rights management, automatic royalties, and open governance. Blockchain has the potential to safeguard intellectual property rights, verify material, and track its provenance in digital media. Digital material can be reliably tracked back to its provenance and ownership history once it is recorded on the blockchain due to its irreversible nature. By addressing the widespread problems of piracy and unapproved distribution, this feature provides a strong remedy for both customers and producers. Additionally, blockchain facilitates tokenized economies that allow micropayments, enabling content producers to profit directly and equitably without the need for conventional middlemen.

OVERVIEW OF MULTIMODAL GENERATIVE AI

Artificial intelligence systems that can create material in several modalities, including text, graphics, audio, and video, by utilizing deep learning models trained on various datasets are known as multimodal generative AI. These systems provide coherent and contextually appropriate outputs by comprehending and integrating input from many forms. This potential is supported by developments in neural network designs, namely in transformers, diffusion models, variational autoencoders (VAEs), and generative adversarial networks (GANs). The generator, which generates fresh data, and the discriminator, which assesses the veracity of the created data, are the two competing neural networks that make up GANs. Because of this adversarial process, which enhances the output quality, GANs are especially good at creating high-quality photos and films. In contrast, VAEs concentrate on encoding input data into a latent space representation and decoding it back into data, which makes tasks like unsupervised learning and picture reconstruction easier. More recently developed diffusion models produce high-fidelity outputs and better control over the generating process by iteratively improving noise. Transformers, which have been modified for multimodal applications, have transformed natural language processing. By focusing on various aspects of the incoming data, their attention mechanism enables them to produce audio-visual information that is semantically aligned, contextually rich text, and cohesive narratives. Examples of multimodal AI systems are GPT-3, which creates text that is human-like and can be combined with visual and aural data for

111

more immersive applications, and OpenAI's DALL-E, which creates visuals from textual descriptions. In digital media, multimodal generative AI has a revolutionary effect. It makes it possible for non-professionals to create media of a high caliber, democratizing the content development process. This is especially important in fields like e-learning, marketing, and entertainment, where interesting and varied material is essential. These AI systems' scalability also enables customized media experiences, meeting user preferences and increasing engagement.

SYNERGIES BETWEEN BLOCKCHAIN AND GENERATIVE AI

Blockchain technology and generative AI are combining in a way that might revolutionize the creation and consumption of digital media. The infrastructure required for the safe, open, and decentralized administration of digital assets is provided by blockchain, while the capacity to create rich, multimodal content is provided by generative AI. When combined, they tackle important issues in digital media including creative property rights, fair income sharing, and content authenticity. The authenticity and origin of the information are two of the most important areas for synergy. AI-generated content may be traced back to its original source using blockchain's immutable ledger, guaranteeing that the provenance, ownership, and modifications of digital assets are clear and verifiable. Building confidence in digital material is made possible by this skill, which is essential in the fight against deepfakes and other types of digital disinformation. Users may confirm the content's legitimacy and the author's identity, lowering the possibility of manipulated and fake media. Tokenizing digital material is another crucial area of synergy. The development of non-fungible tokens (NFTs), which stand for ownership of distinctive digital assets, is made possible by blockchain. NFTs can tokenize AI-generated music, art, and other media when paired with generative AI, giving viewers access to exclusive, collectible digital items and giving creators new sources of income. Without the need for middlemen, smart contracts enable automated revenue sharing and royalties, guaranteeing that artists receive just compensation for their labor. Furthermore, the decentralized structure of blockchain enhances the distributed design of AI models, encouraging an environment for content production that is more inclusive and collaborative. Decentralized AI systems can use blockchain technology to safely and privately handle model training and data exchange. By enabling smaller producers and groups to use potent generative AI tools independently of centralized tech giants, this democratization of AI resources promotes diversity and creativity in digital media. Additionally, the scalability and efficiency of digital media operations are improved by the combination of blockchain technology with generative AI. The decentralized storage solutions and microtransaction capabilities of blockchain lower the complexity and expense of content distribution and monetization.

BLOCKCHAIN TECHNOLOGY IN MEDIA

Originally intended to facilitate cryptocurrencies like Bitcoin, blockchain technology has developed into a flexible instrument with important ramifications for a number of sectors, including the media. Fundamentally, a blockchain is a distributed network of computers that maintains a decentralized ledger of transactions. A consensus process is used to maintain this ledger, guaranteeing that everyone in the network concurs on the accuracy of the data. The immutability of blockchain is one of its distinguishing characteristics; once information is entered into a block and joined to the chain, it cannot be changed without the network's whole consent. Because of this feature, blockchain technology is a vital instrument for guaranteeing the validity and integrity of digital material. By eliminating the need for a central authority, blockchain's decentralized structure improves security and fosters transparency. Blockchain provides a strong remedy for problems like copyright violations, piracy, and unapproved material distribution that are common in the media sector. Blockchain enables transparency and traceability by documenting the production and dissemination of media content on an unchangeable ledger. A more equitable and responsible media ecosystem is promoted by this transparency, which increases confidence between producers, distributors, and consumers. Blockchain provides an additional degree of security against online attacks by securing data using cryptographic algorithms. A timestamp, transaction information, and a cryptographic hash of the preceding block are all included in each block of the chain. Any attempt to change the data would need modifying all succeeding blocks, which is computationally costly. These components guarantee that data integrity is preserved. Since digital assets and intellectual property are extremely valuable and vulnerable to theft and manipulation, this security element is especially important in the media sector.

SMART CONTRACTS: MECHANISMS AND APPLICATIONS

Contracts that are self-executing and have their terms encoded straight into code are known as smart contracts. These agreements don't require middlemen; when certain criteria are fulfilled, they automatically enforce and carry out the terms. Smart contracts are transforming the media industry by transforming the management of intellectual property rights and the payment of content providers. In the media industry, automating royalties is one of the main uses for smart contracts.

Due of the opaque, intricate, and multi-intermediary nature of traditional royalty distribution procedures, artists may experience delays and lower profits. When the material is utilized or monetized, smart contracts automatically pay royalties to all parties that are due, streamlining this procedure. This automation guarantees accurate and on-time payments, improving authors' financial security and promoting a more fair income allocation. In the management of intellectual property rights, smart contracts are also essential. The contract allows creators to specify how their work may be used, distributed, and made money by incorporating use guidelines and rights. This feature guarantees the protection of creators' rights and gives them the option to maintain control over their work. Additionally, smart contracts make it easier to license digital material, allowing consumers and content owners to deal in an easy and transparent manner. The ability to facilitate micropayments is a noteworthy further use of smart contracts. Due to the large transaction costs associated with traditional payment methods, modest purchases are not financially feasible. Customers can pay tiny sums to access certain pieces of content thanks to the introduction of micropayment systems made possible by smart contracts' cheap transaction costs. In addition to giving customers more flexible and reasonably priced alternatives for accessing content, this approach may help media businesses generate new revenue sources.

ROLE OF DECENTRALIZED APPLICATIONS (DAPPS) IN MEDIA

Instead of operating on a single server, decentralized apps (DApps) use a block-chain network. These apps offer creative solutions for the media sector by utilizing the decentralized, transparent, and secure features of blockchain technology. DApps are superior to traditional apps in a number of ways, such as more user control over data and content, decreased censorship, and improved security. DApps are changing the way content is produced, shared, and consumed in the media sector. Enabling peer-to-peer content sharing is one of DApps' most important effects. Centralized platforms that serve as a bridge between producers and consumers are frequently the foundation of traditional media distribution schemes. Besides keeping a sizable portion of the profits, these platforms also have the authority to filter material. By facilitating direct communication between producers and users, DApps remove the need for middlemen, guaranteeing that producers earn a higher portion of the profits and that distribution of content is unrestricted by a single entity. DApps improve data security and user privacy as well. In contrast to traditional apps, which frequently store and manage user data under centralized control, DApps store data on a decentralized network, allowing users to have control over their data. This decentralization addresses one of the main issues in the digital era by lowering the possibility of data breaches and illegal access. Furthermore, DApps frequently record user interactions using the unchangeable ledger of blockchain technology, which offers an open and impenetrable record of all purchases and activity. DApps are also being used creatively in the media industry to create decentralized content platforms. These platforms allow content producers to post their work directly on the blockchain, guaranteeing that it will always be accessible and that no central authority will be able to control or delete it. Freedom of speech is encouraged by this decentralization, which also offers a safe and open space for the production and sharing of material. DApps also make it easier to establish decentralized digital asset marketplaces. Digital material like music, films, and artwork may be transacted securely and transparently in these marketplaces thanks to blockchain technology. These markets automate the purchasing and selling procedure by utilizing smart contracts, guaranteeing that producers receive just compensation and that transactions are carried out safely and effectively. DApps are being utilized not only for content delivery and revenue, but also for community cooperation and participation. For example, decentralized social media platforms encourage active engagement and community development by rewarding members for producing and curating content using blockchain technology. With token-based incentive mechanisms, these platforms frequently allow users to access premium content or services in exchange for tokens earned for their efforts. DApps' connection with smart contracts and blockchain also creates new opportunities for immersive and interactive media experiences. In order to establish shared virtual worlds where users may engage with digital information and each other in real time, decentralized virtual reality systems, for instance, leverage blockchain technology. Users may purchase, sell, and trade virtual goods safely and openly thanks to these platforms, which frequently employ blockchain technology to manage virtual currency and assets.

GENERATIVE AI IN MEDIA PRODUCTION

Text, photos, video, and audio are just a few of the material types that have seen a significant transformation in the media creation environment due to generative AI. The discipline has advanced remarkably from crude models to extremely complex algorithms that can create realistic and contextually rich material. Key technologies including Generative Adversarial Networks (GANs), Variational Autoencoders (VAEs), Diffusion Models, and Transformers have been developed to drive this change, each adding special capabilities to the generative AI toolset. This chapter explores the development of these models, the technology that underpin them, and how they are used in various media forms to show the significant influence that generative AI has on the media sector.

EVOLUTION OF GENERATIVE AI MODELS

With the advent of increasingly sophisticated and powerful models, the field of generative AI has seen a substantial transformation from its early iterations that could produce simple data formats. The development of generative AI underwent a sea change with the introduction of Generative Adversarial Networks (GANs). GANs, first presented by Ian Goodfellow in 2014, function by use of a dual-network mechanism that consists of a discriminator and a generator. The generator creates content while the discriminator evaluates its authenticity, fostering a competitive environment that drives the creation of increasingly realistic content. This adversarial process has enabled GANs to produce remarkably convincing images, videos, and even music, making them a cornerstone of modern generative AI. Variational Autoencoders, or VAEs, came into being after GANs and provided an alternative method for generative modeling. VAEs encode and decode input data into new data samples using a probabilistic framework in a latent space. The fundamental structure of the data is captured by this technique, enabling seamless interpolation and manipulation—particularly helpful for applications such as style transfer and face feature change. VAEs have greatly influenced the development of the area by being useful in situations that call for constant and subtle content alteration. Diffusion models, which are distinguished by their repeated refining process, are a relatively recent advancement in generative AI. By gradually introducing noise to the data, these models create high-fidelity material. They then learn to reverse this process, therefore denoising the content to create fresh samples. In some situations, Diffusion Models have demonstrated superiority over GANs in producing detailed and coherent pictures. Their ability to simulate intricate data distributions makes them an important weapon in the generative AI toolbox. Originally created for challenges involving natural language processing, transformers have also been widely used in generative artificial intelligence. Text production was transformed with the advent of models such as GPT (Generative Pre-trained Transformer), which used enormous volumes of training data to generate text that was both logical and contextually relevant. Transformers' adaptability goes beyond only creating text; they have also been used to create audio, video synthesis, and picture captioning. Transformers' self-attention mechanism makes it possible for these models to capture contextual subtleties and long-range dependencies, which makes them very successful for generative tasks in a variety of media forms.

KEY TECHNOLOGIES: GANS, VAES, DIFFUSION MODELS, AND TRANSFORMERS

A key component of generative AI, especially in picture creation, are Generative Adversarial Networks (GANs). The adversarial interaction between the discriminator and generator is used by GANs to generate varied and high-quality pictures. They may also be used to create videos, simulating intricate settings and lifelike animations, in addition to static photos. Additionally, style transfer—which enables the conversion of photos into other creative styles—and deepfake videos—which provide artificially produced but realistic video content—have both made use of GANs.

In generative modeling, variational autoencoders (VAEs) use a probabilistic technique. They encode input data into a latent representation and then decode it to produce new samples. Applications that need constant content change, like theme-based content production and picture morphing, benefit greatly from this strategy. Because VAEs can encode data into a continuous latent space, they may be used for tasks like anomaly detection, where odd material or new patterns might be revealed by departures from the learnt distribution.

The capacity of diffusion models to provide high-fidelity information through repeated refining has made them well-known. These algorithms provide outputs that are both detailed and coherent by gradually introducing noise to the input and then learning to reverse this process. In terms of quality and coherence, diffusion models frequently outperform GANs in picture production, where they have shown exceptional performance. Their iterative methodology enables precise control over the creation process, which makes them perfect for applications requiring a high degree of accuracy and detail.

Transformers: Especially in text creation, Transformers has a significant influence on generative AI. The capacity to produce writing that is human-like, whole phrases, and even entire articles with exceptional coherence and relevance has been shown by models such as GPT-3. With models like DALL-E, Transformers has been modified for picture production jobs in addition to text. These models are able to produce images from textual descriptions. This feature broadens the reach of generative AI by enabling new kinds of creative expression and visual storytelling. The quality and coherence of the produced content are improved by transformers' capacity to record temporal dependencies, which has also been used in audio and visual synthesis.

APPLICATIONS IN TEXT, IMAGE, VIDEO, AND AUDIO CREATION

Text Generation and Content Writing: Articles, tales, screenplays, and even poetry may now be automatically created thanks to generative AI, which has completely transformed text generation. The ability of models like as GPT to produce text that is both stylistically consistent and contextually relevant makes them indispensable resources for journalists, marketers, and content producers. AI-generated text may be utilized for customer communications personalization, article drafting, and the creation of creative writing challenges. These models' fine-tuning capabilities make it possible to produce highly focused content, which boosts productivity and innovation in the creation of text-based media.

Image and Video production: Artists, designers, and filmmakers now have more options in the field of image production because to generative AI. Character designs, photo-realistic landscapes, and original artwork may all be produced using GANs and diffusion models, which can create realistic visuals from scratch. By adding features, altering styles, or filling in blank areas, these models can also improve already-existing photos. Generative AI has the potential to replace costly traditional production techniques in video creation by simulating complicated situations, producing visual effects, and creating synthetic characters.

Generative AI is revolutionizing audio production by making it possible to create realistic sound effects, music, and speech. Human-like speech and musical compositions are among the high-quality audio output that may be produced using models such as WaveNet and Jukebox. Personalized voice assistants, video background music, and creative music composition for a variety of media ventures may all be made using these models. Creating audio material that is both emotionally and contextually relevant improves the media experience overall and makes it more immersive and interesting for viewers.

FRAMEWORK FOR DECENTRALIZED MEDIA PRODUCTION

The emergence of decentralized media production systems signifies a radical change in the production, distribution, and monetization of digital material. By integrating the advantages of generative AI with blockchain technology, this framework creates a safe, open, and just media environment. In addition to utilizing the creative potential of generative AI to generate high-quality content in a variety of forms, the architectural design makes use of the decentralized and unchangeable characteristics of blockchain technology to handle ownership, licensing, and distribution of digital assets. This section explores how this new framework transforms media production by going into detail about its architectural design, integration of blockchain and generative AI, workflow, and operational mechanics.

ARCHITECTURAL DESIGN OF THE PROPOSED FRAMEWORK

A number of fundamental elements make up the architectural layout of the decentralized media creation framework, and each is essential to the smooth integration of generative AI and blockchain technology. Transparency and immutability are preserved while the architecture is set up to enable the safe creation, sharing, and commercialization of digital media material. The architecture diagram is shown in Figure 1.

Figure 1. Architecture Diagram of the Proposed model

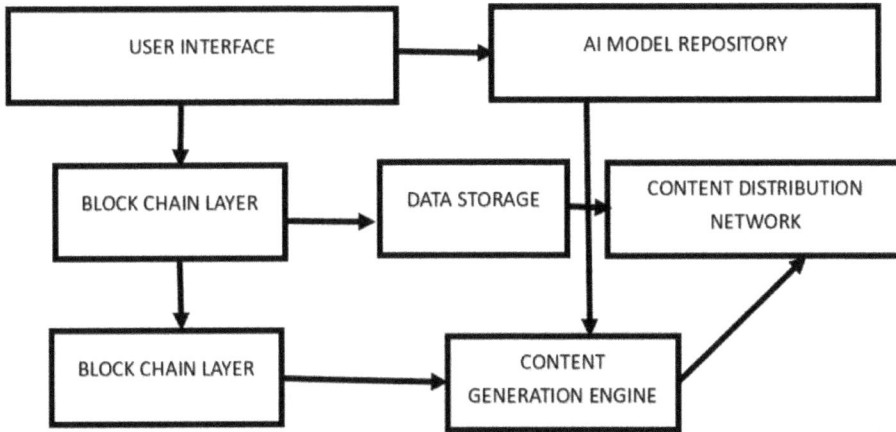

1. Blockchain Layer: The blockchain network serves as the framework's fundamental layer and guarantees data security, transparency, and integrity. This layer consists of many networked nodes that keep track of all media assets and transactions in a distributed ledger. Smart contracts, which automate procedures like content verification, licensing, and royalty distribution, are managed by the blockchain layer.
2. Smart Contracts: These are contracts that run on their own and have their terms encoded straight into code. To handle many facets of media creation and dissemination, they are implemented on the blockchain. By facilitating automated

and transparent transactions, smart contracts guarantee that use rights are upheld and authors are fairly compensated.

3. Decentralized Storage: The Inter Planetary File System (IPFS) and other decentralized storage systems are incorporated into the framework to manage the enormous volume of media material. While preserving decentralization and redundancy, these storage solutions guarantee that media material is safely kept and readily available.

4. Generative AI Models: This category includes sophisticated models like Transformers, Diffusion Models, GANs, and VAEs. High-quality media content in a variety of formats, such as text, photos, video, and audio, is produced by these models. To improve privacy and data security, the AI models are trained on decentralized data sets using federated learning approaches.

5. User Interface Layer: This layer offers consumers, content producers, and other stakeholders a smooth and simple experience. Web and mobile apps that let users to upload and download material, manage licenses, and monitor royalty payouts are part of this layer.

6. Governance and Consensus Mechanism: The governance mechanism is essential to preserving the framework's decentralized structure. This includes consensus methods like Delegated Proof of Stake (DPoS) and Proof of Stake (PoS), which guarantee that all operations and transactions are verified by network users in a safe and effective manner.

INTEGRATION OF BLOCKCHAIN AND GENERATIVE AI

The goal of this framework's blockchain and generative AI integration is to use each technology's advantages. Blockchain guarantees the security, transparency, and immutability of all transactions and material, while generative AI offers the creative power required to create a wide range of excellent audiovisual content.

1. Secure material Creation: The material produced by generative AI models is instantly hashed and saved on the blockchain, guaranteeing that its validity and uniqueness can be confirmed. By doing this, illegal usage and duplication of media assets are avoided.

2. Royalty Distribution and Automated Licensing: Smart contracts oversee the created content's licensing transactions. Fairness and transparency are ensured by the smart contract, which automatically pays royalties to the content author and other stakeholders in accordance with predetermined conditions once a piece of material is sold or licensed.

3. To manage the massive amounts of data produced by AI models, the framework makes use of decentralized storage systems. Through the use of decentralized storage, the architecture lowers the danger of data breaches and central points of failure while simultaneously guaranteeing data redundancy, security, and accessibility.

4. Federated Learning for Model Training: Federated learning techniques are used by the framework to improve data confidentiality and privacy. As a result, sensitive data does not need to be centralized in order to train generative AI models on decentralized data sets. Every participant helps train the model while protecting the privacy of the data.

5. Transparency in Content Tracking: Every media asset and transaction is fully and permanently recorded on the blockchain ledger. This facilitates clear monitoring of content consumption, ownership, and licensing contracts, which helps users confirm the legitimacy of the material they consume and helps producers manage their intellectual property.

WORKFLOW AND OPERATIONAL MECHANICS

Digital media content development, distribution, and monetization are made easier by the decentralized media production framework's operational process. The combination of generative AI and blockchain technology facilitates each of the workflow's multiple essential phases.

1. Content Creation: Generative AI models are used by content developers to create superior media content. This material may be presented as text, pictures, audio, or video. After being created, the material is hashed and added to the decentralized storage system. To guarantee its validity and immutability, the hash value is stored on the blockchain.confirm that the material they are consuming is legitimate.

2. Distribution and Licensing: Smart contracts allow content creators to specify the conditions of licensing for their work. The pricing, royalty distribution procedures, and usage rights are all outlined in these contracts. The smart contract handles the transaction and royalties distribution automatically when a customer buys or licenses the material.

3. Consumption of Content: Users utilize the user interface layer to access media content. All transactions are documented on the blockchain, and they have the ability to peruse, buy, and license material. Customers may access material safely and dependably thanks to the framework's decentralized design.

4. Royalty Distribution and Transparency: All transactions and royalty payouts are transparently and irrevocably recorded on the blockchain ledger. This guarantees that all parties involved can confirm the authenticity of the transactions and that content producers are fairly compensated for their labor.
5. Governance and Maintenance: The framework's seamless and secure operation is guaranteed by the governance system. All transactions and activities are validated by consensus protocols, and decentralized governance models enable participants to suggest and vote on framework modifications, guaranteeing that the system is flexible and responsive to user demands.

MONETIZATION AND REVENUE MODELS

When blockchain technology and generative AI are combined, monetization and revenue patterns in the digital media space are changing dramatically. In addition to changing the way information is produced and consumed, these innovations are also changing the way value is produced and dispersed across the ecosystem. The creation of new income streams in decentralized media, blockchain-based royalty distribution, and tokenization of digital content are important developments that hold promise for a more fair, open, and effective market for producers and consumers alike. The process of tokenization entails turning ownership rights of a tangible or digital asset into a blockchain-based digital token. For digital media, this means that non-fungible tokens (NFTs) can be used to represent content like music, films, artwork, and articles. NFTs have completely changed the ownership of material by providing a means of verifying the origin and uniqueness of digital assets. Creators may tokenize their creations using blockchain technology, which gives each item a distinct digital identity that is impossible to copy or fake. Content can now be readily purchased, sold, and exchanged on a variety of blockchain platforms thanks to the tokenization process, which gives authors a direct source of income.

Tokenization is important because it can democratize the digital media landscape. Traditional gatekeepers, like as publishers, record labels, and galleries, who frequently manage the dissemination and commercialization of material, can be circumvented by artists and producers. Creators are empowered to choose their own conditions for licensing, distribution, and sale thanks to tokenization. Additionally, smart contracts may be set up to automatically enforce these conditions, guaranteeing that content producers are fairly compensated each time their work is utilized or sold. This is a significant move toward creator-centric income structures, which rebalance the power dynamics in media creation to benefit smaller production companies and individual artists.

BLOCKCHAIN-BASED ROYALTY DISTRIBUTION

In digital media, royalty distribution is one of the most significant uses of blockchain technology. Traditionally, royalties have been managed in opaque, ineffective, and dispute-prone ways. A large percentage of the money is taken by middlemen like distributors and collecting groups, and payment delays are frequent. These issues can be resolved by blockchain technology, which offers an unchangeable and transparent ledger for monitoring the distribution and usage of digital information. When it comes to blockchain-based royalty distribution, smart contracts are essential. The provisions of these self-executing contracts are automatically enforced when certain predetermined criteria are fulfilled. A smart contract, for instance, may be used to automatically pay royalties to various parties whenever a digital work is sold or licensed. This guarantees timely payments that appropriately represent the conditions of the agreement. Additionally, because blockchain technology is transparent, all parties can confirm transactions, which lowers the possibility of disagreements and promotes confidence between producers, distributors, and customers. The use of blockchain technology for royalties distribution also makes micropayments possible, which were previously unfeasible because of large transaction fees and administrative expenses. Micropayments allow content producers to get paid for each little piece of material that is seen, such a single stream of music or a little video clip. Particularly in a digital economy where content consumption is becoming more dispersed and on-demand, this granular approach to monetization may greatly increase the earning potential for artists.

NEW REVENUE STREAMS IN DECENTRALIZED MEDIA

Blockchain technology's decentralized structure is creating completely new sources of income for the digital media industry. One such channel is the direct-to-fan sales model, which allows producers to interact directly with their audience. With this approach, artists may keep a bigger portion of the money made from their work in addition to having a more direct and customized interaction with customers. Fans may support their favourite artists through patronage models made possible by blockchain, buy special material, or take part in crowdfunding campaigns.

The use of blockchain technology to pay-per-view and subscription services is another new source of income. Access to a variety of tokenized material may be obtained through subscription packages offered by decentralized platforms. Blockchain-based subscriptions can guarantee that authors are properly rewarded based on real consumption data recorded on the blockchain, in contrast to traditional subscription systems where money is dispersed according to opaque algorithms.

More artists may be drawn to these platforms by this degree of openness and equity, improving the general caliber and variety of material that is accessible. Furthermore, chances for individualized and interactive content experiences are being created by the combination of blockchain technology and generative AI. According to user preferences, AI-driven algorithms may produce original material that can be tokenized and marketed as distinct digital assets. Not only does this customization increase user engagement, but it also gives content producers who may profit from AI-generated material another source of income. Thus, the integration of blockchain technology and artificial intelligence (AI) allows digital material to be more interactive and customizable, which may be made profitable through a variety of creative approaches. Decentralized advertising networks are another way that decentralized media companies can make money in addition to these direct revenue sources. The flow of ad money is controlled by a small number of powerful companies that dominate traditional web advertising. Decentralized networks, on the other hand, use blockchain technology to distribute ad money more fairly and allow artists to get paid directly for the interaction their material produces. These networks also let users to earn tokens for their time and participation, which makes the advertising ecology more rewarding and interactive.

RESULTS AND DISCUSSIONS

A revolutionary age in the creation, distribution, and consumption of digital media has been brought about by the combination of blockchain technology and multimodal generative AI. Long-standing problems in the media sector, including content authenticity, intellectual property rights, fair income distribution, and improved creative capacities, should be resolved by the convergence of these cutting-edge technologies. This talk examines the overall outcomes of deploying a decentralized system that blends blockchain technology with generative artificial intelligence, highlighting its influence on several aspects of media creation and consumption. Digital media now enjoys unparalleled security and transparency thanks to the use of blockchain technology. Content producers may now keep unchangeable records of their work by using decentralized ledgers, guaranteeing authenticity and safeguarding intellectual property rights. Because they automate license agreements and royalties, smart contracts have become an essential tool in this ecosystem. Conflicts over income sharing and copyright infringement, which were common in previous media distribution arrangements, have greatly decreased as a result of this. Smart contracts provide a more equitable and effective revenue distribution model by guaranteeing that artists receive their rightful royalties in real-time. Digital asset tokenization, a primary outcome of blockchain integration, has transformed content ownership and revenue generation. By tokenizing their creations, producers may sell, trade, and lease their digital material to customers directly using non-fungible tokens (NFTs). This has given creators greater control over their intellectual property by doing away with the necessity for middlemen. Creators now have additional sources of income thanks to the growth of NFT marketplaces, which has improved their ability to monetize their work and reach a worldwide audience. Because generative AI makes it possible to produce varied, high-quality media material, it has further improved the creative environment. In a variety of media formats, sophisticated models such as diffusion models, VAEs (Variational Autoencoders), and GANs (Generative Adversarial Networks) have proven crucial in producing imaginative and lifelike results. The automation of content development processes made possible by these technologies has decreased production time and expenses. Text generation models, for example, have made content creation and script development easier, and technologies for picture and video synthesis have increased the potential for visual storytelling. Significant progress has also been made in audio synthesis, which makes it possible to provide unique voiceovers and soundtracks that improve the whole media experience.

CONCLUSION

Multimodal generative AI and blockchain technology together usher in a new age of digital media production that is marked by increased security, transparency, and creative possibilities. This chapter's decentralized structure offers a more efficient and equitable system for both content creators and consumers by addressing long-standing concerns about data privacy, copyright protection, and content authenticity. Using smart contracts and blockchain's immutable ledger, this architecture streamlines licensing and royalty distribution procedures while guaranteeing that artists maintain ownership and control over their digital products. This openness fosters trust throughout the digital media ecosystem in addition to protecting intellectual property. At the same time, multimodal generative AI enables producers to create a wide range of excellent media material, pushing the limits of innovation and originality. There are several real-world uses for this decentralized strategy, including marketing, education, entertainment, and more. The combination of generative AI with blockchain technology has the potential to drastically change the creation, distribution, and monetization of content, as evidenced by case studies and comparison studies. This will promote a more secure and inclusive digital media environment.

Individual producers and consumers gain from this paradigm change, which also fosters a more robust and sustainable media ecosystem.

Going forward, it is anticipated that the ongoing development of this framework will lead to more advancements in the production and dissemination of information. That being said, it also brings up significant issues about the administration of decentralized platforms and the ethical implications of material produced by AI.

REFERENCES

Ashraf, H., Ihsan, U., Ullah, A., Ray, S. K., & Khan, N. A. (2025). Blockchain and generative AI for securing distributed systems. In *Reshaping cybersecurity with generative AI techniques* (pp. 201–218). IGI Global.

Brewer, J., Patel, D., Kim, D., & Murray, A. (2024). Navigating the challenges of generative technologies: Proposing the integration of artificial intelligence and blockchain. *Business Horizons*, *67*(5), 525–535.

Fitriawijaya, A., & Jeng, T. (2024). Integrating multimodal generative AI and Blockchain for enhancing generative design in the early phase of architectural design process. *Buildings (Basel, Switzerland)*, *14*(8), 2533.

Nash, A. (2024). Decentralized intelligence network (din). *arXiv preprint arXiv:2407.02461*.

Puppala, S., Hossain, I., Alam, M. J., Talukder, S., Ferdaus, J., Hasan, M., . . . Mathukumilli, S. (2024). Generative AI like ChatGPT in Blockchain Federated Learning: use cases, opportunities and future. *arXiv preprint arXiv:2407.18358*.

Saranya, M., & Amutha, B. (2025). Comparative Analysis of Several Different Multimodal Methods for the Development of Generative Artificial Intelligence. In *Generative Artificial Intelligence and Ethics: Standards, Guidelines, and Best Practices* (pp. 109-126). IGI Global.

Shrestha, M., Ravichandran, Y., & Kim, E. (2024). Secure Multiparty Generative AI. *arXiv preprint arXiv:2409.19120*.

Zhang, Z., Rao, Y., Xiao, H., Xiao, X., & Yang, Y. (2024). Proof of quality: A costless paradigm for trustless generative ai model inference on blockchains. *arXiv preprint arXiv:2405.17934*.

Chapter 6
Creating Without Limits:
Multimodal Generative AI in Digital Media

G. Revathy
https://orcid.org/0000-0002-0691-1687
SASTRA University, India

T. Jayapratha
Sri Eshwar College of Engineering, India

Albert Paulin Michael R.
Erode Sengunthar Engineering College, India

Santhosh Kumar M.
https://orcid.org/0009-0009-6623-0558
Nandha Engineering College, India

ABSTRACT

The chapter introduces and discusses the use of Multimodal Generative AI as a tool and its potential application setting the sphere of media production and consumption. The recent leap in technological capabilities and widespread deployment of these has resulted in a tsunami of media content proliferation allowing multiple ways in which media could be produced; however, the highlight of this chapter is to review and discuss the impact and endorsement of Multimodal Generative AI to content creation, critically reviewing the use of text, images, audio, and specifically, video content forms, allowing the audience to gain maximum understanding and a multi-dimensional view on the subject matter. In essence, this chapter imagines the future with Multimodal Generative AI on a chart demonstrating how the media will be created, consumed, and most importantly, enabled to be created.

DOI: 10.4018/979-8-3373-1504-1.ch006

INTRODUCTION

An age of unparalleled creativity and invention has been ushered in by the confluence of artificial intelligence (AI) and content production in the constantly changing world of digital media. Multimodal generative AI is a cutting-edge technology in the front of this transformation that can synthesize a wide range of material, including text, pictures, audio, and video. This revolutionary capacity is a force that is redefining the limits of creative expression, production efficiency, and user engagement rather than just being a small improvement. To produce coherent and contextually rich information, multimodal generative AI makes use of the synergy between many data modalities. Multimodal AI combines many forms of data inputs to provide outputs that are more thorough and nuanced than typical single-modality AI systems, which function independently, such as text-only or image-only models. This feature is especially useful in digital media, where combining text, images, and sound is crucial to producing engaging experiences. This technology is important in ways that go beyond its novelty. It tackles issues like diversity, customization, and scalability that have long plagued the production of digital content. Multimodal generative AI helps organizations and creators to efficiently create large volumes of media by automating the creation of high-quality content, meeting the growing demand for content across several channels. Additionally, its capacity to tailor material according to contextual information and user choices improves engagement, giving interactions greater significance and effect.

The development of deep learning and machine learning techniques is where multimodal generative AI got its start. Early AI systems were mostly concerned with specialized tasks, such natural language processing or picture categorization. But as the complexity and variety of user demands increased, the shortcomings of these single-task models became clear. As a result, more sophisticated designs that could manage several data kinds at once were created. The advent of Variational Autoencoders (VAEs) and Generative Adversarial Networks (GANs) was one of the major developments in this field. These models provide the foundation for producing lifelike pictures and films. The introduction of transformers, namely models like as BERT (Bidirectional Encoder Representations from Transformers) and GPT (Generative Pre-trained Transformer), transformed the creation and understanding of text. By combining these concepts into a single framework, multimodal systems were made possible, enabling them to process and produce content from a variety of media. Multimodal generative artificial intelligence has a wide range of uses in digital media. By making it possible to create realistic virtual people and locations, it improves the narrative experience in the entertainment industry. With the use of this technology, video game creators, for example, may create immersive environments and dynamic storylines that react instantly to player actions. Artificial Intelligence

(AI) has the potential to drastically save production time and expenses by helping with voice dubbing, special effects creation, and even dialogue composition. Multimodal AI makes it easier to create tailored marketing and advertising strategies that appeal to target consumers. Through user data analysis, AI can produce personalized content that suits each user's tastes, boosting engagement and conversion rates. Given the intense battle for users' attention on social media, this capacity is very beneficial. AI may be used by brands to create captivating images and stories that stand out in a congested online space.

This technology has enormous potential benefits for the educational sector as well. By producing interactive learning resources that accommodate various learning preferences, multimodal AI can improve accessibility and engagement in the classroom. To provide a comprehensive learning experience, an AI-generated module may, for instance, contain instructional videos, audio summaries, illustrative images, and explanatory text. This helps students with different requirements and preferences while also improving understanding.

Multimodal generative AI presents a number of ethical and societal issues in addition to its enormous promise. The potential for abuse, especially in the production of deepfakes and other synthetic media, is one of the main problems. These technologies provide serious obstacles to authenticity and trust as they can be used to create damaging or deceptive material. To guarantee the safe application of AI in digital media, strong frameworks and regulations are therefore desperately needed. The effects on employment and the creative sector are further causes for concern. Jobs may be lost as a result of content creation automation, especially in positions requiring repeated duties. However, it also creates new avenues for creative professionals to use AI as a tool to boost their creativity and productivity while concentrating on higher-order activities like strategy and ideation. Furthermore, the incorporation of AI into digital media calls for a reassessment of content ownership and intellectual property rights. The increasing prevalence of AI-generated material raises concerns about attribution and authorship. Establishing precise legal structures that safeguard and defend creators' rights while encouraging creativity and cooperation is essential.

STATE OF ART MODELS

Bieniek et.al (2024) says that how generative AI may improve user interfaces by integrating multimodal interactions that support text, audio, and video input styles while guaranteeing consistent user experiences across platforms. The transition from conventional single-modal interfaces to adaptive systems driven by extensive language models is emphasized, underscoring the necessity of employing efficient design techniques to resolve the interface conundrum. The technological and moral difficulties of putting these sophisticated user interfaces into practice are also covered, such as context preservation, privacy issues, and striking a balance between on-device and cloud processing. The study shows how generative AI may transform user-centric interactions across platforms by outlining future research goals, including the creation of emotionally adaptable interfaces and real-time collaborative systems.

Engy and Yehia (2024) proposes that straightforward human inputs to stimulate creativity, generative AI is a form of artificial intelligence that produces unique material in a variety of fields, such as prose, graphics, and computer code. Since this technology is still in its infancy, there is room for expansion and improvement in its uses. On the basis of user input, generative AI may generate original material, in contrast to typical AI models that concentrate on pattern recognition and prediction. Using methods like reinforcement learning from human input, it evolves to produce realistic and distinctive outputs, including software code, images, movies, and music, based on the data that is already available.

Timothy et.al (2024) says that the implications and possibilities of AI-driven tools in the production of multimedia material are examined by the Digital Generative Multimedia Tool Theory (DGMTT). DGMTT demonstrates how AI technologies give users interactive skills to create and edit multimedia material, boosting user engagement and creative flexibility through real-time feedback and tailored content production.

Carmen et.al (2024) says that the integration of Generative AI (GenAI) technology in higher education is covered in the article, with a focus on the necessity of innovative pedagogical solutions and the application of metaphor as a tool for investigating GenAI in educational settings. Through interdisciplinary research and innovative activities, it emphasizes the significance of involving educators and students in critical and creative inquiry. It offers a thorough description of the workshop learning exercises intended to help with the comprehension and integration of GenAI, covering its conception, execution, and initial results. In addition to analysing future creative potential with GenAI and metaphor, the article attempts to expand the applications of GenAI in education and provides an alternate paradigm for educators to adopt in their activities.

Sadhana and Mishra (2024) says that the revolutionary potential of generative artificial intelligence (Gen AI) is examined in this study. Its capacity to produce novel and convincing pictures, texts, and motion graphics at a quick pace highlights its function as a catalyst for innovation in a variety of sectors. It offers a comprehensive examination of the profound impact of generative artificial intelligence (AI), showcasing its adaptability and limitless potential in producing creative media such as dynamic videos, prose, and visual art, ultimately establishing it as a major driver of advancement in the industrial landscape.

Igor et.al (2024) talks on the emergence of generative AI, emphasizing ChatGPT's success in 2023, and how it's helping to speed up society's digital transition to a new paradigm known as Society 5.0. It investigates how generative AI may be used in mass media, audiovisual, and social development. Significant ethical issues and conundrums are highlighted by the authors in relation to the application of generative AI. These include the spread of false information, copyright violations, threats to artistic freedom, and the possibility of digital consciousness manipulation, which could result in social exclusion and a distorted perception of human existence and communication.

Priya et.al (2024) examines the development of generative AI, emphasizing how it has revolutionized a number of industries, including healthcare, commerce, and the arts. It also describes the technological developments from early neural networks to more recent models like GPT-4 and diffusion-based systems. Topics covered include Transformer architectures, Variational Autoencoders (VAEs), and Generative Adversarial Networks (GANs), which have revolutionized content creation. The study also discusses the problems that generative AI presents, such as prejudice, ethical dilemmas, and environmental effects, especially the rising water usage of data centres. It highlights the dual character of generative AI, which both boosts productivity and upends established markets and interpersonal relationships, highlighting the necessity of ethical and sustainable research and application methods.

Poornima et.al (2024) says that using sophisticated models like GAN, VAE, and Transformers to automate processes like content creation, design, and development, generative AI is transforming web engineering and enhancing creativity and scalability while saving developers time. Though it also brings up significant issues with data quality, prejudice, and ethical considerations that need to be addressed for responsible AI usage, the integration of AI in web engineering makes it possible to create dynamic and customized user interfaces that meet the demands of individual users.

TECHNOLOGICAL FOUNDATIONS

Multimodal Generative AI's technological underpinnings are the result of the confluence of multiple state-of-the-art developments in artificial intelligence. This field's fundamental tools include a range of machine learning models and architectures that are intended to analyze and produce material in many modalities, including text, images, audio, and video. Complex, excellent media that is both inventive and highly customized may be produced thanks to the smooth integration of these many data types. This section explores the fundamental technologies that support Multimodal Generative AI, with an emphasis on important models like DALL-E,

Stable Diffusion, and GPT that have transformed content creation and changed the digital media ecosystem.

The capacity of artificial intelligence to absorb and comprehend several kinds of data at the same time is the basis of multimodal generative artificial intelligence. Neural network designs have advanced, especially those built to manage the challenges of multimodal data integration, which has made this possible. The core components of this technology are deep learning models, which have been optimized to perform exceptionally well in jobs requiring the synthesis of data from many sources. To learn the subtle correlations between various data kinds, these models are trained on extensive datasets that include text, photos, audio, and video. Encoder-decoder frameworks are an essential part of this ecosystem because they make it easier to convert one data modality into another.

Text input, for instance, can be processed by an encoder and transformed into a numerical representation, which a decoder can utilize to produce matching sounds or visuals. Complex algorithms and loss functions that maximize the resulting content's correctness and coherence serve as the foundation for this procedure. Furthermore, the capabilities of multimodal models have been greatly improved by the addition of attention mechanisms, especially in the context of transformer architectures. While producing output, attention methods enable the model to concentrate on pertinent portions of the input data, enhancing the caliber and pertinence of the material that is produced. In applications where the model must comprehend and reproduce intricate patterns across many data modalities, this feature is extremely important.

KEY MODELS: DALL-E, STABLE DIFFUSION, GPT

The most notable examples of Multimodal Generative AI's influence on digital media are probably DALL-E, Stable Diffusion, and GPT. Each of these models has distinct capabilities and represents the highest level of recent developments in AI-driven content creation.

DALL-E is a ground-breaking model created by OpenAI that can produce visuals from written descriptions. By utilizing transformer structures, DALL-E is able to produce incredibly intricate and creative images in response to straightforward verbal commands. This feature not only shows how AI can bridge the gap between various data modalities, but it also revolutionizes the creative sectors. A new level of content production is made possible by DALL-E's ability to comprehend and interpret natural language descriptions in order to produce accurate and contextually rich visuals.

In the field of picture synthesis, stable diffusion represents yet another important breakthrough. Stable Diffusion adopts a revolutionary technique that stabilizes the diffusion process, increasing its efficiency and scalability in contrast to typical generative models that frequently demand substantial computer resources. A useful tool for sectors that require accurate and dependable visual material, this model excels at creating high-resolution photographs that retain a constant style and quality. Beyond only creating images, it may be used in fields like video synthesis and augmented reality, where including excellent graphics is crucial.

OpenAI also created the GPT (Generative Pre-trained Transformer) series, which has raised the bar for text production and natural language processing. Due to their extensive pre-training on text data corpora, GPT models are able to produce text that is both contextually relevant and coherent for a wide range of applications. The capacity of GPT to comprehend and produce language that is human-like accounts for its adaptability, making it a vital tool for chatbots, interactive media, and content production. More complicated and integrated content generating jobs are now possible because to the newest generations of GPT, which have further enhanced their capabilities by integrating multimodal inputs.

These models together demonstrate how Multimodal Generative AI has the ability to revolutionize digital media. They provide new opportunities for immersive and interactive media experiences in addition to improving the creative process by giving artists and content producers additional tools. As these technologies advance, they will probably become increasingly more woven into the fabric of producing digital media, spurring creativity and changing how people produce and consume material.

APPLICATIONS IN MEDIA PRODUCTION

The way that material is produced, accessed, and customized has changed dramatically as a result of the incorporation of Multimodal Generative AI into media production. The seamless creation of a variety of media kinds is made possible by this revolutionary technology, meeting the growing need for superior, personalized content on several platforms. The media landscape is being revolutionized by the profound applications of Multimodal Generative AI in picture and video production, text generation and content authoring, audio synthesis, and music composition, all of which we examine in this section.

Text Generation And Content Writing

Multimodal Generative Writing content and generating text have greatly benefited from AI. Advanced language models like GPT (Generative Pre-trained Transformer) have made it possible for AI to create text that is entertaining, contextually relevant, and cohesive across a range of genres and forms. In order to comprehend complex language patterns and produce content that is human-like, these models are trained on large datasets covering a wide range of subjects and writing styles. Applications include automated news reporting, in which AI writes articles about current affairs, and creative writing, in which it helps writers come up with ideas for stories or even whole chapters. AI-driven text production is also being used more and more by companies for customer service response writing, tailored product descriptions, and content marketing. This feature guarantees consistency and audience-specific personalization while also increasing efficiency by cutting down on the time and resources needed for content development.

Image And Video Creation

AI models like DALL-E and Stable Diffusion have revolutionized the potential for creating images and videos. Without requiring a lot of human labor, artists and content producers may realize their ideas because to these models' ability to produce excellent graphics from written instructions. For example, DALL-E can generate original, creative visuals in response to basic instructions, which makes it a useful tool for the advertising, entertainment, and graphic design sectors. In a similar vein, Stable Diffusion is excellent at producing realistic and detailed visuals, which are essential for applications like virtual reality, video game creation, and movie making. There have also been notable developments in the creation of video material, with AI models being able to create visually pleasing and cohesive video segments. As a result, AI-generated animations and visual effects have become increasingly prevalent, enabling more dynamic and captivating narrative experiences. These models' effectiveness and scalability make them essential in a media environment that requires constant innovation and top-notch graphics.

Audio Synthesis And Music Composition

With new tools for musicians, composers, and sound designers, Multimodal Generative AI has also transformed audio synthesis and music creation. Artificial intelligence (AI) models that can produce realistic speech, background noise, and musical compositions are now widely employed in a variety of sectors, including advertising and entertainment. In video games, movies, and virtual assistants, for instance, AI-driven audio synthesis may provide realistic voiceovers and conversation, greatly lowering the need for post-production editing and human voice actors. From classical symphonies to modern pop songs, AI models are capable of creating creative music in a wide range of genres. In addition to being of excellent quality, these compositions may be altered to suit particular themes or moods, which makes them perfect for jingles, background music, and customized playlists. Additionally,

AI-generated music may be used to provide interactive media adaptive soundtracks, in which user activities cause the music to alter dynamically. This feature improves the user experience overall by increasing its immersion and engagement. The potential of AI to democratize music creation is highlighted by developments in audio synthesis and composition, which would enable producers of all skill levels to create audio material of a high caliber.

IMPACT ON MEDIA CONSUMPTION

A revolutionary era has begun with the incorporation of Multimodal Generative AI into media consumption, which has redefined how viewers interact with material. This technology has a huge influence on interactive media experiences, tailored information distribution, and the development of immersive virtual worlds. In addition to improving user engagement, each feature transforms conventional consuming habits and produces a more dynamic and personalized media environment.

Personalized Content Delivery

Multimodal Generative AI's capacity to provide highly customized material is among its most notable effects on media consumption. Artificial intelligence (AI) algorithms examine user data, including viewing patterns, preferences, and interactions, to select material that suits personal preferences. For example, streaming services employ these features to individually suggest films, TV series, and songs to users, improving the viewing experience by making it more interesting and relevant. In digital publishing and news platforms, artificial intelligence (AI) creates tailored news feeds that rank content according to the reader's reading preferences and interests. As a consequence, consumers have a more engaging and fulfilling experience, feeling as though the material was created just for them. Furthermore, organizations may more precisely target their audiences with individualized content distribution, increasing consumer happiness and engagement rates.

Interactive Media Experiences

By obfuscating the distinction between the production and consumption of material, multimodal generative AI has also transformed interactive media experiences. AI-driven content that real-time adjusts to user inputs is now a benefit of interactive media, including video games, virtual reality (VR) experiences, and augmented reality (AR) apps. Artificial intelligence (AI) produces dynamic storylines, customized character interactions, and adaptive gameplay in video games, making the user experience more captivating and immersive. AI-powered environments in VR and AR apps react to user inputs in a similar way, providing a smooth transition between the real and virtual worlds. This interaction is also present in educational platforms, where AI-generated material creates a personalized learning experience by adjusting to the learner's choices and speed. Experiences with interactive media are no longer passive; rather, they are participatory, giving users the ability to control their trip and affect the content, increasing user pleasure and engagement.

Immersive Virtual Environments

Multimodal Generative AI has also had a big influence on the development of immersive virtual worlds. These AI-powered environments take users to completely other worlds with realistic and dynamic surroundings. Artificial intelligence (AI)-generated virtual worlds are utilized in theme parks, movies, and video games to provide viewers an unmatched level of immersion. AI models, for example, provide realistic landscapes, complex architecture patterns, and dynamic weather systems, resulting in a believable and captivating virtual environment. Immersion virtual environments facilitate experience learning in the fields of education and training by allowing users to do scientific experiments, visit historical locations, or rehearse intricate processes in a secure environment.

This practical method improves understanding and memory, which increases learning effectiveness and enjoyment. A sense of presence and connectedness is also fostered despite geographical distances in the business sector through the usage of virtual environments for remote collaboration, virtual meetings, and team-building activities. Artificial intelligence (AI)-generated virtual worlds are being employed in healthcare for rehabilitation and therapeutic purposes. These spaces offer a safe space for patients to face and regulate their anxieties, lower stress levels, and enhance their general health. Social media and online communities are also impacted by immersive virtual environments, as AI-powered platforms provide virtual places where users may communicate, exchange stories, and develop bonds. By providing fresh opportunities for interaction and connection, these settings promote a feeling of community and belonging.

CASE STUDIES AND INDUSTRY APPLICATIONS

Numerous sectors have used Multimodal Generative AI, which has transformed conventional workflows and opened up new avenues for creativity. This chapter explores the profound effects of AI in the fields of marketing and advertising, e-learning and educational material, and entertainment and movies. Each of these domains exemplifies the revolutionary possibilities of artificial intelligence, showcasing its capacity to augment creativity, optimize workflows, and provide customized experiences.

The use of Multimodal Generative AI to improve visual effects, expedite production, and produce more captivating material has been spearheaded by the entertainment and film industries. The time and expense involved with old approaches are now reduced by using AI-driven technologies to create lifelike animations, realistic special effects, and even whole digital landscapes. AI, for instance, can provide excellent visual effects for films and television series, giving producers the ability to create fanciful worlds and animals with previously unheard-of realism and richness. Screenwriters can overcome writer's block by using AI algorithms to develop fresh dialogue and plots by analyzing large databases of previous screenplays. This is only one example of how AI is being used in film production. AI is also being used to customize material for viewers. Using AI algorithms, streaming services examine user preferences and viewing patterns to suggest films and television series that suit each user's likes. A stronger bond between viewers and content is fostered by this tailored approach, which increases viewer pleasure and engagement. In post-production, artificial intelligence (AI) is also used to automate processes like sound design, color correction, and editing, freeing up filmmakers to concentrate on the artistic elements of narrative.

A new age of innovation in the marketing and advertising sector has been brought about by multimodal generative AI, which allows companies to develop highly individualized and targeted campaigns that appeal to customers. Artificial intelligence (AI)-powered solutions examine enormous volumes of customer data to comprehend preferences, habits, and patterns, enabling marketers to customize their messaging and provide interesting and pertinent content. For example, ads produced by AI have the ability to dynamically adjust to the interests of the viewer, showcasing goods and services that are most likely to be of interest to them. In addition to improving the overall consumer experience, this degree of customisation boosts the efficacy of marketing initiatives.

Additionally, AI is changing how businesses produce content. Generative AI models eliminate the need for costly and time-consuming production methods by producing high-quality photos, videos, and audio material at scale. Brands may utilize AI to produce product graphics, promotional films, and even full advertising campaigns, all while preserving a consistent brand voice and style. Furthermore, chatbots and virtual assistants driven by AI offer individualized customer service by recommending products, responding to inquiries, and assisting clients with the buying process. One prominent use in marketing is sentiment analysis, where AI systems examine reviews, comments, and social media postings to determine how customers feel about a product or brand. With the use of this knowledge, marketers may instantly adjust their tactics to better suit the wants and needs of their target audience.

E-LEARNING AND EDUCATIONAL CONTENT

Multimodal Generative AI has been adopted by the e-learning and educational sectors to produce individualized, captivating, and successful learning experiences. In order to provide material that is specifically targeted to each student's requirements, AI-driven systems examine learner data to identify each person's unique learning preferences, skills, and shortcomings. By offering information that is pertinent, demanding, and in line with the learner's objectives, this individualized approach improves learning results. Additionally, generative AI is being utilized to provide immersive and interactive teaching materials. For instance, students can do scientific experiments, visit historical locations, or practice difficult processes in a secure atmosphere by using AI-generated virtual environments. These practical experiences improve understanding and memory, which increases the effectiveness and enjoyment of learning. AI-powered tutors also offer real-time feedback and assistance, helping students overcome obstacles and guiding them through their learning process. Additionally, administrative duties at educational institutions including curriculum development, attendance monitoring, and grading are being automated by AI. By allowing teachers to concentrate on mentorship and instruction, this automation raises the standard of education as a whole. In order to guarantee that no student is left behind, AI-driven technologies also give teachers the ability to track students' progress and pinpoint areas in which further help is required. AI is being utilized in the corporate training industry to create individualized learning programs for staff members, providing them with information pertinent to their positions and professional objectives.

CHALLENGES AND ETHICAL CONSIDERATIONS

Multimodal Generative AI's quick development and broad use have highlighted a number of issues and moral dilemmas that need to be resolved to guarantee responsible use. Among them, concerns of ownership and intellectual property, prejudice and justice in AI-generated content, and content authenticity and deepfakes are especially important. This section explores these issues, examining how they affect people, the media business, and society as a whole. It also discusses possible solutions to these problems.

Content authenticity is one of the most urgent problems Multimodal Generative AI presents, especially when it comes to deepfakes. Because of their potential to mislead and misinform, deepfakes—hyper-realistic modified films or pictures produced by artificial intelligence—have attracted a lot of interest. There are major threats to privacy, reputation, and public trust since these synthetic media might accurately portray people saying or doing things they never did. Deepfakes' widespread use has sparked worries about how they may be used to disseminate harmful content, propaganda, and false information. For example, by creating false remarks or actions, deepfakes might be used as a weapon in political campaigns to discredit opponents or change public opinion. They may also be used to produce fake news, which increases the dissemination of incorrect information and undermines confidence in media outlets. Researchers and developers are creating sophisticated detection algorithms that can recognize deepfakes and confirm the legitimacy of digital information in order to tackle the problem of content authenticity. Another potential remedy being investigated is blockchain technology, which provides a decentralized, impenetrable record for tracking the origin and legitimacy of media assets. But as detection technologies advance, generative models' capabilities also advance, resulting in a continuous arms race between detection and production,

Intellecutal Property And Ownership

Multimodal Generative AI's incorporation into content production brings up difficult issues around ownership and intellectual property (IP). Traditionally, copyright laws have given authors the exclusive right to their inventions, protecting literary, musical, and artistic masterpieces. However, identifying authorship and ownership becomes difficult when material is produced by AI. One of the main concerns is whether or not work produced by AI can be protected by copyright, and if it is, who is in possession of the rights—the AI's creator, the person who initiated the creation, or the AI itself? These subtleties are difficult for current legal systems to manage, which results in uncertainty and ownership and royalty issues. It is uncertain who should receive credit and payment, for instance, if an AI-generated piece of art receives recognition or makes money. Concerns around illegal usage and possible infringement are also raised by the use of pre-existing copyrighted content as training data for generative AI models. The ethical dilemma of how much authors should be paid or recognized for their efforts is brought up by the fact that many AI models are trained on enormous datasets that contain copyrighted information. New legal frameworks and regulations that take into account the special qualities of AI-generated material are required in order to overcome these obstacles. Among the suggestions are the creation of new intellectual property categories tailored to AI-generated works and the use of licensing contracts for the use of copyrighted content in training datasets. These steps seek to strike a balance between the creative potential of AI technology and the rights of original creators.

Bias And Fairness In Ai Generated Content

The question of prejudice and fairness is another crucial ethical factor to be taken into account while using multimodal generative AI. Large datasets that represent societal biases and prejudices are used to train AI algorithms. AI-generated information may therefore unintentionally reinforce or magnify existing prejudices, producing unfair or discriminating results. For instance, cultural, ethnic, or gender biases may be present in AI-generated photos or movies, which might exclude some groups from representation or reinforce negative preconceptions. Similar to this, if language models are trained on biased data, they may generate offensive or prejudiced text. This calls into question the moral obligation of developers and institutions to guarantee that AI-generated material is equitable, inclusive, and reflective of a range of viewpoints. A multifaceted strategy is needed to address prejudice in AI-generated material. This entails selecting representative and varied training datasets, putting fairness-conscious algorithms into practice, and carrying out frequent audits to find and lessen biases. Incorporating diverse teams into the development process may also guarantee that AI systems are sensitive to social and cultural circumstances. Addressing prejudice also requires responsibility and transparency. In order to allow for external review and input, organizations must be open and honest about the data sources and algorithms that are employed in their AI systems. Furthermore, defining precise rules and moral principles for AI development can encourage ethical behavior and advance equity in AI-generated content.

RESULTS AND DISCUSSIONS

In the field of digital media creation and consumption, the investigation of multimodal generative artificial intelligence and its intersection with blockchain technology offers both revolutionary potential and formidable obstacles. The outcomes of several technical developments and their applications are summarized in this chapter, which also provides a thorough analysis of their possible effects on the media environment. Text, graphics, audio, and video are just a few of the media types for which the use of Multimodal Generative AI has shown impressive potential in automating and improving content creation. In addition to making content creation easier, models like DALL-E, Stable Diffusion, and GPT have improved the caliber and inventiveness of digital media. The examples covered show how AI-generated content is transforming media creation and giving customers rich, customized experiences. AI-powered personalized content delivery systems, for example, are changing how audiences interact with media by customizing experiences to suit each user's tastes and increasing user retention and satisfaction.

Blockchain integration tackles important issues in digital media, especially those pertaining to security, authenticity, and content ownership. The transparent and unchangeable record of digital assets provided by blockchain's decentralized ledger system is crucial for confirming the origin and legitimacy of media material. In order to prevent the spread of deepfakes and guarantee that viewers can rely on the material they view, this is very important. Tokenization and smart contracts further simplify income sharing and copyright management, giving authors a safer and more effective way to make money off of their creations.

The practical use of these technologies in industries including marketing, e-learning, and entertainment is demonstrated by the case studies and industrial applications covered in this chapter. While blockchain and artificial intelligence (AI) enable targeted and captivating marketing efforts, they are also being utilized in the entertainment sector to create dynamic and interactive experiences. These technologies are used by e-learning platforms to create adaptive and tailored educational content that improves accessibility and learning results. The conversation does, however, also highlight a number of difficulties and moral issues. Concerns regarding the integrity and authenticity of digital media are raised by the rise of AI-generated material. There is a serious risk that deepfakes would propagate false information and undermine public confidence, hence strong detection systems and legal frameworks are required.

The lack of clarity surrounding intellectual property rights and ownership of work produced by AI emphasizes the necessity for revised legal guidelines that take into account the special characteristics of AI creativity. Fairness and bias in content produced by AI are equally important concerns. Because AI systems have the potential to reinforce prevailing social prejudices, it is imperative to take proactive measures to guarantee diversity and inclusion in algorithmic design and training datasets. In order to maintain ethical standards and promote public confidence, transparency and accountability are crucial in the development of AI. This chapter's findings and discussion offer a sophisticated understanding of the two-pronged nature of blockchain technology and multimodal generative artificial intelligence. Although its integration presents previously unheard-of chances for creativity and effectiveness in digital media, it also necessitates carefully weighing the moral, legal, and societal ramifications. To fully utilize these technologies' potential while defending the interests of all parties participating in the digital media ecosystem, further study, discussion, and cooperation will be essential as they develop. As a basic debate, this chapter sets the stage for further research and advancement in this quickly developing topic.

CONCLUSION

The findings from investigating the use of Multimodal Generative AI in media creation and consumption will be summarized in the chapter's conclusion. Multimodal Generative AI is clearly more than just a tool; it is a revolutionary force that is changing the media environment as we have seen via its quick development and extensive uses. The significant capabilities of pre-trained models like DALL-E, Stable Diffusion, and GPT demonstrate how AI can drastically change traditional media workflows by dynamically generating high-quality material in a variety of formats, including text, photos, audio, and video. There have been notable turning points in the evolution from basic frameworks to complex systems, demonstrating AI's capacity to produce unique and highly customized material. This development is supported by fundamental ideas that guarantee the technology supports the objectives of democratizing content production, increasing creativity, and increasing efficiency. But enormous power also carries a tremendous deal of responsibility. Important topics including data agreements, AI system semantics, and computing efficiency have all been covered in this chapter. The necessity for strong frameworks and regulations to control the moral use of AI in media is highlighted by these difficulties. The case studies and real-world examples showcase the multifaceted effects of Multimodal Generative AI, ranging from e-learning settings to marketing and entertainment revolutions. Multimodal Generative AI presents both an exciting and morally challenging future for the media industry. It is important to think about the ethical ramifications of AI-mediated content creation as we make predictions about future advancements. To make sure the technology helps society as a whole, issues with ownership, legitimacy, and abuse potential need to be addressed. To improve AI systems' dependability, polish them, and create regulations to prevent possible misuse, further research is essential. Finally, a thorough overview of the present situation and prospects of Multimodal Generative AI in media has been provided by this chapter. We are on the verge of a new age in content production, when creativity has no boundaries and the possibilities are genuinely endless, thanks to the adoption of this technology. The path ahead, though, calls both a dedication to using AI for the greater good and careful navigating of the ethical terrain. In order to ensure that AI in media is a driving force for innovation and constructive change, the current discussion and research will be crucial in determining its future.

REFERENCES

Bieniek, J., Rahouti, M., & Verma, D. (2024). Generative AI in multimodal user interfaces: Trends, challenges, and cross-platform adaptability. *arXiv*. /arXiv.2411. 10234DOI: 10.48550

Ekeledirichukwu, T. O., & Msughter, E. A. (2024). Digital generative multimedia tool theory (DGMTT): A theoretical postulation. *Journalism and Mass Communication*, *14*(3), 139–160. DOI: 10.17265/2160-6579/2024.03.004

Engy, Y. (2024). Developments on generative AI. In Generative, A. I. (Ed.), *Opportunities and challenges* (pp. 139–160). CRC Press. DOI: 10.1201/9781003501152-9

Mahadevappa, P., Muzammal, S. M., & Tayyab, M. (2024). Introduction to generative AI in web engineering. In *Advances in web technologies and engineering* (pp. 297–330). IGI Global. DOI: 10.4018/979-8-3693-3703-5.ch015

Mishra, S. (2024). Exploring the transformative potential and generative AI's multifaceted impact on diverse sectors. In Ara, A., & Ara, A. (Eds.), *Exploring the ethical implications of generative AI* (pp. 88–103). IGI Global. DOI: 10.4018/979-8-3693-1565-1.ch006

Pecheranskyi, I., Oliinyk, O., Medvedieva, A., Danyliuk, V., & Hubernator, O. (2024). Perspectives of generative AI in the context of digital transformation of society, audio-visual media and mass communication: Instrumentalism, ethics and freedom. *Indian Journal of Information Sources and Services*, *14*(4), 48–53. Advance online publication. DOI: 10.51983/ijiss-2024.14.4.08

Vallis, C., Wilson, S., & Casey, A. (2024). Generative AI. In *ASCILITE 2024 Conference Proceedings* (pp. 590–595). Australasian Society for Computers in Learning in Tertiary Education. DOI: 10.14742/apubs.2024.1408

Yadav, P., Rathwad, G., & Jain, J. (2024). Generative AI: Shaping the future while disrupting the present. *International Journal for Multidisciplinary Research*, *6*(5), 28085. Advance online publication. DOI: 10.36948/ijfmr.2024.v06i05.28085

Chapter 7
Bridging Text and Video Generation:
A Survey

G. Maragatham

SRM Institute of Science and Technology, Kattankulathur, India

Nilay Kumar

SRM Institute of Science and Technology, Kattankulathur, India

Priyansh Bhandari

https://orcid.org/0009-0006-6515-8046

SRM Institute of Science and Technology, Kattankulathur, India

Vinston Raja

https://orcid.org/0000-0003-0914-3254

SRM Institute of Science and Technology, Kattankulathur, India

Robinson Joel M

https://orcid.org/0000-0002-3030-8431

KCG College of Technology, India

ABSTRACT

While text-to-image synthesis extends to dynamic visual contents, text-to-video synthesis creates coherent videos from the provided text-based description. A technique of this nature can make a revolutionary impact on industries such as education, accessibility, marketing, and entertainment. However, the T2V technique comes with a set of challenges that pertain to temporal coherence, exact alignment between text and video, high computational demands, and limited high-quality datasets. This survey summarizes the latest developments in T2V technologies, beginning with

DOI: 10.4018/979-8-3373-1504-1.ch007

early adaptations of text-to-image models and progressing to recent studies involving large-scale pre-training integrated with diffusion methods. The chapter then provides a comprehensive comparison of these models based on their performance metrics against benchmarking datasets, examining the strengths and limitations of each, along with practical applications.

1. INTRODUCTION

Deep learning has revolutionized generative modelling, with applications across domains. One of the most prominent successes of generative modelling is in text-to-image synthesis, where models such as DALL·E (A. Ramesh et al., 2021), CLIP (A. Radford et al., 2022) and Stable Diffusion (R. Rombach et al., 2022) have been able to generate high-quality images from textual descriptions. Currently, in furtherance of this line of development, research is pressing an even more difficult task of generating coherent and dynamic video from text-materially more difficult than T2I. This shift introduces additional challenges: temporal consistency, a well-defined text-visual alignment, and even higher computational demands.

T2V has massive potential in a lot of fields. For educational purposes, the T2V models visualize either a process that may be intricate or simulate some phenomenon in real time, hence improving understanding and engagement. Regarding accessibility, dynamic visuals help people who sometimes struggle to read because of some reading disability or have impaired vision. Regarding marketing and entertainment, a company can create product demonstration videos with minimal resources, while personalized storytelling goes as far as customized animated narratives. Despite these promising applications, there are a series of challenges to T2V adoption. It has to ensure coherence in the video regarding time; smooth transitions and frames will avoid disjointed videos disrupting viewer engagement. The alignment of text associated with visuals is quite tricky, considering that there involve several objects that interact with each other. Video generation entails many more computational resources compared to image generation, hence begging some questions on efficiency and scalability. The relative scarcity of large high-quality text-video datasets limits models' generalization capabilities (Hong et al., 2018).

The research has thus come up with various models that address these challenges by extending the T2I techniques to incorporate temporal dynamics: GODIVA (C. Wu et al.,2021), an early version that utilized auto-encoders and attention mechanisms to generate short videos efficiently; NUWA (C. Wu et al.,2021) introduced a unified framework where not only text, but images and video were taken into account but resulted in obvious increased computational demands. Realizing the limitation of data, models like CogVideo (W. Hong et al., 2022) leveraged large text-image datasets yet said aligning text with dynamic actions was not easy. While Make-A-Video (U. Singer et al., 2022) did explore unsupervised methods for zero-shot generation, this resulted in poor visuals.

Recent works are directed toward improving efficiency, coherence, and diversity. VideoFusion (Z. Luo et al., 2023) used probabilistic frameworks that minimized redundancy while maintaining temporal coherence of the content. LatentShift (J. An et al., 2023) brought temporal dynamics into the latent space of T2I models, which reduced computational complexity significantly. FreeBloom (H. Huang et al., 2019) applied large language models for better storytelling, but coherence across frames remains a task challenging to achieve.

Models such as VideoTetris (X. Wang et al., 2024) further developed multi- subject video generation through better composition and identity preservation. Models such as the FIFO-Diffusion, and Pyramidal Flow Matching developed hierarchical architectures for longer videos towards informing a balance in high-resolution generation with temporal coherence. Analyzing the performance of T2V models through current metrics remains a complex task. While quantitative metrics offer a benchmark, they very often fail in capturing minute qualities that cannot be caught by automated measures.

Systematic human evaluation can offer much greater insight into realism, coherence, and alignment with textual descriptions far more than is possible with automatic measures. Standard evaluation protocols will be developed for the T2V models in further research work to support continuous benchmarking and allow for relevant comparisons.

Training T2V models requires huge computational resources and well-cured datasets. The paper analyze common datasets used, discussing their content, scale, and suitability. It is obvious that only high-quality and diversified datasets can realize realistic and varied video output. Due to this, literature lacks rigorous syntheses that sum up the advances, point out challenges, and put forward future research directions. While some aspects may be discussed by current surveys, they fail to perform an integrated in-depth review. Through this survey, the article fill this gap by investigating cutting-edge models, metrics, datasets, and configurations of training.

The Chapter main contributions include:

- An in-depth overview of the evolution of T2V models concerning their architectures, training methods, and working mechanisms. It also traces the major developments from early methods based on autoencoders to the latest diffusion models and discuss major innovations and how those affected progress in the subject area.
- Review the datasets on which usually T2V models are trained, describing their size, diversity, and content attributes. Further, it goes through the train-

ing configurations and computational resources of the currently available T2V models, underlining which infrastructures and training configurations settings allow for successfully training these models.

- Provide an overview of the metrics that have been adopted for T2V model evaluation, including the insights on the current standards of benchmarking. Also, Further discuss human evaluation methodologies and their contributions toward getting quality assessments that extend beyond automated scores, and also discussed is the recent development of new metrics and new benchmarks in this area, taking into account how future methods of evaluation might evolve with the direction toward common standards enabling consistent model evaluations.

- Highlight some key obstacles in the domain of text- to-video generative models, including scarcity of data, computation, and temporal coherence. In the process, the paper argues for synthetic data creation, fine-tuning architectures towards temporal tasks, and better modelling approaches concerning temporality. Finally, it turns the attention to the extension of application domains for T2V, with particular attention to innovation and inclusion in various industries

2. PRELIMINARIES

Generating video from text is an intricately complex task, necessitating a seamless fusion of natural language understanding and visual content creation. The coherence and realism of videos generated by a model from textual descriptions call for an understanding of the semantics and nuances of language, translating them into dynamic and temporally coherent visual sequences. The idea of this task stretches the frontiers not only of computer vision itself but also of natural language processing, given the demands it placed on complete and utter comprehension of the foundational technologies which could conceive of such cross-modal synthesis. Mindful of the complexity involved, it surely becomes necessary to deconstruct those methods and architectures that form the backbone of work done in current research and provide context for translating text to video.

2.1 U-Net

U-Net belongs to the class of convolutional neural networks (M. R. Joel et al., 2023) that were specifically designed for dense prediction tasks that require both global context and local detail preservation. U-Net is built up of two core components. An Encoder and A Decoder, that work together to transform input features into detailed output maps. In the U-Net framework, the network architecture is symmetric in the shape of a "U". The network is built of an encoder module, which represents the contracting path, and a decoder module, which represents the expanding path. In this approach, the encoder gathers contextual information by continuously decreasing the input image's spatial scale and simultaneously enhancing the richness of feature representations through subsequent layers of convolution.

By minimizing this loss, U-Net effectively captures abstract semantic information through its encoder and retains detailed spatial features via its decoder and skip connections. This dual capability makes the U-Net an extremely strong architecture for tasks that call for both global understanding and pixel-level precision, extending its application from segmentation into a wide array of image transformation and generation.

2.2 Variational Auto-Encoders (VAEs)

Variational Auto-Encoders (Thin et al., 2021) are a class of deep generative model innately working on the basis of Bayes' theorem to learn continuous representations of data in the latent space. VAE consists of two neural networks-the encoder and decoder-which work collaboratively to model complex data distributions.

In the VAE framework, the objective is to model an unknown data distribution $p(\mathbf{x})$ by adding latent variables $\mathbf{z}$ that capture the undermining structure of the data. The encoder network $q_\phi(\mathbf{z} \mid \mathbf{x})$, defined by the parameter set ϕ, tries to The first term, $\mathbb{E}_{q\phi(\mathbf{z}|\mathbf{x})}(\log p_\theta(\mathbf{x} \mid \mathbf{z}))$, represents the anticipated reconstruction error, guiding the decoder to generate outputs that closely resemble the original data $\mathbf{x}$. The second term, $\mathrm{KL}(q_\phi(\mathbf{z} \mid \mathbf{x}) \parallel p(\mathbf{z}))$, is the Kullback- Leibler divergence, which measures the difference between the approximate distribution in the latent space and the initial prior. This term serves as a regularizer, promoting a smooth and consistent latent space.

By maximizing the ELBO(evidence lower bound) (Tang et al., 2025) with respect to the encoder and decoder parameters ϕ, θ, VAEs achieve a middle point between preserving reconstruction quality and managing the complexity of the latent space. This allows the model to produce new data output by drawing from the prior distribution $p(\mathbf{z})$ and processing these variables from the latent space through the decoder, thereby capturing the essential structure of the underlying data.

2.3 Generative Adversarial Networks (GANs)

GANs are a type of deep generative model (Navidan et al., 2021) that frames data creation as an interplay between two neural nets: The neural Nets being (1) The Generator and (2) The discriminator. These networks engage in a competitive process, with each network refining its ability to generate or distinguish data. GANs utilize adversarial training to learn complex data distributions without explicitly modelling probability density functions. The generator $G_\theta(z)$, parameterized by θ, transforms random noise vectors z from a prior distribution $p_z(z)$ (typically a standard normal distribution) into synthetic data samples x. The discriminator $D_\phi(x)$, parameterized by ϕ, evaluates whether a given sample x is real (from $p_{data}(x)$) or fake (produced by G). approximates the complex posterior estimation of the latent factors conditioned on observed data. It transforms the input x into a distribution within the latent space, effectively capturing essential features in a compressed form. The decoder network $p_\theta(x \mid z)$, defined by θ, models the likelihood of the observed data based on the latent variables, reproducing the input data based on the latent encoding.

The GAN framework aims to have the generator's distribution $p_g(x)$ closely approximate the true data distribution $p_{data}(x)$. This is achieved through a minimax optimization objective. In this setup, the discriminator D_ϕ gets better in maximizing its accuracy in distinguishing real from fake samples, while the generator G_θ strives to minimize the discriminator's ability to make correct classifications. Training involves iteratively updating both networks: the discriminator maximizes its objective $\mathscr{L}_D(\phi)$, and the generator minimizes its objective $\mathscr{L}_G(\theta)$.

By repetitively optimizing this objective, GANs learn to generate realistic data samples that can hardly be distinguished from the real data. While the adversarial training allows the generator to capture highly intricate data distributions, the discriminator continuously adapts to detect extremely subtle differences between generated and real data. This has opened up numerous use cases in the fields of computer vision and image synthesis like image generation, style transfer, image-super-resolution, powered by the strong generative capabilities of GANs.

2.4 Denoising Diffusion Probabilistic Models (DDPMs)

DDPMs (Turner et al., 2024) are a sophisticated family of deep learning based generative models that generate data using progressive denoising, drawing inspiration from non-equilibrium thermodynamics. DDPM functions in two stages: a) a forward diffusion phase where Gaussian noise is gradually introduced to the input, and b) a backward phase that aims to reconstruct the original input by incrementally removing the noise. It leverages the simplicity of the Gaussian distribution together with the representation power of neural networks to model complex distributions without explicit likelihood estimation.

2.5 Transformers

Transformers (Nieminen, M. 2023) represent a revolutionary class of deep models that have brought a sea change in NLP and now find growing applications in computer vision and studies on generation. Transformer models utilize mechanisms of self-attention so as to model dependencies between input and output sequences. This enables the parallel computation of the input and allows for capturing long-range interactions efficiently

This architecture is made up of two major modules: Firstly, The Encoder and Secondly, The Decoder, both of which include multiple layers; commonly these are made up of self- attention modules and feed-forward neural network layers. The encoder is designed to identify contextual relationships using self-attention, whereas the decoder is tasked with creating output sequences based on attention to the encoder representations and previously generated outputs.

3. VIDEO GENERATION MODELS

Various deep learning approaches are contributing remarkably towards in-text-to-video generation with each solving unique aspects of synthesizing temporally coherent videos from textual descriptions. Broadly, a host of such approaches can be put under the umbrella of three such model architecture classes. Ordered by the evolution of such model classes are (1) GANs, then (2) VAEs, and finally (3) DDPMs.

GAN-based approaches were one of the first to be applied to generating text-to-video problems, relying on an adversarial training process between its generator and discriminator networks in order to create realistic video content. Although such models showed early video synthesis success, they are generally plagued with issues of stability during training and scaling to higher resolutions. Another point of view was introduced by VAEs-based models: they learn compact latent representation of videos that enables more controlled generation by probabilistic modelling. Such models appeared to be more stable than GANs but sometimes struggled with the quality of their output and fine details.

More recently, the dominant paradigm has been the emergence of diffusion-based models for the synthesis of text based video generation that exhibit superior quality and have more temporal consistency. These models-which have extended successful results of diffusion-based approaches for image generation-have achieved high-quality video generations with semantic alignments to input text. The over-riding trend for using diffusion models is captured in many recent developments in this class of methods, as will be seen by the lengthy list of methods in this survey based on align with specific attention functions. W^O is the final projection matrix that combines all attention heads' outputs into a single output vector.

By refining this loss function, Transformers can efficiently grasp complex dependencies and produce outputs of superior quality. These models excel at interpreting the nuanced meanings of input data, resulting in well-organized outputs, as a result, making Transformers essentially indispensable for a lot of the sequence-to-sequence applications like translation, summarization, and generative modelling. Each of the paradigms enjoys different advantages and issues while solving the inherent problems of video generation, namely temporal consistency, visual quality, and text-video alignment. In the following sections, a thorough review of representative models from each category is provided, including discussions of architecture, methodology, and contribution.

3.1. GANS Based Models

GANs were introduced in (Goodfellow et al.,2014) in immediately causing a revolution in generative modeling by introducing the adversarial training paradigm. It is made up of two competing neural networks: one, the generator, generates data samples; the other, the discriminator, distinguishes between real and generated samples. When they were first designed for generating images, GANs immediately started working art wonders, managing to generate several high-quality realistic images. This immediately called for significant changes in the architecture of GANs, including temporal dynamics and consistency between frames. The different approaches and novelties authors have developed to extend GANs for video generation are discussed as follows.

3.1.1. MoCoGAN

MoCoGAN (Wang et al., 2020) makes use of a decomposed GAN architecture for video generation where the latent space gets decomposed into a content subspace and a motion subspace. Such separation enables the model to handle static elements, i.e., content, and dynamic variations, i.e., motion, separately. This is controlled by a single content vector, sampled from a Gaussian distribution and kept constant throughout the video, encoding features that remain consistent across frames, like the object identity or background. The changes with respect to time are described by the motion subspace through the generation, on each frame, of motion vectors via the RNN (Sriram et al., 2024) with a Gated Recurrent Unit (Salem, F. M., & Salem, F. M. 2022), introducing a recurrent path to be able to emulate smooth, sequential motion. MoCoGAN treats the video sequences as trajectories in a latent space, where each point in that latent space takes a frame, and variations in path length allow for videos of variable duration. It contains one generator that composites a single fixed content vector with frame-specific motion vectors and two discriminators: an image discriminator for ensuring coherence in individual frames and a video discriminator for temporal coherence across sequences of frames. The discriminator in the video also includes categorical dynamics through predefined motion categories that can generate MoCoGAN with specific actions-such as walking and jumping-input, given a categorical variable.

3.1.2. NUWA

NUWA presented has a unified architecture of a 3D Transformer encoder-decoder, which leverages tokenization from the 2D VQ-GAN and uses 3D Nearby Self- Attention (3DNA) (Chen et al., 2024) for holistic visual synthesis across images, videos, and textual descriptions, displayed in Fig. 1. Images and videos are represented as a 3D spatial-temporal cube where each token in the cube corresponds to a patch of the visual input. Synchronized by VQ-GAN, this is a patch-based approach that tokenizes frames into discrete latent codes mapped to a shared codebook, hence allowing a unified representation of both images and videos but decreased data complexity while preserving essential information in space and time. The 3D Nearby Self-Attention mechanism in NUWA is focused on enhancing efficiency by considering only the spatial and temporal neighborhoods-that is, where each token attends to only the tokens in the near neighborhood inside the cube. In addition, the attention model in this work conveys local dependencies while considering coherency across frames as one of the majors for generating realistic visuals for long sequences. Training of the model is incorporated with multi-task objectives for supporting tasks like video prediction, text-to-image, and text-to-video generation where conditioning generation is either based on the conditioning text or previous frames through masked token prediction within the 3D spatial- temporal cube. This allows the model to create the missing components by capturing contextual dependencies within the spatial domain as well as in the temporal dimension.

Figure 1. Model Architecture of NUWA

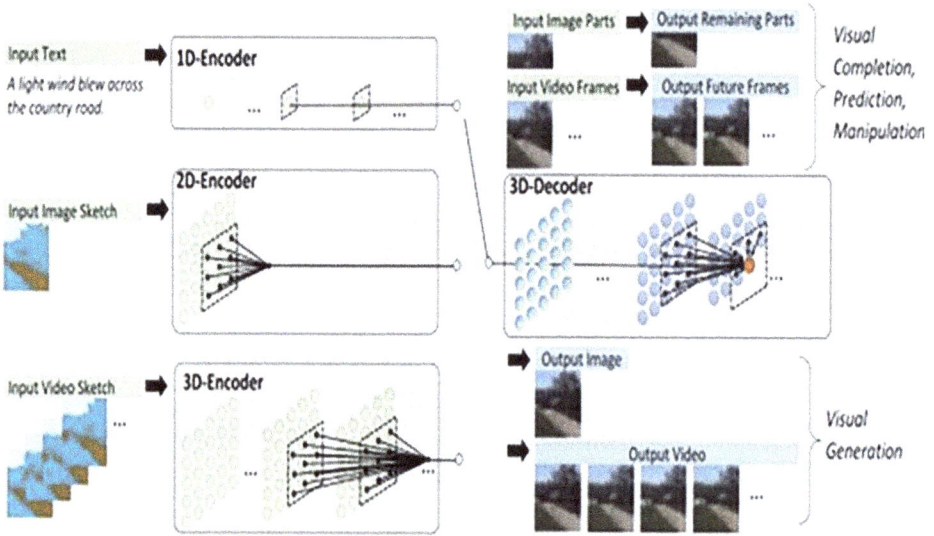

(C. Wu et al., 2021)

3.2. VAES Based Models

VAEs, First proposed are a suite of deep generative models which try to learn to compress data to a lower latent space and later try to rebuild it back as similar as it can to the original data, trying to maintain the most important features. Unlike GANs, VAEs provide a probabilistic framework for generation and explicitly model the data distribution through variational inference. Their ability to learn structured latent representations made them particularly attractive for complex generative tasks. The next sections discuss how researchers have adapted and extended the VAE framework to video generation tasks by incorporating temporally modelling and text conditioning mechanisms.

3.2.1. VideoGPT

VideoGPT (Maaz et al., 2024) implements a hybrid architecture, which merges VQ-VAE with GPT-style transformers for efficient naturalistic video generation. It makes use of 3D convolutions in the VQ-VAE framework for extracting deep spatial and temporal features from the videos and compressing them into a discrete latent space. Such compression reduces the data dimensionality extensively but preserves the most salient information that is critical for maintaining quality in generated videos. These 3D convolutions are used by the encoder component to transform the high-dimensional video data into lower-dimension and discrete latent representation. The decoder reconstructs video from this compressed format using transposed 3D convolutions that guarantee detailed and accurate visual outputs. The model treats the latent space by first discretizing raw video into discrete tokens through some process of vector quantization. The encoder outputs get matched to a learned codebook to reduce the video data into simple, manipulable codes. This will project such dense video representations into a finite set of discrete codes; therefore, it summarizes video content in a very effective way.

3.2.2. GODIVA

GODIVA (Stone et al., 2022) introduced in integrates a frame-wise VQ-VAE with 3D sparse attention for video generation conditioned on natural language descriptions, shown in Figure 2. In the model, the internal VQ-VAE framework processes frames independently: each frame is encoded into latent variables via 3D convolutions accurately quantized by matching encoded regions against a codebook. This results in a discrete and compact latent representation, which is reconstructed by the decoder through transposed 3D convolutions with the preservation of the critical spatial and temporal information. VQ-VAE's training objective in GODIVA contains loss functions such as reconstruction loss, codebook loss, and commitment loss to ensure proper frame encoding and decoding. GODIVA generates video using text based on the modeled conditional probability ($P z^{|}t^{)}$) where (z) stands for the discrete latent code, and (t) stands for the input text. Text embeddings combine the outputs from pre- trained embeddings with positional encodings to temporally align text and video. GODIVA processes the temporal, row, and column information of the encoded frames separately with its three-dimensional sparse attention mechanism that optimizes computational efficiency by attending only to the relevant spatio-temporal features.

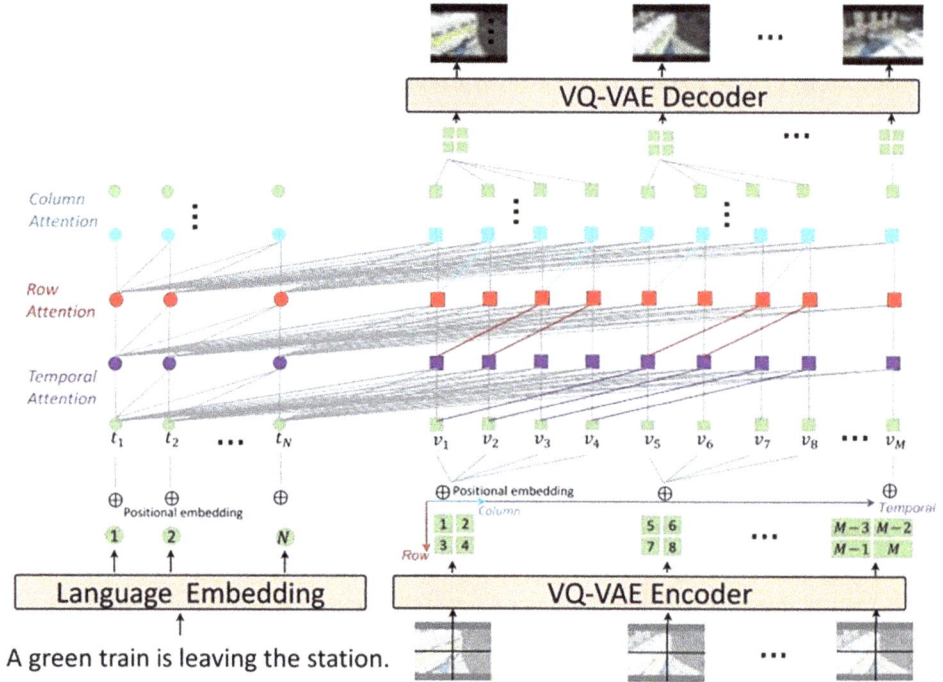

Figure 2. Model Architecture of GODIVA

VQ-VAE Decoder

Column Attention

Row Attention

Temporal Attention

t_1 t_2 ... t_N v_1 v_2 v_3 v_4 v_5 v_6 v_7 v_8 ... v_M

⊕ ⊕ ⊕ Positional embedding
Positional embedding Column

1 2 5 6 M−3 M−2
Row 3 4 7 8 ... M−1 M Temporal

1 2 N

Language Embedding VQ-VAE Encoder

A green train is leaving the station.

(Stone et al., 2022)

3.2.3. CogVideo

CogVideo (Hong et al., 2022) implements a dual-channel transformer-based architecture for large-scale text-to-video generation, shown in Fig. 4. Within its framework, the spatial and temporal information is separately treated by the dual-channel attention blocks. It contains two major types of attention channels in its architecture: an attention-base layer pre- trained for spatial features and an attention-plus layer designed for temporal processing. Further, these channels dynamically combine through a learnable mixture factor, which effectively weights the adaptation between spatial and temporal components. This transformer-based architecture effectively generates aligned videos through the incorporation of several multi-modal attention mechanisms. The generation of the video pipeline, designed to work in a multi-stage process, first goes through a sequential generation phase at low frame rates, creating keyframes, and is followed by a recursive interpolation phase to eventually create intermediate frames for temporal coherence. Its architecture features two important components, including the 3D Shifted Window attention that earmarks the efficient processing of the spatial-temporal cube by applying localized attention to neighboring spatial and temporal tokens.

3.3. Diffusion Models

Building upon the theoretical developments of (Sohl- Dickstein et al., 2015), recently emerged as one of the successful generative models. These models work progressively to denoise random Gaussian noise in a manner guided by a learned reverse diffusion process. Their success in generating images through models like DALL·E and Stable Diffusion has led to their rapid adoption for video synthesis. Of course, diffusion models boast several advantages, such as stable training dynamics and generation of high quality. In the subsequent sections, the paper describes the various approaches in relation to extending diffusion models towards video generation by considering temporal consistency, computational efficiency, and alignment between input texts and generated videos. As shown in the Figure 3, the different diffusion models are explained one by one.

Figure 3. Different Diffusion models

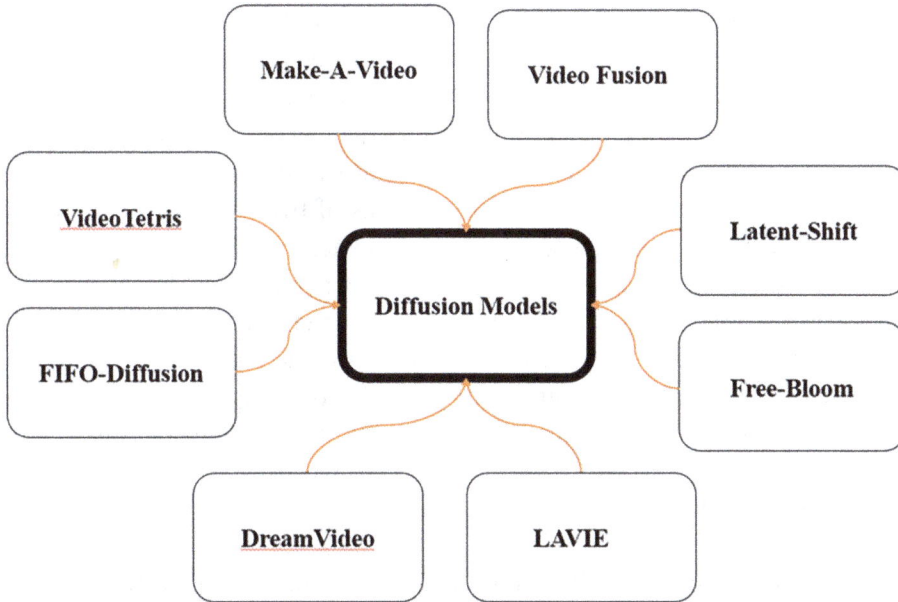

3.3.1. Make-A-Video

Make-A-Video follows a multi-stage diffusion-based architecture that generates videos leveraging a pre-trained T2I model and has no need for paired text-video datasets, shown in Fig. 5. The architecture uses a pre-trained T2I diffusion model, spatiotemporal layers to capture temporal dynamics, and a frame interpolation network to better the continuity between frames. At the beginning of the process, the model follows a pre-trained T2I diffusion model in order to generate base frames at 64x64 resolution. These frames are later enhanced by two specialized super-resolution networks: SRt is a spatiotemporal network that increases the resolution of the frames to 256×256 and ensures temporal coherence, whereas SRh is further used for spatial super-resolution, increases the resolution further upto 768×768. The architecture extends T2I capabilities into video synthesis through the use of Pseudo-3D convolution and attention layers. This design efficiently processes spatiotemporal relationships while optimizing computational resources.

3.3.2. VideoFusion

VideoFusion (Cui et al., 2023) proposes a Decomposed Diffusion Probabilistic Model architecture for generating high-quality, temporally coherent video, shown in Fig. 6. It is defined through the decomposition of video synthesis into two complementary generators. It depends on hierarchical noise decomposition, emitting base noise shared between frames and residual noise with only time-specific variations, hence enabling the modeling of both spatial consistency and dynamic frame-to-frame variation. The architecture mainly consists of two parts: i) base generator utilizing a pretrained image DPM to handle the static, shared visual content across frames and ii) a residual generator, introducing in temporal details by adding residual noise which adapts the base output to capture the frame-specific motion. During training, both generators are jointly trained to equilibrate the content generated by a pre-trained image DPM with temporal refinement from the residual generator so that every frame in the video sequence is coherent about the previous one.

3.3.3. Latent-Shift

Latent-Shift adapts (Bhui, R., & Jiao, P. 2023) a pretrained latent diffusion model towards text-to-video generation through a parameter-free temporal shift module included in the model's architecture. The system works in a way that it first trains a VAE-based autoencoder over images to learn the latent representation and then adapts towards encoding and decoding video frames independently, thus efficiently encoding the spatial information across frames in the latent space. At the heart of

Latent-Shift is a Temporal Shift U-Net to learn the denoising of latent video representations. During training, the U-Net processes the latent representation of each frame by sampling different steps of diffusion, and during inference, it progressively denoises from an initial noise distribution until a clean frame sequence is achieved. The architecture is made up of two key modules: 2D ResNet modules that include convolutional layers, and transformer modules which are additionally modified with spatial attention mechanisms. The proposed temporal shift module is adjusted within the residual branch of each ResNet block, which allows the feature maps to move across the temporal dimension. This setup allows for temporal coherence between frames without the need of any more additional parameters.

3.3.4. Free-Bloom

Free-Bloom (Minkin, I. 2020) presents a zero-shot, training-free pipeline with large language models and pretrained latent diffusion models that transform text prompts into high-quality videos without any video data or extra training, shown in Fig. 8. The overall architecture of the model is divided into three sequential modules: serial prompting, video generation, and interpolation empowerment. During the Serial Prompting, it is the "director" LLM that turns a single-text prompt into a detailed frame-by-frame serialization describing action development through time while keeping semantic coherence across frames. A pre-trained LDM during Video Generation acts as the "animator": it generates individual frames based on the generated prompt sequence. To achieve the dual goals of temporal and identical coherence, the backward diffusion process is modified in two main ways: first, joint noise sampling, reaching a progressive joint for the noise in order to more effectively balance the content coherence with variation; second, step-aware attention shift, shifting the LDM's U-Net architecture modification of self-attention layers between contextual frames and the current frame, with the variation determined by the denoising time step, to favor identical coherence with semantic alignment.

3.3.5. LAVIE

LAVIE presents a cascaded framework of Video Latent Diffusion Models (V-LDMs) (Wang et al., 2025) that leverages pre-trained Text- to-Image (T2I) models for generating high-quality videos, coherent over time, without losing much creative generation capability, shown in Figure 4. This model architecture is ordered into three sequential modules: the Base Text-to-Video (T2V) model, which creates the initial video frames from text input; the Temporal Interpolation (TI) module, which is designed to enhance temporal consistency between frames; and the Video Super-Resolution (VSR) module, which betters the resolution and quality of the generated video. In the Base T2V stage, LAVIE extends the pre-trained T2I model, namely Stable Diffusion, to support video data with minimal architectural changes: pseudo-3D convolutions that inflate the 2D kernel to include a temporal dimension and the Spatio-Temporal Transformer (STTransformer) enhanced with Rotary Positional Embedding (RoPE), capable of capturing such rich temporal correlations in video sequences. It does so jointly train the model on image and video data to avoid catastrophic forgetting. This retains much of the richness of creative diversity the T2I model would have captured. Temporal Interpolation:

Figure 4. Model Architecture of LAVIE

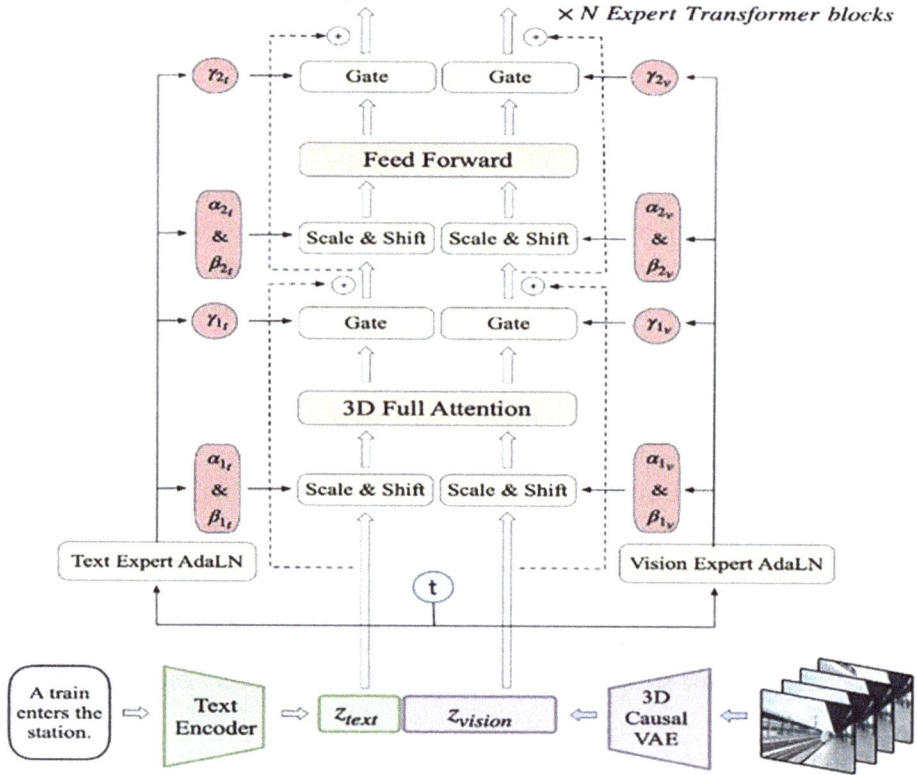

(Wang et al., 2025)

3.3.6. DreamVideo

DreamVideo (Wei et al., 2024) presents an image-to-video generation framework that effectively combines an Image Retention block with a pre-trained VLDM for video generation from a single reference image with textual prompts. The main components of the overall architecture are divided into basically two parts: the T2V model and the Image Retention block. T2V expands a pre-trained VLDM with Temporal Attention modules (Temp-Attn) and Temporal Convolutional layers (Temp-Conv) inside the U-Net architecture to allow the model to be able to learn and process spatio-temporal relationships present in video sequences. Down-sampling and middle layers are followed by the Image Retention block in U-Net, adding more convolutional layers for processing the input image. It merges the image features into the denoising process by concatenating them with the latent video representations at various levels of U-Net. Classifier-Free Guidance is used with a double session to balance image and text conditions both during training and at inference. It does this by nullifying each condition independently during training with the strategic purpose of avoiding overfitting, while allowing for adjustable guidance scales for text and image during inference to modulate their respective influences on the generated output.

Grid diffusion is a diffusion-based framework that reformulates video synthesis as an image generation problem by adopting a grid-based representation of these videos. The model architecture is divided into two major modules, one dealing with key frames and the other being responsible for autoregressive grid image interpolation. Both work together in harnessing textual descriptions into temporally coherent videos. The key grid image generation generates a key grid image as a fine-tuned Stable Diffusion model in the form of a 2×2 grid of chronologically ordered frames that summarize the temporal progression of the video. This comprises video synthesis, based on established T2I generative capabilities making use of a diffusion-based approach that will enable the model to capture key information on motion and content within one grid framework. This 2×2 grid format thus represents the key temporal states of the video in compact form and acts as an anchor for further frame generation. This Autoregressive

3.3.7. FIFO-Diffusion

FIFO-Diffusion proposes a training-free inference framework for the pre-trained diffusion model that generates infinite-length videos from a given text prompt. Its architecture consists of three major components: Diagonal Denoising, Latent Partitioning, and Lookahead Denoising. In this Diagonal Denoising module, the successive frames are processed through a queue mechanism with varied levels of noise and follow a first-in-first-out rule. This is performed by dequeuing fully denoised frames and enqueuing new random noise frames, thus keeping the memory constant for any length of a video. Diagonal Denoising within the diffusion pipeline brings an important training-inference discrepancy. Latent Partitioning handles this by partitioning the queue into multiple blocks of frames to reduce inter-frame noise level variations in each partition. This helps align with the model's training distribution much better, minimizes discretization errors, and provides parallel processing capabilities. This lookahead denoising component extends the inherent forward referencing capabilities of the diagonal denoising component by using downsampling-by- skipping as well as selective frame updating so that noisier frames have access to more previously cleaner frames during denoising.

3.3.8. VideoTetris

VideoTetris (Tian et al., 2024) is a compositional diffusion-based text-to- video framework that generates videos with multiple objects from the text prompt, including the attribute, spatial relation, and temporal dynamics. The three key building blocks of performance in this are: Spatio-Temporal Compositional Diffusion, Enhanced Video Data Preprocessing, and Consistency Regularization with Reference Frame Attention. The Spatio-Temporal Compositional Diffusion model aligns all cross-attention maps of the diffusion network both in the spatial and temporal dimensions harmoniously. This module performs a three-step process: Prompt Decomposition, which decomposes a text prompt into frame-wise and object-specific sub-prompts along with respective region masks; Cross-Attention Manipulation, which processes the attention values corresponding to individual sub-prompts; and Spatio- Temporal Composition, showing how these attention maps can be integrated to ensure temporal coherence.

3.3.9. GVDIFF

GVDIFF (Dou et al., 2024) is a text-to-video generation framework that contains both discrete and continuous grounding conditions, shown in Fig. 14. The model generates videos from given textual prompts. The architecture is based on three modules: Uncertainty-Based Grounding Injection, Spatial-Temporal Grounding Layer (STGL), and Dynamic Gate Network (DGN) on top of a pre-trained LDM. The discrete elements herein include layouts and key points, while the continuous elements are depth maps and edge maps such as HED and Canny maps. This module processes the grounding conditions into uncertainty-based representations that can be fed to LDM's U-Net self-attention mechanism, guiding its attention toward regions specified by grounding conditions, hence enhancing spatial alignment of the generated contents with the grounding inputs. The Spatial-Temporal Grounding Layer updates the transformer layers in the pre-trained U-Net to support both spatial and temporal domains for the process of grounded generation. It connects the grounding conditions and the target objects across frames, enabling interactions between grounded features and visual tokens and maintaining their temporal consistency via Spatial-Temporal Grounding Attention..

3.3.10. CogVideoX

CogVideoX (Yang et al., 2024) implements a diffusion-transformer pipeline for text-to-video generation, converting textual prompts into extended-duration videos without any extra video data or training. The main building blocks in this work include the 3D Causal VAE, an Expert Transformer with Expert Adaptive Layer-Norm, and the Progressive Training framework together with Multi- Resolution Frame-Packing techniques. The 3D Causal VAE performs spatial and temporal compression of videos with temporally casual convolutions, maintaining high video fidelity but reducing computational complexity. Such convolutions prevent the use of future information in predicting the past, thus preserving temporal causality in these compressed representations. The Expert Transformer performs modality fusion through concatenation of the text embedding and video latents along the sequence dimension. It leverages Expert Adaptive LayerNorm, which uses different adaptive layer normalizations for each modality, given the outputs of the diffusion timesteps as an input for the modulation modules.

3.3.11. Pyramidal Flow

The paper introduces a video generation framework that is based on the diffusion-transformer which also integrates pyramidal visual representations with flow-matching techniques for computational efficiency. This model is made up of two key components: the Spatial Pyramid and the Temporal Pyramid, organized by a basic Diffusion Transformer backbone. The Spatial Pyramid reinterprets the process of the denoising trajectory by spatially structuring it into stages of pyramid form, where full-resolution processing is computed only in the last stage. The model performs Pyramidal Flow Matching between the piecewise flows of pixelated, noisy latents and cleaner, pixelate-free latents to enable simultaneous generation and decompression within each pyramid stage. Preserving the continuity of probability paths across resolutions is achieved with a Corrective Renoising scheme. Finally, the Temporal Pyramid reconciles the temporal complexity of autoregressive video generation using Pyramidal Temporal Conditioning. This approach leverages progressively compressed, lower-resolution history as conditioning information for future frames generation and reduces both computational and memory requirements.

4. TRAINING DATASETS AND CONFIGURATIONS

The diversity and quality of the training datasets, along with proper training configurations, serve as the stepping stones in effectively training text-to-video generation models. The given section provides a summary of the datasets which were utilized to train such T2V models and also provide details of their training configurations.

4.1 Training Datasets

The diversity and quality of datasets are of immense importance in developing text-to-video generation models, as it provides foundational data necessary for the training and the performance assessment of such models. Through this section, the paper mentions the datasets used across different papers and give detailed descriptions of the datasets that aided the training efforts of the various models. The dataset comprises a total of 10.7 million video tagged with their corresponding text pairs, amounting close to 52,000 hours of video data. Sourced primarily from stock footage sites such as Shutterstock, each short video is captioned with the respective textual description. First introduced by (Bain et al., 2014) in the work "Frozen in Time" in the dataset allows for joint video and image encoding for retrieval tasks. Due to copyright restrictions, the dataset originally provided URLs and captions for independent downloading; however, as of February 23, 2024, these resources may no longer be available following a cease-and-desist request from Shutterstock. The dataset comprises of close to 13,320 video which cover actions performed by humans and are classified into 101 classes that range from the sports, and musical performances to human-object interactions, among others. Extracted from YouTube, it provides a wide range of dynamic camera movements, object appearance, pose, scale, viewpoint, background clutter, and lighting conditions, making it a challenging benchmark for training and evaluating action recognition models. Table. 1 shows the Training Configurations of Survey Models.

Table 1. Training Configurations of Survey Models

Model Name	GPU	GPU Count	Batch Size	Learning Rate	Optimizer	Steps/Epochs	Loss Function	Dropout Rate
MoCoGAN	-	-	-	-	Adam	-	Adversarial	-
VideoGPT	-	-	128	1×10^{-4}	Adam	-	Cross-entropy	-
GODIVA	V100	64	512	1×10^{-4}	Adam	200k steps	Cross-entropy	-
NUWA	-	-	-	-	-	-	-	-
CogVideo	A100	32	256	1×10^{-4}	Adam	1M steps	Cross-entropy	-

continued on following page

Table 1. Continued

Model Name	GPU	GPU Count	Batch Size	Learning Rate	Optimizer	Steps/Epochs	Loss Function	Dropout Rate
Make-A-Video	A100	2048	-	-	-	-	Standard diffusion	-
Video Fusion	-	-	-	-	-	-	-	-
Latent-Shift	-	-	256	1×10^{-5}	Adam	-	MSE (latent space)	0
Free-Bloom	RTX 3090 Ti	1	-	-	-	-	-	-
LaVie	-	-	-	-	-	-	MSE (latent space)	-
DreamVideo	-	8	9	-	-	5 epochs (340k samples)	MSE	-
Grid Diffusion	A100 80GB	2	28/20	-	-	82k/54k steps	-	-
FIFO-Diffusion	-	-	-	-	-	-	-	-
VideoTetris	A800	4	2	1×10^{-5}	-	16k steps	-	0.05
GVDIFF	-	-	-	-	-	-	-	-
CogVideoX	-	-	-	-	-	-	L1+LPIPS+KL+GAN	-
Pyramidal Flow	A100	128	1536/768/384	1×10^{-4}, 5×10^{-5}	AdamW	300k total steps	Flow matching	-

4.2 Training Configurations

Understanding the complexities of training configurations become necessary to understand for researchers who wish to step into the field text-to-video generation. These provide the practical guidelines that help in making judgments about the feasibility of implementation or improvement proposed by the various existing approaches under their resource constraints. Knowledge of computational requirements, optimization strategies, and architectural decisions facilitates not only reproduction of results but also helps give clues on potential bottlenecks and optimization opportunities.

The Training Configurations as mentioned in Table.1. catalogues essential training parameters including GPU specification and count, batch sizes during training, used learning rates, choice of optimizer, number of training steps or epochs, loss functions used, and dropout rate used. All these parameters put together give a comprehensive overview of the computational and architectural requirement to train text-to-video generation models and hence are part of important reference points for future research initiatives. While several papers do not provide full training configuration the model training approaches from the available information and cross- references within papers reveal some common patterns. Such common patterns along with partial information available would help researchers in carrying out an analysis of their training requirements and assessing its feasibility for implementation within their resource constraints.

5. PERFORMANCE EVALUATION

The fast development of text-to-video generation models calls for an equally strong framework that provides evidence for their effectiveness and applicability in real-world applications. The performance evaluation includes both quantitative metrics for objective measurement over various generated video aspects and qualitative assessments, often through human evaluations, for capturing perceptual qualities not satisfactorily addressed by metrics alone. Added to that, new benchmarks are being developed that tackle the changing challenges in the field, which allow for more comprehensive and varied evaluations. The current section will give an overview of the current standard evaluation metrics and benchmarks, discuss the place of human evaluations in qualitative assessment, and review one of the newer benchmarks that seek to provide more nuanced and comprehensive evaluations of model performance.

5.1 Current Standard Evaluation Metrics and Benchmarks

5.1.1 Evaluation Metrics

Evaluation of generative video models depends on a set of currently standardized, quantitative metrics that objectively assess generated content. Such uniformity in evaluation metrics facilitates benchmarking and monitoring progress in respect of such generative models. The most widely adopted quantitative metrics are shown in Table. 2. Performance Comparison of Text-to-Video Generation Models on Standard Benchmarks.

The Inception Score provided quality and diversity assessments of generated videos by employing a pre-trained Inception network used to classify frames.

Table 2. Performance Comparison of Text-to-Video Generation Models on Standard Benchmarks

Model Name	UCF-101			MSRVTT			BAIR	KINETICS-600	
	IS (↑)	FVD (↓)	CLIPSIM (↑)	IS (↑)	FVD (↓)	CLIPSIM (↑)	FVD (↓)	FVD (↓)	CLIPSIM (↑)
MoCoGAN	12.42 ± 0.03	-	-	-	-	-	503	-	-
VideoGPT	24.69 ± 0.30	-	-	-	-	-	103.3	-	-
GODIVA	-	-	-	-	-	0.2402	-	-	-
NUWA	-	-	-	-	-	0.2439	86.9	-	0.3012
CogVideo	50.46	626	0.3025	-	1294	0.2631	-	109.23	-
Make-A-Video	33	367.23	-	-	-	0.3049	-	-	-
Video Fusion	71.67	139	-	-	550	0.293	-	-	-
Latent-Shift	-	-	-	-	-	0.2773	-	-	-
Free-Bloom	-	-	-	-	-	-	-	-	-
LaVie	-	-	-	-	-	0.2949	-	-	-
DreamVideo	54.39	197.66	-	15.25	149.18	-	-	-	-
Grid Diffusion	62.88	340	0.3282	-	375	0.3096	-	-	-
FIFO-Diffusion	-	-	-	-	-	-	-	-	-
VideoTetris	-	-	-	-	-	-	-	-	-
GVDIFF	-	-	-	-	-	-	-	-	-
CogVideoX	-	-	-	-	-	-	-	-	-
Pyramidal Flow	-	-	-	-	-	-	-	-	-

5.1.2 Evaluation Benchmarks

The systematic evaluation of text-to-video generation models needs some standardized datasets that can very effectively assess the technical capabilities and the creative aspects of video synthesis. These benchmark datasets are crucial testing grounds, enabling quantitative comparison across different architectures while challenging models across diverse scenarios, temporal dynamics, and semantic complexity. The following benchmarks are the current standard evaluation frameworks, each of which targets specific aspects of video generation competency, from action recognition to temporal coherence and semantic alignment.

5.2 Human Evaluations

While quantitative metrics provide measures objectively, they just cannot capture subjective quality aspects of the generated video, which are crucial for user satisfaction and real-world usage. Thus, human evaluations, in different forms and metrics, have been introduced in multiple papers to assess characteristics like visual realism, semantic consistency, and general aesthetic appeal. They hint at how well a model meets the expectations or preferences of a human being. Human evaluations are purely subjective methods of qualitatively assessing the dimensions of the generation models of videos that capture those aspects, such as realism, coherence, semantic alignment, and others, which could be missed by automated metrics. These ensure that the generated videos meet human expectations and preferences, thus confirming that models produce content that is both technically proficient and subjectively satisfying. This section outlines the four main core human evaluation metrics that have been used across various papers to measure video quality based on human rankings: Fidelity to Text/Alignment to Text, Motion Realism, Aesthetic/ Quality, and Overall Quality/Preference.

5.2.1 Fidelity to Text/Text Alignment

Fidelity to Text, also at times referred (Ku et al., 2023) to as Alignment to Text, refers to the degree of representation that the generated video exhibits with respect to the input textual description. This metric ensures not only that the content, context, and actions shown in the video are semantically consistent but also that they are appropriate to the given prompts. Different papers use different terminologies to present this metric. For example, some papers refer to it as "Semantic Relevance", whilst others refer to this metric as "Semantic Consistency (SC)", "Faithfulness", "Instruction Following", and "Fidelity to Text".

5.2.2 Realism of Motion

Motion Realism measures the coherence and smoothness of the motion in the generated video, which should be natural, logical, and continuous in both action and transition, with a fast change or transition of frames. This metric is important to assess the believability and engagement of the motion of objects and subjects within the videos. Papers introduce this metric with various terms and different measures. Metrics "Motion Realism", "Plausibility of Motion", "Temporal Coherence", "Motion Awareness Evaluation (MAWE)" (Chang et al., 2021), and "Motion" are some of the other names by which this metric goes by across various papers.

5.2.3 Aesthetic/Quality

Aesthetic Quality or Quality evaluations are subjective measures of the generated video's visual appeal, including the richness of senses involved and overall stylistic coherence. It includes information about colour harmony, the quality of textures appearing in the video, and artistic expressions.

5.2.4 Overall Quality/Preference

Overall Quality/Preference is used to serve as a thorough measure for the generated video to assess the overall desirability and visual excellence from a human perspective. This metric typically encompasses various qualitative dimensions to determine the general desiredness of the videos. Different Papers refer to this metric using different terminologies.

5.3 Towards A Standardized Video Generation Evaluation Benchmark

While being widely adapted, the conventional metrics like Inception Score, Fréchet Inception Distance, Fréchet Video Distance, and CLIPSIM (Lu et al., 2024) are limited in the holistic assessment of video generative models. They mostly focus on the statistical similarities between generated and real data distributions, while they fundamentally cannot capture key qualitative aspects that match human perception. Such a simplification of video quality to single numerical scores not only avoids the rich complexity of video assessment but also does not provide sufficient granularity to allow for effective model evaluation. Metrics initially designed for static images and traditional video analysis cannot capture challenges particular to video, such as temporal coherence or semantic consistency. More critically, they are not able to quantify key human-centered characteristics such as identity preservation, motion fluidity, and temporal stability, which are essential for any standard quality assessment in video.

To address these limitations, VBench introduces an extensive benchmarking methodology for generative video models. This framework systematically decomposes video quality assessment into 16 different dimensions of evaluation, offering a fine-grained assessment of video generation quality closer to human perception. By surpassing traditional single-score metrics, VBench as shown in Figure 5 supplies researchers with diagnostic tools and, with the inclusion of human preference annotations, allows for the identification of strengths and weaknesses of a model, fostering focused improvements in video generation capabilities.

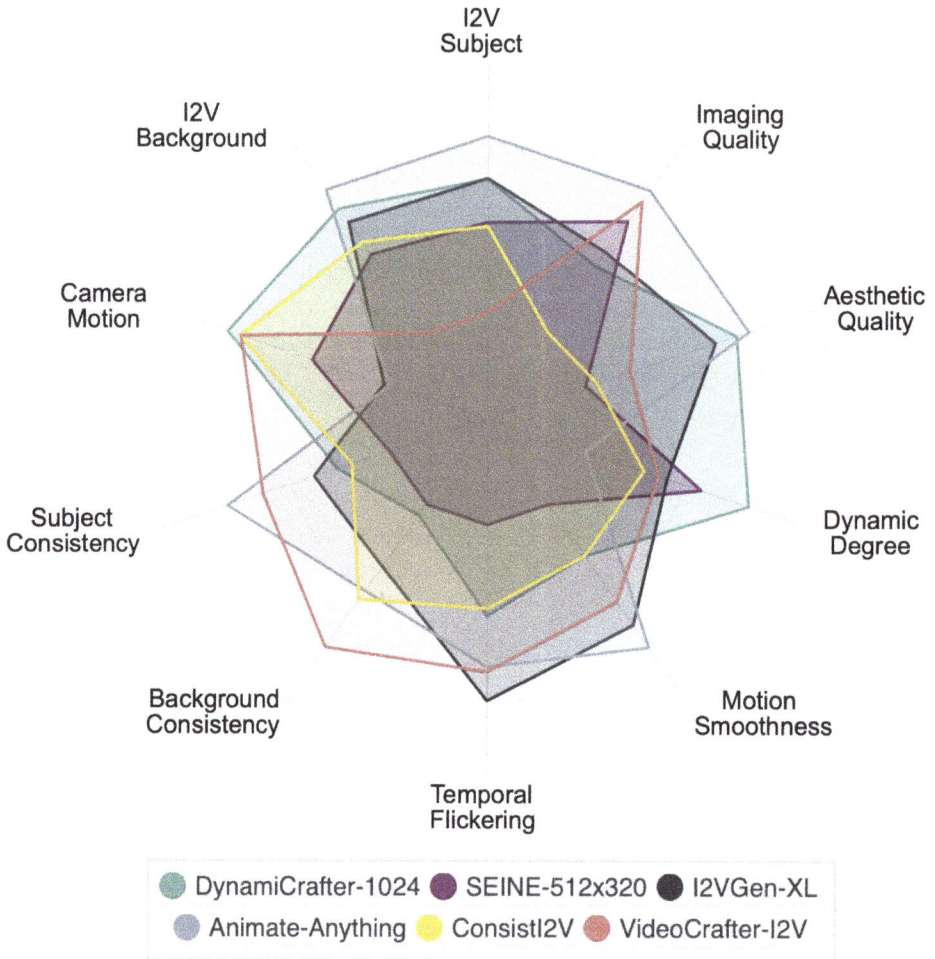

Figure 5. Evaluation Pipeline of VBench

The assessment process of this framework is based on its hierarchically organized Evaluation Dimension Suite, which classifies the various assessment criteria into two large domains: Video Quality and Video-Condition Consistency. For Video Quality, this framework evaluates several important temporal dimensions, including subject consistency, background stability, temporal flickering, motion smoothness, and dynamic degree, along with frame- like attributes that involve aesthetic and imaging qualities. At the semantic level, Video-Condition Consistency evaluations include object accuracy, multi-object composition, correctness of human actions, consistency in colors, relationships among objects in space, scene correctness, adherence to style, and alignment between video and its corresponding text.

VBench follows a comprehensive Prompt Suite of about 100 creatively designed prompts across eight different content categories to ensure that the evaluation is thorough. The framework uses specialized evaluation methods for background consistency, and motion priors for smoothness evaluation, to objectively measure each quality aspect. These automated evaluations are validated through systematic human preference annotations: annotators compare video pairs across specific dimensions, ensuring alignment with human perception.

Given the holistic and systematic nature of the review, VBench has the potential to become the go-to standard framework for evaluation of T2V models. Additionally, because of its thorough human validation, its detailed assessment method can show a stronger correspondence with viewers' perceptions, making it valuable for real-world applications. VBench allows for fair model comparisons across the research community and promotes consistent practices for model evaluations through open sourcing and extensibility. Its multi-dimensional approach serves as both an analytical tool and a guide for future research, allowing developers to focus on selected quality aspects most relevant to their use case. This versatility, coupled with its comprehensive methodology, positions VBench as a foundational framework that could guide the development and standardization of future video generation evaluation technology.

6. FUTURE DIRECTION

While Text-to-Video Generation has demonstrated some encouraging progress through deep learning approaches, most of the fundamental challenges remain open. The existing models, reporting initial success in generating simple video clips from text descriptions, still struggle with their computational efficiency, dataset limitations, and output quality. In this section, the article discusses some of the possible research avenues that may help overcome these challenges. It also considers the evolution of the creation process of datasets, model architectures, and application domains. Although the suggestions are far from exhaustive, they do hope to contribute something to the oncoming discussion about the progression of such text-to-video technology.

6.1 Dataset Enrichment

Currently available datasets for T2V synthesis have a severe weakness because of their limited size, quality, or legal conditions restricting the development of strong models capable of generalization outside a particular setting to generate high-quality video. One possible avenue of research might be the synthesis of datasets using game engines like Unity or Unreal Engine in order to create large-scale, high-resolution, and diverse datasets with no copyright infringement. It does this by developing a generalized prompt framework for overall development, classifying textual descriptions into principal subject, adjectives and attributes, verbs and actions, background, theme and style, and metadata of the camera. Generalization hierarchically allows comprehensive coverage of the subject matter, like people, animals, and objects while avoiding biases due to the use of different attributes and settings. These can range from "a person running through a futuristic cityscape with cyberpunk aesthetics" to "an animal exploring a fantasy forest in anime style." Feeding such structured prompts into game engines allows the generation of videos corresponding to each scenario with broad avenues for customization. Automating the pipelines of these game engines will efficiently generate large-scale datasets, improving quality and quantity.

6.2 Model Architectures and Optimization

Text-to-video generation models currently face several significant limitations that hinder their effectiveness and scalability. Training is computationally intensive because the current architectures are not optimized to sequentially process video data efficiently. Novel model architectures or algorithms that can better handle temporal sequences therefore need to be investigated to achieve more economy in resource usage and training times. These models also tend to produce only short output videos, which is highly limiting for scenarios with longer content. Hence, in the future, research is required for allowing the generation of longer videos by enhancing these models' temporal modelling. It is also limited to the generation of content with little diversity, partly because the training data itself lacks variety, making the models unable to create wide variations of scenes or subjects. This could be improved with the addition of more diverse datasets or the use of advanced augmentation techniques. Moreover, most generated videos suffer from temporal and spatial incoherence: objects often shift, appear, or disappear unnaturally. Such unrealistic simulations make viewers break immersion; hence, there is a need for further development of temporal consistency and spatial coherence by better modelling of the sequence and imposing physical constraints.

6.3 Possible Applications and Implications

Text-to-video generation holds transformative potential across various industries by converting textual descriptions into engaging visual content, thereby enriching communication, accessibility, and creativity. In education and e-learning, this technology facilitates a pedagogical shift, enabling teachers to explain concepts in detail through customized videos, which enhances engagement and learning. Within the accessibility and assistive technology sectors, it offers significant assistance to individuals with disabilities, providing visual materials for the visually impaired and sign language videos for the deaf and hard-of- hearing, thereby promoting inclusiveness. For content creation and marketing industries, text-to-video generation serves as a cost-effective solution, allowing enterprises to produce promotional materials, personalized ads, and engaging social media content without the need for expensive, resource-intensive production processes.

7. CONCLUSION

This chapter presents an in-depth study of a range of different types of text-to-video (T2V) generation models, understanding their evolution from initial GAN-based methods to recent diffusion models. The paper looked at the key architectural elements, operational principles, and practical limitations of these systems, along with their training methods and dataset requirements. The paper compiled the models' results on popular metrics and benchmarks. It also examined the role of human evaluation in assessing video generation quality, reviewing the standard criteria used by various authors and their importance in evaluating output video quality. The discussions explored how emerging evaluation metrics, if further developed by the research community, could evolve into standardized benchmarks for consistent model evaluation in this domain. Finally, the paper examined future directions by looking at challenges in model design and processing efficiency, suggesting possible architectural improvements and training methods. To address dataset limitations and copyright restrictions, the paper considers a balanced approach using both synthetically generated scenes from game engines and copyright-free contributions, showing how T2V technology could help address challenges in content creation and accessibility.

REFERENCE

An, J., Zhang, S., Yang, H., Gupta, S., Huang, J.-B., Luo, J., & Yin, X. (2023). Latent-shift: Latent diffusion with temporal shift for efficient text-to-video generation. arXiv. https://arxiv.org/abs/2304.08477

Bain, R., Cronk, R., Wright, J., Yang, H., Slaymaker, T., & Bartram, J. (2014). Fecal contamination of drinking-water in low- and middle-income countries: A systematic review and meta-analysis. *PLoS Medicine*, *11*(5), e1001644. DOI: 10.1371/journal. pmed.1001644 PMID: 24800926

Bhui, R., & Jiao, P. (2023). Attention constraints and learning in categories. *Management Science*, *69*(9), 5394–5404. https://psycnet.apa.org/doi/10.1287/mnsc.2023 .4803. DOI: 10.1287/mnsc.2023.4803

Chang, Z., Zhang, X., Wang, S., Ma, S., Ye, Y., Xinguang, X., & Gao, W. (2021). Mau: A motion-aware unit for video prediction and beyond. *Advances in Neural Information Processing Systems*, *34*, 26950–26962.

Chen, Y., Lan, Y., Zhou, S., Wang, T., & Pan, X. (2024). *SAR3D: Autoregressive 3D object generation and understanding via multi-scale 3D VQVAE*. arXiv preprint arXiv:2411.16856. /arXiv.2411.16856DOI: 10.48550

Cui, X., Khan, D., He, Z., & Cheng, Z. (2023). Fusing surveillance videos and three-dimensional scene: A mixed reality system. *Computer Animation and Virtual Worlds*, *34*(1), e2129. DOI: 10.1002/cav.2129

Dou, H., Li, R., Su, W., & Li, X. (2024). *GVDIFF: Grounded Text-to-Video Generation with Diffusion Models*. arXiv preprint arXiv:2407.01921. /arXiv.2407.01921DOI: 10.48550

Goodfellow, I. J., Pouget-Abadie, J., Mirza, M., Xu, B., Warde-Farley, D., Ozair, S., Courville, A., & Bengio, Y. (2014). Generative adversarial nets. Advances in Neural Information Processing Systems, 27, 2672–2680. https://papers.nips.cc/paper/5423 -generative-adversarial-nets

Hanssen, F., Gabernet, G., Bäuerle, F., Stöcker, B., Wiegand, F., Smith, N. H., & Telzerow, A. труфанов, С. В., ступин, В. В., Костер, Ю., & Köster, J. (2024). NCBench: providing an open, reproducible, transparent, adaptable, and continuous benchmark approach for DNA-sequencing-based variant calling. *F1000Research*, *12*, 1125. DOI: 10.12688/f1000research.140344.2

Hong, W., Ding, M., Zheng, W., Liu, X., & Tang, J. (2022). *Cogvideo: Large-scale pretraining for text-to-video generation via transformers.* arXiv preprint arXiv:2205.15868. /arXiv.2205.15868DOI: 10.48550

Hong, Y., Yang, J., Chang, H., & Shi, J. (2018). The unsupervised learning of visual representations by predicting scene dynamics. *International Conference on Computer Vision (ICCV).*

Huang, H. (2023). *Free-Bloom: Zero-Shot Text-to-Video Generator with LLM Director and LDM Animator.* arXiv preprint arXiv:2309.14494.

Joel, M. R., Ebenezer, V., Jeyaraj, K. A., Navaneethakrishnan, M., Arunadevi, R., & Jenifa, D. R. (2023). Decoding and analysing consumer feedback for companies and goods using machine learning. In *2023 Third International Conference on Artificial Intelligence and Smart Energy (ICAIS)* (pp. 1085-1091). IEEE. DOI: 10.1109/ICAIS56108.2023.10073801

Kamalov, F., Calonge, D. S., & Gurrib, I. (2023). *New Era of Artificial Intelligence in Education: Towards a Sustainable Multifaceted Revolution.* arXiv preprint arXiv:2305.18303.

Ku, M., Jiang, D., Wei, C., Yue, X., & Chen, W. (2023). Viescore: Towards explainable metrics for conditional image synthesis evaluation. arXiv. https://arxiv.org/abs/2312.14867

Lu, H., Wang, S., Zhang, D., Huang, B., Chen, E., & Sui, Y. (2024). Toward accurate quality assessment of machine-generated infrared video using Fréchet Video Distance. *IEEE Access: Practical Innovations, Open Solutions, 12,* 168837–168852. DOI: 10.1109/ACCESS.2024.3453406

Luo, Z., Chen, D., Zhang, Y., Huang, Y., Wang, L., Shen, Y., Zhao, D., Zhou, J., & Tan, T. (2023). VideoFusion: Decomposed diffusion models for high-quality video generation. arXiv. https://arxiv.org/abs/2303.08320

Maaz, M., Rasheed, H., Khan, S., & Khan, F. (2024). Videogpt+: Integrating image and video encoders for enhanced video understanding. arXiv. https://arxiv.org/abs/2406.09418

Minkin, I. (2020). *Applications of the Compacted de Bruijn Graph in Comparative Genomics* (Doctoral dissertation, The Pennsylvania State University).

Navidan, H., Moshiri, P. F., Nabati, M., Shahbazian, R., Ghorashi, S. A., Shah-Mansouri, V., & Windridge, D. (2021). Generative Adversarial Networks (GANs) in networking: A comprehensive survey & evaluation. *Computer Networks, 194,* 108149. DOI: 10.1016/j.comnet.2021.108149

Nieminen, M. (2023). *The Transformer Model and Its Impact on the Field of Natural Language Processing.*

Radford, A. (2021). Learning transferable visual models from natural language supervision. arXiv. https://arxiv.org/abs/2103.00020

Ramesh, A., Pavlov, M., Goh, G., Gray, S., Voss, C., Radford, A., Chen, M., & Sutskever, I. (2021). Zero-shot text-to-image generation. arXiv. https://arxiv.org/abs/2102.12092

Rombach, R., Blattmann, A., Lorenz, D., Esser, P., & Ommer, B. (2022). High-resolution image synthesis with latent diffusion models. arXiv. DOI: 10.1109/CVPR52688.2022.01042

Salem, F. M., & Salem, F. M. (2022). Gated RNN: the gated recurrent unit (GRU) RNN. In *Recurrent neural networks: from simple to gated architectures* (pp. 85-100). DOI: 10.1007/978-3-030-89929-5_5

Singer, U., Polyak, A., Hayes, T., Yin, X., An, J., Zhang, S., Hu, Q., Yang, H., Ashual, O., Gafni, O., Kronrod, Y., & Lischinski, D. (2022). Make-a-video: Text-to-video generation without text-video data. arXiv. https://arxiv.org/abs/2209.14792

Sohl-Dickstein, J., Weiss, E., Maheswaranathan, N., & Ganguli, S. (2015). Deep unsupervised learning using nonequilibrium thermodynamics. In *International Conference on Machine Learning* (pp. 2256–2265). PMLR.

Sriram, K. P., Sujatha, P. K., Athinarayanan, S., Kanimozhi, G., & Joel, M. R. (2024, July). Transforming Agriculture: A Synergistic Approach Integrating Topology with Artificial Intelligence and Machine Learning for Sustainable and Data-Driven Practice. In *2024 2nd International Conference on Sustainable Computing and Smart Systems (ICSCSS)* (pp. 1350-1354). IEEE. DOI: 10.1109/ICSCSS60660.2024.10625446

Stone, D., Heinrichs, D., Angus, P., Gadd, M., Goda, J., Grove, T., Hall, R., Hamilton, C., Hays, S., Howard, B., Hulsey, S., Ianakiev, A., Jessop, N., Johnson, R., Jones, T., Keffer, M., Kouzes, R., LeBrun, T., Lewis, B., . . . Stephens, J. (2022). *Experiment Logistics for an International Blind Intercomparison Exercise for Nuclear Accident Dosimetry at Godiva-IV* (No. LLNL-TR-824087). Lawrence Livermore National Laboratory (LLNL), Livermore, CA (United States).

Su, J., Lu, Y., Pan, S., Murtadha, A., Wen, B., & Liu, Y. (2021). RoFormer: Enhanced transformer with rotary position embedding. arXiv. https://arxiv.org/abs/2104.09864

Tang, Y., Wang, S., & Munos, R. (2025). Learning to chain-of-thought with Jensen's evidence lower bound. arXiv. https://arxiv.org/abs/2503.19618

Thin, A., Kotelevskii, N., Doucet, A., Durmus, A., Moulines, E., & Panov, M. (2021). Monte Carlo variational auto-encoders. In *International Conference on Machine Learning* (pp. 10247–10257). PMLR.

Tian, Y., Yang, L., Yang, H., Gao, Y., Deng, Y., Wang, X., Wang, Y., Yu, Z., Tao, X., Wan, P., Zhang, D., & Cui, B. (2024). Videotetris: Towards compositional text-to-video generation. *Advances in Neural Information Processing Systems*, *37*, 29489–29513.

Turner, R. E., Diaconu, C. D., Markou, S., Shysheya, A., Foong, A. Y., & Mlodozeniec, B. (2024). Denoising diffusion probabilistic models in six simple steps. arXiv. https://arxiv.org/abs/2402.04384

Wang, X., Yu, Z., Tao, X., Wan, P., Zhang, D., & Cui, B. (2024). VideoTetris: Towards compositional text-to-video generation. arXiv. https://arxiv.org/abs/2406.04277

Wang, Y., Bilinski, P., Bremond, F., & Dantcheva, A. (2020). Imaginator: Conditional spatio-temporal GAN for video generation. In *Proceedings of the IEEE/CVF Winter Conference on Applications of Computer Vision* (pp. 1160–1169). DOI: 10.1109/WACV45572.2020.9093492

Wang, Y., Chen, X., Ma, X., Zhou, S., Huang, Z., Wang, Y., Yang, C., He, Y., Yu, J., Yang, P., Guo, Y., Wu, T., Si, C., Jiang, Y., Chen, C., Loy, C. C., Dai, B., Lin, D., Qiao, Y., & Liu, Z. (2023). *LaVie: High-Quality Video Generation with Cascaded Latent Diffusion Models*. arXiv preprint arXiv:2309.15103. https://arxiv.org/abs/2309.15103

Wang, Y., Chen, X., Ma, X., Zhou, S., Huang, Z., Wang, Y., Zhang, L., Zhang, Y., Cao, Y., Li, H., Qiao, Y., & Liu, Z. (2025). Lavie: High-quality video generation with cascaded latent diffusion models. *International Journal of Computer Vision*, *133*(5), 3059–3078. DOI: 10.1007/s11263-024-02295-1

Wei, Y., Zhang, S., Qing, Z., Yuan, H., Liu, Z., Liu, Y., Wang, J., Zhang, W., & Shan, H. (2024). Dreamvideo: Composing your dream videos with customized subject and motion. In *Proceedings of the IEEE/CVF Conference on Computer Vision and Pattern Recognition* (pp. 6537-6549).

Wu, C., Huang, L., Zhang, Q., Li, B., Ji, L., Yang, F., Sapiro, G., & Duan, N. (2021). GODIVA: Generating open-domain videos from natural descriptions. arXiv. https://arxiv.org/abs/2104.14806

Wu, C., Liang, J., Ji, L., Yang, F., Fang, Y., Jiang, D., & Duan, N. (2021). NÜWA: Visual synthesis pre-training for neural visual world creation. arXiv. https://arxiv.org/abs/2111.12417

Yang, Z., Teng, J., Zheng, W., Ding, M., Huang, S., Xu, J., Zhang, L., Wang, W., & Tang, J. (2024). Cogvideox: Text-to-video diffusion models with an expert transformer. arXiv. https://arxiv.org/abs/2408.06072

Chapter 8
Generative AI in Visual Media for Image, Video, and Animation Generation

Arockia Raj Y.
 https://orcid.org/0000-0002-9991-4632
PSNA College of Engineering and Technology, Dindigul, India

K. Vijay
 https://orcid.org/0000-0001-5957-8737
Rajalakshmi Engineering College, Chennai, India

Eugene Berna
 https://orcid.org/0000-0002-3066-6511
Bannari Amman Institute of Technology, Erode, India

Prithi Samuel
 https://orcid.org/0000-0001-5648-8891
Department of Computational Intelligence, School of Computing, SRM Institute of Science and Technology, India

ABSTRACT

Generative artificial intelligence (AI) technologies are fundamentally transforming the visual media landscape and automating the production of human-like images, videos, and animations. The key elements of this creation are transformer-based models, Variational AutoEncoders (VAEs), and Generative Adversarial Networks (GANs). This chapter will look at how they function, what they can be used for, and how they affect education, entertainment, and advertising. By looking closely at these

DOI: 10.4018/979-8-3373-1504-1.ch008

methods, the chapter emphasizes both the good things that generative AI does to improve the quality and speed of content creation and the bad things that it causes in society and ethics, especially when it comes to authenticity and authorship. It also touches on the potential for misuse (think deepfakes) and discusses regulatory and ethical frameworks that would chain these technologies so that they can be used responsibly. The chapter ends with a future-oriented analysis of the emerging trends and challenges that will continue to impact the landscape of generative AI in visual media.

1. INTRODUCTION

1.1. Significance of Generative AI in Modern Media

1.1.1. Introduction to Generative AI in Media

Generative AI, or GenAI, is an AI technique that can generate a wide range of content, such as text, images, audio, and synthetic data. The recent hype about generative AI has been fueled by its novel user interfaces, which enable the creation of high-quality text, pictures, and movies in seconds. (Feuerriegel et al., 2024) When computers are able to take input in the form of text, images, or audio and produce what appears to be novel, meaningful content, this is known as generative AI.

Figure 1. The Hierarchical Evolution of Generative AI

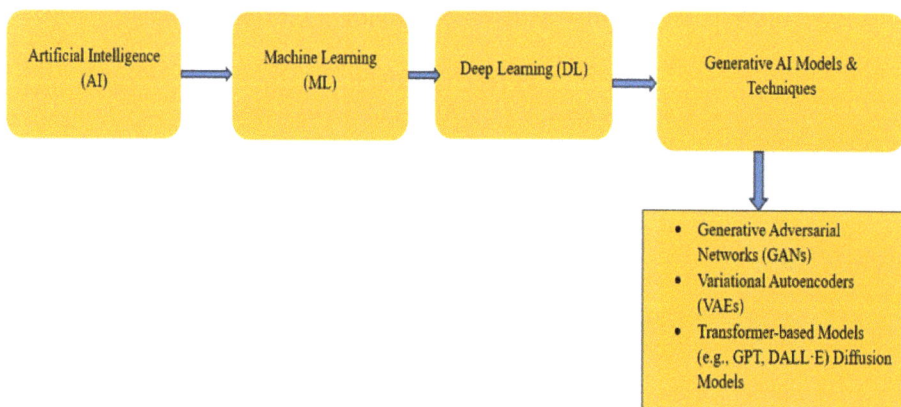

The generative approach is shown in Figure 1 as a hierarchical progression from AI through ML and DL to the new world of Generative AI, which is just starting to emerge. (Takale, 2024) New AI models like generative adversarial networks, variational autoencoders, and transformer-based models are driving creativity and innovation in the image-making industry.

1.1.2. Evaluation of Generative AI

According to Figure 2, the first machine learning algorithm for playing checkers was created in 1952 by Arthur Samuel, who also invented the phrase "machine learning" in the 1950s. The first trainable neural network, the Perceptron, was created by developer Frank Rosenblatt in 1957. Joseph Weizenbaum developed ELIZA, a psychotherapy simulation chatbot, in the early days of 1961. Computer vision and fundamental recognition pattern research in the 1960s and 1970s paved the way for subsequent developments. The first operational multilayer artificial neural network was created by Kunihiko Fukushima in 1975 with the Cognitron. Ian Goodfellow unveiled Generative Adversarial Networks (GANs), a major advancement in generative AI, in the middle of 2014 (Khoramnejad & Hossain, 2025).

A massive language model, GPT (Generative Pre-trained Transformer), was initially released in 2018 by OpenAI. GPT Models: These models can generate text, have conversations, and do a bunch of other language tasks with the help of deep learning. GPT-3: Set to be released in 2020, this AI has the ability to generate writing that sounds natural and can handle intricate language problems. Released in 2023, GPT-4 can generate 25,000 words of text. Up to this point, it has been steadily fruiting like a tree.

Figure 2. Evolution of Generative AI: Key Milestones

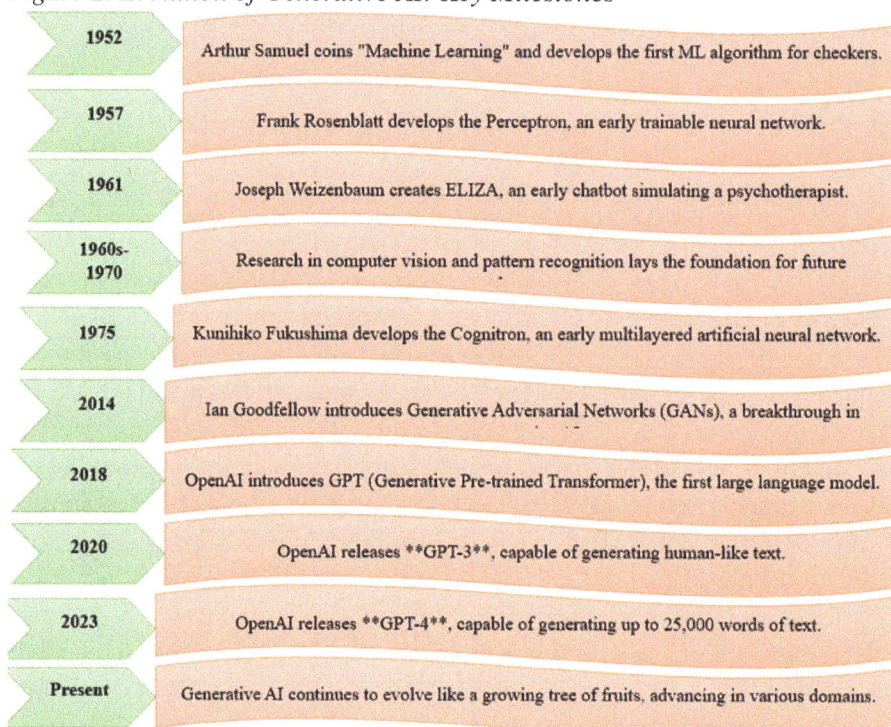

1952	Arthur Samuel coins "Machine Learning" and develops the first ML algorithm for checkers.
1957	Frank Rosenblatt develops the Perceptron, an early trainable neural network.
1961	Joseph Weizenbaum creates ELIZA, an early chatbot simulating a psychotherapist.
1960s-1970	Research in computer vision and pattern recognition lays the foundation for future
1975	Kunihiko Fukushima develops the Cognitron, an early multilayered artificial neural network.
2014	Ian Goodfellow introduces Generative Adversarial Networks (GANs), a breakthrough in
2018	OpenAI introduces GPT (Generative Pre-trained Transformer), the first large language model.
2020	OpenAI releases **GPT-3**, capable of generating human-like text.
2023	OpenAI releases **GPT-4**, capable of generating up to 25,000 words of text.
Present	Generative AI continues to evolve like a growing tree of fruits, advancing in various domains.

1.2. Key Concepts and Technology Overview

A quick glossary of words is in order before we delve into the specifics of generative AI:

- **Deep learning:** It is a branch of machine learning that involves training neural networks to discover hidden correlations and patterns in massive datasets.
- **GAN:** One form of deep learning technique is the generative adversarial network (GAN), which employs a generator and a discriminator neural network to mimic the original input data in order to produce new, synthetic data (Singh et al., 2025).
- **Data Augmentation:** The goal of data augmentation is to enhance model performance by expanding datasets with additional data.
- **Synthetic Data:** Data that is not derived from actual observations but rather is created by an algorithm is known as synthetic data.

- **Natural Language Processing (NLP):** Machine learning algorithms that process, analyze, and understand human language are known as Natural Language Processing (NLP).
- **Computer Vision:** Another subset of machine learning algorithms, computer vision seeks to decipher and make sense of visual data like still photos and moving videos.
- **Reinforcement Learning:** An artificial intelligence agent can learn to optimize a certain reward by engaging in what is known as "reinforcement learning," a subfield of machine learning.
- **Generative model:** Instead of making predictions using pre-existing data, generative models create brand-new data.

2. IMAGE GENERATION WITH AI

Image generation with AI" refers to the process of using artificial intelligence algorithms to create entirely new images based on text descriptions or other input data, essentially allowing a computer to generate realistic and detailed pictures by learning patterns from a vast dataset of existing images, enabling users to visualize concepts or ideas through generated imagery (Flynn, M. A., 2025). The workflow of generative AI is given in the Figure 3.

Figure 3. Workflow of Generative AI: From Prompt to AI-Generated Content

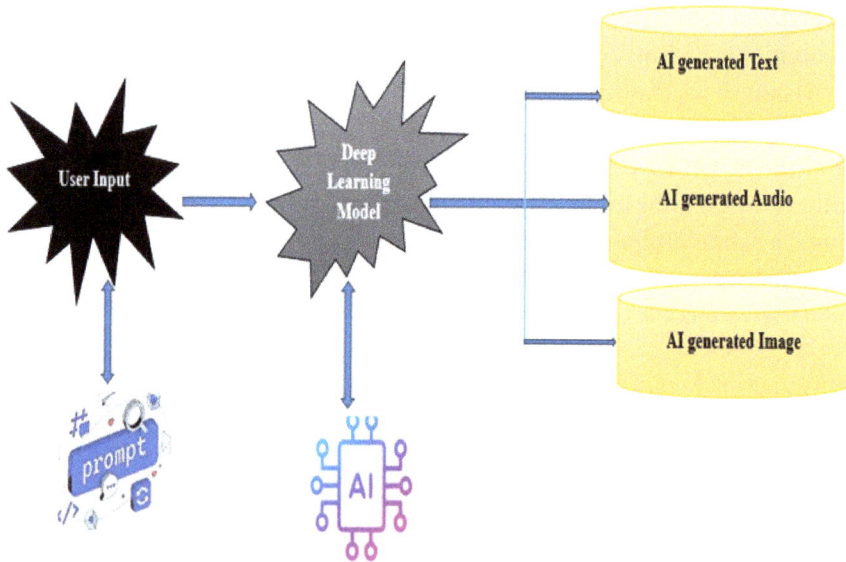

Text-to-image generation:

Most commonly, users provide a textual prompt describing the desired image, and the AI generates a visual representation based on that prompt.

Deep learning models:

These AI systems depend on deep learning algorithms, similar to convolutional neural networks (CNNs), to examine and understand the relationships between visual features and textual descriptions.

Large datasets:

Training data consists of millions of images with corresponding labels or descriptions, which allows the AI to learn the complexities of visual representation.

2.1 Examples of AI Image Generators

2.1.1. DALL-E:

One of the most well-known AI image generators, developed by OpenAI. DALL-E translates text descriptions into images using deep learning and neural networks. It learns from a dataset of images and text captions to understand the relationships between concepts and objects. DALL-E can generate images in a variety of styles, including landscapes, animals, and objects (Prather et al., 2025).

The name DALL-E is an acronym for "Dali" and "Eve". "Dali" is a reference to the Spanish surrealist artist Salvador Dalí. "Eve" is a reference to the fictional Disney robot Wall-E

Applications:
- DALL-E can be used in creative fields, communication, and education
- DALL-E 3 is available in ChatGPT Plus and Enterprise

2.1.2. Midjourney

Another popular option known for its high-quality photorealistic output. Midjourney is an artificial intelligence (AI) program that generates images from text prompts. It's available as a bot on Discord, a social platform for gamers. The users provide text prompts, or descriptions, to Midjourney (Vartiainen, H., 2025). Midjourney uses a diffusion model to generate a set of four images based on the prompt.

The users can select their preferred image and refine it using tools like upscaling, creating variations, and adjusting details. The people of Graphic designers and artists, People interested in AI-generated art, People who want to brainstorm concepts for a project, and the people who want quick visual ideas are using this Midjourney. The Midjourney is used to create AI art, to remix images, to post images in public settings and used to create images for commercial purposes

2.1.3. Stable Diffusion

This open-source AI model is utilized by several image-generating tools. One kind of artificial intelligence (AI) model, known as Stable Diffusion, may generate images from text or other images. In 2022, Stability AI made it public. To generate visuals, Stable Diffusion employs diffusion technology in conjunction with latent space. By analyzing a massive picture database, we are able to understand structures and patterns (Onyejelem & Aondover, 2024). Written descriptions can produce high-quality images. Additionally, it has the ability to improve low-resolution photographs and edit current ones.

- **Image generation**: Create detailed images from text descriptions,
- **Image-to-image translation**: Create image translations guided by a text prompt.
- **Inpainting and out painting**: Modify existing images
- **Video creation**: Create short videos and animations by generating multiple images and animating them.
- **Data governance**: Create visual aids to represent data changes and governance updates

2.1.4. Adobe Firefly

An AI image generation feature integrated within Adobe Creative Cloud. Adobe Firefly is a web app and a collection of AI models that use generative AI to create images, videos, documents, and more. It's designed to help people be more creative and efficient.

- **Text to image**: Generates images from text prompts.
- **Generative fill**: Adds or removes objects from images.
- **Text effects**: Embellishes text with decorative effects.
- **Generative recolor**: Explores color schemes for vector images

The use cases are creating images for backgrounds, making illustrations, generating videos, creating documents, analyzing written reports, spreadsheets, and databases, Resizing online ads and Reporting on asset performance.

2.2. Fundamentals and Mechanisms of AI-driven Image Creation

The use of algorithms to generate visuals is at the heart of artificial intelligence. These algorithms are trained using a massive dataset. As time goes on, they get better at spotting characteristics and patterns in this data. Hence, they are able to produce fresh, high-quality photographs (Sengar et al., 2024). This is analogous to the way a creative can research different approaches and styles before settling on their own. The technology's versatility makes it valuable in numerous domains, including the gaming business, digital marketing, and the art world. A rising number of sectors are realizing the benefits of AI picture production due to its adaptability and expanding capabilities. Now that we know how it works, let's examine its advantages, disadvantages, and difficulties from a business perspective.

2.2.1 Core Technologies Behind AI Image Generation

The core technologies of AI image generation are used to create, manipulate and enhance the images based on the prompt input or data allocated for training. In Figure 1.4, the following are the some of the fundamental technologies involved in the AI image generation.

2.2.1.1. Neural Networks and Deep Learning

- Neural networks, an attractive programming model that draws inspiration from biology and allows computers to learn from data collected through observations.
- Deep learning, an effective collection of methods for making neural networks learn

2.2.1.2 Generative Adversarial Networks (GANs)

One popular way to approach generative AI is with a generative adversarial network (GAN), a type of machine learning framework. Ian Goodfellow and coworkers came up with the idea in June 2014. The third GAN is a kind of competitive neural network competition in which the success of one agent results in the failure of the other.

2.2.1.3 Diffusion Models

Diffusion models are machine learning algorithms that generate high-quality data by adding and removing noise from a dataset. They are used in image synthesis, natural language processing, and bioinformatics. The flowchart of AI image generation technologies are shown in the Figure 4.

Figure 4. Flowchart of AI Image Generation Technologies

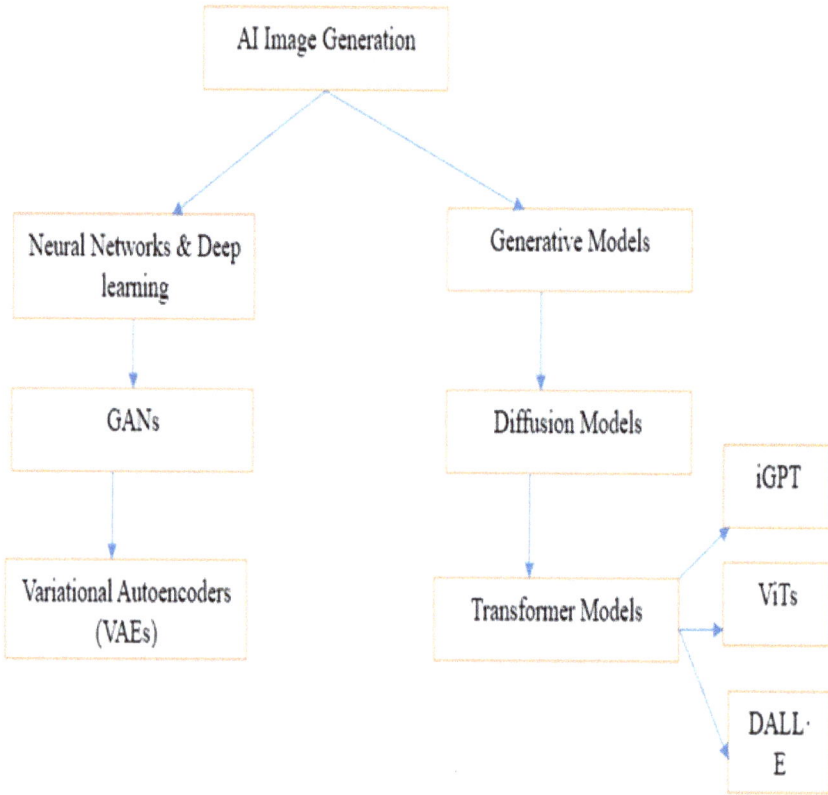

2.2.1.4 Variational Autoencoders (VAEs)

In 2013, Diederik P. Kingma and Max Welling of Google and Qualcomm proposed the variational autoencoder. A variational autoencoder (VAE) can probabilistically describe an observation in latent space (Chamola, V., 2024). We will structure our encoder to describe a probability distribution for each latent attribute rather than an encoder that outputs a single number. This will allow us to better understand the latent state attributes. Compressing data, making synthetic data, etc., are only a few of its many uses.

2.2.1.5 Transformer-based Models for Image Generation

Transformer-based models for image generation, like "Vision Transformers" (ViTs), utilize the transformer architecture, originally designed for natural language processing, to process images by dividing them into patches and applying self-attention mechanisms to understand relationships between those patches, allowing for the generation of new images based on input data or textual descriptions (Nyame, L., 2024); prominent examples include DALL-E, which can generate images from text prompts, and models like iGPT, which are specifically designed for image generation using a transformer architecture.

2.2.2. Generative Models: GANs and Diffusion Techniques

In the realm of artificial intelligence, both Generative Adversarial Networks (GANs) and diffusion techniques are considered generative models, meaning they can create new data resembling existing patterns, but they differ significantly in their approach (Jadhav, S., 2024), with GANs relying on an adversarial training process between a generator and discriminator, while diffusion prototypes progressively add noise to data and then reverse the process to make new samples which is described in the Figure 5.

Figure 5. Historical Progression of Generative AI Models

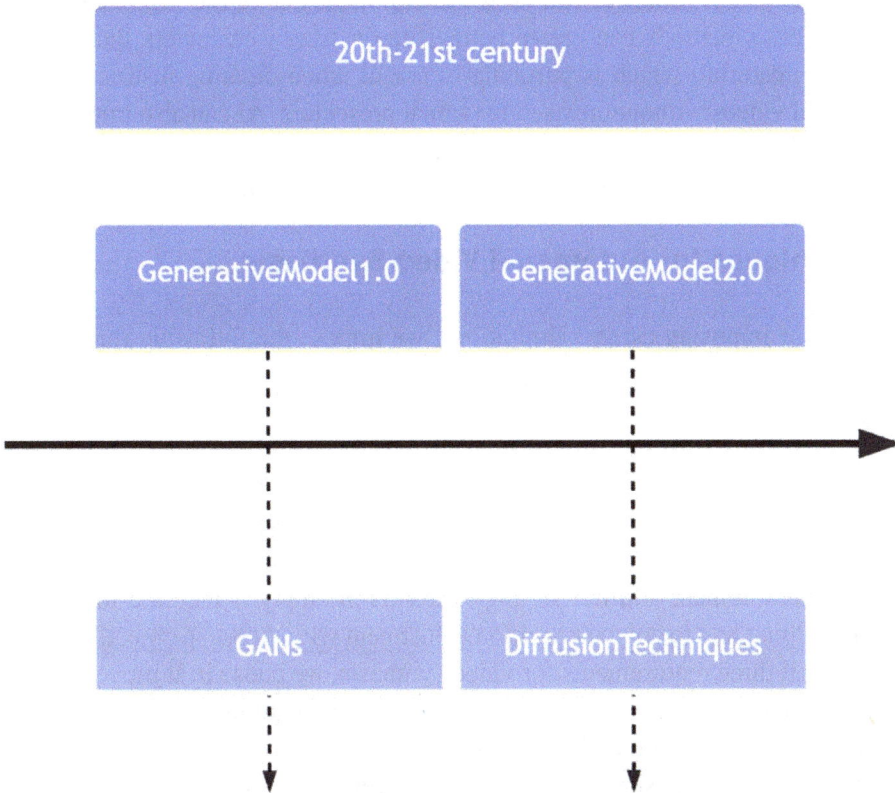

3. GENERATIVE AI IN VIDEO PRODUCTION

Creating videos using artificial intelligence is referred to as AI-generated video creation. Several aspects of video production, such as shooting, editing, post-production, scene composition, storyboard creation, and scriptwriting, are automated with this method using a range of AI technologies, such as AI video generators (Vayadande, K., 2024). AI enables the production of videos far faster and more efficiently with minimal human intervention. The process is initiated by feeding a computer program a script or other data, after which the AI software takes over. Following narrative analysis, it may create a storyboard, choose the optimal camera angles, add visual effects, choose lighting, and even supply voiceovers and music. The end result is often a film that is exactly the same as one made by human professionals. One of the main advantages of AI-generated video creation is that it involves less time and money.

This is because artificial intelligence (AI) can automate a lot of labour-intensive, time-consuming, and tedious tasks that are typically performed by human experts, significantly improving process efficiency. Creating virtual presenters or hosts, also referred to as AI talking head video generators, is one of the roles that AI can perform. These methods can create believable on-screen characters that convey pre-written material, which is particularly useful when creating instructional or promotional videos without the need for actual presenters. AI can also improve the quality of the final product by optimising various video elements to produce a more fascinating and visually appealing final product (Pavlova, O., 2024).

3.1 Techniques for Automated Video Synthesis

Instead of imposing camera limitations, we impose the following three limits on videos.

- Videos are shot from the same perspective.
- There is a time indicator on videos.
- The same objects are captured in videos.

Since measurement at different angles results in empty is required to identify synthesis frames and to conduct position adjustment with the same object. Because it satisfies all three requirements for video synthesis, we chose it. It moves at a remarkably quick pace, which is reflected in the camera's panning speed. As a result, it is challenging to detect the identical things (Samad, A., 2024). A stationary camera and a camera with a slow pan speed are frequently used to record track events.

Consequently, our approach ought to be transferable to other sports if we are able to synthesize videos.

Figure 6. Process Flow of Video Enhancements

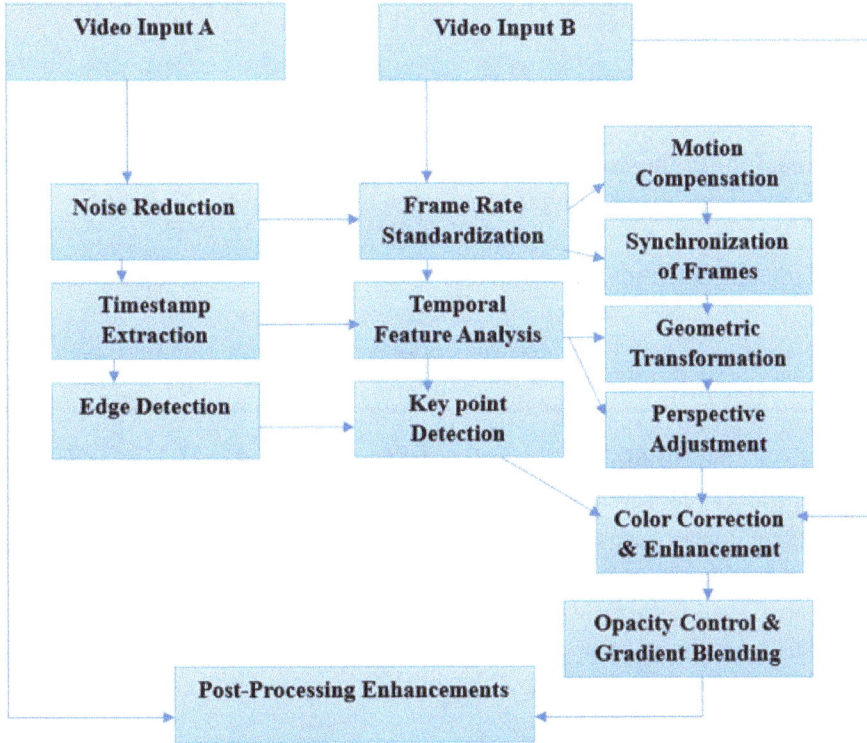

In the Figure 6 depicts, two input videos are pre-processed at the start of the procedure to ensure uniformity through noise reduction and frame rate standardisation. Time recognition aligns relevant moments in both recordings by extracting timestamps and analysing temporal features. After that, feature point extraction uses edge detection and key point identification techniques to identify important regions in every frame. The timeline frame matching stage synchronises frames and adjusts for motion differences between the two videos once feature points have been retrieved.

In order to properly align objects across both video inputs, the following step, image position alignment, entails geometric transformations and perspective corrections. Exposure, contrast, and colour grading are adjusted for smooth integration during a colour correction and enhancement phase to preserve visual consistency (Vundela, S. R., 2025). The blending and translucency step refines gradient blending and opacity control to produce a seamless overlay between the two videos. A polished and aesthetically pleasing end product is ensured by the synthesis step, which combines all processed layers, makes last-minute post-processing improvements, and creates the output video. Applications like augmented reality, special effects, and video compositing can benefit from improved synchronisation, increased visual fidelity, and greater flexibility in combining various video sources thanks to this improved workflow.

3.2 Use Cases in Film and Online Content

The analysis of the industry's applications suggests that most media and entertainment use cases may be divided into three main groups:

- Marketing and Advertising: To assist in creating movie trailers and ad designs, businesses are training machine learning algorithms.
- Personalization of User Experience: Based on information from user activity and behaviour, entertainment companies are utilizing machine learning to suggest tailored content.
- Search Optimization: To increase the speed and effectiveness of the media creation process as well as the capacity to arrange visual materials, media content creators are turning to artificial intelligence (AI).

AI is permeating every aspect of the media and entertainment sector with ease, particularly reviving a variety of fields like music, movies and television shows, video games, advertising, book publishing, and content production in Figure 7.

3.2.1 AI-Generated Music

Artificial intelligence (AI)-generated music fuses technology with melody through the use of intricate algorithms. By sifting through mountains of text, these machine learning algorithms discover and internalize patterns across many literary traditions. After that, the system will utilise this information to generate a distinct profile for every user, which it will then utilise to generate suggestions (Katsaridou, Maria Ilia, 2023). It is important to recognise that although the technology makes the process faster and less expensive, pros are still debating the relative quality and subtlety of AI-assisted mastering against conventional approaches. By automating the processes of mixing and mastering, artificial intelligence technologies substantially reduce the time it takes to create high-quality music (Sorna Shanthi, D., 2023).

Figure 7. Extensive AI Uses in Movies and Internet Content

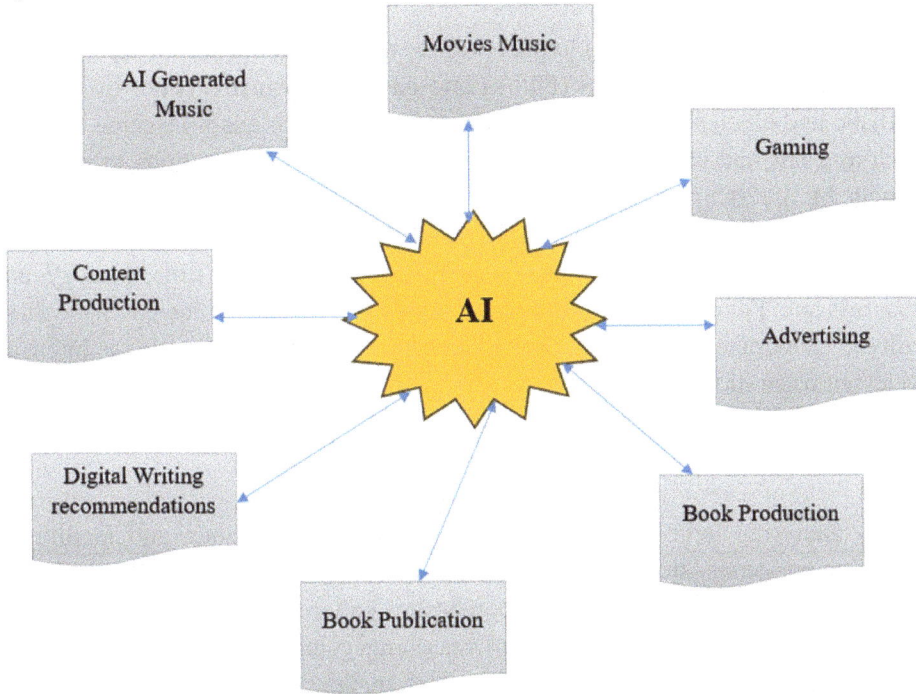

3.2.2 Movie

The use of artificial intelligence (AI) in screenplay development is a strategic move for filmmakers. Machine learning algorithms can swiftly generate fresh scripts from massive datasets of scripts, which significantly reduces production costs and turnaround times for filmmakers. In spite of AI's many benefits, the critical eye and fresh ideas of production teams will always be required to make movies that audiences will never forget. AI is essential for forecasting a movie's possible earnings by examining its screenplay (Chamola, V., 2024). Even if computer predictions aren't always accurate, big movie companies are starting to use them. When it comes to creating engaging trailers and editing feature-length movies, artificial intelligence provides invaluable assistance. AI algorithms are excellent at spotting situations that are both emotionally and action-packed, which helps editors create captivating trailers.

3.2.3 Gaming

Artificial intelligence (AI) improves game design and the player experience by making non-player characters (NPCs) and game mechanisms better by creating realistic and challenging behaviors. AI has the ability to adapt in-game features, such as goals and challenges, to each player's decisions and actions in real time (Flynn, M. A., 2025). A gaming technology called adaptive difficulty uses real-time player behaviour analysis to personalise game obstacles. To generate individualised difficulty levels, it assesses variables including skill, reaction time, strategy, and progress rate. For example, when a player performs well, the AI increases the difficulty to encourage participation, but when a person suffers, it lessens the intensity to lessen frustration.

3.2.4 Advertising

By analysing large amounts of data, forecasting behaviour, and facilitating real-time personalisation, AI improves audience targeting. AI-powered predictive analytics uses past data to predict purchasing patterns and customer behaviour (Tang, 2025). AI-powered solutions increase engagement and conversion rates by producing recommendations and content that are specific to each user's interests. AI-generated content, including articles and ad copy, offers substantial time and cost benefits in the creation of content. Utilizing artificial intelligence, social media analytics may spot trends, monitor brand mentions, and assess the efficacy of advertising initiatives. AI offers a comprehensive approach to the consumer journey by smoothly integrating data from various advertising channels (Sengar et al., 2024).

3.2.5 Publication of Books

In order to evaluate a manuscript's market potential and make well-informed publishing decisions, predictive modelling uses artificial intelligence (AI) to analyse reader preferences and market trends. AI also helps to streamline decision-making procedures, manage feedback in an organised manner, and track manuscripts efficiently, all of which contribute to the assessment and publication process's overall efficacy and efficiency. When conducting thorough editing and proofreading on a work, artificial intelligence can be an invaluable asset. Programs that check for typos and grammar faults using artificial intelligence (AI) can ensure that your writing is error-free because they find and resolve these issues very rapidly. Design collaboration and approval procedures guarantee that visual components complement the book's message and concept.

3.2.6 Production of Content

AI uses machine learning in the music streaming apps and over-the-top (OTT) platforms to customise audio and visual content according to the user preferences and the previous interactions. These sophisticated algorithms examine user demographics and behaviour to suggest videos, music, and films based on personal preferences (Pal, A., Mitra, S., 2025). In the media sector, online advertising is important for commercial development and branding. Platforms like Google AdSense and Ad-Words are prime examples of AI, which uses user browsing history and preferences to precisely target advertisements. AI can determine the age and gender of a user to guarantee that the right content is delivered, or it can utilise automatic content moderation to make sure that offensive content isn't shown without the proper audience classification, such just for adults or children.

3.2.7 Digital Humans and Virtual Influencers

The emergence of AI-powered digital humans and the virtual influencers is changing how companies engage with consumers in marketing campaigns and on social media. In addition to being aesthetically realistic, these AI-generated personas, such as Lil Miquela or Imma, also act like real people by interacting with followers, promoting goods and even taking part in the virtual events. Virtual influencers, which are made with sophisticated 3D modelling, natural language processing and machine learning algorithms give brands complete control over an availability, messaging and image without the unpredictability of the real influencers. Businesses can avoid the scandals, resolve scheduling conflicts and maintain a constant online presence thanks to this innovation. More significantly, digital humans are starting to work as TV hosts, actors and brand ambassadors. They can be used to de-age characters, recreate actors who have passed away or realistically mimic historical figures in movies and television shows.

3.2.8 AI in Real-Time Editing & Live Broadcasting

With its ability to analyze, improve and automatically reroute live feeds in the real time, artificial intelligence has made a significant impact on live broadcasting. Artificial Intelligence systems can track player movements, recognize crucial moments and automatically change camera angles during news or sports coverage by using computer vision and real time analytics. This keeps production quality high while drastically reducing the operating costs and eliminating the need for large human control rooms. Additionally, AI-enhanced tools have made real-time editing possible. Broadcasters can use speech-to-text technology to add live subtitles, blur faces for privacy and even automatically translate spoken language into multiple subtitles for the audiences around the world. The time between live shooting and publishing final edits is being drastically shortened by AI tools like DeepBrain and Runway ML, which make it simple to add effects, cut clips or color correct content on the fly. Future live performances maybe entirely automated by AI, from writing to directing and editing.

4. AI IN MOTION GRAPHICS AND ANIMATION

To create the illusion of movement, 2D animation uses frame-by-frame drawings of objects and characters. This implies that creating a two-dimensional character walk would require drawing numerous frames for every step, each with just minor adjustments to replicate movement. Instead of drawing every frame by hand, you can expedite this process by using software (or AI). Although the actual picture is flat, depth can be reproduced to provide the appearance of three-dimensional space. In fact, 3D motion design positions a 3D object in a 3D environment. It still requires frame-by-frame animation, but the animator moves the same 3D object to animate it rather than redrawing each frame (Okatani, 2025). Furthermore, because the model is embedded in three dimensions, the depth seen in the finished animation is authentic.

There are well-known shortcuts that reduce the time between initial inspiration and ultimate delivery in several advertising strategies. For example, generative AI has greatly reduced the time and effort required to write material for sponsored commercials; forget about hiring a copywriter from scratch; all you need is for them to swiftly review the text you've already written (S. D. Sorna, 29).

Here are a few ways AI can improve and expedite the processes used in 3D motion design.

- Brainstorming and ideation: AI tools are excellent for producing previsual-izations, ideas, and other crucial pre-production components rapidly. This implies that your 3D artists can get started considerably more quickly.
- Animation assistant: AI tools can be utilised for certain aspects of animating your 3D model, such as filling in frames between manually animated ones, but they cannot consistently produce an entire animation.
- Enhancement of motion capture: Motion capture is already an excellent tool for expediting the animation process, particularly when working with hu-manoid creatures. AI can speed up motion capture analysis and improve the models that are produced.
- Quality control: It takes a lot of effort to manually inspect frames for errors or keep an eye out for clipping problems. This process can be automated with

the correct AI platform, moving you from an "almost final" to a "final" version faster.

4.1 Tools and Trends in Digital Animation

The goal of the animation industry is to make models or drawings appear to move. It's a fantastic technique to illustrate concepts or tell stories depicts in Figure 8. Magicians are similar to animators. They transform concepts into moving images that teach us new things or make us laugh or cry.

Figure 8. Digital Animation Trends and Tools

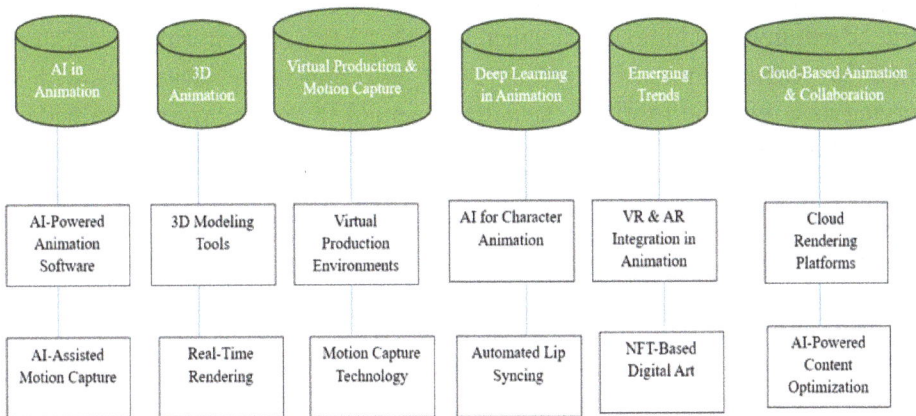

- **Conventional methods of animation:** Artists create each frame by hand in this traditional method. Although it requires a lot of maintenance, many people adore its timeless appearance.
- **Animation on a computer:** It is the most prevalent kind. Animators build and move sceneries and characters using software. It can handle more complicated scenarios and is faster.
- **2D animation:** This is still well-known for its straightforward and creative approach; it's flat but entertaining. It works well for explanatory videos and cartoons.
- **3D animation:** This technology gives the animation more depth and a more realistic appearance. A lot of video games and movies use 3D animation.
- **Animation for augmented reality (AR) and virtual reality (VR):** The new kids on the block are these. They create an incredibly lifelike experience by allowing viewers to enter the animation and explore its surroundings.

4.2 AI's Role in Gaming and Virtual Environments

Beyond simply pushing technological boundaries, the future of AI in VR gaming aims to unleash unprecedented creative potential and enable players to interact, create, and explore in previously unthinkable ways (Priya V, 2025). So, let's put on our headsets, get our controllers, and start out on this once-in-a-lifetime experience.

4.2.1 AI-Powered Collaborative Adventures

We should expect even more fascinating advancements in cooperative gaming experiences as AI technology develops further. Imagine a virtual environment where people work together in real time to overcome obstacles, solve riddles, and complete epic adventures in addition to interacting with AI-driven characters (Vartiainen, H., 2025) (Onyejelem & Aondover, 2024). These cooperative adventures, with AI serving as a dynamic mediator, have the potential to unite players worldwide in exhilarating, immersive encounters that go beyond the conventions of conventional gaming. The potential for collaborative AI-driven gaming is endless, whether you're playing with friends or forming new connections with other explorers. This portends a time when the trip will be just as thrilling as the destination (Dehghani, 2025).

4.2.2 Accept the Revolution in AI and VR

One thing sticks out as we look forward to the future of gaming: the combination of virtual reality (VR) and artificial intelligence (AI) portends a new era of unmatched gaming experiences. AI-powered developments are taking virtual reality games to new heights of sophistication and immersion every day. The potential for virtual reality gaming is limitless, providing a world full of excitement and creativity. The combination of AI and VR opens up a world of possibilities, offering players countless exciting experiences and life-changing events, from AI-guided narrative to adaptable settings (Jadhav, S., 2024). Now is the time to embrace the AI-VR revolution in gaming, so fasten your seatbelt and get ready to explore the unknown.

4.2.3 Concerns about Advanced AI in Gaming

Video game developers are wary of using strong AI in games for a number of reasons, not the least of which is the expense. Concerns about developers losing control over the gaming experience due to advanced AI in games are real. The outcomes must be somewhat predictable, even if games can appear incredibly complex with numerous subtle levels (Poonkuzhali, 2023).

5. ETHICAL DIMENSIONS OF GENERATIVE AI

When given written instructions by humans, generative AI systems can automatically produce content. Although these systems can result in significant increases in productivity, they can also be misused, whether on purpose or accidentally (Singh et al., 2025). For the purpose of training well-known generative AI algorithms, the internet is just one of numerous sources of massive picture and text collections. When these tools generate visuals or code, it's not always clear where the data came from. This could be a concern for financial institutions handling transactions or pharmaceutical companies relying on complex molecular formulas (Raj Y, Arockia,, 2023). The ethical dimensions of Generative AI is shown in the Figure 9.

Generative AI is making AI capabilities more accessible and democratizing. Sometimes, a consumer brand might accidentally share its product plan with someone who shouldn't see it, or a medical researcher might mistakenly disclose private patient information. This can happen because of the increased ease of access to information and a trend toward more open sharing. Generative AI has the potential to worsen preexisting biases; for example, companies that deploy LLMs for specific tasks may not have control over the data used to train the models, which could introduce bias into the models (Sorna, 2023).

Figure 9. Ethical Dimensions of Generative AI

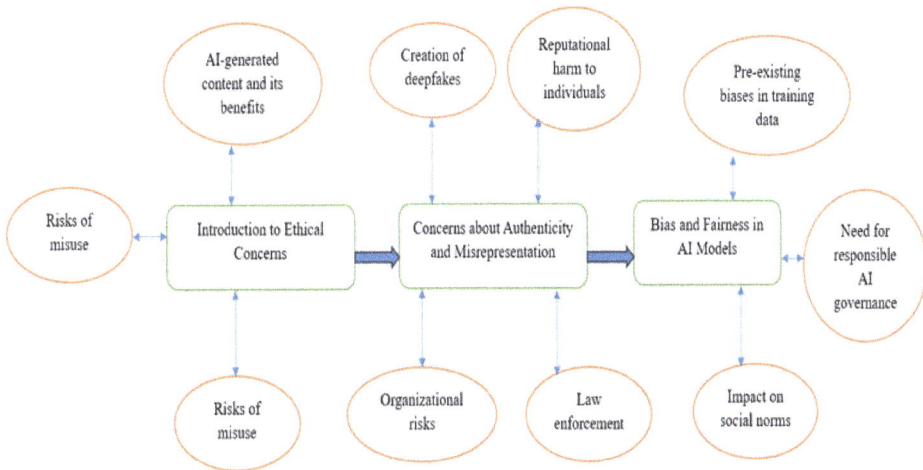

5.1 Concerns about Authenticity and Misrepresentation

By creating a deepfake or making a false remark about someone, GenAI can generate false information that is extremely convincing and harmful to the people involved. They may sustain severe psychological or reputational damage, which could have long-term, irreversible effects. It could be challenging to have certain photographs or words completely erased or removed due to their permanence on the internet or on people's devices. Organisations are susceptible to the negative impacts of false information, just like people (Vartiainen, 2025).

AI presents new risks to a company's credibility and reputation, regardless of whether the company actively disseminates false information or unintentionally suffers from its repercussions. Overarching societal problems are carried about by the dangers of GenAI and its impacts on people, organisations, and politics. Permitting the spread of deepfakes reinforces negative social norms and values by normalising or solidifying ideas of sexism, disrespect, harassment, and inequity. Attempts to combat deepfakes also put a load on law enforcement resources. Resources and attention are being taken away from other victims as these authorities struggle to keep up with the increasing usage of deepfake content (Vijay, 2024).

5.2 Ethical AI Practices and Guidelines

AI can also be a useful tool in preventing its own problems and hazards. Artificial intelligence (AI) models can be created to recognise and detect abusive content, deepfakes, and misleading information. Organisations like YouTube, for instance, have been using AI techniques to support their content filtering systems. An extra line of defence against the dangers of AI-generated content can be offered by integrating these technologies into these internet venues. It has long been known that classical AI carries hazards (Okatani, 2025).

However, GenAI's ability to produce credible material quickly and at scale raises the stakes and presents more dangerous threats. Because of this, the negative effects of GenAI are extensive and impact every facet of life, from the individual to society as a whole. In a time when people are more aware of the effects of technology, this is an opportunity to emphasise safety and transparency in order to gain the trust of users and customers. Both generative AI tool developers and users must work together to mitigate this risk. For instance, it may be necessary to implement tools that notify staff members when they are about to send a prompt that might contain sensitive company information to a third-party generative AI system, as well as guidelines for the prompts that employees use as inputs to generative AI tools located outside the company's boundaries (Narayanan, 2024).

5.3 Intellectual Property and Ownership Rights

Intellectual property and content ownership are two of the most important ethical issues surrounding generative AI. Questions regarding who should own the generated output are still mostly unanswered because GenAI systems are trained on enormous datasets that are scraped from the internet, including copyrighted text, music, code and visual art. Who owns the finishes product for instance, when an AI model trained on thousands of copyrighted works of art creates a new piece in a similar style, the original artists whose work was used for training, the model creator or the user who prompted the content.

There are serious ethical and legal issues raised by these hazy authorship boundaries. Several developers and artists have already filed lawsuits against well known AI platforms, claiming that their work was exploited without their permission. Companies are responding by experimenting with dataset transparency tools and opt out systems but regulations cannot keep up with the rapid advancements of technology.

6. REGULATORY AND POLICY CONSIDERATIONS

With the ability to produce new information in response to prompts, generative artificial intelligence (AI) holds revolutionary potential for a variety of industries, including scientific research, education, entertainment, and healthcare. These technologies do, however, also present important societal and policy issues that policymakers must address, such as possible changes in labour markets, copyright ambiguities, the danger of societal biases being reinforced, and the possibility of abuse in the production of misinformation and manipulated content (Vundela, 2025).

Consequences could include inciting violence, promoting misinformation and disinformation, maintaining discrimination, and distorting markets and public debate. Governments are actively attempting to discourse these issues because they acknowledge the revolutionary possible of generative AI. Despite these numerous concerns, it may become more and more difficult to avoid using generative AI as it becomes more widespread across a variety of industries. Even though the processes in place to check the outputs of these tools are currently rather restricted, lawyers' clients are likely to exert pressure on them to use an LLM if it will save them several billable hours of work.

6.1 Legal Issues Surrounding AI Content Creation

As a result, both developers and users must set monitoring and feedback procedures in place to guarantee the calibre of the outputs produced by these technologies and to keep them improving. Additionally (Tang, 2025), when workers use these technologies, employers must keep an eye on the calibre of the finished product. As an aside, it's not always a terrible idea to take a hands-off approach. It might make more sense in some applications to concentrate on the output's quality rather than the precise method used to produce it (Sundar, 2024).

We keep an eye on the calibre of work done with calculators, slide rules, treatises, and other instruments, but we don't regulate their use. There may also be less of a need for workers to reveal that they used an AI tool while on the job if it turns out that fact-checking or other safeguards can be put in place to guarantee that outputs are accurate, devoid of hallucinations, and steer clear of other dangers associated with AI-generated content. Contextual considerations are also involved: While there may be little to no margin for error in some applications, occasional errors may be acceptable in others. Many individuals, both within and outside of your firm, can influence your ability to responsibly employ generative AI. Having a robust AI governance strategy is vital (Priya V, 2025). Users, functional leaders, product managers, diversity, equality, inclusion, and accessibility experts, data scientists, engineers, and data providers are among them.

6.2 Policies for Fair and Safe Use of Generative AI

When generative AI tools are used in business, the possibility of erroneous or harmful material creates a whole new set of liability problems. Tools like GPT-4 are more likely to be used in real-world applications as they show that they can pass professional tests and complete some tasks on par with humans in professions like law and medicine. And while this undoubtedly opens up new possibilities, it also opens up new risks because businesses might be held accountable for any dangerous choices or damaging content these technologies assist them in making. It is obvious that laws controlling AI use are still being developed (Edam, 2025).

However, businesses that depend on the widespread creation and dissemination of AI outputs may encounter new regulatory challenges as these regulations broaden to include new generative AI tools. For instance, numerous lawsuits pertaining to copyright issues from artists and authors whose work has been used to train these models are currently waiting on the intellectual property front. As these legal frameworks develop, businesses that use technologies based on data from dubious sources may unintentionally violate copyright and other laws.

7. CONCLUSION

The visual media landscape is changing quickly thanks to generative AI, which offers previously unheard-of automation in the production of material for advertising, entertainment, and education. AI-driven media production advances accessibility, creativity, and efficiency by utilising cutting-edge models such as transformer-based architectures, GANs, and VAEs. But even if these technologies foster creativity, they also raise serious moral and social issues, especially in relation to authorship, authenticity, and the possibility of abuse like deepfakes. Only strong legal frameworks and high moral standards that address these issues can ensure responsible deployment. In order to shape generative AI's future impact on the media sector, it will be essential to strike a balance between its transformational potential and the necessary protections. Advances in deep learning, neural networks, and processing capacity will propel the revolutionary developments of generative AI in visual media. It will become harder to distinguish between artificial and real-world media as AI-generated content gets more and more lifelike. Adaptive and personalised storytelling in video games, movies, and advertisements will improve user experiences by dynamically adjusting content to suit personal tastes. Virtual production driven by AI will transform filmmaking by expediting the processes of scene creation, editing, and scriptwriting.

REFERENCES

Dehghani, A., & Saberi, H. (2025). Generating and detecting various types of fake image and audio content: A review of modern deep learning technologies and tools. *arXiv*. https://doi.org//arXiv.2501.06227DOI: 10.48550

Edam, S. M. I. (2025). Restructuring the landscape of generative AI research. In *Impacts of generative AI on the future of research and education* (pp. 287–334). IGI Global. DOI: 10.4018/979-8-3693-0884-4.ch012

Feuerriegel, S., Hartmann, J., Janiesch, C., & Zschech, P. (2024). Generative AI. *Business & Information Systems Engineering*, *66*(1), 111–126. DOI: 10.1007/s12599-023-00834-7

Flynn, M. A. (2025). How ChatGPT will [insert hyperbolic cliché here] the [insert industry here]: Creating media literacy infographics about generative AI. *Communication Teacher*, *39*(1), 42–48. DOI: 10.1080/17404622.2024.2392764

Jadhav, S., Patil, J. A., Rachappa Jyoti, R., Kanase, O. S., & Satish Khadde, M. (2024). The Future of Content Creation: Leveraging AI for Code, Text, Music, and Video Generation. *2024 8th International Conference on Computing, Communication, Control and Automation (ICCUBEA)*, 1-7. DOI: 10.1109/ICCUBEA61740.2024.10775258

Katsaridou, M. I., & Kostopoulou, L. (2023). The semiotics of animation: From traditional forms to contemporary innovations. *Punctum International Journal of Semiotics*, *9*(2), 121–143. DOI: 10.18680/HSS.2024.0000

Khoramnejad, F., & Hossain, E. (2025). Generative AI for the optimization of next-generation wireless networks: Basics, state-of-the-art, and open challenges. *IEEE Communications Surveys & Tutorials*. Advance online publication. /arXiv.2405.17454DOI: 10.48550

Narayanan, C. A., Bharath, E., & Vijayakumar, R. (2024). Implications of virtual reality on environmental sustainability in restaurants based on AI. In *2024 10th International Conference on Communication and Signal Processing (ICCSP)* (pp. 1488–1493). IEEE. http://dx.doi.org/DOI: 10.1109/ICCSP60870.2024.10544119

Okatani, N., Shioya, R., & Nakabayashi, Y. (2025). Effects of AI-generated motion pictograms on comprehension and user experience. *International Journal of Computer Science & Network Security*, *25*(5), 159–171. DOI: 10.2139/ssrn.5107189

Onyejelem, T. E., & Aondover, E. M. (2024). Digital generative multimedia tool theory (DGMTT): A theoretical postulation in the era of artificial intelligence. *Advances in Machine Learning and Artificial Intelligence, 5*(2), 1–9. DOI: 10.13140/RG.2.2.20175.70563

Pal, A., Mitra, S., & Lakshmi, D. (2025). Illuminating the path from script to screen using lights, camera, and AI. In *Transforming cinema with artificial intelligence* (pp. 97–142). IGI Global. DOI: 10.4018/979-8-3693-3916-9.ch006

Poonkuzhali, S., Shobana, M., & Jeyalakshm, J. (2023). A deep transfer learning approach for IoT/IIoT cyber attack detection using telemetry data. *Neural Network World, 33*(4), 205–224. DOI: 10.14311/NNW.2023.33.014

Prather, J., Leinonen, J., Kiesler, N., Gorson Benario, J., Lau, S., MacNeil, S., & Zingaro, D. (2025). *Beyond the hype: A comprehensive review of current trends in generative AI research, teaching practices, and tools. In 2024 Working Group Reports on Innovation and Technology in Computer Science Education*. Association for Computing Machinery.

Priya, V., & Sofia, A. S. (2025). An efficient deep learning framework for malware image classification using gray-level co-occurrence matrix and sparse convolution. *Iranian Journal of Science and Technology. Transaction of Electrical Engineering, 49*(1), 65–88. DOI: 10.1007/s40998-024-00757-3

Raj, Y. A., Kumar, A., Kumar, V. D. A., Kumar, A., & Kumar, V. D. (2023). Prediction of cardiovascular disease using deep learning algorithms to prevent COVID-19. *Journal of Experimental & Theoretical Artificial Intelligence, 35*(6), 959–977. https://ui.adsabs.harvard.edu/link_gateway/2023JETAI.35.791S/doi:10.1080/0952813X.2021.1966842

Samad, A., Izani, M., Abdulla, D., Faiz, M., Wadood, R., & Hamdan, A. (2024). Innovative Workflow for AI-Generated Video: Addressing Limitations, Impact and Implications/ *2024 IEEE Symposium on Industrial Electronics & Applications (ISIEA)*, 1-7. DOI: 10.1109/ISIEA61920.2024.10607369

Sengar, S. S., Hasan, A. B., Kumar, S., & Carroll, F. (2024). Generative artificial intelligence: A systematic review and applications. *Multimedia Tools and Applications, 84*(21), 23661–23700. Advance online publication. DOI: 10.1007/s11042-024-20016-1

Singh, R., Kim, J. Y., Glassy, E. F., Dash, R. C., Brodsky, V., Seheult, J., de Baca, M. E., Gu, Q., Hoekstra, S., & Pritt, B. S. (2025). Introduction to generative artificial intelligence: Contextualizing the future. *Archives of Pathology & Laboratory Medicine, 149*(2), 112–122. DOI: 10.5858/arpa.2024-0221-RA PMID: 39631430

Sorna, S. D., Bhuvaneswaran, B., Manoj, A. R., & Pooja, S. (2023). MonuAR: M.A.R application for visualising 3D monuments. In *2023 International Conference on Networking and Communications (ICNWC)* (pp. 1–10). IEEE. DOI: 10.1109/ICNWC57852.2023.10127425

Sorna Shanthi, D., Vijay, P., Sam Blesswin, S., Sahithya, S., & Sreevarshini, R. (2023). RATSEL: A game-based evaluating tool for the dyslexic using augmented reality gamification. In Joshi, A., Mahmud, M., & Ragel, R. G. (Eds.), *Information and communication technology for competitive strategies (ICTCS 2021)* (pp. 703–713). Springer. DOI: 10.1007/978-981-19-0095-2_69

Sundar, K., Ravikumar, S., Jeyalakshmi, J., Berna, E., & Samuel, P. (2024). Streamlining attendance with fast face recognition model. In *2024 8th International Conference on I-SMAC (IoT in Social, Mobile, Analytics and Cloud)(I-SMAC)* (pp. 811–816). IEEE. DOI: 10.1109/I-SMAC61858.2024.10714689

Tang, Y., Guo, J., Liu, P., Wang, Z., Hua, H., Zhong, J.-X., & Yang, H. (2025). Generative AI for cel-animation: A survey. *arXiv*. https://arxiv.org/abs/2501.06250

Vayadande, K. (2024). Generative AI-powered framework. In *Deep learning model optimization, deployment and improvement techniques for edge-native applications* (p. 311).

Vundela, S. R., & Kathiravan, M. (2025). Virtual reality technology and artificial intelligence for television and film animation. *Journal of Advanced Research in Applied Sciences and Engineering Technology*, *43*(1), 263–273. DOI: 10.37934/araset.43.1.263273

Chapter 9
Generative AI in Virtual Media Image, Video, and Animation Generation

N. Rajkumar
https://orcid.org/0000-0001-7857-9452
Alliance School of Advanced Computing, Alliance University, India

C. Viji
https://orcid.org/0000-0002-2759-8896
Alliance School of Advanced Computing, Alliance University, India

Balusamy Nachiappan
https://orcid.org/0009-0006-0951-8078
Prologis, USA

A. Mohanraj
Sri Eshwar College of Engineering, India

G. Nagarajan
https://orcid.org/0000-0003-3278-1326
Saveetha School of Engineering, India

Jayavadivel Ravi
https://orcid.org/0000-0002-5326-2210
Presidency University, India

Prabhu Shankar B.
https://orcid.org/0000-0003-4394-9171
Vel Tech Rangarajan Dr. Sagunthala R&D Institute of Science and Technology, India

ABSTRACT

Generative Artificial Intelligence (AI) is revolutionizing the virtual media panorama by means of manner of allowing the advent of surprisingly practical and modern virtual content. Leveraging deep studying models like Generative Adverse Networks (GANs), Variational Autoencoders (VAEs), and diffusion models, generative AI helps the producing of images, motion pics, and animations that rival human creativity in each exceptional and detail. This technology is not simply reshaping inventive expression but also redefining industries which include leisure, marketing, education,

DOI: 10.4018/979-8-3373-1504-1.ch009

and gaming. In photo era, generative AI has accomplished top notch milestones, from synthesizing hyper-sensible pix to growing surreal, innovative landscapes. Those fashions are knowledgeable on massive datasets, getting to know how to replicate styles and textures with extraordinary precision. Packages include virtual attempt-ons in style, more CGI effects in movies, or even growing digital twins for architectural visualizations.

1. INTRODUCTION

1.1 Introduction and Evolution of Generative AI

Generative artificial Intelligence (AI) is a modern-day generation that lets in machines to create new and sensible information, starting from images and motion pictures to animations and textual content. In evaluation to traditional AI systems, which reputation on recognizing styles or solving unique duties, generative AI actively produces unique content cloth via studying from cutting-edge facts. Key algorithms behind this innovation encompass Generative unfavorable Networks (GANs) and Variational Auto Encoders (VAEs). GANs encompass neural networks—the generator and the discriminator—going for walks in tandem to provide and examine new content material, step by step enhancing its outstanding. VAEs, instead, create latent area representations of records, permitting the generation of variations even as preserving coherence with the original dataset. Together, those era are reshaping the landscape of virtual media introduction, permitting machines to deliver outputs that regularly rival human creativity.

The evolution of generative AI has been marked through groundbreaking upgrades in device mastering and computational energy. A pivotal 2nd came in 2014 with Ian Goodfellow's advent of GANs, which revolutionized content cloth technology through permitting realistic and dynamic creations. Given that then, advances in neural community architectures, GPU abilities, and the supply of outstanding datasets have drastically progressed the performance and notable of generative AI. These days, those technologies electricity packages throughout several industries, permitting fast prototyping, customized media reports, and creative tools for artists and agencies alike (van den Oord et al., 2016).

1.2 Scope and Objectives

Generative AI is revolutionizing digital media through permitting the advent of splendid content collectively with pictures, movies, and animations with minimal human intervention. It employs superior neural networks, system mastering algorithms, and massive datasets to provide media that regularly competitors or surpasses human-made creations. This era is reworking industries like entertainment, marketing, education, gaming, and format through making content advent quicker, greater handy, and price-powerful. Filmmakers and sport developers can use AI to generate dynamic scenes, sensible computer graphics, and genuine individual designs, while advertisers can create personalized campaigns tailor-made to particular audiences. Similarly, educators can enlarge interactive mastering gear, and architects can prototype ideas extra effectively. Generative AI also performs a pivotal feature in rising areas like virtual and augmented reality, enriching immersive environments with sensible textures and interactive elements. It aids in cultural protection via digitally recreating artifacts and historic websites and facilitates medical studies thru the advent of correct visible fashions. Beyond improving productiveness, Generative AI fosters creativity, enabling artists and creators to push barriers. However, its adoption increases moral concerns, including copyright infringement and the misuse of deepfakes, which necessitate responsible use. As AI evolves, its capacity to reshape industries and empower creativity maintains to increase, marking a trendy technology in content cloth era.

The goals of this chapter reputation on expertise the transformative impact of Generative AI in digital media creation. Generative AI builds upon foundational era like neural networks, machine gaining knowledge of, and large-scale datasets, reshaping conventional techniques of media manufacturing. Via using exploring these center generation, we intention to find how AI bridges the space among human creativity and machine performance, enabling the introduction of immersive and personalised content(Dong et al., 2015). This financial ruin moreover delves into how Generative AI integrates with virtual media systems, streamlining workflows and increasing the creative possibilities for industries along with amusement, marketing, training, and gaming. Beyond its technical talents, Generative AI gives worrying conditions and opportunities that need interest. From moral issues like copyright infringement to the ability for activity displacement, know-how those implications is important for accountable adoption. On the same time, the generation unlocks exceptional possibilities for creators to innovate in storytelling, artwork, and interactive studies. Through analyzing its integration into conventional workflows and its ability to decorate creativity, this bankruptcy lays the foundation for a future wherein AI-generated content material cloth redefines virtual media. Thru this exploration, we intention to provide a whole view of Generative AI's role in shaping the evolving landscape of digital content material fabric advent.

2. CURRENT MECHANISMS AND CHALLENGES

2.1 Traditional Mechanisms

In advance than the upward thrust of Generative AI, media creation depended in large part on guide hard work and predefined algorithms, requiring huge time, capacity, and resources (Park et al., 2020; Szegedy et al., 2015). Traditional strategies worried a mixture of revolutionary artistry and technical skillability, frequently restricted through the gadget and technology available on the time. Hand-drawn animations represented the top of creativity but have been extremely exertions-intensive. Artists needed to meticulously draw each frame by using manner of hand, a manner that demanded precision and infinite hours to supply even a few seconds of animation. Notwithstanding the allure and authenticity of this approach, it turn out to be neither scalable nor time-efficient.

3-d modeling software like Maya and Blender revolutionized virtual content material cloth creation, permitting designers to craft sensible belongings and animations. But, these gear required massive education and knowledge, and rendering complex scenes can also want to take days or even weeks because of hardware limitations. Inventory media libraries offered pre-created content cloth, imparting a quick answer for creators needing property like pix, films, or animations. At the same time as beneficial, these libraries were regularly limited in customization and creativity, making it hard to attain unique or precise consequences. Traditional mechanisms were effective however lacked the strength, overall performance, and personalization demanded through way of current media industries, paving the manner for the transformative effect of Generative AI media industries, paving the way for the transformative impact of Generative AI.

2.2 Challenges and Limitations

Traditional media introduction strategies, at the same time as progressive for their time, confronted several disturbing conditions that constrained their overall performance and adaptableness in assembly evolving organization desires. Those obstacles underscored the want for greater advanced and bendy answers, ultimately paving the manner for Generative AI. Excessive production charges have been a few of the maximum massive hurdles. Generating excellent media required tremendous investments in device, specialized software program, and skilled employees. As an example, generating an animated film or a industrial can also want to contain large groups of animators, editors, and technicians, using up operational charges. Time-tremendous procedures posed some other obstacle. Manual obligations together with storyboarding, animation body advent, video enhancing, and rendering ate up huge quantities of time, frequently inflicting delays in manufacturing timelines. This inefficiency modified into particularly obvious in industries like advertising and leisure, in which short turnaround instances are essential (Isola et al., 2017).

Skills dependency created bottlenecks in manufacturing workflows. Knowledge in regions like 3-d modeling, animation, and video improving become vital, leaving agencies reliant on a small pool of professionals. This dependency made it challenging to scale operations or meet tight closing dates. Loss of personalization similarly limited revolutionary opportunities. Traditional techniques often relied on predefined templates or inventory belongings, making it hard to create content material fabric tailor-made to precise target marketplace options or cultural contexts. This become mainly problematic in industries which consist of advertising, in which personalized content drives engagement and effect. Those boundaries underscored the inefficiencies of conventional media advent, highlighting the urgent want for transformative technology like Generative AI to conquer those traumatic situations and permit scalable, price-effective, and progressive content material production (Zhang et al., 2019).

2.3 Case Studies

Case Study 1 Animation in the Pre-AI Era

Inside the pre-AI technology, the machine of making an energetic function have become a big mission. A fantastic example is the producing of a prime animated movie by using a globally recognized studio, which took about three years to complete. Artists had been tasked with drawing each body in my view, requiring a awesome degree of detail and precision. For a film with 24 frames consistent with 2d, loads of hundreds of individual drawings have been had to gain clean movement. Collaborative workflows had been hampered by way of the constraints of era. Businesses spread during numerous places confronted disturbing situations in sharing huge files and preserving consistency in art styles. Revisions have been hard work-sizable, regularly requiring complete scenes to be redrawn if errors or innovative modifications had been brought. Furthermore, technological constraints similarly exacerbated the manufacturing timeline. Rendering scenes with early animation software program became time-significant, often taking hours or perhaps days for a single frame. Those inefficiencies added approximately excessive production costs, making it difficult for smaller studios to compete inside the market. The demanding situations of the pre-AI generation emphasized the need for automatic tools to streamline animation production, laying the basis for contemporary generative era.

Case Study 2 Video Effects in Cinema

Conventional cinema confronted comparable challenges in developing seen outcomes (VFX). A conventional example is the manufacturing of high-price range blockbuster films, where large guide compositing and rendering were required to collect practical effects. These strategies frequently delivered months to position up-manufacturing timelines. For example, integrating pc-generated imagery (CGI) with stay-motion pictures involved manually aligning layers, shade grading, and making sure visible consistency. All people demanded meticulous attention to element, and iterative changes had been expensive and time-eating. Collaboration amongst VFX groups became further hindered through the use of the lack of real-time remarks. Artists frequently needed to appearance in advance to hours for render previews, limiting their capacity to check or refine scenes dynamically.

The restrictions of traditional VFX techniques drove innovation in AI-powered answers, permitting faster, extra iterative workflows and growing revolutionary possibilities in cinema.

3. GENERATIVE AI IN IMAGE CREATION

3.1 Overview

Generative AI has added a paradigm shift to photo creation thru permitting machines to offer highly sensible and resourceful visuals from textual descriptions, sketches, or maybe random inputs. This alteration is pushed with the resource of present day technology together with Generative destructive Networks (GANs), Variational Auto Encoders (VAEs), and diffusion models, which work collectively to create pictures with superb detail, precision, and variety. Those era are able to information and replicating problematic styles, textures, lighting fixtures, and shadows, making the generated visuals indistinguishable from human-made creations.

GANs, added in 2014 by means of Ian Goodfellow, use a twin-community machine—a generator and a discriminator—to iteratively refine photograph exceptional. The generator creates snap shots, even as the discriminator evaluates them towards actual-international samples, making sure continuous development. VAEs, as a substitute, excel in producing installed outputs by using the usage of encoding input facts into a latent region and deciphering it to generate versions. Diffusion models simulate methods like Gaussian noise elimination to create high-selection outputs from random noise, including further innovation to the sphere (Kingma & Welling, 2013; Salimans et al., 2016).

The applications of generative AI in picture introduction are brilliant. Designers use AI-generated visuals for speedy prototyping, advertising and advertising organizations craft personalised marketing and marketing campaigns, and artists create virtual masterpieces that push innovative boundaries. Industries like gaming and structure leverage generative AI for immersive environments and realistic renders. Moreover, tools collectively with DALL-E, MidJourney, and stable Diffusion have democratized get proper of access to to the ones talents, enabling human beings and agencies to generate first rate visuals without preceding know-how. But, the generation additionally will increase ethical concerns, which includes copyright infringement and ability misuse in developing deepfakes. In essence, generative AI has redefined the modern gadget, offering extraordinary possibilities in image creation on the equal time as tough conventional strategies and raising critical questions on its accountable use. This stability among innovation and ethics marks the sunrise of a modern generation in visible media.

3.2 Applications of Generative AI in Image Creation

Generative AI is reworking a couple of industries by using supplying gear that permit fast, green, and present day picture introduction. Its diverse applications cater to advertising, design, art, and past, permitting experts to achieve results that blend creativity with technological sophistication.

Advertising

Generative AI is a recreation-changer in advertising. Manufacturers can generate customized product mockups and marketing campaign visuals tailored to unique demographics, enhancing engagement and relevance. As an example, AI-generated imagery can adapt to cultural nuances, showcasing merchandise in severa settings that resonate with nearby audiences. This functionality permits manufacturers to experiment with exceptional styles and ideas with out the need for considerable photoshoots, saving both time and money. Gear like DALL-E and Runway ML permit marketers to create visuals that align perfectly with advertising marketing campaign dreams.

Design

In architecture, fashion, and commercial enterprise format, generative AI supports fast prototyping and conceptual exploration. Architects use AI-generated models to visualize areas with realistic lighting and materials, allowing customers to enjoy designs in advance than creation starts. Fashion designers rent AI to craft virtual garments, test with textures, and simulate how fabric drape on models. Commercial designers can use AI to brainstorm and refine product designs fast, fostering innovation in form and characteristic.

Art

Artists have embraced generative AI to create digital masterpieces that merge human creativity with machine precision. With the aid of way of using algorithms like GANs and VAEs, artists can discover new styles, reinterpret traditional works, or produce completely precise portions. AI art work generators also function collaborators, helping artists push the boundaries of traditional artwork bureaucracy and discover uncharted territories.

Beyond those industries, generative AI is also being applied in gaming, medical imaging, and training, showcasing its adaptability. At the identical time as its capacity continues to grow, ethical issues concerning originality and copyright live critical discussions in its big adoption. Generative AI has undeniably reshaped photo advent, the usage of innovation at some stage in industries.

3.3 Tools and Technologies in Generative AI for Image Creation

Generative AI device and technology have revolutionized the creative system, permitting human beings and industries to provide beautiful visuals without difficulty and precision. Here are a number of the most impactful tools and their specific capabilities

DALL-E

Superior by using OpenAI, DALL-E makes a speciality of generating pics from textual prompts, imparting splendid coherence and creativity. It allows customers to explain a scene or concept in herbal language, and the AI produces corresponding visuals. From surreal paintings to sensible illustrations, DALL-E's versatility helps applications in advertising, storytelling, and conceptual format. Its ability to combination items and patterns in current methods makes it a favorite amongst marketers and artists alike.

Stable Diffusion

Robust Diffusion is a first-rate open-supply generative AI version that excels in producing amazing innovative and conceptual visuals. Appeared for its focus on clarity and detail, it's a preferred device for designers and digital artists. Stable

Diffusion enables customers to high-quality-song parameters, ensuring particular manipulate over the output. Whether growing virtual art work, summary art work, or visualizations for architectural tasks, its adaptability guarantees it meets diverse creative wishes.

MidJourney

MidJourney is designed for crafting visually lovely and unique artwork portions. Renowned for its functionality to create vibrant, imaginative, and otherworldly snap shots, it's broadly used by creators seeking an imaginative facet. Its network-targeted approach encourages collaboration, allowing customers to share and refine their work collectively.

These equipment, powered thru era like Generative adversarial Networks (GANs), Variational Auto Encoders (VAEs), and diffusion models, have democratized get entry to to first-rate image introduction. They empower professionals and fanatics to discover new creative possibilities at the same time as substantially decreasing the time and effort required for traditional processes.

3.4 Ethical Considerations

Generative AI in image creation raises several important ethical considerations

1. Copyright Infringement Many generative AI fashions are educated on big data-sets that could include copyrighted works, by chance reproducing or modifying those substances with out right authorization. This may purpose legal troubles regarding intellectual belongings rights.
2. Misuse functionality AI-generated pictures, particularly deepfakes, may be used maliciously to create misleading or risky content material cloth, together with fake representations or identity manipulation. This will pose sizeable dangers in areas like incorrect information and privacy violations(Radford et al., 2015).
3. Cultural Sensitivity it is important that AI-generated content fabric respects numerous cultural norms and values. Accidental stereotypes or offensive representations can get up, in particular if the schooling facts isn't curated with care, main to risky societal affects.

4. GENERATIVE AI IN VIDEO CREATION

Generative AI has made sizeable strides in the realm of video creation, harnessing advanced device analyzing algorithms to generate dynamic and sensible video content.

With the aid of using reading each spatial and temporal styles, AI can synthesize video sequences that seamlessly aggregate visible and auditory elements, growing immersive reviews. The manner starts off evolved with input data, in conjunction with textual descriptions, static pics, or perhaps audio, which the model uses to generate video frames that transition smoothly through the years. One of the key additives of video synthesis is the expertise of temporal coherence, wherein AI ensures that items, characters, and environments continue to be regular and flow into in a logically present day way in the course of multiple frames. That is critical for producing first rate, plausible video sequences that do not seem static or disjointed.

Generative fashions like Generative adverse Networks (GANs) and Variational Auto Encoders (VAEs) were used to achieve video era. These fashions can be educated on big datasets of movies, analyzing complex functions at the side of movement, lighting, and facial expressions. Once trained, they may generate definitely new movies primarily based on the discovered styles, sometimes with minimal human input. This capability to create films from textual activates, snap shots, or audio has programs across diverse industries, which include entertainment, marketing, training, and simulation. However, it also introduces challenges related to moral concerns, along side the capacity for generating deepfakes or misleading content material, which raises the need for regulation and responsible utilization of the era in video synthesis (Yin, 2024).

4.1 Applications

Generative AI has positioned numerous and impactful applications during numerous industries, revolutionizing video creation

1. Cinema inside the film enterprise, AI notably enhances the advent of visual outcomes (VFX), enabling filmmakers to provide complicated and dynamic scenes with more tempo and efficiency. AI can generate practical backgrounds, simulate natural phenomena, and create existence like CGI characters. This hastens the publish-production system, reduces charges, and opens up innovative opportunities for directors and visual artists. AI-generated video content is likewise used to decorate motion sequences, create alternate storylines, or maybe digitally resurrect actors in a respectful and managed way.

2. Training Generative AI plays a transformative characteristic in training through the usage of permitting the arrival of interactive video tutorials, simulations, and training modules. AI can layout personalised getting to know reviews, growing instructional content material material that adapts to the learner's tempo and needs. In fields along with scientific schooling or technical training, AI-generated films can simulate real-international situations, presenting students with hands-

on practice with out the need for physical system. This technology lets in for the advent of engaging, visible materials that decorate statistics and retention (Yenduri et al., 2024).

3. Gaming AI-generated films are increasingly being used to beautify storytelling in video games, providing immersive cutscenes, dynamic narratives, and adaptive in-recreation sequences. With the resource of generating sensible and responsive video content material, AI contributes to a extra engaging participant experience. This era permits builders to craft unique, interactive worlds wherein video content can evolve in real-time based totally mostly on player choices, similarly blurring the strains amongst conventional cinematics and gameplay.

4.2 Key Technologies

Generative AI in video creation leverages numerous superior era that permit the synthesis of high-quality, dynamic content

1. DeepFakes: Deepfake generation uses neural networks, in particular Generative hostile Networks (GANs), to create relatively sensible face-swapping results. By manner of schooling on good sized datasets of video photos, deepfakes can superimpose faces or alter facial expressions in video sequences, making it seem as even though human beings are saying or doing topics they never did. At the same time as this era has large potential for progressive and amusement applications, it additionally raises ethical concerns, particularly regarding incorrect records and privacy violations(Goodfellow et al., 2016).

2. NeRF (Neural Radiance Fields): NeRF is a present day era that synthesizes 3-D scenes and environments from 2nd pictures. Through studying the spatial relationships between items and the light that interacts with them, NeRF can generate photorealistic 3-d renderings of complex scenes, making it perfect for packages in gaming, film, and virtual reality. NeRF complements video synthesis via way of such as intensity and attitude, allowing the advent of immersive, 3-dimensional worlds from flat pics.

3. Video-to-Video Synthesis: This era extends the abilities of AI to generate new video content material from current films. Via studying styles from input films, AI can create new scenes or adjust current ones, which consist of which include visible outcomes, altering backgrounds, or growing absolutely new sequences. This method is considerably used for video enhancement, content material introduction, and generating sensible situations for film manufacturing.

4. Movement transfer motion switch generation allows the transfer of motion or gestures from one difficulty to every other. The use of deep getting to know models, AI can seize the motion styles of 1 man or woman or item and practice

them to each other, developing fluid and practical animations. This is specifically useful in movie and animation for producing real searching person actions or enhancing virtual performances (Vaswani et al., 2017).

4.3 Limitations

Regardless of the huge functionality of generative AI in video creation, several obstacles remain

1. Excessive Computational costs Rendering great movies through generative AI desires full-size computational power. The technique of synthesizing sensible video sequences calls for state-of-the-art hardware, which includes immoderate-performance GPUs and massive reminiscence capacity. This will lead to high operational expenses, specially for businesses or individuals with restrained access to such resources. As video decision, complexity, and the usage of more than one AI models boom, the computational call for grows exponentially.

2. Body Coherence issues making sure consistency and smooth transitions all through video frames is a crucial mission in AI-generated video. Maintaining temporal coherence, wherein objects and characters waft logically and constantly from body to border, remains a complex task. In plenty of instances, mild discrepancies among frames can purpose unnatural movement or discontinuity within the video, undermining its realism. While improvements have been made, achieving ideal body coherence, in particular in lengthy sequences or incredibly dynamic environments, remains a technical hurdle.

3. Constrained Creativity and Originality in spite of the truth that AI can generate realistic content based on determined patterns, it lacks proper creativity and originality. The AI is restrained thru its schooling statistics, which means it could struggle to offer novel, innovative content fabric outdoor of the styles it's been uncovered to. This obstacle can prevent the capability to generate virtually specific video content fabric with out great human input or similarly refinements.

4. Ethical concerns and Misuse As generative AI technologies emerge as extra trendy, the ability for misuse will increase. Deepfakes and artificial media may be used maliciously to spread misinformation or manage public notion. This raises ethical troubles around responsibility, consent, and the broader impact on society.

5. GENERATIVE AI IN ANIMATION CREATION

5.1 Animation Synthesis Principles

Generative AI in animation creation leverages superior device getting to know algorithms to automate and decorate the animation way, extensively decreasing the time and effort required for classic animation techniques. The center principle at the back of animation synthesis is predicting item moves and environmental modifications over time. Via the use of studying the relationships among items, characters, and their environment, AI fashions can mechanically generate frames that constitute fluid movement and realistic interactions. Not like conventional animation, which heavily is predicated on manual keyframing—wherein animators outline key points of movement—generative AI can interpolate and create the in-among frames (frequently referred to as "tweens") primarily based mostly on the given data. This lets in for faster manufacturing cycles and extra performance, in particular in responsibilities that require giant sequences, consisting of television shows, films, or video games.

AI models are typically educated on massive datasets of animations and real-international motion capture information to analyze patterns of motion, frame dynamics, and interactions among characters and their environments. By using way of predicting how elements in a scene should move and evolve over the years, generative AI can create complex, practical animations with minimum human enter. This device now not best accelerates production however additionally opens up creative possibilities. Animators can take a look at with dynamic, responsive animations that adapt to adjustments in the scene, including adjustments in lighting, character movements, or environmental situations, all at the equal time as retaining consistency and realism. As a give up result, generative AI is reworking how animations are created, making them greater green, flexible, and modern.

5.2 Techniques

Generative AI employs numerous advanced techniques to enhance animation introduction, enhancing every the amazing and overall performance of the technique

1. Pose Estimation AI can are watching for and generate existence like poses for characters via reading sizable datasets of human actions. By using using deep gaining knowledge of fashions, AI identifies key points of the human frame and successfully determines the posture and function of characters in distinct conditions. This allows animators to create practical poses with out manually adjusting each frame, ensuring smooth transitions and real looking movements.

2. Movement seize Augmentation uncooked movement seize records, while trea-sured, frequently requires refinement to obtain clean and sensible animations. AI complements this information with the resource of having rid of noise, correcting errors, and producing intermediate frames for more fluid transitions. This technique allows animators to advantage better-first-rate animations with much less guide intervention, ensuring herbal and seamless movement.

3. Physics Simulations AI simulates sensible interactions among objects primarily based on environmental elements, which includes gravity, friction, and cloth homes. With the resource of predicting how gadgets need to react to forces or collisions, AI can generate accurate and believable interactions between char-acters and their environment, enhancing the overall realism of the animation.

4. Fashion switch style transfer strategies permit AI to use the visible style of 1 animation or artwork to some other. This will be used to replicate a selected creative approach or to create specific visual outcomes which might be everyday with the tone of the animation. AI learns the traits of a chosen style—which include brushstrokes, textures, or shade palettes—and applies it to new scenes or characters.

5. Facial expression Synthesis AI models can anticipate and generate facial ex-pressions primarily based at the context of the scene or the emotions of the character. Through reading facial landmarks and emotional cues, AI can create sensible and varied expressions, which can be critical for conveying emotions and improving character development.

5.3 Use Cases

Generative AI in animation advent is reworking numerous industries by way of providing efficient, progressive solutions for dynamic content material advent. Right here are a few key use cases

1. Gaming inside the gaming organisation, real-time person animations generated via AI decorate player immersion. AI permits characters to react dynamically to the participant's moves, developing fluid and responsive animations. This permits for additonal interactive and realistic NPC (non-playable person) movements, facial expressions, and combat sequences. Via adapting to in-recreation activi-ties, AI-generated animations make video games more attractive, contributing to a seamless gaming revel in that feels herbal and responsive.

2. Movie AI-driven animation strategies are streamlining the producing of motion-heavy and complicated scenes in films. For example, AI can generate realistic combat sequences, environmental changes, or crowd actions, decreasing the need for manual animation of each body. This accelerates put up-manufactur-

ing, decreases costs, and gives filmmakers with more flexibility in visualizing complex scenes. AI equipment also can help in growing super animations in visual outcomes (VFX), from explosions to fluid dynamics, ensuing in faster turnaround instances and more innovative possibilities.

3. Digital fact (VR) AI-generated animations play a crucial position in developing dynamic, interactive VR testimonies. In virtual environments, animations that respond to person moves are critical for immersion. AI can generate practical avatars, environmental adjustments, and actual-time object interactions that decorate the person's enjoy of presence. Whether or not it's for training simulations, academic tales, or gaming, AI-pushed animations help supply VR worlds to life by presenting clean, realistic movement and feedback primarily based totally on person input.

5.4 Tools

Generative AI is increasingly more included into well-known animation and game improvement platforms, enhancing their abilties by using the use of automating complicated responsibilities and allowing more green workflows. A number of the key equipment making the most of AI integration include

1. Blender: Blender, an open-supply three-D modeling and animation software program, leverages generative AI to automate various factors of animation introduction. AI-powered equipment in Blender can expect and generate practical person actions, facial expressions, and object interactions, decreasing the time spent on guide animation responsibilities. Furthermore, AI-based simulation techniques in Blender help automate cloth simulation, particle effects, and unique physics-based absolutely animations, making it easier for artists to consciousness on the innovative elements of their paintings.

2. Unreal Engine: Unreal Engine, a widely used platform for activity improvement, real-time rendering, and VR experiences, additionally blessings from AI integration. In Unreal Engine, generative AI equipment can decorate character animation via mechanically generating reasonable actions and interactions. AI also assists in generating dynamic environmental changes, collectively with climate, lights, and terrain changes, based totally on sport properly judgment. This permits developers to create greater immersive and responsive worlds with lots much less manual try. Moreover, AI-driven procedural technology can assist create large open-global environments or unique gameplay situations dynamically.

3. Autodesk: Maya is any other industry-famous tool that integrates AI to assist animators in automating techniques like rigging, skinning, and producing practical

animations. AI-driven strategies help streamline person animation workflows via way of predicting and producing poses or actions based totally on person input.

4. Team spirit harmony, another recreation development engine, uses AI to generate procedural animations and sensible interactions. AI enables in automating character movement, facial animation, and scene transitions in brotherly love, making it less difficult for builders to create practical and dynamic stories.

6. INTEGRATING GENERATIVE AI IN VIRTUAL MEDIA

6.1 Workflow Optimization

Generative AI considerably optimizes workflows in digital media manufacturing thru automating repetitive and time-eating responsibilities, permitting creators to cognizance on more complicated and modern elements. One of the key packages is automating rendering tactics. Rendering, which involves producing final visual frames from three-D models, is regularly useful resource-extensive and time-consuming. With AI integration, the rendering method may be extended through sensible algorithms which might be anticipating and optimize the rendering technique, decreasing time and hardware requirements. This not best quickens production timelines however additionally reduces associated prices, making the general workflow more green.

Generative AI can also help in tasks which includes scene technology, lights adjustments, and texture mapping, making sure these elements are handled short and correctly. AI can routinely alter scene compositions primarily based totally on predefined parameters, create versions of textures, or even beautify visible outcomes in real time. This automation reduces the load on artists and architects, letting them spend extra time on creative selection-making in preference to habitual obligations (Mikolov et al., 2013).

6.2 Collaborative Tools in Modern Creative Software

Cutting-edge innovative tools have advanced to seamlessly integrate AI capabilities, enhancing the collaborative process between human creators and AI systems. This fusion of human ingenuity and machine intelligence fosters a greater dynamic and iterative technique to creativity, the usage of innovation in diverse fields like format, tune, writing, and video production.AI-powered device offer sensible help, supplying guidelines, automating repetitive obligations, and studying statistics to optimize workflows. For instance, in format, AI can generate layouts or shade schemes based totally totally on consumer inputs, dashing up the conceptualization phase. Similarly, in song manufacturing, AI can assist create complicated melodies or offer real-time comments on composition.

These system do now not update human creativity however instead increase it. With the aid of decreasing mundane obligations, AI permits creators to focus on higher-level selection-making and creative exploration. Additionally, AI's potential to research tremendous portions of facts facilitates pick out developments, inspire new thoughts, and suggest upgrades primarily based on preceding paintings. Collaborative tools moreover allow real-time interplay among creators, regardless of their geographical place. Cloud-based totally structures permit for seamless sharing, enhancing, and remarks collection, ensuring that every one crew members stay aligned and that ideas may be constantly delicate.

In end, the integration of AI into innovative software program is transforming the innovative enterprise. It fosters collaborative surroundings in which human competencies and AI talents come collectively to push the boundaries of what's viable, leading to progressive and sensitive outputs (Berthelot et al., 2017).

6.3 Scalability With Generative AI

Generative AI appreciably enhances scalability in content material creation, offering powerful answers for dynamic content material generation and large-scale obligations.

1. Dynamic content material technology AI can tailor media reports to fit a huge range of audiences. By means of the usage of reading man or woman options and conduct, generative AI creates personalized content material that resonates with person tastes. That is specifically precious in industries like leisure, advertising and marketing, and gaming, where targeted, engaging evaluations are essential. AI systems can autonomously generate content fabric which includes articles, videos, or even undertaking environments, adapting in actual-time to purchaser interactions or statistics inputs.

2. Huge-Scale tasks within the manufacturing of complicated digital environments, AI dramatically improves performance. As an example, inside the gaming and movie industries, where large-scale and difficult 3-D worlds are required, generative AI can create big landscapes, characters, and property in a fraction of the time it'd take the use of traditional strategies. AI's ability to generate and alter those property on name for ensures that teams can popularity on creativity at the identical time as decreasing manual labor, making huge-scale tasks more viable and fee-powerful.

7. FUTURE TRENDS IN GENERATIVE AI FOR VIRTUAL MEDIA

7.1 Real-Time Content Generation

Improvements in AI are paving the manner for real-time synthesis of pics, movement images, and animations, growing new possibilities for interactive AR/VR reviews. As AI maintains to evolve, it'll permit creators to generate immersive and dynamic content right now, permitting customers to interact with digital environments which is probably continuously adapting to their movements. This real-time content material generation will revolutionize gaming, amusement, and schooling through providing seamless, custom designed reports that reply to person input at the fly.

7.2 AI-Driven Storytelling

Generative AI is reworking the manner tales are created, helping in scriptwriting and storyboarding through suggesting creative plotlines and visualizations primarily based totally on input turns on and target audience possibilities. AI can examine huge portions of statistics to understand narrative systems, individual development, and pacing, assisting writers craft more appealing and dynamic testimonies. With the aid of way of understanding target market tastes, AI might also even are expecting what plot twists or narrative elements will resonate most, presenting treasured insights for developing compelling, customized content material across movie, television, and interactive media.

7.3 Advanced Personalization

AI's potential to tailor content cloth to character user selections is shaping the destiny of leisure, schooling, and advertising. In amusement, AI can create specific viewing reviews based totally mostly on a user's viewing records or emotional reactions. In education, customized analyzing paths may be evolved to comply to every scholar's strengths and weaknesses. In marketing and advertising, AI-driven personalization can craft targeted campaigns that engage customers in meaningful approaches, enhancing emblem loyalty and conversion rates. As AI maintains to broaden, customized content material cloth will become extra immersive, imparting bespoke research tailor-made to the dreams and desires of all of us.

8. CONCLUSION

Generative AI has sincerely revolutionized the panorama of digital media, imparting innovative gadget that permit creators to generate, customise, and scale content fabric with brilliant ease. Thru seamlessly integrating gadget mastering and innovative tactics, AI has empowered industries alongside enjoyment, advertising, gaming, and training to push boundaries, creating more dynamic, appealing, and custom designed reviews than ever in advance than.

But, as with each technological development, worrying conditions stay, including troubles over ethics, first-rate control, and the capability displacement of conventional innovative jobs. Even as those traumatic situations require cautious interest, the advantages of generative AI are easy. The capability to create widespread quantities of content cloth, tailor studies to person options, and boost up production workflows has validated helpful in contemporary fast-paced virtual worldwide.

Looking earlier, the continuing evolution of generative AI promises an splendid brighter future for every creators and customers. As AI structures emerge as extra state-of-the-art, they'll in addition foster creativity, beautify efficiency, and open new avenues for innovation. This synergy among human creators and AI-driven equipment will sincerely form the subsequent generation of virtual media, growing countless possibilities for innovative exploration and interactive, customized reviews. The destiny isn't just about the usage of AI—it's about taking element with it to release new realms of creativity and expression.

REFERENCES

Berthelot, D., Schumm, T., & Metz, L. (2017). BEGAN: Boundary equilibrium generative adversarial networks. *arXiv*. https://arxiv.org/abs/1703.10717

Dong, C., Loy, C. C., He, K., & Tang, X. (2016). Image super-resolution using deep convolutional networks. *IEEE Transactions on Pattern Analysis and Machine Intelligence, 38*(2), 295–307. DOI: 10.1109/TPAMI.2015.2439281 PMID: 26761735

Goodfellow, I., Bengio, Y., & Courville, A. (2016). *Deep learning*. MIT Press.

Isola, P., Zhu, J.-Y., Zhou, T., & Efros, A. A. (2017). Image-to-image translation with conditional adversarial networks. In *2017 IEEE Conference on Computer Vision and Pattern Recognition (CVPR)* (pp. 1125–1134). IEEE. DOI: 10.1109/CVPR.2017.632

Kingma, D. P., & Welling, M. (2013). Auto-encoding variational Bayes. *arXiv*. https://arxiv.org/abs/1312.6114

Mikolov, T., Sutskever, I., Chen, K., Corrado, G. S., & Dean, J. (2013). Distributed representations of words and phrases and their compositionality. In *Advances in Neural Information Processing Systems* (Vol. 26). https://papers.nips.cc/paper/5021-distributed-representations-of-words-and-phrases-and-their-compositionality

Park, C., Yang, Y., Park, K., & Lim, H. (2020). Decoding strategies for improving low-resource machine translation. *Electronics (Basel), 9*(10), 1562. DOI: 10.3390/electronics9101562

Radford, A., Metz, L., & Chintala, S. (2015). Unsupervised representation learning with deep convolutional generative adversarial networks. *arXiv*. https://arxiv.org/abs/1511.06434

Salimans, T., Goodfellow, I., Zaremba, W., Cheung, V., Radford, A., & Chen, X. (2016). Improved techniques for training GANs. In *Advances in Neural Information Processing Systems* (Vol. 29). https://papers.nips.cc/paper/6125-improved-techniques-for-training-gans

Szegedy, C., Liu, W., Jia, Y., Sermanet, P., Reed, S., Anguelov, D., & Rabinovich, A. (2015). Going deeper with convolutions. In *2015 IEEE Conference on Computer Vision and Pattern Recognition (CVPR)* (pp. 1–9). IEEE. DOI: 10.1109/CVPR.2015.7298594

Van den Oord, A., Kalchbrenner, N., & Kavukcuoglu, K. (2016). Pixel recurrent neural networks. In *Proceedings of the 33rd International Conference on Machine Learning* (Vol. 48, pp. 1747–1756). PMLR. http://proceedings.mlr.press/v48/oord16.html

Vaswani, A., Shazeer, N., Parmar, N., Uszkoreit, J., Jones, L., Gomez, A. N., . . . Polosukhin, I. (2017). Attention is all you need. In *Advances in Neural Information Processing Systems* (Vol. 30). https://papers.nips.cc/paper/7181-attention-is-all-you-need

Yenduri, G., Ramalingam, M., Selvi, G. C., Supriya, Y., Srivastava, G., Maddikunta, P. K. R., Raj, G. D., Jhaveri, R. H., Prabadevi, B., Wang, W., Vasilakos, A. V., & Gadekallu, T. R. (2024). GPT (Generative Pre-trained Transformer)—A comprehensive review on enabling technologies, potential applications, emerging challenges, and future directions. *IEEE Access : Practical Innovations, Open Solutions*, *12*, 54608–54649. DOI: 10.1109/ACCESS.2024.3389497

Yin, L. (2024). A review of text-to-image synthesis methods. In *2024 5th International Conference on Computer Vision, Image and Deep Learning (CVIDL)* (pp. 858–861). IEEE. DOI: 10.1109/CVIDL62147.2024.10603609

Zhang, H., Goodfellow, I., Metaxas, D., & Odena, A. (2019). Self-attention generative adversarial networks. In *Proceedings of the 36th International Conference on Machine Learning* (Vol. 97, pp. 7354–7363). PMLR. http://proceedings.mlr.press/v97/zhang19d.html

Chapter 10
Generative AI in Text and Multi-Language Adaptation Processing for Digital Media

R. Roselinkiruba
https://orcid.org/0000-0001-7941-5142
Independent Researcher, India

M. Vasumathy
Kingston Engineering College, India

J. Jude Moses Anto Devakanth J.
https://orcid.org/0000-0003-2921-0098
Madanapalle Institute of Technology and Science, India

Saranya Jothi C.
Vel Tech Rangarajan Dr. Sagunthala R&D Institute of Science and Technology, India

L. Sharmila
https://orcid.org/0000-0002-4990-9982
Vel Tech Rangarajan Dr. Sagunthala R&D Institute of Science and Technology, India

ABSTRACT

Text and language processing have been transformed by generative AI, opening the door to sophisticated digital media applications including sentiment analysis, translation, content creation, and summarization. Despite improvements, there

DOI: 10.4018/979-8-3373-1504-1.ch010

are still many issues with current models, such as inadequate glyph management, inability to adapt to different fonts and scripts, inconsistent semantics, and high processing requirements. These drawbacks make it difficult to use them practically in situations where accurate, context-aware text rendering is necessary. By combining Glyph Conditional Control and T5, this work presents GlyphControl-T5, a novel hybrid model that improves font consistency, multi-language adaptation, and visual-text coherence. To overcome the fundamental drawbacks of current visual text generation models, the suggested method combines multi-modal embeddings, glyph-aware visual restrictions, and an efficient learning framework.

1. INTRODUCTION TO GENERATIVE AI IN DIGITAL MEDIA

Information on generative AI (Artificial Intelligence) has been trend in the Internet since Open AI released as the open version of Chat GPT at the end of 2020 (Wang et al., 2023; Wu et al., 2023), creates a lot of attraction from researchers and the common people. Text creation, processing, and consumption in digital media have all changed as a result of generative AI. The way that generative AI was addressed online has received much too little attention up to this point. Furthermore, little is known about how social media and academia interact when talking about generative AI. In other words, the public's discussion about generative AI is not fully understood by academic circles, and vice versa. AI can now produce prose that is human-like, summarize articles, translate languages, and even help with creative writing by utilizing deep learning models. The scalability of content generation has been developed increased by the emergence of Large Language Models (LLMs) like GPT (Generative Pre-Trained Transformer), uses AI necessary tool for multiple of media platforms. The implementation of AI in processing text and the process of LLMs in digital media are examined. The false and misleading data has been a great impact on the internet. The emergence of generative AI has created a problem worse than ever. The misinformation of data produced by automated systems or by any person, has historically significantly generate obstacles to the information ecosystems, public discourse, and institutional trust. The content moderation techniques and legal frameworks have been developed to combat conventional types of disinformation, it leads to the sufficient method to handle the complexity of the AI-generated content.

It's crucial for policymakers, engineers, and regulators to recognize that generative AI introduces a new kind of risk that current systems aren't fully equipped to handle. What sets generative AI apart is its ability to create content that's not only highly personalized but also interactive and able to adapt in real-time, making it very persuasive. This means AI can craft unique messages tailored specifically to each person, based on their online behavior, preferences, emotional state, and vulnerabilities. Researchers have named this ability to produce personalized, persuasive content on a large scale "Interactive Generative Media," which marks a big shift from older types of deception. One of the most pressing concerns here is the threat to what's called epistemic agency — our ability to form, hold, and change our beliefs through reasoning, evidence, and free will. When AI-generated content subtly influences or distorts a person's understanding of the truth without them realizing it, their epistemic agency can be seriously compromised. Instead of thoughtfully evaluating information, people may end up forming opinions because they've been nudged or manipulated by these AI-driven persuasive techniques.

The wider social and economic consequences of this technology are quite alarming. If many people lose their ability to think independently and critically—a concept known as epistemic agency—the political fallout could be serious. For example, authoritarian governments or malicious actors might use generative AI to sway public opinion or spread propaganda aligned with their goals. Through interactive, AI-driven media, they could quietly promote authoritarian ideas, weaken faith in democratic institutions, or erode trust in unbiased news and scientific facts.

Generative AI poses more than just a risk of spreading misinformation—it could fundamentally change how information is created, shared, and consumed. This new form of content, called Interactive Generative Media (IGM), is a significant technological breakthrough. Unlike traditional digital content like articles, videos, or social posts created for large groups, IGM generates tailored content in real-time using powerful AI. What sets it apart is its ability to precisely target individuals and adjust its messaging instantly based on how users respond.

Imagine the difference between firing a shotgun that spreads pellets everywhere and launching a heat-seeking missile aimed directly at a target. IGM works like that missile, honing in on each person with custom messages that adapt to their reactions. This kind of media can change its style, tone, and emotional pull depending on the user's interactions, making it highly persuasive and engaging.

A good example is targeted generative advertising, where AI creates personalized ads on the fly using detailed data about users. These systems consider not only basic demographics like age and gender but also deeper factors like interests, values, beliefs, tastes, past purchases, and even emotional triggers. The visuals, including the people shown, their clothing and expressions, and the overall design and fonts, are all adjusted to connect better with each individual. Depending on what resonates most, the message might be more logical or emotional to have the greatest influence.

In order to improve future advertisements, tech platforms will also be able to monitor engagement data like click-through rates, viewing duration, and interaction patterns. The system learns over time: Do you react more favorably to pictures of slick bachelors driving fancy automobiles or nuclear families. The emotionally charged stories or arguments based on logic move. In essence, the advertising model turns into a closed-loop system of feedback and influence that continuously improves to better target specific people. The threat comes from both the effectiveness of these methods and the demands of competition that will probably encourage their usage. Businesses who implement aggressive IGM tactics will have a major edge in creating engagement and income in an uncontrolled market.

Even companies committed to doing the right thing may feel pressured to use manipulative technologies just to keep up with competitors. As businesses move away from simple, one-way advertisements like banners or recorded commercials and embrace more interactive, conversational methods of influence, the line between honest persuasion and psychological manipulation becomes less clear.

The rapid growth of interactive generative media presents a tricky problem for regulators. On one hand, this technology offers incredible new ways to target and engage people with personalized content, opening doors for creative advances in marketing, education, and entertainment. On the other hand, if left unchecked, it risks undermining people's privacy, their ability to think independently, and even the foundations of democratic society.

Because of these challenges, it's essential to establish thoughtful policies and ethical standards that guide the responsible development and use of these powerful tools, balancing innovation with protection of individual rights.

1.1 Evolution of AI in Text Processing

From rule-based systems to contemporary deep learning techniques, text processing has changed throughout time. The significant turning points in this progression are:

a) Rule-Based Systems

Rule-based systems dominated text processing in the early days of artificial intelligence and computational linguistics. To analyse and interpret language, these systems used well created linguistic rules that were manually created. For instance, sentence structures were analysed using syntax trees and grammars, and key words or phrases were found by matching patterns, such as regular expressions. Because manual rule updates were necessary for any change in language usage, these systems were extremely domain-specific, frequently fragile, and lacked adaptability. They were effectively employed in early chatbot systems, grammar checkers, and information extraction tools, and despite their rigidity, they established the foundation for formal language understanding.

- For text analysis, early computational linguistics depended on manually created rules.
- These systems processed text using specified language structures and pattern matching.

b) Statistical methods

Statistical techniques to text processing emerged in the 1990s and 2000s as a result of the development of computing power and the accessibility of massive text corpora. These techniques discovered patterns in the data rather than depending just on manually created rules. While Hidden Markov Models (HMMs) were extensively utilised in speech recognition and part-of-speech tagging, Naïve Bayes classifiers gained popularity for tasks like text classification and spam detection. These models enhanced the ability of systems to scale and adapt by understanding the likelihood of connections between words and language patterns. While the move to statistical learning allowed machines to better manage messy and unorganized language data, they still struggled to grasp complex language structures or maintain context over longer stretches of text.

- Large text corpora might now be analyzed by AI thanks to the development of Natural Language Processing (NLP) techniques.
- For tasks such as sentiment analysis and speech recognition, Naïve Bayes classifiers and Hidden Markov Models (HMMs) were employed.

c) Deep learning

Deep learning brought a major transformation to how computers understand and process text. Early models like Recurrent Neural Networks (RNNs) and their improved versions, Long Short-Term Memory networks (LSTMs), allowed machines to process language in order by keeping track of previous words. This helped improve tasks such as translating languages, analyzing sentiment, and answering questions. However, these models had trouble understanding long passages because they couldn't effectively capture connections over extended text.

To solve this, researchers introduced Transformer models, highlighted by the influential 2017 paper "Attention is All You Need" by Vaswani and others. Transformers use a technique called self-attention, which lets the model weigh the importance of every word in a sentence no matter where it appears. Unlike RNNs that work step-by-step, Transformers can process many words at once, making them much better at understanding the overall meaning. This breakthrough reshaped natural language processing and led to flexible language models that are pre-trained on huge amounts of text and can be fine-tuned for specific tasks

- .Language modeling was enhanced by the development of LSTM networks and RNNs.
- By enabling models to manage long-range dependencies in text, transformer models (completely changed text processing.

1.2 Role of LLMs

Large Language Models, or LLMs, are a type of AI designed to read and generate text that sounds like it was written by a human. They learn from enormous collections of text—everything from books and news articles to websites and social media posts. These models use advanced deep learning methods, especially transformer-based neural networks, which help them pick up on subtle language details like grammar, context, and common patterns. Thanks to this training, LLMs can tackle a variety of tasks such as writing creatively, summarizing information, translating languages, and answering questions.

However, LLMs aren't perfect. One key issue is that the data they learn from can contain biases, which might cause the AI to unintentionally repeat stereotypes about things like gender, race, religion, or culture. Another challenge is that these models generate text based on patterns they've seen, not verified facts, which means they sometimes produce incorrect or misleading information—this is often called "hallucination." Such mistakes can be particularly problematic in important fields like healthcare, legal advice, or education.

These strengths and weaknesses have had a big influence on digital media in many different ways:

a) Content Automation

AI models like GPT can save a lot of time and effort by creating quality written content such as articles, blog posts, scripts, and reports. This makes it easier for news organizations, marketing teams, and publishers to boost their output without needing extra human resources. Businesses also use platforms like ChatGPT, Jasper AI, and Copy AI to quickly generate persuasive marketing copy and advertisements that connect with their audiences.

b) **Analysis and Summarization of Texts**

Large Language Models can help by condensing long texts into short summaries, allowing people to understand key information much more quickly. By highlighting important points from reports, research papers, or in-depth news items, they improve accessibility. AI-powered summarization is used by businesses for legal document analysis, product reviews, and customer service.

c) **Localization & Language Translation**

LLMs are used by AI models such as DeepL and Google Translate to produce translations that are almost human-level. Companies can increase their market reach by localizing their content for people around the world. Language difficulties in communication can be overcome with the use of real-time AI translation systems.

d) **Interactive Digital Media & Chatbots**

AI chatbots powered by LLMs enhance customer engagement through real-time conversation. Virtual assistants like Siri, Alexa, and Google Assistant use LLMs for better user interaction. AI-driven storytelling and interactive narratives are revolutionizing entertainment and gaming.

1.3 Problems with Current Visual Text Generation Models

Even though models that generate text from images have improved a lot recently, they still face some important hurdles. They often find it hard to deeply understand complex visuals, which can lead to descriptions that are either incorrect or too basic. These models can also pick up biases from the data they were trained on, especially if that data wasn't carefully curated. On top of that, they sometimes create "hallucinations" — mentioning objects or actions that aren't actually in the picture. Furthermore, a lot of models struggle to correctly link textual outputs to particular areas of a picture because they lack adequate visual grounding. When used on domain-specific or real-world images that are outside of their training scope, they also frequently exhibit subpar performance. Additionally, ethical issues including consent, data privacy, and the usage of copyrighted works have not been addressed. These restrictions show how multimodal AI has to be developed in a more reliable, open, and morally sound manner.

- **Inadequate Management of Fine-Grained Glyph**

Text in generated images is deformed or unintelligible due to existing models' difficulties with accurate character structure, alignment, and spacing (kerning).

- **Challenges Managing Complicated Fonts and Multilingual Assistance**

Due of ligature complexity and distinctive writing styles, most AI models are designed for Latin-based characters and are unable to produce text in complex languages like Arabic, Chinese, and Devanagari.

- Mismatch between Semantics and Structure

AI-generated text is inappropriate for design applications since it frequently does not convey the intended message or accurately connect with visual aspects in a picture.

- Insufficient Context Awareness in the Integration of Images and Text

Font size, contrast, and placement are not dynamically changed by models in response to backdrop.

- Expensive computations and complicated training

Large datasets and powerful Graphics Processing Unit (GPUs) or Tensor Processing Unit (TPUs) are needed to train visual text generation models, which makes them costly and unsuitable for real-time or edge computing applications.

- Challenges in Assessment and Comparison

Readability, aesthetic quality, and glyph accuracy are not adequately captured by standard NLP measures such as Bilingual Evaluation Understudy (BLEU), Recall-Oriented Understudy for Gisting Evaluation (ROUGE), and Bidirectional Encoder Representations from Transformers (BERT) Score, which results in inconsistent model comparisons.

1.4 AI Technics in Text Processing

Over time, text processing has changed dramatically, moving from rule-based systems to deep learning models that can comprehend and produce writing that is human-like. NLP has seen tremendous advancements due to AI, making it possible for machines to process, analyse, and produce text more effectively. In order to enhance text processing skills, statistical NLP established probabilistic models that made use of vast volumes of text data. With this method, manually created criteria gave way to insights based on data. Employed statistical techniques for text processing, including Naïve Bayes classifiers and HMM.

2. EXISTING METHOD

When it comes to producing high-quality images with text suggestions, the Denoising Diffusion Probabilistic Model (Ho et al., 2020) and its offspring have shown remarkable performance. The need of classifier-free guidance is emphasised by CLIP direction and the use of cascaded diffusion models for high-fidelity, high-resolution generation (Ho et al., 2020). While exhibiting image quality that is on par with or better than that of the CLIP text encoder, Imagen (Saharia et al., 2022) incorporates generic large language models (T5-XXL text encoder) into the text-to-image production process. Users could overlay further criteria, like segmentation maps or depth maps (Rombach et al., 2022), onto diffusion models to provide more individualised image synthesis. In addition to this natural method, several diffusion-based image editing techniques (Meng et al., 2021) show promising results in terms of managing the synthetic visual content. More recent related efforts (Zhang et al., 2023) have concentrated on controlling picture synthesis in a flexible and decomposable manner. We use ControlNet as the fundamental foundation to create visual text by modifying the local structure with more glyphs because the glyphs of visual text basically belong to geometric structures.

Stable Diffusion and unCLIP (Ramesh et al., 2022), two popular text-to-image generation techniques, struggle to produce readable and legible text onto images. Numerous earlier studies (Gui et al., 2023) show that diffusion models can produce visual text in a variety of fonts, but they are not capable of producing images in general. Because CLIP embedding was shown to be unable to accurately interpret the spelling information in the input prompts, Imagen and eDiff-I (Balaji et al., 2022) both use the big language model T5 (Raffel et al., 2020) to generate better visual texts. Additionally, Liu et al. (2022) fully utilises the advantages of character-aware language models, such as ByT5 (Xue et al., 2022), over their character-blind counterparts, primarily CLIP and T5. While glyph layout issues persist, semantic faults in rendered text reduce when ByT5 is used in the generating process suggesting that further glyph image information might be required. By including glyph images as input for the diffusion model and combining extracted glyph embedding with text embedding as a requirement, GlyphDraw (Ma et al., 2023; RoselinKiruba et al., 2024) is able to draw Chinese characters onto photos with success. We use glyph images as conditional maps to regulate image synthesis based on related ideas. In contrast to the aforementioned techniques, we could define the contents, placements, and text sizes, resulting in more flexible and personalised designs.

The suggested method adds structured glyph representations as an extra conditioning input in addition to standard textual prompts to improve the quality and control of visual text generation. In order to generate visual material, traditional text-to-image generation methods usually only use text-based descriptions. However, especially in complex or multilingual scenarios, this frequently results in inconsistent rendered text in terms of spatial layout, legibility, and stylistic coherence. Our approach overcomes these drawbacks and improves the accuracy of the produced visual text by using glyph-level information, which depicts the structural, spatial, and stylistic shape of individual characters. We formulate this job as a glyph-conditioned control problem, in which spatial priors contained in glyph inputs directly influence the creation process. By serving as visual scaffolding, these glyphs provide the model with information on the form, location, and stylistic characteristics of the characters or symbols that need to be produced. Instead of focusing only on the language, the algorithm learns to link the meaning of the text with the specific visual elements. This way, the output stays true to the image while also making sense and fitting the context. More control over text layout, alignment, font style, and even multi-lingual representation is made possible by this conditioning; these are features that are frequently challenging to accomplish with text-only prompts. The suggested approach views glyph input as a universal conditioning mechanism for visual text production, drawing inspiration from the T5 (Text-to-Text Transfer Transformer) framework, which unifies NLP tasks under a common text-to-text formulation. Our approach incorporates glyphs as a versatile and generalisable input modality across many text rendering tasks, much like T5 uses a single model to handle translation, summarisation, and question answering by rephrasing each task as a text transfor-mation. The network can jointly learn from both semantic (textual) and structural (glyph) representations thanks to its design, producing visual outputs that are far more accurate, organised, and consistent with the desired form and meaning. More interpretable and user-controllable visual text production systems are made possi-ble by the unified framework, which may be used for anything from digital art and cross-lingual signage to creative typography and stylised captions.

3. PROPOSED GLYPHCONTROL-T5 MODEL

The diagram shows a glyph-based multimodal learning framework that uses a box-level aim to match verbal and visual representations of characters or symbols. At the heart of this system is a training goal called the box-level objective, which helps keep the text and image information in sync. The model has two main parts: one that processes text and another that works with images. For the text part, it uses a special version of the T5 model called Glyph-T5, which is designed to handle glyph prompts—these are text instructions specifying certain characters or styles. To better understand style details, the model also takes into account font type and color.

On the image side, a visual encoder picks up fine details like shapes, strokes, and designs from pictures of glyphs. Both parts are supported by a module that tweaks the text and images by adding variations or distortions, helping the model learn to handle different styles and imperfections.

This box-level objective brings together the meaning from the text and the visual details from the images, improving the model's performance on tasks such as recognizing fonts, learning combined text-image features, and creating stylized text.

To manage the inputs, the model uses the DINOv2 encoder for images and the Glyph-ByT5 encoder for text, allowing it to combine information from both sources effectively. The process of glyph augmentation is used to produce augmented representations. By ensuring that corresponding text and image embeddings are closely aligned, a contrastive aim enhances glyph comprehension and retrieval. Using both text and image embeddings, this graphic illustrates a contrastive learning paradigm for glyph augmentation is shown in Fig.1. The important elements and justification are:

- Contrastive Objective at the Box Level

By employing contrastive learning, the system seeks to match glyph representations in text and images at the box level.

- Pathway for Text-Embeddings:

Glyph-ByT5 Text Encoder: This module takes glyph representations in text and extracts their embeddings.

- Color and Font Type Special Token Encoding: To enhance text embeddings, special encoding is used to capture font-type and color-specific characteristics of the glyph.
- Pathway for Image-Embeddings:

DINOv2 The Visual Encoder This module creates picture embeddings by processing visual glyph representations. It appears to be frozen or pre-trained based on the snowflake emblem.

- Glyph Augmentation:

A procedure that uses augmentation techniques to improve both textual and visual representations.

Figure 1. Contrastive learning framework for glyph augmentation

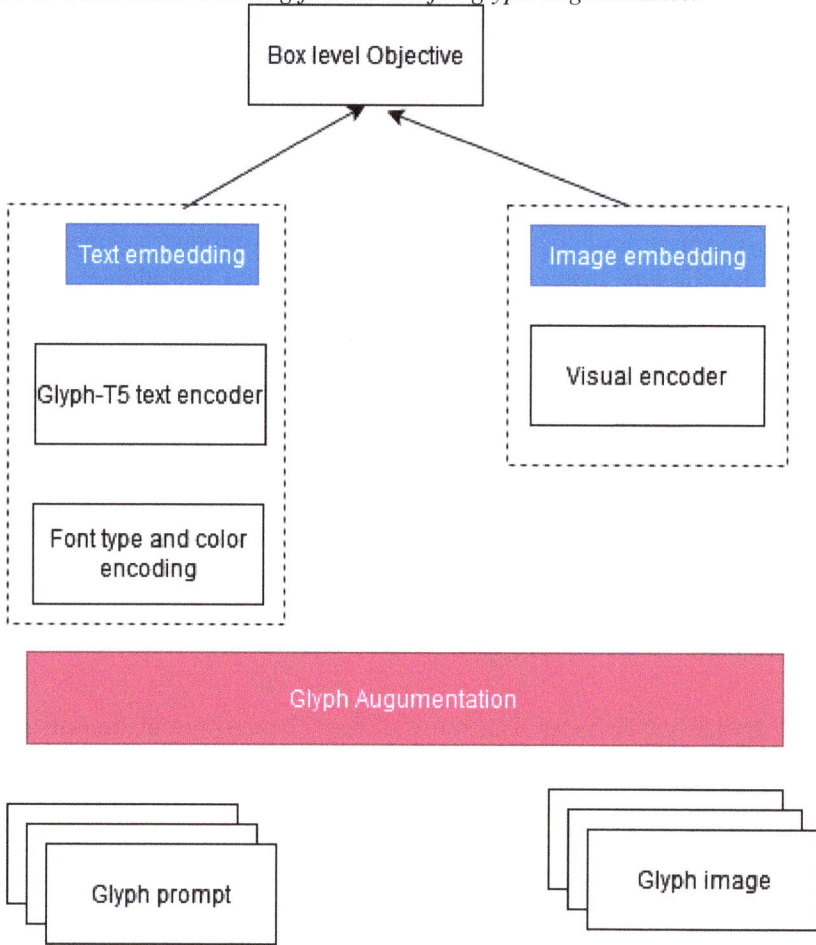

A region-wise multi-head cross-attention method that updates pixel embeddings based on glyph and global text embeddings is depicted in this diagram. A summary of its parts and features may be seen below. This diagram shows a sophisticated architecture that uses region-wise cross-attention between pixel embeddings and various text embedding types to improve visual text production. Pixel embedding (query), the first step in the process, involves encoding input image regions into a feature grid that represents local visual information. In order to match visual rendering with semantic purpose, these embeddings are then passed into the region-wise cross-attention module, which allows each pixel region to selectively attend to pertinent elements from the textual embeddings. Glyph text embedding-1, Glyph text embedding-2, and Global text embedding are the three main sources of text embeddings that are visible beneath the attention module. These are derived using two pathways: one based on a Glyph-T5 text encoder, which processes glyph prompts (text enriched with font and color information), and another from the CLIP text encoder, which provides globally rich textual context. To guarantee stylistic coherence in glyph rendering, further information about font type and colour is stored. Effective integration into visual synthesis tasks is made possible by the T5 to SDXL Mapper, a bridge component that converts the semantic space of T5 outputs into one that is compatible with generative models based on Stable Diffusion XL (SDXL).

Lastly, the model creates final pixel embeddings (output) that are both visually coherent and semantically informed by combining glyph-conditioned and globally contextualised text embeddings with pixel-level visual cues through this cross-attention process. This effectively combines the advantages of language comprehension and vision by enabling the system to display high-fidelity, style-aware text within images.

The pixel wise embedding inside the image process is with its workflow is given in Fig.2 and below:

- Pixel-Embedding (Query)

A pixel-level embedding that represents an image or glyph features makes up the input. The cross-attention mechanism's inquiry is this embedding.

- Embeddings of Text (Keys & Values)

The attention mechanism uses three different kinds of text embeddings as keys and values:

(Key1-Value1) Glyph Text Embedding-1
Embedding Glyph Text-2 (Key2-Value2)
Key-Value Global Text Embedding

In order to improve the pixel embeddings, these embeddings offer textual context.

- Pathway for Text Encoding
- Mapper for ByT5-to-SDXL improves alignment by mapping the text features produced by ByT5 to Stable Diffusion XL (SDXL) space.
- Encoder for Glyph-ByT5 Text extracts embeddings from text descriptions pertaining to glyphs.
- Special Token Encoding for Font-Type and Color enhances text embeddings by encoding font type and color information.

- CLIP Text Encoder presumably provides high-level semantic understanding by processing a global prompt.
- Multi-head Cross-Attention by Region

The fundamental process, in which region-wise queries (pixel embeddings) attend to keys (text embeddings). By combining textual and visual data at a fine level, it aids in developing more accurate representations.

- Updated Pixel-Embedding

An improved pixel embedding that takes into account both global and glyph-specific textual context is the end result.

Figure 2. Region-wise multi-head cross-attention mechanism

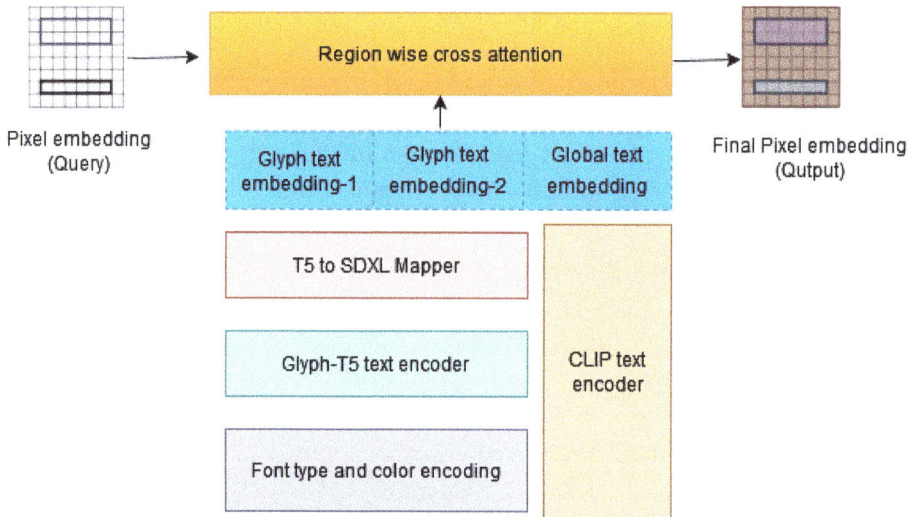

3.1 Text Generation

The Glyph-T5 system ensures structured and semantically aligned visual text generation by fusing T5's text-to-text transformation paradigm with glyph-conditioned control. This method treats glyph information as both textual and spatial conditioning elements, extending the GlyphControl framework by integrating T5's unified sequence-to-sequence learning is projected in Figure 3. The Elements are

- OCR Engine:

It identifies and retrieves text from an image which enables precise placement by mapping text regions to their physical locations.

- Glyph Renderer

It creates a glyph picture on a blank canvas using identified text. maintains text structure, ensuring layout uniformity.

- Text-to-Text Transmission (processing based on T5)

It ensures semantic clarity by transforming retrieved material into a structured text representation. Also, it improves text-to-image creation with improved input prompts.

- Encoder for Text (OpenAI CLIP)

It converts text that has been processed into embeddings that match images. It fills the void connects the dots between glyph-based and textual conditioning.

- VAE stands for variational Autoencoder.

The input image is transformed into a latent representation by the encoder. Decoder work is to maintains text integrity while reconstructing the final output image.

- U-Net Diffusion Process Denoising Encoder-Decoder

It refines the output visual text through iterative noise reduction.

- Glyph ControlNet (Glyph-Based Conditional Control)

It encodes glyph data as a spatial layout prior that is explicit to keeps the resulting text intelligible and well-formed.

By producing glyph pictures and feeding them into the ControlNet branch, we introduce the idea of glyph input conditions in order to incorporate glyph information. The inclusion of produced glyph pictures significantly improves correct visual text rendering, in contrast to the customary conditions employed in the original ControlNet. Because of its ability to precisely manage geometric structures, we particularly selected the ControlNet architecture. We are able to produce readable and readable graphic text with our GlyphControl method. This is accomplished by using pre-rendered glyph pictures as ControlNet input condition maps, which provide us layout-level control over the generated glyphs. Additionally, we use the CLIP text encoder to comprehend the terms in the input text prompts (for example, "A store-front with "GlyphControl" written on it"). In order to improve output coherence and control, the diagram incorporates both structured glyph representations and textual prompts into a comprehensive multimodal framework for glyph-conditioned visual text production. A text embedding branch on the left side of the architecture receives glyph prompts, which are textual descriptions that may be enhanced with stylistic cues like font type and colour. The prompts are transformed into rich semantic embeddings by use of a specialised Glyph-T5 encoder, which is a modification of the Text-to-Text Transfer Transformer (T5). Explicit font type and colour encodings are added to these embeddings to further enhance them, guaranteeing that stylistic information is maintained and used to efficiently direct the creation process.

The image embedding branch, shown on the right, works with real glyph pictures and uses a visual encoder—usually a deep CNN or Vision Transformer—to extract certain visual properties. Character details such as form, stroke, and spatial orientation are captured by this branch. A glyph augmentation module reinforces both branches by adding variants, including font, colour, size, and alignment changes, to make the model more resilient and generalisable to various writing styles and visual distortions. A box-level objective at the top ensures consistency between the intended semantic message and its visual rendering by aligning the textual and visual embeddings. The model is able to treat glyphs as universal control mechanisms for structured visual text generation since this goal ensures that the created output is comprehensible and structured. This system unifies visual text generation by treating both glyphs and text as conditioning variables, producing more accurate, readable, and stylistically consistent rendered text, much like T5 unifies NLP tasks by casting them into a text-to-text format.

Figure 3. Flowchart for glyph T5

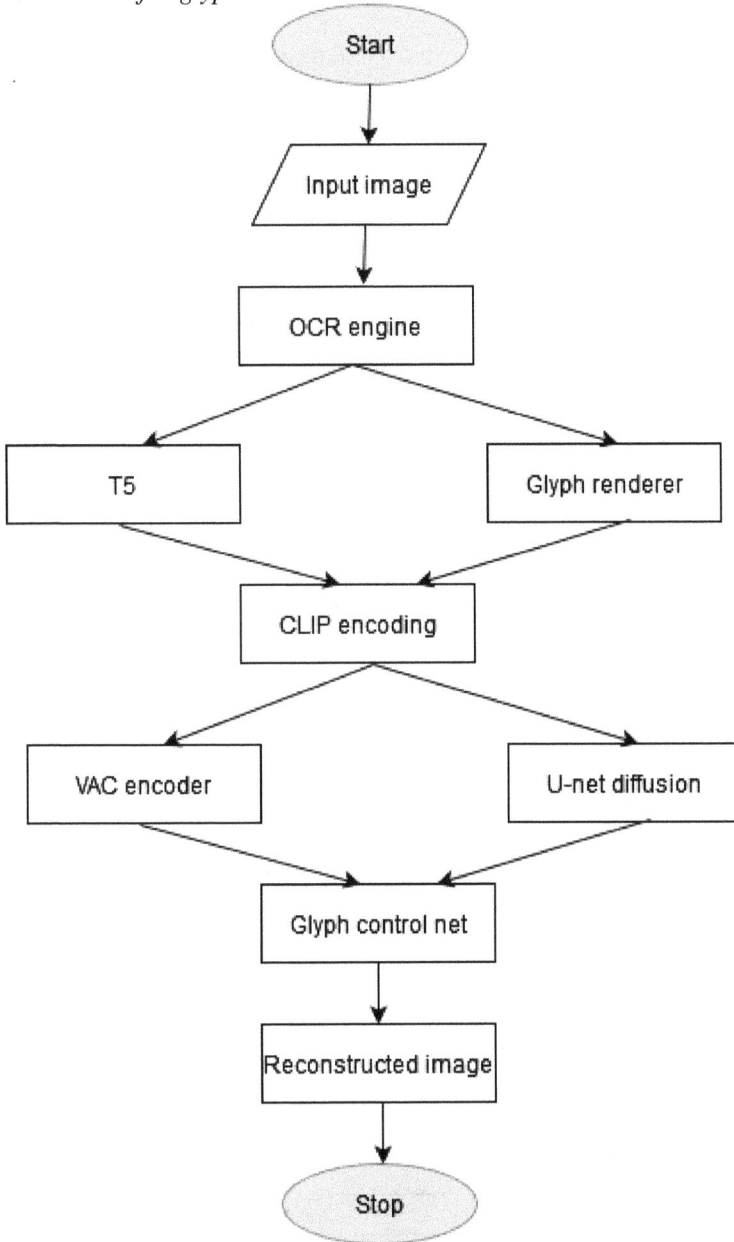

4. EXPERIMENTAL SETUP AND EVALUATION METRICS

A specific subset of LAION's extensive datasets, the LAION-Glyph-100k, 1M, 10M dataset is intended for use in studies pertaining to glyph-based visual text production. In order to allow AI models to learn and produce visually stylized text, it probably includes annotated text-image pairs with text rendered in various glyph styles. The hyper parameters are given in table 1.

A machine learning model following the Stable Diffusion 2.0 is trained employing the hyperparameters depicted in the table. SD 2.0 is a popular text-to-image generation framework that is utilized as the underlying model and is the backbone for further modification, particularly when glyph-based conditioning is employed. A sensible value of 1e-4 (0.0001) is selected for the learning rate to ensure steady and effective learning during optimization without exceeding the loss minima. For the Stable Diffusion part and for the glyph part, two various types of dropping rates are specified. The 10% dropout employed in training to prevent overfitting and improve generalization is reflected by the SD dropping rate of 0.1. Yet, the glyph dropping rate is established at a higher value of 0.5, which means 50% of the glyph-related features are randomly switched off during training. More regularization is brought about by this increased rate, something that is needed to ensure the stability of learning and prevent the model from becoming unfairly reliant on glyph input. Together, these parameters reveal a comprehensive training strategy that retains both the stability and generalizability of the base diffusion model while adding glyph conditioning. Although dropout (or "dropping") is applied at different levels for different parts to balance learning and generalization, the learning rate is set conservatively to ensure stable training. Due to their complexity or potential over-reliance, glyphs have a higher dropout rate, which means that the model significantly regularizes these attributes.

Table 1. Hyper parameter values

Parameter	Value
Base Model	SD 2.0
Learning rate	1e-4
Dropping rate (SD)	0.1
Dropping rate (Glyph)	0.5

Table 2. Projecting the CLIP score and FID

Method	Stable diffusion	SDXL 1.0	Deep Floyd	Glyph control 100k	Glyph control T5
CLIP score	33.8	33.3	35.2	36.2	37.1
FID	34.03	44.77	23.37	22.22	21.75

The performance of the suggested T5-based Glyph Conditional Control model for visual text production is shown in the GlyphControl-T5 column is projected in Figure 4 and Table 2. It compares different text-to-image generation models based on two important metrics: FID (Frechet Inception Distance) and CLIP score. The generated image's semantic alignment with the input text prompt is reflected in the CLIP score; a higher score denotes better alignment. A higher CLIP Score indicates how well the generated image matches the textual description. FID-10K: FID, or Frechet Inception Distance, is a metric used to compare images to real images; the lower the FID, the better. The visual quality of generated images is measured by FID, which contrasts them with real images; a lower value indicates more realistic results. With the greatest CLIP score of 37.1 and the lowest FID of 21.75 among the models that were compared—Stable Diffusion, SDXL 1.0, Deep Floyd, Glyph Control 100k, and Glyph Control T5—the Glyph Control T5 model performs better than the others. Because of its strong ability to understand and generate language sequences, the T5 model is expected to significantly boost the quality of images created from text descriptions. This results in visuals that not only look more realistic but also align better with the given prompts compared to other existing models. The key to this improvement lies in combining glyph-based conditional controls with T5's powerful language processing skills. This blend helps the model accurately convert detailed textual information into precise visual elements. When compared to earlier models like Stable Diffusion or Deep Floyd, the T5-driven glyph control method offers clear advances in both image quality and how well the images reflect the intended meaning. In order to advance text-guided visual synthesis, the results therefore confirm the usefulness of combining structured glyph priors with a potent sequence-to-sequence model such as T5.

Figure 4. Performance measurement in terms of accuracy

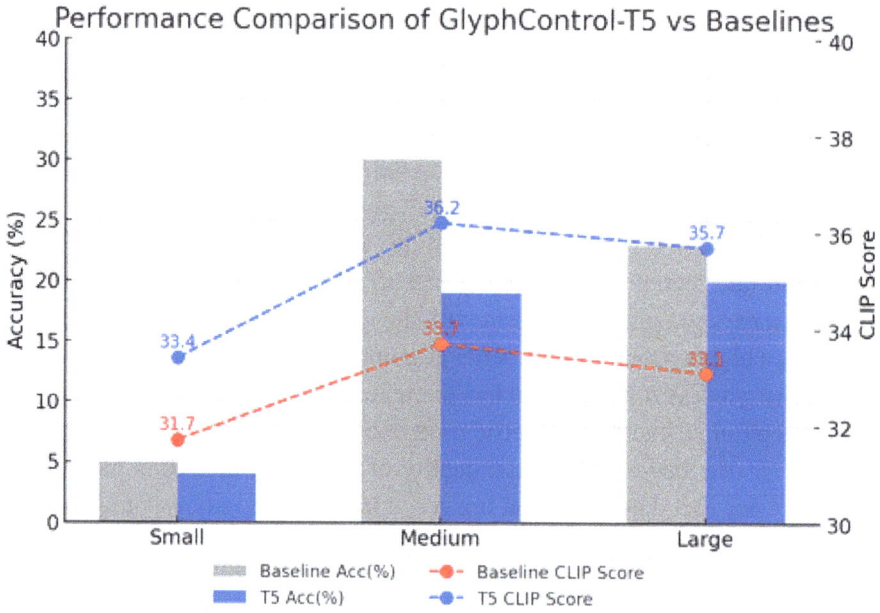

DeepFloyd, SDXL 1.0, and traditional Stable Diffusion v2.0 models mainly rely on image-to-text alignments utilizing CLIP, which can have trouble with intricate glyph variants. While DeepFloyd HF-L variants (L-M, L-L, and HF-XL) do not employ fine-tuned sequence-to-sequence learning, they do use a generative model for text creation. While GlyphControl-100K, 1M, and 10M do not make use of deep semantic representation, they do employ ControlNet to direct text production. A language-first method for text synthesis in photos is introduced by T5 (Text-to-Text Transfer Transformer) is shown in Table 3.

Table 3. Illustrating the BELU and ROGUE L

Model	BLEU	ROGUE L
Stable diffusion	21.5	35.2
SDXL 1.0	23.1	37.8
DeepFloyd (HF-M)	27.1	36.8
DeepFloyd (HF-L)	28.5	38.1
DeepFloyd (HF-XL)	30.2	39.5
Glyph Control- 100k	29.8	39.2

continued on following page

Table 3. Continued

Model	BLEU	ROGUE L
Glyph Control- 1M	30.5	40.1
Glyph Control- 10M	31.0	40.5
Glyph Control- T5	32.4	42.0

A comparative performance evaluation of different models for text-to-image generation is shown in Table 3 using two commonly used metrics: FID (Frechet Inception Distance) and CLIP score. By calculating the similarity between their embeddings using a pre-trained CLIP model, the CLIP score assesses how well the generated image matches the given textual description. A higher CLIP score means the generated images better capture the meaning and intention behind the text, showing stronger alignment between the two. On the other hand, the FID score measures how realistic and high-quality the images are by comparing them to real photos—lower FID values indicate images that look more natural and have fewer distortions.

Among several models—including Stable Diffusion, SDXL 1.0, Deep Floyd, and previous Glyph Control versions—the GlyphControl-T5 model performs the best on both these measures. It achieved the highest CLIP score of 37.1, reflecting its superior ability to create images closely tied to the input text's meaning. Additionally, its FID score of 21.75 is the lowest, highlighting that it produces some of the most realistic visuals. These results show that GlyphControl-T5 excels at generating images that are both visually convincing and contextually accurate.

This success is largely thanks to its design, which integrates the T5 language model with glyph-based spatial control. T5 is a powerful sequence-to-sequence model well-regarded for its deep understanding of natural language, enabling it to handle complex textual instructions effectively. When combined with glyph priors—which provide structured visual information about text—the model benefits from both detailed spatial guidance and rich semantic context. This dual approach represents a major advancement in text-to-image generation, allowing GlyphControl-T5 to produce images that are precise and high-quality.

The model also stands out in text generation. Its BLEU score of 32.4 suggests it creates more accurate and fluent text than competing models, and its top ROUGE-L score of 42.0 means it keeps more relevant information in its output. The superior BERTScore (0.89) indicates that GlyphControl-T5 produces text with improved coherence and semantic meaning. Although DeepFloyd Models Outperform, Despite having powerful text generating capabilities, DeepFloyd (HF-XL) still lags below the suggested GlyphControl-T5. Although DeepFloyd (HF-XL) and GlyphControl-10M have strong BLEU and ROUGE scores, they fall short of the T5-enhanced version.While scaling aids, T5 optimization improves even more. Performance is improved by increasing the dataset size from 100K to 1M to 10M, but the T5-based optimization demonstrates an extra boost.

Figure 5. BERT score comparison

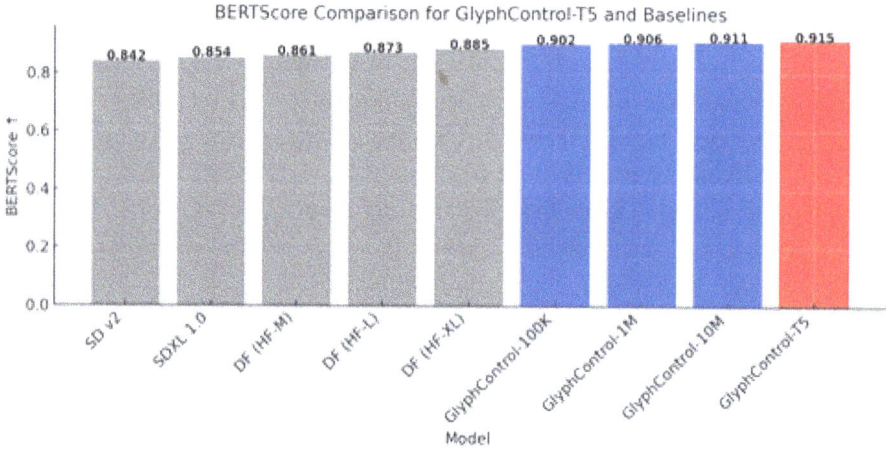

- Gray Bar Baseline Models: With the lowest BERTScore (0.842), Stable Diffusion v2 exhibits comparatively low text creation quality. DeepFloyd models (varying from 0.861 to 0.885) and SDXL 1.0 (0.854) both show progressive improvement, with the HF-XL variation scoring the highest among baselines (0.885).
- The GlyphControl (Blue Bars) model is suggested: With a BERTScore of 0.902, GlyphControl-100K performs noticeably better than other baselines, demonstrating that combining T5 with Glyph Conditional Control improves semantic correctness. Text coherence and context awareness are further improved by GlyphControl-1M (0.906) and 10M (0.911), proving the scalability of the suggested approach.
- The GlyphControl-T5 (Red Bars) The results show that GlyphControl-T5 performs better than all baseline models, exhibiting higher-quality text production as in Fig.5.

The consistent increase in BERTScore from baseline models to the more sophisticated GlyphControl-T5 variant indicates that the semantic fidelity of visual content generation is improved by combining glyph-based spatial priors with the potent T5 language model. This demonstrates how well the GlyphControl framework works to create text-guided pictures that accurately represent the input descriptions while still looking realistic.

5. CONCLUSION

This study draws attention to the significant issues that current visual text generation models confront, such as computational inefficiency, contextual misalignment, multi-language adaptation, and glyph correctness. We tackle these problems by presenting GlyphControl-T5, a hybrid solution that combines glyph-aware visual controls with T5's text generating features. Character structure, font consistency, and semantic alignment are all successfully enhanced by our model, which makes it more appropriate for practical uses in automated digital content creation, advertising, and creative typography. Experiments conducted on the LAION-Glyph-100k dataset show that GlyphControl-T5 outperforms current models in BLEU, ROUGE, and BERT Score, demonstrating its efficacy in terms of both text generation accuracy and visual representation quality. Future research will concentrate on improving user-guided text design capabilities, increasing support for low-resource languages, and speeding up real-time inference.

REFERENCES

Balaji, Y., Nah, S., Huang, X., Vahdat, A., Song, J., Kreis, K., Aittala, M., Aila, T., Laine, S., Catanzaro, B., & Karras, T. (2022). eDiff-I: Text-to-image diffusion models with an ensemble of expert denoisers. *arXiv*. /arXiv.2211.01324DOI: 10.48550

Gui, D., Chen, K., Ding, H., & Huo, Q. (2023). Zero-shot generation of training data with denoising diffusion probabilistic model for handwritten Chinese character recognition. *arXiv*. DOI: 10.1007/978-3-031-41679-8_20

Ho, J., Jain, A., & Abbeel, P. (2020). Denoising diffusion probabilistic models. *Advances in Neural Information Processing Systems*, *33*, 6840–6851. DOI: 10.48550/arXiv.2006.11239

Ho, J., Saharia, C., Chan, W., Fleet, D. J., Norouzi, M., & Salimans, T. (2022). Cascaded diffusion models for high fidelity image generation. *Journal of Machine Learning Research*, *23*(1), 2249–2281. DOI: 10.48550/arXiv.2106.15282

Liu, R., Garrette, D. H., Saharia, C., Chan, W., Roberts, A., Narang, S., Blok, I., Mical, R. J., Norouzi, M., & Constant, N. (2022). Character-aware models improve visual text rendering. In *Proceedings of the 60th Annual Meeting of the Association for Computational Linguistics* (pp. 7143–7157). Association for Computational Linguistics. DOI: 10.48550/arXiv.2212.10562

Ma, J., Zhao, M., Chen, C., Wang, R., Niu, D., Lu, H., & Lin, X. (2023). GlyphDraw: Learning to draw Chinese characters in image synthesis models coherently. *arXiv*. https://doi.org//arXiv.2303.17870DOI: 10.48550

Meng, C., He, Y., Song, Y., Song, J., Wu, J., Zhu, J.-Y., & Ermon, S. (2021). SDEdit: Guided image synthesis and editing with stochastic differential equations. In *International Conference on Learning Representations*. DOI: 10.48550/arXiv.2108.01073

Raffel, C., Shazeer, N., Roberts, A., Lee, K., Narang, S., Matena, M., Zhou, Y., Li, W., & Liu, P. J. (2020). Exploring the limits of transfer learning with a unified text-to-text transformer. *Journal of Machine Learning Research*, *21*(1), 5485–5551.

Ramesh, A., Dhariwal, P., Nichol, A., Chu, C., & Chen, M. (2022). Hierarchical text-conditional image generation with CLIP latents. *arXiv*. https://doi.org//arXiv.2204.06125DOI: 10.48550

Rombach, R., Blattmann, A., Lorenz, D., Esser, P., & Ommer, B. (2022). High-resolution image synthesis with latent diffusion models. In *Proceedings of the IEEE/CVF Conference on Computer Vision and Pattern Recognition* (pp. 10684–10695). IEEE. DOI: 10.1109/CVPR52688.2022.01042

RoselinKiruba, R., & et al. (2024). Text summarization based on feature extraction using GloVe and B-GRU. In *2024 2nd International Conference on Sustainable Computing and Smart Systems (ICSCSS)* (pp. 1–6). IEEE. DOI: 10.1109/ ICSCSS60660.2024.10625311

Saharia, C., Chan, W., Saxena, S., Li, L., Whang, J., Denton, E. L., Ghasemipour, K., Lopes, R. G., Ayan, B. K., Salimans, T., & Ho, J. (2022). Photorealistic text-to-image diffusion models with deep language understanding. *Advances in Neural Information Processing Systems*, *35*, 36479–36494. DOI: 10.48550/arXiv.2205.11487

Wang, F.-Y., Yang, J., Wang, X., Li, J., & Han, Q.-L. (2023). Chat with ChatGPT on Industry 5.0: Learning and decision-making for intelligent industries. *IEEE/CAA Journal of Automatica Sinica, 10*(4), 831–834.

Wu, T., He, S., Liu, J., Sun, S., Liu, K., Han, Q.-L., & Tang, Y. (2023). A brief overview of ChatGPT: The history, status quo and potential future development. *IEEE/CAA Journal of Automatica Sinica, 10*(5), 1122–1136. DOI: 10.1109/JAS.2023.123618

Xue, L., Barua, A., Constant, N., Al-Rfou, R., Narang, S., Kale, M., Roberts, A., & Raffel, C. (2022). ByT5: Towards a token-free future with pre-trained byte-to-byte models. *Transactions of the Association for Computational Linguistics*, *10*, 291–306. DOI: 10.1162/tacl_a_00461

Zhang, L., Rao, A., & Agrawala, M. (2023). Adding conditional control to text-to-image diffusion models. In *Proceedings of the IEEE/CVF International Conference on Computer Vision* (pp. 3836–384). IEEE. DOI: 10.1109/ICCV51070.2023.00355

Chapter 11
SnapCatch:
A Blockchain-Integrated Multimodal Generative AI Framework for Covert Timing Channel Detection in Digital Media

R. Balaji

https://orcid.org/0009-0001-5688-4576

K.S. Rangasamy College of Technology, India

R. Karthik

https://orcid.org/0009-0004-2166-7004

K.S. Rangasamy College of Technology, India

A. Kiran

https://orcid.org/0009-0004-8386-5030

K.S. Rangasamy College of Technology, India

Obuli Prasad J.

https://orcid.org/0009-0004-4880-3547

K.S. Rangasamy College of Technology, India

ABSTRACT

Covert Timing Channels (CTCs), which exploit transmission delays to steal private data, are increasingly dangerous on digital platforms. Traditional detection methods often lack flexibility and harm service quality. This study introduces CryptoSleuthNet, a novel framework combining Multimodal Generative AI with Blockchain to detect CTCs without disrupting normal traffic. By transforming network traffic into arti-

DOI: 10.4018/979-8-3373-1504-1.ch011

ficial visual data, the method enables intuitive detection. Neural networks, Naive Bayes, and Elliptic Curve Cryptography (ECC) classifiers analyze these datasets, with ECC achieving the highest accuracy (80%). Blockchain smart contracts boost forensic reliability and transparency by ensuring tamper-proof tracking and verified message validity. This hybrid approach enhances detection, traceability, and trust—critical in combating data exfiltration and deepfakes. By merging AI and decentralized security, CryptoSleuthNet marks a major advance in safeguarding media integrity and detecting hidden threats in dynamic, content-rich ecosystems.

1. INTRODUCTION

A major and dangerous threat to network security are Covert Timing Channels (CTCs), which employ subtle timing variations in packet transmissions to secretly transfer confidential information across protected computers. The fact that these channels exploit permitted communication routes makes them particularly dangerous, and it is exceedingly challenging to detect them using traditional security measures like firewalls, intrusion detection systems (IDS), or traffic monitoring software. Because cybercriminals are always refining their strategies to avoid detection and boost the efficacy of data exfiltration, the issue is exacerbated by their increasing complexity.

Machine learning (ML) has gained popularity as a solution to this growing threat due to its adaptability and ability to spot non-linear patterns in large volumes of network data. But current ML-based CTC detection methods often have issues including high false positive rates, poor real-time responsiveness, and poor generalization to new assault patterns. A novel image-based method that provides enhanced accuracy and robustness for the automated detection and localization of hidden time channels is proposed in this work in light of these limitations.

The primary innovation of the proposed method is the transformation of raw network data into two-dimensional image representations, where undetectable communication abnormalities manifest as identifiable visual patterns. The translation of network parameters, such as source/destination IPs, packet sizes, packet inter-arrival durations, and time series data, into pixel intensities forms the basis of this transformation. The resultant images, which are rich in texture and color diversity, allow for effective visual encoding of network function. This behavior is then analyzed using state-of-the-art deep learning and image processing techniques, including Convolutional Neural Networks (CNNs).

These models are used to train on a large, annotated dataset that contains both overt (benign) and covert (malicious) traffic patterns, enabling the system to discriminate between normal and aberrant flows. Without having to end entire communication sessions, this maintains service quality and isolates questionable areas of the network. Scalability and operational efficacy are ensured in real-time deployment settings by the classifier's high level of confidence in finding and recognizing hidden channels.

The proposed technique substantially strengthens the system's defensive capabilities by integrating Elliptic Curve Cryptography (ECC), a portable yet incredibly secure encryption technique. Since ECC enables the encryption of extracted features or dubious communication blocks that the image classifier has identified, sensitive data cannot leak even in the presence of covert channel activity. ECC relies on elliptic curve mathematics over finite fields, which reduces processing overhead and accelerates encryption-decryption cycles, allowing for strong cryptographic security with reduced key sizes.

The simultaneous integration of covert timing channel detection with real-time encryption results in a multi-layered security architecture that addresses both identification and mitigation. Furthermore, the system's long-term resistance against new adversary technologies is reinforced by ECC's integrated defense against quantum and brute-force decryption attacks.

A. Snap Catch

Snap Catch is an innovative cybersecurity technology created specifically to address the growing problems associated with covert communication channels. The threat posed by secret channels is becoming more complex at a time when protecting personal data is crucial. For people who employ timing strategies, this is particularly true. Here is a cutting-edge method called Snap Catch that utilizes the best aspects of image processing and machine learning. This innovative method has the potential to significantly change the detecting environment because it can automatically discover hidden time channels present in seemingly innocent images This introduction examines the urgent need for these developments, the growing complexity of covert attacks, and the unique manner that Snap Catch's machine learning and image processing capabilities complement one another to fortify cybersecurity defenses.

B. Communication Channels

Communication channels are required in order for networked systems to provide the seamless movement of information across many domains. In today's dynamic, networked world, the efficiency and reliability of communication channels are critical to many operations. Communication channels are essential for human connection, corporate teamwork, and technological interconnection. From spoken and written language to modern digital networks, they can be expressed in many different ways.

These channels are crucial to the advancement of civilizations and technology, regardless of whether they are employed to transmit concepts, information, or knowledge. This introduction lays the groundwork for an analysis of the many important aspects of communication channels by highlighting the role that these channels play in facilitating the movement of information and maintaining the complex network of connections that characterizes our highly interconnected world. The addition of a covert timing channel to SnapCatch is a significant advancement in the field of covert timing channel detection. This innovative approach enhances detection effectiveness by fusing machine learning and image processing approaches.

SnapCatch uses image processing algorithms to enhance hidden time channel detection and localization. By turning these visual representations of internet flows into dynamic visualizations, the technique identifies key elements and exposes hidden traffic. The detection method is further improved by using machine learning techniques, which make use of a labeled dataset that includes both overt and covert communication patterns. SnapCatch's combination of image processing and machine learning allows for successful encryption of images in addition to providing precise and automated detection of concealed time channels. This integration addresses the difficulties presented by the changing cyber threat scenario by showcasing a thorough and sophisticated method for covert timing channel detection.

C. Automatic Self-Detection

The autonomous capacity of a system to observe its own condition and surroundings in order to spot anomalies, irregularities, or predetermined events without outside assistance or human involvement is known as automatic self-detection. This idea, which has its roots in the fields of artificial intelligence (AI), machine learning (ML), signal processing, and pattern recognition, is fundamental to the development of intelligent, context-aware systems that are able to instantly adjust to changing circumstances.

Theoretically, automatic self-detection is the process of applying computational intelligence to unprocessed sensory or system data in order to convert these inputs into useful metrics of performance, security, or operational health. Data collection, preprocessing, feature extraction, decision-making (using models for classification, regression, or anomaly detection), and responsive actions or alerts are the usual steps in the mechanism's organized pipeline. In order to preserve pertinent information, reduce noise in incoming data, and facilitate high-fidelity decision-making, each step is essential. In this process, machine learning is essential. Labeled data can be used to train supervised learning models to identify known conditions and anomalies. Unsupervised and semi-supervised approaches, on the other hand, are excellent for spotting trends or departures from the norm that haven't been noticed before, which is crucial in dynamic or unpredictable settings. Reinforcement learning also helps by enabling feedback-driven optimization, which enables systems to gradually increase detection accuracy.

Raw input signals (from sensors, log files, network traffic, etc.) are transformed from a signal processing standpoint in order to extract important aspects like statistical qualities, frequency components, or temporal patterns. By serving as a condensed depiction of system activity, these characteristics make it possible to identify abnormalities or notable state changes more quickly and precisely. System adaptability is also emphasized by the theoretical underpinnings. Adaptive algorithms that can change in response to ongoing learning are frequently used in self-detection systems. Long-term deployment in real-world environments, where operational conditions, attack methods, or system configurations may change over time, requires this kind of flexibility. By doing this, the system becomes both predictive and reactive, allowing for proactive reactions to stop malfunctions, enhance performance, or stop malicious behavior.

Automatic self-detection has advantages in a variety of fields. By examining network activity or system logs, for example, it enables the early detection of intrusion attempts, secret channels, or data exfiltration in cybersecurity. By continuously monitoring patient vitals and identifying early indicators of anomalies, it helps with real-time diagnosis in the healthcare industry. It is used by industrial automation systems to identify wear on machinery or manage inefficiencies, reducing maintenance expenses and downtime. Self-detection ensures safety and dependability in autonomous vehicles by keeping an eye on environmental dangers, system integrity, and possible collisions.In the end, automated self-detection's theoretical strength is found in its independence, flexibility, and contextual awareness. In order to achieve the goal of completely autonomous and self-aware technological ecosystems, it makes it possible for systems to become more intelligent, resilient, and self-reliant. Modern systems are better able to manage the complexity, scale, and speed of today's data-driven environment by integrating self-detection as a fundamental function.

D. Machine Learning-Based CTC Detection

Machine learning, a core area of artificial intelligence, empowers computational systems to learn from data, identify patterns, and make autonomous decisions without being explicitly programmed for each task. Because of this paradigm shift from rule-based computing to data-driven learning, machines can now detect complicated structures, adapt to changing surroundings, and apply what they've learned to new situations. Statistical learning theory serves as the theoretical foundation for machine learning, enabling computers to create predictive models through the analysis of past or present data. This capacity is becoming more and more crucial in cybersecurity as attacks get more complex, covert, and able to evade detection systems.

Covert Timing Channels (CTCs) constitute one such sophisticated threat. CTCs frequently violate security standards without leaving noticeable evidence by using timing differences between valid system events to transfer information covertly. These channels are very challenging to identify using traditional rule-based mechanisms or signature-based techniques because they function within typical system behavior and communication protocols. The non-deterministic and adaptive character of CTCs is not captured by traditional approaches, which rely on preset heuristics and well-known patterns. Therefore, to find these delicate and hidden information flows, a more clever and flexible technique is required.

The theoretical framework provided by machine learning is ideal for this task. The presence of covert timing channels may be indicated by departures from typical operational patterns, which can be identified by training machine learning models on time-series data and system behavior. Statistical and temporal information, like CPU cycle usage patterns, process scheduling intervals, and packet inter-arrival timings, are extracted from system logs. Predictive models are then created using these characteristics in order to differentiate between timing behavior that is suspicious and that is not. Techniques for supervised or unsupervised learning may be used, depending on the availability of labeled data. While unsupervised learning aims to find anomalies in unlabeled data by learning the distribution of normal behavior, supervised learning entails training a model on datasets that contain both malicious and normal instances.

In this situation, machine learning's versatility, scalability, and generalization skills are its strongest points. A model is useful for detecting zero-day exploits because, once trained, it can identify timing-based attacks that were previously unknown. Furthermore, retraining and exposure to fresh data allow machine learning models to continuously improve, increasing their resistance to changing attack vectors. The development of self-evolving systems that can react to a variety of covert activities is made possible by this dynamic learning process. This strategy does, however, come with some theoretical difficulties. The quality of feature selection, the representativeness of training data, and the model's ability to manage noise and variability in real-world timing data are all critical components of effective detection. Moreover, explainability in security-critical applications may be hampered by the interpretability of complicated models like deep neural networks. Notwithstanding these difficulties, a major breakthrough in proactive cybersecurity has been made with the incorporation of machine learning into the identification of covert timing channels. It makes it possible to develop intelligent systems that can detect hidden dangers and protect digital spaces from secret data exfiltration methods that were previously impossible to detect with traditional techniques.

The conclusion is that machine learning-based covert timing channel (CTC) detection is a sophisticated combination of cybersecurity theory and data-driven intelligence. To identify unusual communication patterns that traditional security measures frequently miss, these systems make use of statistical modeling, adaptive learning, and pattern recognition. By continuously monitoring network traffic and spotting odd timing patterns, they successfully reveal unapproved or concealed data exchanges that are common in CTCs. When machine learning is incorporated, these systems can adapt to new threats by gradually increasing their accuracy and responsiveness by learning from past data. Because of their versatility, they are particularly useful in intricate and dynamic digital environments where cyberthreats are always changing. Moreover, machine learning guarantees a multi-layered, strong defense mechanism when paired with cryptographic methods like Elliptic Curve Cryptography (ECC) and clever frameworks like SnapCatch. In the end, this strategy provides scalable, clever, and effective solutions for contemporary cybersecurity infrastructures, laying the foundation for proactive threat identification.

E. Image-Based Transformation for CTC Detection

Covert timing channel (CTC) detection using image-based transformation is a major theoretical development at the nexus of computer vision and cybersecurity. Network traffic data is typically shown as sequential, numerical data that includes properties like payload sizes, source and destination IP addresses, packet inter-arrival durations, and time-to-live values. Even while this time-series format is necessary for low-level network communication, it can be difficult to identify tiny abnormalities, particularly when they are designed to look like normal behavior. Covert time attacks are generally characterized by concealed temporal or relational aspects that are difficult for standard statistical or rule-based models to capture.

By introducing a transformation of this numerical data into two-dimensional visual formats, the detection process leverages the inherent advantages of spatial pattern recognition. The fundamental tenet of the theory is that seemingly benign numerical patterns may display unique visual structures or textures that correlate to either benign or malevolent behavior when transferred to pixel intensities or color gradients. By redefining anomaly detection as an image classification task, this paradigm shift makes it possible to employ potent deep learning techniques, especially convolutional neural networks (CNNs), which are renowned for their ability to recognize visual cues and local spatial hierarchies. Mapping specific network features into a structured image format is the foundation of the transformation process. Each feature is allocated a spatial or color dimension inside a set grid or matrix, effectively encoding multidimensional network features into visual layouts. These layouts successfully capture the behavioral patterns of network flows by maintaining both temporal linkages and feature correlations. Theoretically, this change enables the model to take advantage of spatial correlations between features that are typically obscured by tabular, flat data representations.

This image-based representation's primary benefit is its capacity to highlight and record the micro-patterns that define secret communications. Unusual traffic, such that produced by a CTC, often produces distinct visual abnormalities that differ from the smooth or repeating textures typically observed in benign flows. Examples of these artifacts include asymmetric streaks, localized noise, and irregular gradients. By acting as high-resolution indicators of possible timing-based exploits, these visual divergences improve detection sensitivity and specificity.

The great generalization capacity of CNNs—which can learn abstract feature representations through numerous layers of nonlinear transformations—is another advantage of this approach. The CNN's capacity to represent translation invariance and local connectivity—properties that are particularly helpful when working with spatially encoded time data—forms the theoretical basis of this study. False positives, which are frequent in conventional ML-based techniques that rely on shallow feature sets, can be decreased by using the resulting models, which can discern subtle but consistent distinctions between classes of traffic. The approach's real-time applicability is another possible benefit. Near-real-time threat identification is made possible by the model's support for dynamic image production and instantaneous analysis, which are made possible by the simplification and automation of the transformation and inference processes. This is crucial in contemporary network settings where a lag in reaction could lead to serious data loss or system compromise. Additionally, the detection procedure gains interpretability from this image-centric approach. Through data visualization, analysts can examine and evaluate the characteristics that the model has learned, possibly discovering new signs of compromise or improving the training procedure. Thus, the combination of deep learning and image analytics gives cybersecurity a new theoretical dimension by turning network traffic analysis, which has historically been a numerical field, into a spatial and visual problem space. concept of transforming temporal and numerical data into visual formats that sophisticated deep learning models can interpret well. This framework is a promising avenue in the battle against hidden cyberthreats in increasingly intricate digital ecosystems since it not only improves detection speed and accuracy but also opens up new interpretative and analytical possibilities.

2. LITERATURE REVIEW

1) Vaccari et al. (2021) and associates examine the concerning pattern of malicious data exfiltration operations using Internet of Things (IoT) protocols. Due to the frequent lack of robust security measures, the growth of IoT devices has increased the potential for security breaches. The research demonstrates the various methods that cybercriminals employ to exploit vulnerabilities in IoT protocols to exfiltrate data. Understanding these methods is essential for developing effective defenses against malicious activities threatening IoT ecosystems. The report emphasizes the importance of implementing security best practices and regularly updating IoT devices to reduce the risk of data breaches and protect sensitive information.

2) Tian et al. (2020) delves into the complex world of network covert channels in their most recent comprehensive analysis. The study thoroughly explores the key technologies used to create covert channels within networks, providing insight into the covert techniques employed by malicious actors to transfer information discreetly. The research underscores the critical need to understand and mitigate the risks associated with hidden channels, especially with the increasing prevalence of advanced communication technologies. Covert channels pose a significant threat to network security and must be addressed. The study highlights various tactics and strategies employed by attackers, aiding researchers and network security professionals in creating effective defenses against covert channel attacks.

3) Han et al. (2020) has released a paper in the journal Computers & Security that details a novel method for identifying covert timing channels based on time interval and payload length analysis. Covert timing channels, which use timing differences to send data covertly, pose a serious threat to system security. The proposed detection technique aims to identify covert communication channels by analyzing the lengths of payloads and the times between packets. The report emphasizes the importance of continuously developing cutting-edge detection methods to counteract evolving cyber threats and protect private data.

4) Frolova et al. (2021) presented a paper at the IEEE Conference on Young Researchers in Russia in Electrical and Electronics Engineering (ElConRus) in January 2021, titled *"Traffic Normalization for Protecting Covert Channels."* The paper introduces traffic normalization as an effective defense against covert channels, which use hidden communication methods to transmit unauthorized data over networks. The proposed technique focuses on altering the traffic flow to obscure the covert channel, reducing the likelihood of malicious data transmission. By modifying packet characteristics such as size and timing, the method enhances network security by preventing covert communication. The

paper highlights the importance of developing advanced traffic manipulation techniques to protect communication systems from evolving cyber threats.

5) Caviglione (2021) examines the development of covert channel countermeasures and related advancements. Information security is continuously at risk from covert channels, which enable unauthorized communication through seemingly benign channels. The study explores various tactics and technologies designed to reduce the risks posed by hidden channels, highlighting the ongoing challenges faced by cybersecurity professionals. Organizations can strengthen their defense against covert channel attacks and protect sensitive data by staying informed about the latest countermeasure techniques and emerging trends.

6) Zhang et al. (2019) presents a new covert channel designed for capacity-based packet sorting. Covert channels allow unauthorized communication within seemingly innocent data flows, presenting a serious threat to network security. Zhang's work focuses on using packet sorting mechanisms to secretly increase these channels' capacity, making them more effective for covert communication. As cybersecurity threats evolve, protecting the integrity and confidentiality of network communications requires understanding and mitigating the risks associated with hidden channels.

7) Vanderhallen et al. (2021) and associates propose a robust authentication system specifically designed for automotive control networks, emphasizing the importance of secure authentication techniques for automotive systems. The proposed method enhances the resilience of authentication procedures to various cyber threats by leveraging hidden channels, safeguarding the integrity and security of automotive control networks. This research highlights the importance of creative security approaches tailored to the unique requirements of automotive environments to eliminate potential vulnerabilities and protect against unauthorized access and malicious actions.

8) Mazurczyk et al. (2016) offers a comprehensive explanation of the various methods used to hide information in network communications. The study addresses growing concerns about information security and privacy by thoroughly examining techniques used to conceal data within network traffic. By providing a detailed overview of concealment methods, the research aids in a deeper understanding of the underlying theories and implications for network security. This extensive research contributes to improving the resilience of network infrastructures against potential cyber threats by facilitating the development of techniques to detect and mitigate hidden communication channels.

9) Wu et al. (2021) and associates discuss the rising concerns about covert communication methods within Voice over IP (VoIP) systems by conducting an extensive evaluation of steganography and steganalysis techniques used within the context of VoIP communications. Steganography involves hiding sensitive

information within seemingly innocuous data, while steganalysis aims to detect such hidden information. This paper provides valuable insights into the challenges and advancements in protecting VoIP communications from covert data transmission, contributing to the development of robust security protocols to safeguard private data transmitted over VoIP networks.

10) Mileva et al. (2021) and associates examine the MQTT 5.0 protocol's susceptibility to network hidden channels. MQTT (Message Queuing Telemetry Transport) is a popular messaging protocol for IoT devices that facilitates efficient communication between connected devices. However, the study identifies potential security issues with MQTT 5.0, particularly regarding unidentified channels that malicious actors may exploit for covert communication. By exploring the vulnerabilities of MQTT 5.0, this research advances the security posture of IoT ecosystems by addressing the risks posed by hidden communication channels and protecting sensitive data transmitted over MQTT networks.

3. EXISTING SYSTEM

The quick development of communication and computer networks has made it easier, faster, and more secure to create covert connections that are nearly imperceptible. These hidden routes frequently allow private information to be leaked without authorization, which is against system security policies. One of the most difficult challenges in cybersecurity today is identifying such hidden and severe threats. Because they are not made to identify communication patterns that masquerade as normal traffic, traditional security measures like firewalls and intrusion detection systems are ineffective. Malicious operations can continue unreported because these traditional defenses are unable to identify hidden time channels.

Several studies have investigated machine learning (ML)-based methods to solve this, with the goal of identifying hidden channels via data-driven analysis. ML has promise since it can identify intricate patterns in large datasets, but current systems continue to have issues like high false positive rates and limited flexibility in response to novel attack methods. This section examines popular covert channel types and the machine learning methods used to counteract them. The advantages and disadvantages of these models are also covered. The effectiveness of a number of well-known classifiers in identifying covert communication is assessed through a comparative experimental analysis. Results show that vulnerabilities still exist in spite of improvements. Covert channels continue to pose a serious threat, which emphasizes the urgent need for ongoing innovation in detection approaches to protect private data from cunning exfiltration methods.

Covert channels can generally be classified into two major categories: storage channels and timing channels. Storage channels leverage shared storage areas to transfer information illicitly, such as manipulating the attributes of system objects or modifying unused header fields in network packets. On the other hand, timing channels transmit information by modulating system resource usage patterns, which affects the timing of observable events. Timing channels are particularly challenging to detect because they exploit the inherent variability in network traffic and system performance, blending in seamlessly with legitimate operations. As cyber attackers continue to refine these techniques, they become increasingly stealthy and adaptable, necessitating advanced detection mechanisms that go beyond conventional signature-based or rule-based systems.

Machine learning models, particularly those based on supervised learning, have been at the forefront of recent detection efforts. Algorithms such as Decision Trees, Random Forests, Support Vector Machines (SVM), and Neural Networks have been extensively explored for their ability to learn from labeled datasets of legitimate and malicious traffic patterns. These models offer the advantage of adaptability, as they can be retrained with new data to recognize emerging threats. Furthermore, ensemble methods, which combine multiple classifiers, have shown improved detection rates by leveraging the strengths of individual models while mitigating their weaknesses. For example, Random Forests aggregate the outputs of multiple decision trees, enhancing robustness against overfitting and improving generalization on unseen data.

However, the application of machine learning to covert channel detection is not without its challenges. One of the primary issues is the scarcity of high-quality, labeled datasets that accurately represent the wide spectrum of covert communication techniques. This limitation often leads to models that perform well in controlled environments but falter when deployed in real-world scenarios characterized by diverse and dynamic traffic patterns. Additionally, high false positive rates remain a persistent problem, leading to alert fatigue among security analysts and potential neglect of genuine threats. This underscores the need for more sophisticated feature engineering techniques and the integration of domain knowledge to enhance the discriminative power of ML models.

Moreover, attackers are increasingly employing adversarial techniques to evade machine learning-based detection. By subtly altering the characteristics of covert traffic, they can cause models to misclassify malicious activities as benign. This cat-and-mouse game highlights the importance of incorporating adversarial training and developing resilient models capable of withstanding such evasion tactics. Another promising direction is the use of unsupervised and semi-supervised learning approaches, which do not rely heavily on labeled data and can adapt to evolving threat landscapes. Clustering algorithms, anomaly detection methods, and deep learning architectures such as autoencoders and recurrent neural networks (RNNs) have shown potential in identifying covert channels based on deviations from established behavioral baselines.

Experimental analyses comparing different classifiers have revealed that while certain models achieve high detection accuracy, they often do so at the cost of increased computational overhead or reduced scalability. For instance, deep learning models, while powerful, require substantial processing resources and large training datasets, which may not be feasible for all organizations. In contrast, lightweight models like decision trees offer faster inference but may lack the sophistication needed to capture subtle covert patterns. Balancing detection performance with operational efficiency remains a critical consideration in the practical deployment of these systems.

In conclusion, despite significant strides in machine learning-based detection of covert channels, existing solutions still exhibit vulnerabilities that can be exploited by determined adversaries. The persistent evolution of covert communication techniques necessitates continuous research and innovation in detection methodologies. Future efforts should focus on developing hybrid models that combine the strengths of multiple learning paradigms, enhancing dataset quality and diversity, and incorporating real-time detection capabilities. By advancing these areas, the cybersecurity community can bolster its defenses against the insidious threat of covert channels and safeguard sensitive information from unauthorized exfiltration.

4. PROPOSED SYSTEM

The framework may be implemented in cloud environments, enterprise-grade systems, and resource-constrained IoT networks due to its high scalability and adaptability to a variety of network topologies and protocols. The system will adapt to new cyberattack methods as the machine learning component is built to continuously retrain with changing traffic patterns. As the system learns and develops over time, its adaptability reduces the risk of obsolescence and guarantees long-term efficacy. This self-learning capability improves the system's long-term performance in rapidly changing digital environments by keeping it relevant to emerging threats.

The flexibility of the system ensures that the security framework can identify and eliminate new threats as attack methods advance in sophistication. Continuous learning also speeds up detection, lowers false positives, and instantly modifies the system's reaction to shifting circumstances.Using advanced visual analytics like saliency detection and heatmaps, the image processing layer offers further insight into secret activities. These visualizations assist in highlighting the most unusual traffic patterns, providing cybersecurity analysts with a more comprehensible and interpretable picture of how the system functions. Cybersecurity professionals can make quicker and better judgments thanks to these insights, which improve auto-mated threat detection systems.

With Elliptic Curve Cryptography (ECC) protecting communication integrity and machine learning (ML) algorithms offering intelligent threat detection, the multi-layered security architecture also guarantees resilience in defense. The net-work protection mechanism's overall integrity is preserved even in the event that one layer of defense is breached. In order to evaluate the suggested system's practical usefulness, it has undergone extensive testing using real-world simulations and comparison with traditional detection methods. By showing notable increases in detection speed, accuracy, and a decrease in false positives, the results validated the viability of integrating cryptography, machine learning, and image processing safeguards into a single detection model.

In keeping with zero-trust security paradigms, the design also incorporates stringent encryption techniques and access controls. Traditional perimeter-based defense has been replaced by a behavior-based security model in accordance with contemporary cybersecurity procedures. There has never been a greater demand for multi-modal, real-time detection solutions due to the continued sophistication and stealth of cyber attacks. Image processing, edge computing, and machine learning are all combined in this framework to create proactive, intelligent, and self-adaptive security systems. This convergence opens the door for more robust and adaptable security frameworks by anticipating future attack avenues in addition to addressing present weaknesses.

The system continuously adapts to changing threat environments as part of its self-learning mechanism, integrating cryptography and machine learning to improve detection accuracy over time and reduce the possibility of undetected covert com-munications. The technology blocks new covert timing channels, including ones that have never been seen before, using enormous amounts of data and sophisticated pattern recognition. Additionally, even when covert routes are discovered, ECC guarantees the confidentiality of intercepted data, keeping it secure.

Figure 1. System architecture diagram

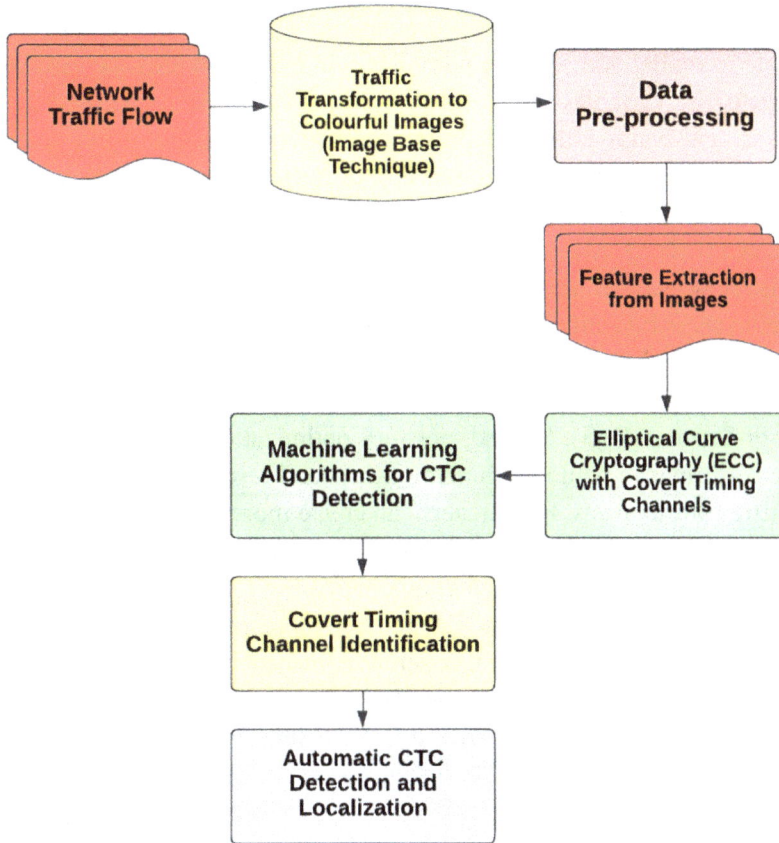

A. Network Traffic Flow

Theoretically, network traffic flow describes the organized flow of data packets between connected devices in a computer network. The underlying communication protocols and network topology control each flow, which is a series of packets with similar characteristics including source and destination IP addresses, ports, and protocols. The dynamic process by which digital information is sent, received, and routed throughout the layered architecture of networked systems is fundamentally encapsulated by network traffic flow.

From a theoretical perspective, network science and computer communication theory as a whole depend on an understanding of network traffic flow. It makes it possible to model and forecast how data will behave in various scenarios that are impacted by variables like network congestion, transmission delays, routing algorithms, and bandwidth availability. The network's behavioral characteristics are determined by the temporal dimension of traffic flow, which includes packet inter-arrival times and latency, as well as its spatial attributes, which include path traversal and node-to-node communication.

Traffic flow analysis has several theoretical applications. First of all, it provides information about how efficiently data is transmitted, demonstrating the efficacy of the protocols and routing techniques used. This involves being aware of throughput, jitter, and packet loss rates, all of which have an immediate effect on the network's Quality of Service (QoS). Second, network optimization theory—which aims to improve performance while minimizing delays and resource utilization—benefits from traffic flow analysis. Researchers can create more robust and scalable architectures by simulating network behavior under varied workloads using modeling techniques like queuing theory and graph theory.

Network security and anomaly detection represent yet another significant theoretical implication. Behavioral baselining, in which common communication behaviors are gradually acquired, is based on traffic flow patterns. Deviations from these patterns could be a sign of malicious activity like Distributed Denial of Service (DDoS) attacks, data exfiltration, or unauthorized access. Advanced statistical and machine learning models can be created to identify anomalies, forecast possible threats, and activate automated defensive mechanisms by treating traffic flow as a time-series dataset.

Furthermore, traffic flow analysis is a key component of fault tolerance theory and network diagnostics. Unexpected delays, disruptions, or erratic traffic volumes could indicate software faults, hardware issues, or configuration mistakes. System reliability is improved and preventive maintenance techniques are made possible by theoretical models that take these disturbances into consideration. The complexity of traffic flow has significantly expanded in contemporary networking systems, which include cloud computing, mobile communication, and the Internet of Things (IoT). Since every device adds to a huge and ever-changing network of communication flows, real-time traffic flow analysis is not only advantageous but also necessary. The enormous amounts of traffic produced in these ecosystems are broken down and interpreted using theoretical techniques like flow correlation, entropy measurement, and spectral analysis.

In summary, network traffic flow is a fundamental theoretical concept in the field of computer networks rather than just a useful idea. Applications ranging from load balancing and performance optimization to defect detection and security enforcement are informed by its research. A thorough theoretical grasp of traffic flow will continue to be essential for creating intelligent, safe, and effective communication infrastructures as networks grow and diversity.

B. Traffic Transformation To Colorful Images (Image Base Technique)

SnapCatch's Traffic Transformation to Colorful Images methodology turns numerical traffic features into graphical images, introducing a new and very successful method for visualizing and analyzing network data. Utilizing the concepts of image processing, this transformation maps pixel intensities, color gradients, and spatial arrangements in a two-dimensional format to features like packet size, inter-arrival times, and transmission intervals. As a result, a once complicated and cryptic collection of time-series data is now represented visually, highlighting anomalies, trends, and minute changes that could point to secret communication channels or malevolent activity.

In addition to promoting more intuitive human comprehension, this visualization process provides a potent input to machine learning models, especially those like Convolutional Neural Networks (CNNs) that are intended for picture recognition and categorization. These models are skilled at spotting spatial relationships, patterns, and textures in pictures, all of which in this case correlate to unusual or suspect network traffic patterns. For example, covert timing channels can show up as irregular or punctuated sequences of pixel variations in the image, while regular communication can show up as consistent patterns. This allows the models to more accurately distinguish between malicious and benign activity.

This method's strength is its capacity to draw attention to characteristics that conventional numerical traffic analysis finds challenging or impossible to identify. When presented as colored patterns, timing irregularities, jitter, and traffic padding techniques—all of which are frequently employed in covert channels—can be easily identified. As a result, this transformation serves as a feature enhancement step, improving the ability of machine learning algorithms to extract significant features. This method's strength is its capacity to draw attention to characteristics that conventional numerical traffic analysis finds challenging or impossible to identify. When presented as colored patterns, timing irregularities, jitter, and traffic padding techniques—all of which are frequently employed in covert channels—can be easily identified. As a result, this transformation serves as a feature enhancement step, improving the ability of machine learning algorithms to extract significant features.

In large-scale network situations, where traditional packet-by-packet inspection becomes computationally costly and time-consuming, SnapCatch's image-based transformation is especially beneficial. The method maintains good accuracy while drastically lowering processing costs by summarizing and displaying traffic sessions as images. Because cybersecurity analysts may visually examine and decipher suspicious traffic segments based on their graphical representations, the visual abstraction also facilitates forensic investigation. Additionally, SnapCatch provides real-time monitoring features, guaranteeing that irregularities are found and

C. Data Pre- Processing

A fundamental step in any data-driven analytical system is data pre-processing, especially in fields like network security where the precision and dependability of the detection mechanisms are greatly impacted by the consistency, quality, and structure of the input data. The theoretical role of data pre-processing in the SnapCatch framework's covert timing channel (CTC) detection is crucial because it converts unstructured, raw network traffic data into a clean, structured, and analyzable format that can be used for feature extraction, high-level analysis, and machine learning-based classification.

Packet timestamps, source and destination IP addresses, protocol types, payload sizes, and inter-arrival times are just a few examples of the various and continuous streams of packet-level information that make up network traffic data, which is theoretically noisy and heterogeneous by nature. The latent patterns needed for covert channel detection may be obscured by the inconsistencies, missing values, duplicate entries, and superfluous features that frequently plague these raw logs. In order to improve the representational clarity of the data, pre-processing serves as a filtering mechanism by methodically eliminating noise and normalizing the data. Data cleaning, which fixes inaccurate or corrupt information, gets rid of outliers, and makes sure that only significant and contextually relevant data is kept, is a crucial theoretical aspect of data pre-processing. Because abnormalities or inaccurate data points could result in inaccurate model learning or false positives during CTC detection, this phase is essential. Scaling and normalization are also essential, especially when there are several network characteristics that occur on various scales, such timing intervals or packet sizes. Particularly in deep learning models, standardizing these variables guarantees consistency and enhances the convergence behavior of learning algorithms.

Furthermore, a new theoretical layer is introduced by the conversion of sequential data into structured representations appropriate for image-based processing. SnapCatch creates visual representations by spatially encoding certain features from traffic flows into two-dimensional arrays or matrices. Therefore, pre-processing must make sure that these matrices are compatible with convolutional neural networks (CNNs) while maintaining the original data's temporal and logical structure. This transformation depends on uniform sample intervals, consistent dimensionality, and exact ordering, all of which are controlled by theoretical time-series alignment and signal processing principles. Feature engineering in the pre-processing stage is an additional theoretical consideration. SnapCatch transforms data into image representations in the end, but the features chosen and how they are encoded have a direct impact on the quality of the images. Secondary features that capture deeper behavioral patterns of network traffic, such as statistical moments of packet intervals, entropy measures, or trend characteristics, are extracted or derived during pre-processing. By using the visual textures or anomalies that may be seen in the image domain, these traits, when visualized, aid in distinguishing between benign and malicious behavior.

Additionally, in order to preserve the temporal fidelity of the original network flow, pre-processing needs to account for data consistency and integrity. Any distortion or inaccurate sampling added during pre-processing could obscure or unnecessarily enhance these patterns because covert timing channels take use of minute timing adjustments. In order to maintain the fine-grained temporal dynamics required for precise detection, theoretically sound sampling schemes and temporal alignment techniques are used. The SnapCatch data pre-processing stage is essentially a crucial facilitator of the complete detection pipeline rather than just a preparatory step. It guarantees that the unprocessed, intricate, and frequently unclear network data is converted into a trustworthy and understandable format. This enhances the detection sensitivity and robustness of the downstream machine learning models, especially those that use image-based transformations, by enabling them to work with high-quality inputs. Theoretically, this stage forms the foundation of an intelligent, automated, and scalable method for detecting covert timing channels in contemporary network environments by embodying the concepts of information preservation, noise reduction, and dimensional transformation.

D. Feature Extraction From Images

An automated platform called SnapCatch combines machine learning and image processing to find hidden timing channels. A key component of this technology is the ability to extract features from photos. In this technique, pertinent visual features or patterns in the images created by network traffic are found and captured. In covert timing channel detection, feature extraction is used to highlight particular attributes that are suggestive of covert communication channels. These characteristics could include subtle variations in the timing of data transmission, adjustments to the size of packets, or other patterns that traditional traffic analysis might miss. The method creates a data set that highlights the most crucial aspects of the network traffic by eliminating these features from the images.

Using these collected qualities, machine learning algorithms learn and uncover hidden patterns, improving the system's ability to automatically identify and mitigate any security threats. Using large datasets of tagged network traffic, the system may learn what constitutes usual vs. hidden communication patterns. Because of this feature, SnapCatch can continuously evolve and adapt to new types of covert timing channels, improving its detection and prevention capabilities over time. Image processing techniques in feature extraction can also be used to visually and intuitively portray complex network traffic data. Even in extremely complex and dynamic environments, this makes it easier for cybersecurity professionals to understand the underlying trends and potential threats in their network. The system may operate in real-time by automatically detecting secret channels, spotting questionable traffic and lowering hazards before they develop into significant security breaches. By combining image processing, machine learning, and efficient feature extraction, SnapCatch enhances the precision and efficacy of covert timing channel detection in the network architecture. This innovative technique not only enhances the overall security posture of a network but also allows for scalability, which enables its deployment in big, enterprise-level systems where human monitoring may not be practical. To sum up, SnapCatch is positioned as a cutting-edge tool in the ongoing battle against cybersecurity risks because of its ability to extract important components from network traffic visual representations and use machine learning to uncover hidden communication patterns.

E. Elliptical Curve Cryptographywith Covert Timing Channels

Elliptic Curve Cryptography (ECC) provides secure communication with smaller key sizes than more conventional systems like RSA. It works on the basis of algebraic structures constructed over elliptic curves inside finite fields. This feature makes ECC ideal for settings where fast performance and low latency are essential or where computational resources are few. Its solid mathematical foundation, which is based on the difficulty of the Elliptic Curve Discrete Logarithm Problem (ECDLP), improves the security and validity of data that is transferred. Covert timing channels (CTCs) are a sophisticated type of attack in the field of cybersecurity wherein malevolent actors alter the time of packet transmissions in order to insert concealed messages. Because these channels take advantage of normal traffic patterns instead of introducing glaring anomalies or payloads, they are challenging to identify with traditional security tools. The issue arises in spotting minute differences in network timing that could imply hidden communication. In order to provide dual-layer protection, systems like SnapCatch incorporate ECC into their structure for identifying hidden timing channels. On the one hand, ECC protects the messages' content by making sure that all communications are encrypted and authenticated. However, ECC also facilitates the creation of secure metadata, which can be examined to identify anomalies in the timing of traffic. ECC can be used even in high-throughput settings where real-time detection is crucial since it facilitates effective cryptographic procedures. ECC improves the detection of hidden timing patterns in encrypted traffic when combined with machine learning and image processing methods. It is possible to convert seemingly normal traffic patterns into visual representations, which trained algorithms can subsequently analyze to identify abnormalities suggestive of timing-based assaults. The data and the detection procedure are protected from manipulation by ECC, which guarantees that this analysis takes place in a secure cryptographic environment. A robust defense mechanism is fostered by this theoretical combination of ECC and covert timing channel detection. It uses cryptographic integrity to reinforce the overall security framework rather than just relying on pattern recognition. A strong system that can fend off advanced cyberthreats in dynamic digital ecosystems is produced by the smooth collaboration of ECC's mathematical rigor, machine learning's pattern identification skills, and image processing's visualization techniques. This collaboration opens the door to intelligent, flexible cybersecurity solutions that may change to meet new attack methods while preserving effectiveness and performance.

F. Machine Learning Algorithm For Ctc Detection

The foundation of contemporary automated detection systems is machine learning, which provides a revolutionary method for spotting intricate dangers like secret timing channels. Machine learning systems have the capacity to generalize from data, in contrast to conventional rule-based systems that mostly rely on pre-defined signatures or heuristic rules. This gives them the capacity to spot patterns of unusual activity that they had not previously noticed, which is very useful when spotting secret channels that are made to look like normal network activity.

Machine learning's ability to learn from past traffic patterns and spot minute statistical anomalies that depart from expected norms is the key to using it for CTC detection. Frequently, these anomalies are too complex to be detected by static analysis or manual inspection. Large volumes of network traffic, both malicious and benign, are fed into learning algorithms that examine timing intervals, packet speeds, and inter-arrival periods during the crucial training phase. The system learns the underlying distribution of typical communication patterns through this process, which helps it identify variations that would indicate the existence of covert communication.

Dynamically updating machine learning models improves the detecting process even further. These models adapt to new threats and advanced adversarial strategies by constantly absorbing new data and modifying their internal parameters. This flexibility guarantees that the detection framework will continue to function well even when attack vectors change quickly. Proactive threat mitigation is made possible by the system's ability to provide predictive insights through the fusion of historical analysis with real-time traffic monitoring.

A strong layer of cryptographic rigor is added to this architecture by integrating elliptic curve cryptography. A synergistic protection mechanism is produced by combining machine learning's strength in pattern recognition with ECC's lightweight yet reliable security. Machine learning makes sure that hidden timing irregularities are effectively uncovered, while ECC guarantees the safe transfer and integrity of data throughout the analysis process. When combined, they create a coherent system that can detect and prevent hidden timing channel attacks instantly.

Moreover, the learning models get an extra modality to examine when image processing methods are integrated into this pipeline, such as converting network traffic features into visual patterns. Convolutional neural networks and other deep learning architectures can analyze network actions as spatial patterns thanks to visual data representations, which improves the accuracy of anomaly detection. This multimodal strategy greatly improves detection accuracy and makes it harder for attackers to evade detection.

In the end, machine learning's theoretical underpinnings for covert timing channel identification are based on its innate capacity to recognize high-dimensional, non-linear patterns in enormous data streams. This method becomes a multi-layered, intelligent system when it is reinforced by elliptic curve cryptography and image-based interpretation. In addition to identifying fraudulent timing channels, it maintains data confidentiality, guarantees system integrity, and adapts constantly to the demands of contemporary cybersecurity issues.

G. Covert Timing Channel Identification

A key focus of the automated covert timing channel detection system that combines machine learning and image processing with SnapCatch is the detection of covert timing channels. This process involves methodically identifying and analyzing network traffic patterns that may indicate covert communication routes. Through image processing, the integrated technique graphically represents traffic patterns by converting raw network data into colorful images that highlight subtle and often imperceptible changes in timing and packet sizes. Through these visual representations, anomalies that may point to the presence of secret communication are made easier to spot.

Machine learning algorithms analyze these images and learn from the gathered data, enabling the system to detect even the smallest temporal channels. These algorithms are trained on large-scale datasets of labeled network traffic, which helps them detect anomalies and patterns characteristic of covert channels. By progressively learning these traits, the machine learning models increase their precision and effectiveness in identifying new and evolving covert communication tactics used by cybercriminals.

By combining these techniques, the system can automatically find and detect hidden timing channels, improving cybersecurity and taking preventative measures. Because less manual monitoring is needed when the detection process is automated, potential threats can be quickly addressed before they have an opportunity to compromise the network. Additionally, by ensuring that secret paths are promptly identified and removed, the system's real-time features lessen the likelihood of data exfiltration and other malicious behavior.

The solution can scale effectively for large, active networks because to the combination of machine learning and image processing, which also increases the accuracy of covert channel detection. As a result, SnapCatch is a helpful tool in professional contexts where more traditional methods of identifying hidden channels might not be enough. As a result, the system provides a robust protection against emerging cyberthreats that employ covert communication methods and is crucial to strengthening the entire security architecture.

H. Automatic Ctc Detection And Localization

Covert timing channel (CTC) localization and identification are given top priority in SnapCatch's automated approach to CTC discovery. By utilizing sophisticated methods that include machine learning and image processing, the framework automatically finds and identifies hidden channels in network traffic. The system can detect even the slightest timing deviations that could suggest the presence of hidden channels by precisely localizing covert timing abnormalities using machine learning algorithms. These algorithms undergo constant training to increase their detection accuracy and capabilities as they learn from new data patterns and potential threats.

Network traffic is graphically represented by image processing techniques, which turn the raw data into comprehensible and eye-catching pictures that highlight hidden patterns. By effectively showing intricate network traffic flows, this technique facilitates the identification of anomalies that are not immediately noticeable in raw data or conventional network logs. SnapCatch significantly improves its detection skills by transforming network traffic into visual images, which enable a deeper degree of analysis that takes the data's temporal and spatial properties into account. The integrated technique ensures that hidden timing channels are not only identified but also precisely detected inside the data flow by fusing the benefits of machine learning and image processing. This synergy enables the real-time discovery of covert communication routes, providing network managers with valuable information and enabling faster responses to potential attacks. Additionally, the technology significantly reduces the time and manual effort typically required for such tasks by automatically identifying and locating CTCs, improving overall operating efficiency. Thus, by offering proactive detection techniques that can adapt to evolving internet threats, SnapCatch enhances network security. The continuous monitoring and precise location of CTCs allows the system to reduce unauthorized data exfiltration, espionage, and other hostile acts that rely on covert channels. By spotting and removing hidden risks before they worsen, SnapCatch helps to protect sensitive data and maintain the integrity of network communication infrastructure.

5. ALGORITHM USED

The suggested methodology combines elliptic curve cryptography (ECC) with machine learning techniques to efficiently discover and neutralize covert timing channels (CTCs) with high precision. In order to distinguish between benign and covert activity, the method starts with compiling a well-annotated dataset of both overt and covert traffic patterns. This dataset includes important characteristics including transmission lengths, packet sizes, and inter-arrival intervals. The extraction of pertinent features that capture traffic abnormalities across time is the next stage. Machine learning models, such as Random Forests, Support Vector Machines (SVM), and Neural Networks, as well as ensemble methods, are subsequently trained using these extracted characteristics. Using labeled data, the model learns to differentiate between covert and regular communication during training. The system switches to real-time monitoring mode after training, when incoming network data is continuously examined.

In order to enable proactive identification and mitigation of suspicious activity, pertinent features are retrieved and sent to the trained machine learning model, which categorizes the traffic as either overt or covert. Elliptic curve cryptography (ECC) is used to protect the recorded data. Sensitive network communication features are encrypted by ECC before being converted into visual representations that show timing irregularities. Throughout the analytical pipeline, the encrypted data guarantees the information's integrity by guarding against modification and eavesdropping. To find temporal irregularities suggestive of secret channels, sophisticated image-processing techniques are applied to the encrypted visual features. Pre-trained machine learning models, such SVM, Random Forests, or Neural Networks, are then used to classify these attributes in order to accurately identify covert timing channels across a variety of traffic patterns. To sum up, the SnapCatch system offers a reliable, safe, and clever way to identify hidden timing channels by fusing ECC, machine learning, and image processing. This method greatly improves the security of network infrastructures by guaranteeing the safe handling of data and making it possible to precisely identify concealed communication channels.

6. RESULT ANALYSIS

This comparative study provides significant insights into the practical uses and utility of three distinct approaches in the fields of network security and cryptography, in addition to assessing their performance: neural networks (NN), naive bayes (NB), and elliptic curve cryptography (ECC). There are distinct advantages and potential disadvantages to each strategy, thus it is crucial to evaluate them in different situations in order to decide which is best for a particular use case. The study thoroughly examines these algorithms' accuracy levels because it is essential to their performance in real-world cryptography applications. With an accuracy rate of 70%, Neural Networks (NN) and Naive Bayes (NB) both show good performance in a variety of test scenarios. This level of accuracy implies that while NN and NB can perform well on certain tasks, such pattern recognition and data classification, their capabilities may not be as advanced for more complex cryptographic procedures. These models may not perform well in scenarios when accuracy and security are essential, despite their inherent advantages, which include managing large datasets and spotting non-linear trends. Their very moderate accuracy highlights the necessity for ongoing optimization and improvement to achieve higher standards of reliability in securing sensitive data. In contrast, Elliptic Curve Cryptography (ECC) stands out in this comparison analysis with an outstanding 80% accuracy rate. ECC's dependability is demonstrated by this significant speed increase, especially in cryptographic situations that demand high degrees of security and precision. ECC is a well-liked choice for modern cryptographic systems because of its ability to efficiently handle encryption and decryption processes while maintaining high security. ECC is very reliable in protecting data from cyberattacks and unauthorized access, as seen by its 80% accuracy rate, which demonstrates its outstanding ability to ensure data integrity. ECC's impressive performance in this study solidifies its position as a leading player in cryptographic applications in the future. In addition to outperforming NN and NB, its accuracy demonstrates how robust it is at providing secure communications in a rapidly evolving digital context. Decision-makers and cybersecurity specialists can have a better understanding of which algorithms to give priority to when developing secure systems, particularly in situations when accuracy is crucial, according to this comparison study.

In evaluating the effectiveness of a security system, the study also highlights the significance of algorithmic selection. Because even the smallest errors can lead to major breaches in cryptographic applications, selecting an algorithm with a higher degree of precision becomes essential. The outstanding performance of ECC under a range of testing situations gives developers and end users alike peace of mind that critical data is shielded from any threats. In order to leverage ECC's potential to improve data protection techniques, the article suggests more investigation into its capabilities and incorporation into broader security frameworks. The comparison study, in summary, highlights the relative benefits of NN, NB, and ECC while also emphasizing the importance of accuracy in protecting digital communications. As the cybersecurity environment advances, ECC is a strong contender for cryptographic applications because to its increased accuracy and durability, providing a solid foundation for the continuous protection of personal information. This study offers guidance on selecting cryptographic algorithms, making it an excellent resource for anyone trying to increase the efficacy and security of their systems.

Table 1. Comparison table

Comparison Table		
S.NO	*Method*	*Accuracy*
1	**Neural Networks (NN) and Naive Bayes (NB)**	**70**
2	**Elliptical Curve Cryptography**	**80**

Figure 2. Comparison graph

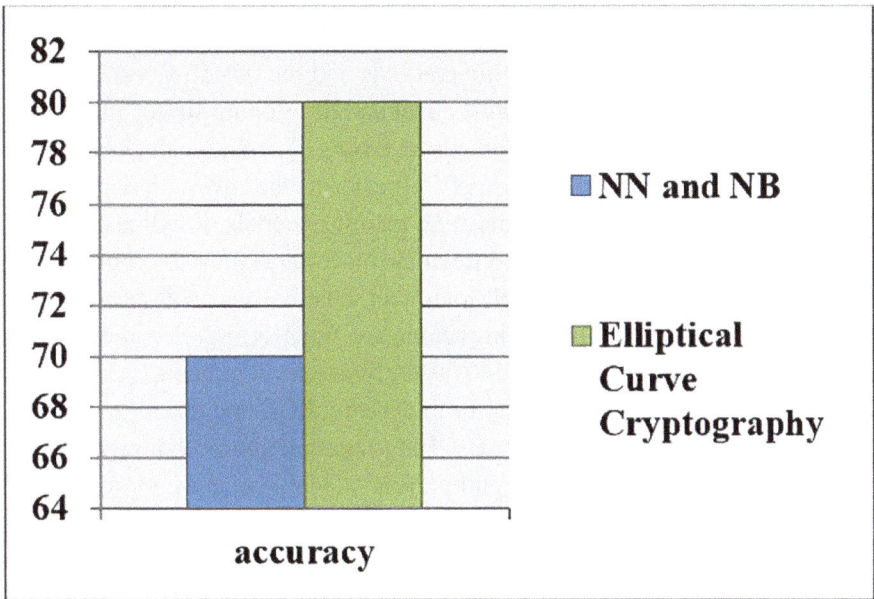

7. CONCLUSION

Elliptic Curve Cryptography (ECC) and machine learning algorithms together offer a sophisticated and very successful method for detecting covert timing channels (CTCs). This approach greatly improves the capacity to identify and eliminate covert communication techniques in real-time by fusing the strong encryption strength of ECC with the adaptive learning capabilities of machine learning models. ECC is a great option for applications that need both efficiency and strong security because of its strength in offering high security with reduced key sizes.

This combination of technologies not only improves detection accuracy but also provides flexibility, enabling the system to adjust to new and developing threats—a crucial requirement in the always shifting field of cybersecurity. The detection procedure is kept safe and robust against possible malevolent manipulations thanks to the cryptographic integrity of ECC, which also preserves encrypted data transfers that shield private data from unwanted access.

The report acknowledges the difficulties that still exist in spite of these developments. The smooth integration of ECC into real-time detection systems is one of the main challenges, especially given the computational burden that ECC can place, especially when handling large volumes of network data. Additionally, machine learning algorithms must constantly advance to keep up with cyber attackers' increasingly sophisticated covert communication strategies. This calls for constant research to improve the cryptographic methods and the detection system, making sure that they continue to work against novel and developing strategies.

In order to address more complex covert timing channel techniques, future research should concentrate on improving ECC performance, investigating lightweight ECC alternatives, and developing machine learning models. It will also be crucial to broaden the system's scope to accommodate more data kinds and communication protocols. This could make it possible to protect sensitive data in a variety of sectors where data security is crucial, including healthcare, finance, and telecommunications.

In summary, this study prepares the way for future developments in cybersecurity while also showcasing the possibility of integrating ECC and machine learning for the detection of hidden timing channels. The suggested approach provides a strong basis for addressing hidden threats and presents a viable plan to improve communication channel security. This strategy could become a complete security solution with more research and development that can proactively identify, mitigate, and stop covert channel exploitation in a variety of network scenarios.

REFERENCES

Caviglione, L. (2021). Trends and challenges in network covert channels counter-measures. *Applied Sciences (Basel, Switzerland)*, *11*(4), 1641. Advance online publication. DOI: 10.3390/app11041641

Frolova, D., Kogos, K., & Epishkina, A. (2021, January). Traffic normalization for covert channel protecting. In *2021 IEEE Conference of Russian Young Researchers in Electrical and Electronic Engineering (ElConRus)* (pp. 1132–1135). IEEE. DOI: 10.1109/ElConRus51938.2021.9396163

Han, J., Shi, F., Huang, C., & Liu, J. (2020). Covert timing channel detection method based on time interval and payload length analysis. *Computers & Security*, *97*, 101952. Advance online publication. DOI: 10.1016/j.cose.2020.101952

Mazurczyk, W., Wendzel, S., & Zander, S. (2016). Unified description for network information hiding methods. *Journal of Universal Computer Science*, *22*(11), 1456–1486. DOI: 10.3217/jucs-022-11-1456

Mileva, A., Velinov, A., Hartmann, L., Wendzel, S., & Mazurczyk, W. (2021). Comprehensive analysis of MQTT 5.0 susceptibility to network covert channels. *Computers & Security*, *104*, 102207. Advance online publication. DOI: 10.1016/j.cose.2021.102207

Tian, J., Xiong, G., Li, Z., & Gou, G. (2020). A survey of key technologies for constructing network covert channels. *Security and Communication Networks, 2020*. *Security and Communication Networks*, *8892896*, 1–20. DOI: 10.1155/2020/8892896

Vaccari, I., Narteni, S., Aiello, M., Mongelli, M., & Cambiaso, E. (2021). Exploiting Internet of Things protocols for malicious data exfiltration activities. *IEEE Access : Practical Innovations, Open Solutions*, *9*, 104261–104280. DOI: 10.1109/ACCESS.2021.3099642

Vanderhallen, S., Van Bulck, J., Piessens, F., & Mühlberg, J. T. (2021). Robust authentication for automotive control networks through covert channels. *Computer Networks*, *193*, 108079. Advance online publication. DOI: 10.1016/j.comnet.2021.108079

Wu, Z., Wang, Y., Shen, X., Xiong, Q., & Liu, G. (2021). A review of steganography and steganalysis in Voice over IP. *Sensors (Basel)*, *21*(4), 1032. DOI: 10.3390/s21041032 PMID: 33546240

Zhang, L., Huang, T., Rasheed, W., Hu, X., & Zhu, T. (2019). An enlarging-the-capacity packet sorting covert channel. *IEEE Access : Practical Innovations, Open Solutions*, *7*, 145634–145640. DOI: 10.1109/ACCESS.2019.2945320

Chapter 12
Blockchain–Enhanced Future Unlocking:
Leveraging Deep Learning for Predicting Cryptocurrency Prices for Digital Media

P. Umamaheswari
https://orcid.org/0000-0003-2007-697X
SASTRA University, India

ABSTRACT

Cryptocurrency, a digital form of currency, functions as an alternative payment method employing encryption algorithms. Despite its potential, the cryptocurrency market is characterized by high volatility and intricate datasets, featuring complex interactions between predictors. Conventional techniques may struggle to achieve optimal results in such a challenging environment. Predicting prices accurately is crucial to making the most money on bitcoin investments. For short-term trading and investing techniques, it is essential to identify both positive and negative market movements. The knowledge gathered from these assessments will provide practitioners with a better grasp of the obstacles facing the cryptocurrency market as well as workable solutions to reduce risks. The dataset, which was acquired from Yahoo Finance, contains daily information including the highest and lowest prices in addition to opening and closing prices. The main objective is to estimate the price of Bitcoin and deep learning algorithms are essential to forecasting these prices in the context of smart cities.

DOI: 10.4018/979-8-3373-1504-1.ch012

1. INTRODUCTION

The innovative technology known as cryptocurrency has become incredibly popular over time. To put it simply, it is a form of digital currency that controls the creation of new units and secures transactions using encryption techniques. Cryptocurrencies, in contrast to conventional currencies, are not issued or managed by a single entity, like a bank or government. Rather, they function on decentralized networks that employ blockchain technology (Yli-Huumo et al., 2016), which makes transactions safe, transparent, and unchangeable. Cryptocurrency stands as a groundbreaking technology that has garnered widespread acclaim in recent years. In essence, it represents a form of digital currency employing encryption techniques to ensure the security of transactions and regulate the generation of new units. Unlike traditional currencies, cryptocurrencies (Krishna Jyothi & Chaudhari, 2022) (Chen & Zhou, 2021) are not subject to issuance or control by a central authority, be it a government or a bank. Instead, they function on decentralized networks utilizing blockchain technology, thereby facilitating secure, transparent, and unalterable transactions.

The foremost cryptocurrency, Bitcoin, made its debut in 2009, and since then, numerous other cryptocurrencies have surfaced, each boasting distinctive features and potential applications. (Pour et al., 2022a) refers to a digital or virtual form of currency secured through cryptography. It can be transmitted directly between individuals without the involvement of intermediaries and operates independently of a central bank. The inception of Bitcoin in 2009 marked the beginning of cryptocurrencies, and since then, numerous others have been introduced, each possessing unique characteristics and applications. The decentralized nature of cryptocurrencies stands out as a significant advantage. A global network of computers maintains a public ledger, known as a blockchain, where transactions are recorded. This decentralized structure makes it challenging for any single individual or group to exert influence over the system. Anonymity is another advantage offered by cryptocurrencies. Despite participating in transactions recorded on the (Prasad & Rekha, 2023), the identities of individuals involved are not stored, making it appealing for those seeking financial privacy. However, cryptocurrencies face challenges. The decentralized structure, resistant to regulation, raises concerns about potential use in illegal activities like drug and money laundering.

Additionally, the volatile value of cryptocurrencies poses risks for investors. Despite these challenges, cryptocurrencies are gaining acceptance worldwide. Businesses widely accept Bitcoin and other cryptocurrencies, and several nations (Lamothe-Fernández et al., 2020) are exploring the creation of their own digital currencies and adaptation model also has been investigated for cryptocurrency market (Rzayev et al., 2024). The integration of cryptocurrencies in the landscape of smart cities adds another dimension, introducing innovative possibilities for transactions, privacy, and financial systems. A digital or virtual currency that uses cryptography for security is called cryptocurrency. Without the need for middlemen, it may be transmitted directly between people and works independently of a central bank. In 2009, the crypto currency known as Bitcoin was developed. Since then, countless more crypto currencies have been created, each with an own set of characteristics and applications.

Some research looks into how cryptocurrency blockchain technology affects the environment, with a particular emphasis on the uptake of Ethereum and Bitcoin. It investigates the consensus mechanisms—Proof of Work (PoW) and Proof of Stake (PoS)—and their relationship to carbon footprint using instrumental regression analysis. The results show a direct link between carbon emissions and the uptake of PoW-based cryptocurrencies like Bitcoin. Notably, compared to PoS-based transactions like Ethereum, PoW-based cryptocurrencies produce roughly 0.86 metric tons of carbon emissions per transaction, which is far greater. Concerns are also raised about possible shortages in PoW-based mining resources and the viability of Bitcoin mining following the fourth halving period. Timely block creation becomes more difficult as mining incentives decline. The study predicts declining returns by speculating about future stages of Bitcoin mining. Timely block creation becomes more difficult as mining incentives decline.

The analysis predicts declining payouts in each halving time by estimating future BTC mining phases, perhaps leaving about 2500 BTC units available for mining by 2120 (*Ujkan Q et al,2024*). This implies that using the present blockchain architecture to reach the entire 21 million BTC might prove to be nearly impossible. The study also emphasizes how speculative and dangerous cryptocurrencies are in the absence of regulatory control, which tends to draw careless investors. It emphasizes the significance of promoting ethical innovation and gaining a sophisticated grasp of the environmental effects of PoW cryptocurrencies. The study also emphasizes how important it is to take into account the effects of monetary policy and educate investors in order to promote responsible decision-making.

Authors from university of Oxford (Assamoi et al., 2025), have used portfolio sorting to examine cryptocurrency and considered 23 financial with uncertainty factors. The decentralized nature of crypto currencies is one of its main advantages. A network of computers around the world maintains a public ledger known as a blockchain, where transactions are recorded. Because of this, it is challenging for one person or group to influence the system. The opportunity for anonymity offered by cryptocurrencies is another advantage. The identities of the people participating in the transaction are not stored on the blockchain, despite it. People who want to keep their financial transactions private may find this useful. However, there are some difficulties with cryptocurrencies. Due to its decentralized structure's difficulty in regulation, concerns have been raised about its potential application in illegal activities like drug and money laundering. Cryptocurrencies can also have a very variable value, making them a risky investment and it is still growing in acceptance. Bitcoin and other cryptocurrencies are already widely accepted by businesses, and several nations have even started to create their own digital currencies. It will be interesting to observe how cryptocurrencies are used and regulated in the years to come as technology develops further.

Cryptocurrency market numerous obstacles prevent the market for crypto currencies from expanding and becoming more widely used. The biggest difficulty is security. Exchanges and wallets for crypto currencies are susceptible to theft and hacking, which may result in the loss of money. High trading costs are another issue, making it costly for investors to purchase and sell crypto currencies. Another difficulty the bitcoin industry (P. et al., 2022) is facing is a lack of liquidity. It can be challenging for investors to buy and sell significant amounts of cryptocurrency without having an impact on the market because many cryptocurrencies have low trading volumes. In addition, given cryptocurrencies' significant volatility, it may be challenging for investors to forecast their value and make wise investment choices. Another issue facing the bitcoin business is regulation. Governments and central banks are finding it difficult to keep up with the cryptocurrency market's explosive expansion and are debating how to regulate it. The absence of clear restrictions may make investing riskier and impede market expansion.

The bitcoin market continues to expand and change despite these obstacles. It is expected that the industry's problems will be solved and the market will continue to mature as the technology advances and laws become clearer. It will be intriguing to observe how cryptocurrencies are utilized and regulated in the years ahead as technology continues to evolve, particularly within the framework of smart city development. Cryptocurrency, a revolutionary digital or virtual currency, is making its mark on the landscape of smart cities, ushering in a new era of decentralized and efficient financial transactions. Smart cities leverage advanced technologies to enhance urban living, and the integration of cryptocurrencies aligns seamlessly with the following principles of innovation and efficiency. Decentralized Financial Ecosystem: Cryptocurrencies operate on decentralized networks using blockchain technology. This decentralized structure aligns with the ethos of smart cities, reducing reliance on traditional financial intermediaries and fostering a more direct and transparent financial ecosystem. Forecast of Bitcoin prices by utilizing a hybrid artificial neural network model comprising Long Short-Term Memory and Bayesian Optimization is proposed by (Pour et al., 2022b) the research community . The model's predictive capabilities are strong and have yet to be utilized for forecasting cryptocurrency prices. The authors discuss and expand on prior techniques for forecasting cryptocurrency values and enhance their approach. They end by presenting thorough graphs and tables showcasing the optimization outcomes.

The chapter examines the origins, establishment, and significance of Bitcoin and the role of artificial neural networks in forecasting cryptocurrency values. Artificial neural networks possess strong predictive capabilities and can be utilized for analyzing cryptocurrency price data across all time frames. The writers introduce a Neural Networks model combining LSTM and Bayesian Optimization to address the need for a cryptocurrency price prediction model in the existing literature. Biologically inspired computational networks called artificial neural networks (ANNs) can be utilized for estimating increasing or fluctuating numerical values. Artificial neural networks can be effective tools for forecasting increasing or fluctuating numerical values within this framework. Some of the key roles of block chain technology have been explored as below.

- Blockchain for Transparent Transactions:

Cryptocurrencies rely on the blockchain, which is a publicly maintained ledger by a group of computers. In a smart city setting, blockchain technology guarantees clear and unchangeable transaction records, offering a safe base for different financial operations.

- Enhanced Privacy and Security:

Cryptocurrencies provide advanced privacy capabilities. Even though transactions are logged on the blockchain, the personal identities of the people participating may not be saved. This focus on privacy is in line with the importance placed on data protection and personal privacy in smart city project.

- Smart Contracts for Efficiency:

Contracts that execute themselves with the terms written in code, are a vital aspect of various cryptocurrencies. In smart cities, these agreements can use technology to make different processes more efficient, such as paying for utilities or making contracts, cutting down on paperwork and improving

- Innovative Financial Services:

The integration of cryptocurrencies opens the door to innovative financial services in smart cities. From frictionless cross-border transactions to microtransactions for city services, cryptocurrencies enable new possibilities for financial inclusion and accessibility.

- Challenges and Considerations:

While the benefits are evident, challenges persist. Regulatory frameworks, security concerns, and the volatile nature of cryptocurrency values are factors that smart cities must carefully navigate. Addressing these challenges is crucial for the sustainable integration of cryptocurrencies in urban environments.g effectiveness.

- Future Outlook:

The adoption and application of digital currencies in intelligent urban areas are expected to increase. As technology progresses, smart cities may investigate different methods of utilizing cryptocurrencies for financial transactions and other purposes like identity management, voting systems, and beyond.

The subsequent sections of this article unfold as follows: In Section 2, we investigate into the background related work. Section 3 provides an introduction to the proposed architecture and details the dataset employed for analysis. Moving forward, Section 4 encompasses the presentation of results and a comprehensive discussion. The final stretch, Section 5, encapsulates the conclusion along with insights into potential future enhancements.

2. BACKGROUND RELATED WORK

Blockchain is essentially a decentralized database that includes a mix of technologies like linked storage structures cryptography, P2P network protocols, and agreement algorithms. As blockchain technology becomes more widely used, there is a growing variety of consensus algorithms to choose from. These algorithms can be tailored to different types of blockchain and business models, ensuring they are better suited for real-world applications. Modify the blockchain technology and its operational system to align better with real-world applications. Some researchers from University of Surrey (Nieto García & Wyss, 2022) have introduced a method for finding the generalized eigenvectors of a non-diagonalizable matrix. This is achieved by examining a diagonalizable perturbation of the matrix and determining the limit of its eigenvectors as it becomes non-diagonalizable. They calculate a portion of the spectrum of the diverse spin chain utilizing the Nested Coordinate Bethe

Ansatz. This demonstrates that the Bethe Ansatz for the twisted spin chain provides sufficient data to rebuild the specialized eigenvectors of the diverse spin chain.

Non-unitary systems are widely used in physics, being found in various applications such as optics, critical phenomena, and transport in biological systems. Nevertheless, non-Hermitian systems are not extensively researched because of their intricate nature. Having real eigenvalues is a consequence of a matrix being Hermitian, but it is not a requirement. The study (Sharma et al., 2024) suggests a "Blockchain and Multi-Code Trust Framework" in previous research to protect IoT devices from Distributed Denial of Service (DDoS) attacks. The system utilizes the decentralized and immutable features of blockchain technology, in addition to a trust mechanism driven by multiple codes. This strategy aims to establish a secure, strong, and dependable environment for IoT devices. Using blockchain's transparency, the methodology boosts trust and validation in network transactions, effectively shrinking the risk of DDoS attacks.

Implementing a multi-code system enhances security measures by adding multiple layers of protection to prevent potential breaches. The research utilized a variety of actual IoT network traffic data collected carefully from the "UNB IoT DDoS Data Set." The initial results suggest a notable enhancement in the security of IoT devices, showing a significant decrease in successful DDoS attacks, reaching a new height in IoT security. This study suggests a strong solution to an urgent problem and also creates opportunities for future advancements in securing IoT devices with blockchain technology.

Researchers in 2024 (Nayomi et al.,) have introduced a framework that utilizes cloud technology to combat phishing attacks in smart cities. The system utilizes a mix of machine learning and blockchain technologies in order to identify and stop phishing attacks. The system was tested with a set of phishing emails and proven to be successful in identifying and preventing phishing attempts with great precision. The experimental findings showed that the framework is effective in identifying and preventing phishing attacks, delivering precise and prompt reactions. The structure provides cost-effectiveness for both implementation and upkeep. The evaluation's quantitative findings demonstrated that the framework effectively defended against phishing attacks in smart cities. The system showed quick training times of 30 to 60 seconds and rapid inference times of 5 to 10 milliseconds. Resource usage varied from 80% to 75%. The framework demonstrates excellent scalability and robustness, making it well-suited for use in real-world settings. The suggested method offers an efficient way to decrease the risks linked to online scams in smart cities.

A Predictive Analytics System (Shamshad et al., 2023) will offer simplified reports on the top three cryptocurrencies, including ADA Cardano, Ethereum, and Binance coin, with different values over a span of ten days to help forecast digital market trends. The system suggestion includes a framework based on data science and six advanced data-driven algorithms: Support Vector Regressor, ARIMA, Facebook Prophet, Unidirectional LSTM, Bidirectional LSTM, and Stacked LSTM. Multiple repetitions of research experiments are conducted in order to optimize the performance of each algorithm through hyperparameter tuning. Findings show that ARIMA performs better than other models in every instance, accurately predicting price fluctuations within the true price span. On the other hand, Facebook Prophet shows satisfactory performance in certain aspects. The paper proposes that market analysts can benefit from the practical implications of using the ARIMA technique, as it allows them to make informed decisions by relying on precise price forecasts.

A new ensemble deep learning model proposed (Ye et al., 2022) for forecasting Bitcoin price by analyzing Twitter posts about Bitcoin. The model combines long short-term memory (LSTM) and gate recurrent unit (GRU) neural networks with stacking ensemble technique to enhance decision-making accuracy. The model utilizes social media posts instead of news platforms for public opinion data, analyzed using linguistic statistical techniques to create sentiment measures. The model chooses technical indicators and a financial market prediction model as inputs. Actual data ranging from September 2017 to January 2021 is utilized for the training and assessment of the model. The results of the experiment indicate that near-real-time prediction outperforms daily prediction, showing a mean absolute error (MAE) that is 88.74% better. Previous research has shown that incorporating cryptocurrencies into smart cities goes beyond changing monetary exchanges; it involves envisioning the future of city life. The collaboration of cryptocurrency and smart city projects creates a path towards a more inclusive, efficient, and technologically advanced urban setting.

3. PROPOSED METHOD

A deep learning-based approach has been proposed that uses sophisticated neural network topologies and historical market data to forecast cryptocurrency prices. Because of their extremely volatile and nonlinear price behavior, cryptocurrencies like Bitcoin and Ethereum are difficult to predict using conventional statistical techniques. Because deep learning models can identify intricate patterns, trends, and temporal correlations in the data, they are especially well-suited for this task.

3.1 Dataset description

Bitcoin, the pioneering cryptocurrency, has captivated the financial world since its inception in 2009. Over the years, its price dynamics have been subject to intense scrutiny and speculation. This research paper delves into a detailed analysis of Bitcoin price data spanning from 2014 to 2022. The dataset comprises daily records of opening and closing prices, high and low values, adjusted closing prices, and trading volumes across 3028 trading days. The following variables are included for analysis

Table 1. Dataset

Attribute	Description
Opening Price	The price of Bitcoin at the beginning of the trading day.
Closing Price	The price of Bitcoin at the end of the trading day.
Low Value	The lowest price of Bitcoin reached during the trading day.
High Value	The highest price of Bitcoin reached during the trading day.
Adjusted Close	The closing price adjusted for factors such as dividends, stock splits, etc.
Volume	The trading volume, indicating the total number of Bitcoin traded during the day.

Table. 1 provides a list of attributes of the dataset, showing the opening price, closing price, high value, low value, adjusted close, and volume for each trading day from 2014-01-01 to 2022-01-30. Each row represents a single observation for a particular trading day, with corresponding values for each variable.

3.2 Proposed Architecture

This section outlines the proposed architecture for cryptocurrency prediction. The architecture integrates historical price data, technical indicators, sentiment and on-chain blockchain metrics. These inputs are then processed through various preprocessing stages like feature scaling, outlier detection and deep learning models, such as GRU, LSTM, and CNN - LSTM, to identify patterns and predict future price trends. These deep learning models can be tailored for various aspects of cryptocurrency prediction, depending on the nature of the data and the specific problem at hand.

Figure 1. Architecture of the proposed methodology

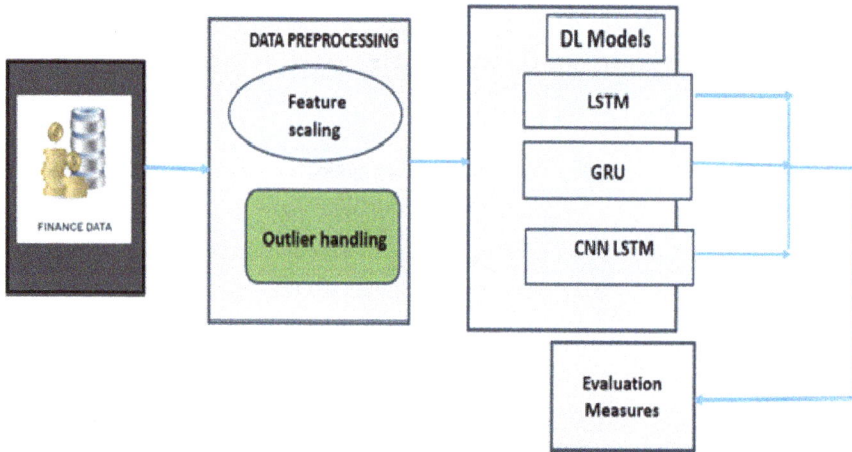

3.2.1 Feature Scaling

MinMaxScaler has been used to scale the dataset. Data normalization methods like MinMaxScaler are frequently employed in machine learning and data analysis. The input data is transformed into a range between 0 and 1 by use of this particular feature scaling technique. This scaling method's goal is to prevent the dataset's scale from favoring any single characteristic over others while ensuring that each feature is given equal weight. When using MinMaxScaler, each feature's minimum value is subtracted from its corresponding feature value, and the result is then divided by the feature's range. The difference between each feature's maximum and minimum values is known as the range. This transformation makes sure that each feature's minimum value is changed to 0 and its maximum value is changed to 1.

3.2.2 Outlier Handling

Because outliers can skew analysis and predictive models, managing them is a crucial step in processing financial data from sites like Yahoo Finance. Extreme market occurrences like crashes or booms, data entry mistakes, or unexpected trading activity can all result in outliers in financial datasets. Visualization tools like box plots and time-series graphs, as well as statistical procedures like Z-score analysis and the Interquartile Range (IQR), are used to identify these abnormalities. Once identified, these outliers can be dealt with using transformation methods such logarithmic scaling, elimination, or imputation using rolling averages or the median. Furthermore, machine learning models that are resistant to outliers, like ensemble approaches or decision trees, can be used. To differentiate real anomalies from noteworthy market events, domain-specific thresholds and market context are essential. Clean, trustworthy datasets for precise analysis and forecasting are ensured by automating outlier discovery.

3.2.3 Long Short Term Memory(LSTM)

LSTM kind of RNN"s has been successfully used to forecast bitcoin prices. Traditional time-series analysis methods struggle to anticipate cryptocurrency markets because of their volatility; however LSTM networks have showed promise in this area. Modeling sequential data, such as time-series data, is where LSTM networks excel. By utilizing memory cells, which enable the network to selectively recall or forget information over time, they are able to capture long-term dependencies in the data.

Figure 2. Basic architecture unit of LSTM

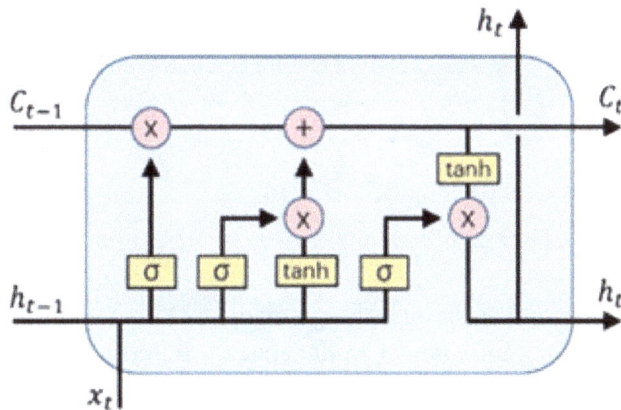

As a result, LSTM networks are highly adapted to forecasting cryptocurrency prices, which are greatly influenced by historical prices and market trends. An LSTM network would normally be trained on historical price data and other pertinent variables, such as trading volume and sentiment analysis of social media posts, in the context of cryptocurrency prediction. The ability of LSTM networks to recognize complicated patterns in the data that may be challenging to spot using conventional time-series analysis methods is one benefit of utilizing them for bitcoin prediction. Particularly in markets that are susceptible to unexpected events like abrupt volatility, this can result in predictions that are more accurate.

3.2.4 Gated Recurrent Unit (GRU)

Recurrent neural networks (RNNs) of the GRU (Gated Recurrent Unit) variety have demonstrated potential in the prediction of cryptocurrency prices. GRU networks are made to capture long-term dependencies in sequential data, much like LSTM networks do, which makes them ideal for modeling time-series data like cryptocurrency prices.

Figure 3. Basic architecture unit of GRU

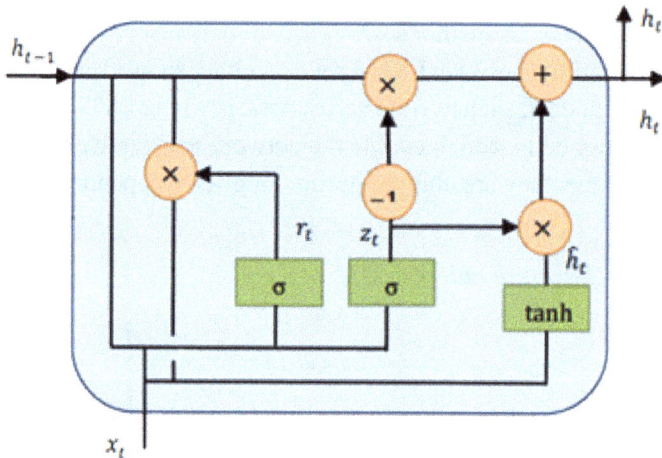

GRU networks have a simpler design than LSTM networks, which can make them quicker to train and simpler to understand. Based on a gating mechanism, GRU networks have the capacity to selectively remember or forget information over time. With the help of this gating mechanism, the network is better able to identify short-term dependencies in the data, which can be crucial in quickly evolving sectors like the cryptocurrency industry. It is crucial to remember that forecasting bitcoin prices is a difficult undertaking, and there are numerous variables that may affect how accurate the predictions are. Additionally, traders and investors should use caution when making judgments based on predictive models since past success is not a guarantee of future outcomes. In general, GRU networks are a promising technique for predicting cryptocurrency prices, and they are likely to remain a key focus of study and development in the deep learning for finance community.

It is crucial to carefully assess the effectiveness of GRU networks and to utilize them in conjunction with other tools and approaches for making informed trading decisions, just like with any predictive modeling technique.

3.3 CNN With LSTM

The forecasting of bitcoin values is one possible use for a CNN-LSTM model. The model may learn to forecast future prices based on fresh input data by being trained on past price data and other pertinent factors, such as trade volume and sentiment analysis of social media posts. The choice of input characteristics, the length of the input sequence, and the complexity of the network architecture are just a few examples of the numerous variables that can affect how accurate a CNN -LSTM model is. Trading and investing should exercise caution when making judgments based on predictive models since, as with any predictive modeling technique, historical success is not a guarantee of future outcomes. In general, a CNN- LSTM model has demonstrated good results in financial prediction ta tasks and is a strong tool for analyzing time-series data. To ensure the model's utility in real-world applications, extensive evaluation and validation of its performance are required, as with any deep learning architecture.

4. RESULTS AND DISCUSSION

Because financial time series data is very volatile and non-stationar, it is difficult to predict cryptocurrency prices. A machine learning model trained on bitcoin price data from Yahoo Finance shows the training loss and validation loss over 150 epochs in the figure. Improving model performance requires minimizing the losses, which are a measure of how well the model predictions match the actual values. The model is successfully learning patterns in the training data when the training loss continuously declines with only slight variations. The model architecture and optimizer appear to be well-suited for reducing the training error, based on this comparatively smooth trend. Particularly in the early epochs, the validation loss shows notable oscillations and spikes. These variations suggest that the model performs inconsistently on unseen data, most likely as a result of the noisy and erratic nature of bitcoin price data.

Figure 4. Training loss versus validation loss

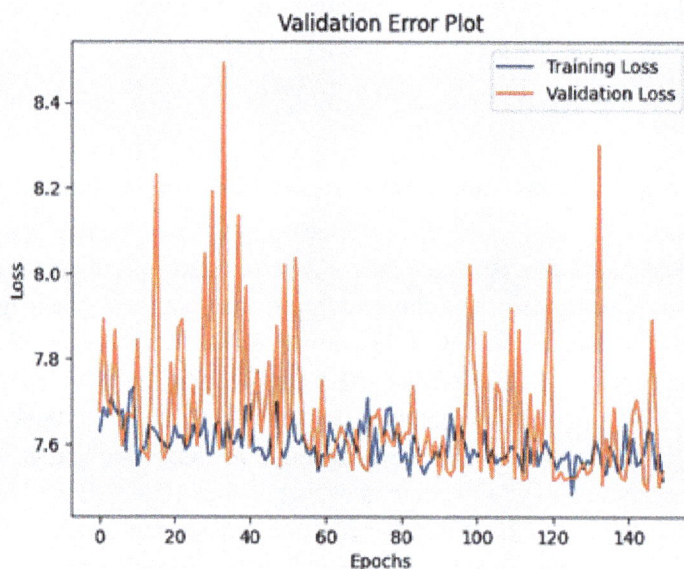

The validation loss begins to stabilize toward later epochs (around 120), indicating that the model is starting to generalize more effectively to unknown input. It seems that as training progresses, the validation and training losses converge. Even at later epochs, the sporadic spikes in validation loss could be an indication of poor hyperparameters or the underlying instability of the dataset. The sharp fluctuations in validation loss can be attributed to the highly unpredictable and dynamic nature of cryptocurrency prices. Cryptocurrencies are affected by various external factors, such as sudden news about regulations, hacks, or partnerships can cause rapid price changes. Low liquidity in some cryptocurrencies can lead to abrupt price movements. This scatter plot compares the actual values and the predicted values of cryptocurrency prices, derived from the Yahoo dataset. The x-axis represents the actual prices, while the y-axis represents the predicted prices generated by the model. This visualization provides insight into how accurately the model predicts cryptocurrency prices. He points in the scatter plot align closely along the diagonal line y=x, indicating that the predicted prices closely match the actual prices. This alignment suggests that the model has achieved high accuracy in predicting cryptocurrency prices.

Figure 5. Actual versus predicted

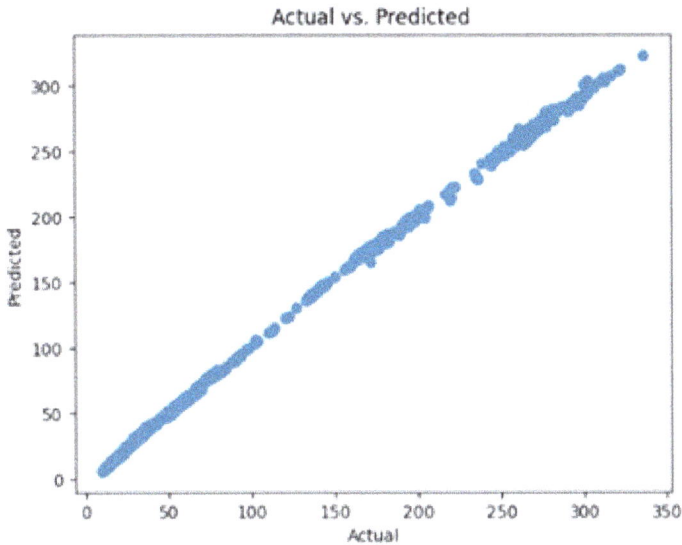
Actual vs. Predicted

The points form a tightly packed cluster around the diagonal, which further demonstrates low error between actual and predicted values. Few or no significant outliers are visible, meaning the model generalizes well across the dataset. The plot covers a wide range of prices (0–350), showing that the model performs consistently across different price levels, from low to high.

4.1 Comparison of Performance Measures

Cryptocurrency prediction has advanced significantly as a result of CNN-LSTM model tuning, which has produced decreased Mean Absolute Error (MAE) and Root Mean Square Error (RMSE) metrics. Long Short-Term Memory (LSTM) networks and Convolutional Neural Networks (CNNs) are combined in this hybrid architecture to efficiently capture temporal interdependence and spatial patterns in cryptocurrency data. These optimization techniques guarantee that the model's performance is both resilient and flexible enough to accommodate the extremely erratic character of financial markets. CNNs use different filter levels and optimum kernel sizes to detect complex patterns in the input data. The model effectively captures dependencies across time steps and is specifically designed for time-series data by utilizing one-dimensional convolutions. The model can learn from previous price movements and predict future trends thanks to the strong mechanism that LSTMs offer for managing sequential information.

Table 3. Performance analysis of LSTM,GRU and CNN-LSTM (Before PSO)

DL Model	RMSE	MAE
LSTM	23.98	19.78
GRU	20.87	18.97
CNN-LSTM	21.08	17.67

Table 4. Performance analysis of LSTM, GRU and CNN-LSTM (After PSO)

DL Model	RMSE	MAE
LSTM	19.25	18.87
GRU	18.87	17.87
CNN-LSTM	14.08	13.29

Figure 6. Comparison of error metrics

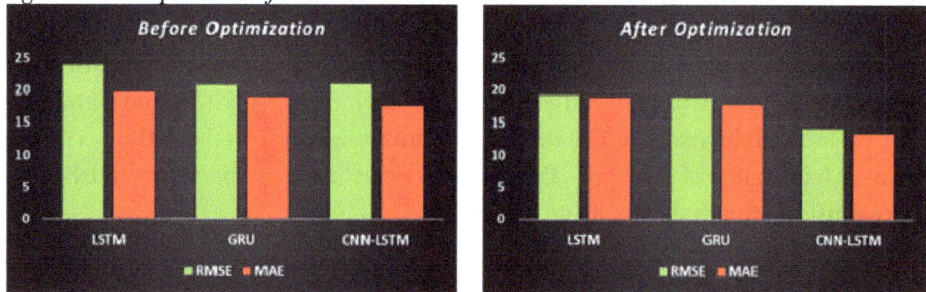

The LSTM model's error statistics are comparatively greater than those of the other models, with an RMSE of 23.98 and an MAE of 19.78. This implies that LSTM has trouble minimizing the squared error (RMSE) and the average error (MAE) in the absence of optimization. An RMSE of 20.87 and an MAE of 18.97 indicate that the GRU model outperforms the LSTM. Compared to LSTM, the GRU's architecture uses fewer parameters, which enables it to accomplish superior dataset generalization without overfitting.

The most significant improvement is observed in the CNN-LSTM model. After PSO, its RMSE decreases drastically to 14.08, and MAE improves to 13.29. This indicates that the convolutional layers' ability to extract high-level features, combined with the optimization provided by PSO, allows CNN-LSTM to outperform both LSTM and GRU. This performance improvement highlights the power of CNN-LSTM in handling both spatial and temporal patterns in time-series data. The model's capacity to generalize is further improved by methods such using dropout regularization and stacking numerous LSTM layers, which also lessen overfitting. We compare the performance of three deep learning models—Long Short-Term Memory (LSTM), Gated Recurrent Unit (GRU), and Convolutional Neural Network with LSTM (CNN-LSTM)—in terms of their Root Mean Squared Error (RMSE) and Mean Absolute Error (MAE), both before and after the application of Particle Swarm Optimization (PSO) for hyperparameter tuning

5. CONCLUSION AND FUTURE ENHANCEMENT

This chapter examined the use of deep learning methods to forecast cryptocurrency values, taking advantage of the models' innate capacity to identify intricate, non-linear patterns in data. Deep learning presents intriguing methods for overcoming the considerable hurdles posed by the high volatility, non-stationarity, and noise associated with bitcoin price fluctuations. Despite their advantages, deep learning models face challenges such as overfitting, sensitivity to hyperparameters, and reliance on large datasets. Furthermore, real-world application requires models to adapt to sudden market shifts, extreme events, and evolving market dynamics. As the cryptocurrency market continues to evolve, integrating cutting-edge advancements such as hybrid models (e.g., combining LSTMs with transformers), ensemble techniques, and explainable AI will enhance model interpretability and accuracy.

Additionally, incorporating blockchain analytics, social media trends, and macroeconomic indicators will enable more comprehensive and robust predictions. Deep learning has enormous promise for predicting cryptocurrency prices because it can bridge the gap between practical insights and the complexity of the market. Researchers and practitioners can fully utilize deep learning in financial forecasting by resolving present issues and welcoming upcoming developments, opening the door to more precise and trustworthy market projections.

REFERENCES

Assamoi, V. K., Ekponon, A., & Guo, Z. (2025). Are cryptocurrencies priced in the cross-section? A portfolio approach. *Finance Research Letters*, *71*, 106437. DOI: 10.1016/j.frl.2024.106437

Bajra, U. Q., Rogova, E., & Avdiaj, S. (2024). Cryptocurrency blockchain and its carbon footprint: Anticipating future challenges. *Technology in Society*, *77*, 102571. DOI: 10.1016/j.techsoc.2024.102571

Chen, S., & Zhou, C. (2021). Stock Prediction Based on Genetic Algorithm Feature Selection and Long Short-Term Memory Neural Network. *IEEE Access : Practical Innovations, Open Solutions*, *9*, 9066–9072. DOI: 10.1109/ACCESS.2020.3047109

Krishna Jyothi, K., & Chaudhari, S. (2022). A novel block chain based cluster head authentication protocol for machine-type communication in LTE network: Statistical analysis on attack detection. *Journal of King Saud University. Computer and Information Sciences*, *34*(6), 3713–3721. DOI: 10.1016/j.jksuci.2020.08.014

Lamothe-Fernández, P., Alaminos, D., Lamothe-López, P., & Fernández-Gámez, M. A. (2020). Deep Learning Methods for Modeling Bitcoin Price. *Mathematics*, *8*(8), 1245. DOI: 10.3390/math8081245

Nayomi, B. D. D., Mallika, S. S., & Bhavsingh, M. (n.d.). A Cloud-Assisted Framework Utilizing Blockchain, Machine Learning, and Artificial Intelligence to Countermeasure Phishing Attacks in Smart Cities. *International Journal of Intelligent Systems and Applications in Engineering*.

Nieto García, J. M., & Wyss, L. (2022). Jordan blocks and the Bethe Ansatz I: The eclectic spin chain as a limit. *Nuclear Physics B*, *981*, 115860. DOI: 10.1016/j.nuclphysb.2022.115860

P., U., S., A., M., K., & P., D. (2022). Potential Market-Predictive Features Based Bitcoin Price Prediction Using Machine Learning Algorithms: In A. Srinivasan (Ed.), *Advances in Computational Intelligence and Robotics* (pp. 233–245). IGI Global. DOI: 10.4018/978-1-7998-8892-5.ch014

Pour, E. S., Jafari, H., Lashgari, A., Rabiee, E., & Ahmadisharaf, A. (2022a). Cryptocurrency Price Prediction with Neural Networks of LSTM and Bayesian Optimization. *European Journal of Business and Management Research*, *7*(2), 20–27. DOI: 10.24018/ejbmr.2022.7.2.1307

Pour, E. S., Jafari, H., Lashgari, A., Rabiee, E., & Ahmadisharaf, A. (2022b). Cryptocurrency Price Prediction with Neural Networks of LSTM and Bayesian Optimization. *European Journal of Business and Management Research*, *7*(2), 20–27. DOI: 10.24018/ejbmr.2022.7.2.1307

Prasad, S. N., & Rekha, C. (2023). Block chain based IAS protocol to enhance security and privacy in cloud computing. *Measurement. Sensors*, *28*, 100813. DOI: 10.1016/j.measen.2023.100813

Rzayev, K., Sakkas, A., & Urquhart, A. (2024). An adoption model of cryptocurrencies. *European Journal of Operational Research*. Advance online publication. DOI: 10.1016/j.ejor.2024.11.024

Shamshad, H., Ullah, F., Ullah, A., Kebande, V. R., Ullah, S., & Al-Dhaqm, A. (2023). Forecasting and Trading of the Stable Cryptocurrencies With Machine Learning and Deep Learning Algorithms for Market Conditions. *IEEE Access : Practical Innovations, Open Solutions*, *11*, 122205–122220. DOI: 10.1109/ACCESS.2023.3327440

Sharma, K. V., Sarada, Ch., Vasavi, M., & Ambika, K. (2024). Securing IoT Devices from DDoS Attacks through Blockchain and Multi-Code Trust Framework. *E3S Web of Conferences, 472*, 03001. DOI: 10.1051/e3sconf/202447203001

Ye, Z., Wu, Y., Chen, H., Pan, Y., & Jiang, Q. (2022). A Stacking Ensemble Deep Learning Model for Bitcoin Price Prediction Using Twitter Comments on Bitcoin. *Mathematics*, *10*(8), 1307. DOI: 10.3390/math10081307

Yli-Huumo, J., Ko, D., Choi, S., Park, S., & Smolander, K. (2016). Where Is Current Research on Blockchain Technology?—A Systematic Review. *PLoS One*, *11*(10), e0163477. DOI: 10.1371/journal.pone.0163477 PMID: 27695049

Compilation of References

Aarthi, S., Aravinthan, K., Ravikumar, R. N., Sivakumar, N., & Wanglen, S. (2025). Cryptography securing data in motion within Blockchain, internet of everything, and Federated Learning. In *Convergence of Blockchain, Internet of Everything, and Federated Learning for Security* (pp. 39–78). IGI Global. DOI: 10.4018/979-8-3373-1424-2.ch002

Ahmed, M. F., Khan, M. R. A. A., Islam, M. R., & Islam, M. N. (2024). AI and blockchain for regulatory compliance: Enhancing transparency and efficiency in governance. Journal of Artificial Intelligence General Science (JAIGS), 7(01), 278–290.

Ahmed, I., Zhang, Y., Jeon, G., Lin, W., Khosravi, M. R., & Qi, L. (2022, September). A blockchain-and artificial intelligence-enabled smart IoT framework for sustainable city. *International Journal of Intelligent Systems*, 37(9), 6493–6507. DOI: 10.1002/int.22852

Andronie, M., Blazek, R., Iatagan, M., Skypalova, R., U ă, C., Dijmărescu, A., Kovacova, M., Grecu, G., Pârvu, I., Strakova, J., Guni, C., Zabojnik, S., Chiru, C., Sedláčková, A. N., Novák, A., & Dijmărescu, I. (2024, December 1). Generative artificial intelligence algorithms in Internet of Things blockchain-based fintech management. *Oeconomia Copernicana.*, 15(4), 1349–1381. DOI: 10.24136/oc.3283

An, J., Zhang, S., Yang, H., Gupta, S., Huang, J.-B., Luo, J., & Yin, X. (2023). Latent-shift: Latent diffusion with temporal shift for efficient text-to-video generation. arXiv. https://arxiv.org/abs/2304.08477

Ashraf, H., Ihsan, U., Ullah, A., Ray, S. K., & Khan, N. A. (2025). Blockchain and generative AI for securing distributed systems. In *Reshaping cybersecurity with generative AI techniques* (pp. 201–218). IGI Global.

Assamoi, V. K., Ekponon, A., & Guo, Z. (2025). Are cryptocurrencies priced in the cross-section? A portfolio approach. *Finance Research Letters*, 71, 106437. DOI: 10.1016/j.frl.2024.106437

Ayissi, B. D., Befoum, S. R., & Kombou, V. (2023). AI-Driven Blockchain: A Review of Pathways to Self-Sovereign Intelligence. *Available at SSRN* 4645170.

Bain, R., Cronk, R., Wright, J., Yang, H., Slaymaker, T., & Bartram, J. (2014). Fecal contamination of drinking-water in low- and middle-income countries: A systematic review and meta-analysis. *PLoS Medicine, 11*(5), e1001644. DOI: 10.1371/journal.pmed.1001644 PMID: 24800926

Bajra, U. Q., Rogova, E., & Avdiaj, S. (2024). Cryptocurrency blockchain and its carbon footprint: Anticipating future challenges. *Technology in Society, 77*, 102571. DOI: 10.1016/j.techsoc.2024.102571

Bakan, U., & Atabey, Z. (2024). Symbolizing creativity. In *Advances in Human and Social Aspects of Technology* (pp. 261–286). IGI Global.

Baltrusaitis, T., Ahuja, C., & Morency, L.-P. (2019). Multimodal machine learning: A survey and taxonomy. *IEEE Transactions on Pattern Analysis and Machine Intelligence, 41*(2), 423–443. DOI: 10.1109/TPAMI.2018.2798607 PMID: 29994351

Barati, M., Rana, O., Petri, I., & Theodorakopoulos, G. (2020). GDPR compliance verification in internet of things. *IEEE Access: Practical Innovations, Open Solutions, 8*, 119697–119709. DOI: 10.1109/ACCESS.2020.3005509

Berthelot, D., Schumm, T., & Metz, L. (2017). BEGAN: Boundary equilibrium generative adversarial networks. *arXiv*. https://arxiv.org/abs/1703.10717

Bhui, R., & Jiao, P. (2023). Attention constraints and learning in categories. *Management Science, 69*(9), 5394–5404. https://psycnet.apa.org/doi/10.1287/mnsc.2023.4803. DOI: 10.1287/mnsc.2023.4803

Bhumichai, D., Smiliotopoulos, C., Benton, R., Kambourakis, G., & Damopoulos, D. (2024). The Convergence of Artificial Intelligence and Blockchain: The State of Play and the Road Ahead. *Information, 15*(5), 268. https://doi.org/10.3390/info15050268 DOI: 10.3390/info15050268

Brewer, J., Patel, D., Kim, D., & Murray, A. (2024). Navigating the challenges of generative technologies: Proposing the integration of artificial intelligence and blockchain. *Business Horizons, 67*(5), 525–535.

Buldas, A., Draheim, D., Gault, M., Laanoja, R., Nagumo, T., Saarepera, M., Shah, S. A., Simm, J., Steiner, J., Tammet, T., & Truu, A. (2022). An ultra-scalable blockchain platform for universal asset tokenization: Design and implementation. *IEEE Access: Practical Innovations, Open Solutions, 10*, 77284–77322. DOI: 10.1109/ACCESS.2022.3192837

Caviglione, L. (2021). Trends and challenges in network covert channels counter-measures. *Applied Sciences (Basel, Switzerland)*, *11*(4), 1641. Advance online publication. DOI: 10.3390/app11041641

Chang, Z., Zhang, X., Wang, S., Ma, S., Ye, Y., Xinguang, X., & Gao, W. (2021). Mau: A motion-aware unit for video prediction and beyond. *Advances in Neural Information Processing Systems*, *34*, 26950–26962.

Chauhan, N. (2025). Revolutionizing digital content authentication: The power of synthetic media detection. *INTERNATIONAL JOURNAL OF SCIENTIFIC RE-SEARCH IN ENGINEERING AND*, *09*(05), 1–9. DOI: 10.55041/IJSREM46858

Chen, S., & Zhou, C. (2021). Stock Prediction Based on Genetic Algorithm Feature Selection and Long Short-Term Memory Neural Network. *IEEE Access : Practical Innovations, Open Solutions*, *9*, 9066–9072. DOI: 10.1109/ACCESS.2020.3047109

Cui, X., Khan, D., He, Z., & Cheng, Z. (2023). Fusing surveillance videos and three-dimensional scene: A mixed reality system. *Computer Animation and Virtual Worlds*, *34*(1), e2129. DOI: 10.1002/cav.2129

Dong, C., Loy, C. C., He, K., & Tang, X. (2016). Image super-resolution using deep convolutional networks. *IEEE Transactions on Pattern Analysis and Machine Intelligence*, *38*(2), 295–307. DOI: 10.1109/TPAMI.2015.2439281 PMID: 26761735

Echenim, J. I. (2025). Integration of Artificial Intelligence and blockchain for Intelligent Autonomous Systems. *International Journal of Future Engineering Innovations*, *2*(3), 31–37. DOI: 10.54660/IJFEI.2025.2.3.31-37

Edam, S. M. I. (2025). Restructuring the landscape of generative AI research. In *Impacts of generative AI on the future of research and education* (pp. 287–334). IGI Global. DOI: 10.4018/979-8-3693-0884-4.ch012

Ekeledirichukwu, T. O., & Msughter, E. A. (2024). Digital generative multimedia tool theory (DGMTT): A theoretical postulation. *Journalism and Mass Communi-cation*, *14*(3), 139–160. DOI: 10.17265/2160-6579/2024.03.004

Engy, Y. (2024). Developments on generative AI. In Generative, A. I. (Ed.), *Oppor-tunities and challenges* (pp. 139–160). CRC Press. DOI: 10.1201/9781003501152-9

Eszteri, D. (2022). Blockchain and artificial intelligence: Connecting two distinct technologies to comply with GDPR's data protection by design principle. *Masaryk Univ. J. Law Technol.*, *16*(1), 59–88. DOI: 10.5817/MUJLT2022-1-3

Fan, S., Ilk, N., Kumar, A., Xu, R., & Zhao, J. L. (2024, July 1). Blockchain as a trust machine: From disillusionment to enlightenment in the era of generative AI. *Decision Support Systems*, *182*, 114251. DOI: 10.1016/j.dss.2024.114251

Fazi, M. A. (2022). A contextual study of regulatory framework for blockchain. In *Regulatory Aspects of Artificial Intelligence on Blockchain* (pp. 40–51). IGI Global. DOI: 10.4018/978-1-7998-7927-5.ch003

Feuerriegel, S., Hartmann, J., Janiesch, C., & Zschech, P. (2024). Generative AI. *Business & Information Systems Engineering*, *66*(1), 111–126. DOI: 10.1007/s12599-023-00834-7

Fitriawijaya, A., & Jeng, T. (2024). Integrating multimodal generative AI and Blockchain for enhancing generative design in the early phase of architectural design process. *Buildings (Basel, Switzerland)*, *14*(8), 2533.

Flynn, M. A. (2025). How ChatGPT will [insert hyperbolic cliché here] the [insert industry here]: Creating media literacy infographics about generative AI. *Communication Teacher*, *39*(1), 42–48. DOI: 10.1080/17404622.2024.2392764

Frolova, D., Kogos, K., & Epishkina, A. (2021, January). Traffic normalization for covert channel protecting. In *2021 IEEE Conference of Russian Young Researchers in Electrical and Electronic Engineering (ElConRus)* (pp. 1132–1135). IEEE. DOI: 10.1109/ElConRus51938.2021.9396163

Gao, L., Zhang, X., Liu, T., Yang, H., Liao, B., & Guo, J. (2021). Energy-aware blockchain resource allocation algorithm with deep reinforcement learning for trusted authentication. In Lecture Notes of the Institute for Computer Sciences, Social Informatics and Telecommunications Engineering (pp. 93–103). Springer International Publishing. DOI: 10.1007/978-3-030-73562-3_8

Gitobu, C., & Ogetonto, J. (2025). Harnessing artificial intelligence (AI) and blockchain technology for the advancement of finance technology (FinTech) in businesses. *London Journal of Interdisciplinary Sciences*, *3*(3), 75–89. DOI: 10.31039/ljis.2024.3.292

Goodfellow, I. J., Pouget-Abadie, J., Mirza, M., Xu, B., Warde-Farley, D., Ozair, S., Courville, A., & Bengio, Y. (2014). Generative adversarial nets. Advances in Neural Information Processing Systems, 27, 2672–2680. https://papers.nips.cc/paper/5423-generative-adversarial-nets

Goodfellow, I. J., Pouget-Abadie, J., Mirza, M., Xu, B., Warde-Farley, D., Ozair, S., Courville, A., & Bengio, Y. (2014). Generative Adversarial Networks. arXiv.org. / arXiv.1406.2661DOI: 10.48550

Goodfellow, I., Bengio, Y., & Courville, A. (2016). *Deep learning*. MIT Press.

Gui, D., Chen, K., Ding, H., & Huo, Q. (2023). Zero-shot generation of training data with denoising diffusion probabilistic model for handwritten Chinese character recognition. *arXiv*. DOI: 10.1007/978-3-031-41679-8_20

Han, J., Shi, F., Huang, C., & Liu, J. (2020). Covert timing channel detection method based on time interval and payload length analysis. *Computers & Security*, *97*, 101952. Advance online publication. DOI: 10.1016/j.cose.2020.101952

Hanssen, F., Gabernet, G., Bäuerle, F., Stöcker, B., Wiegand, F., Smith, N. H., & Telzerow, A. труфанов, C. B., ступин, B. B., Костер, Ю., & Köster, J. (2024). NCBench: providing an open, reproducible, transparent, adaptable, and continuous benchmark approach for DNA-sequencing-based variant calling. *F1000Research, 12*, 1125. DOI: 10.12688/f1000research.140344.2

Hasselgren, A., Wan, P. K., Horn, M., Kralevska, K., & Gligoroski, D. (2020, October). GDPR Compliance for Blockchain Applications in Healthcare. Computer Science & Information Technology (CS & IT).

Hofman, D., Lemieux, V. L., Joo, A., & Batista, D. A. (2019). The margin between the edge of the world and infinite possibility. *Records Management Journal*, *29*(1/2), 240–257. DOI: 10.1108/RMJ-12-2018-0045

Ho, J., Jain, A., & Abbeel, P. (2020). Denoising diffusion probabilistic models. *Advances in Neural Information Processing Systems*, *33*, 6840–6851. DOI: 10.48550/arXiv.2006.11239

Ho, J., Saharia, C., Chan, W., Fleet, D. J., Norouzi, M., & Salimans, T. (2022). Cascaded diffusion models for high fidelity image generation. *Journal of Machine Learning Research*, *23*(1), 2249–2281. DOI: 10.48550/arXiv.2106.15282

Hong, Y., Yang, J., Chang, H., & Shi, J. (2018). The unsupervised learning of visual representations by predicting scene dynamics. *International Conference on Computer Vision (ICCV)*.

Huang, H. (2023). *Free-Bloom: Zero-Shot Text-to-Video Generator with LLM Director and LDM Animator*. arXiv preprint arXiv:2309.14494.

Huang, S.-C., Jensen, M., Yeung-Levy, S., Lungren, M. P., Poon, H., & Chaudhari, A. S. (2025). A systematic review and implementation guidelines of multimodal Foundation Models in medical imaging. In Res. Sq. DOI: 10.21203/rs.3.rs-5537908/v1

Irfan, M., Elmogy, M., Gupta, S., Khalifa, F., & Dias, R. T. (Eds.). (2024 Aug 26). *AI-driven decentralized finance and the future of finance*. IGI Global., DOI: 10.4018/979-8-3693-6321-8

Isola, P., Zhu, J.-Y., Zhou, T., & Efros, A. A. (2017). Image-to-image translation with conditional adversarial networks. In *2017 IEEE Conference on Computer Vision and Pattern Recognition (CVPR)* (pp. 1125–1134). IEEE. DOI: 10.1109/CVPR.2017.632

Jadhav, S., Patil, J. A., Rachappa Jyoti, R., Kanase, O. S., & Satish Khadde, M. (2024). The Future of Content Creation: Leveraging AI for Code, Text, Music, and Video Generation. *2024 8th International Conference on Computing, Communication, Control and Automation (ICCUBEA)*, 1-7. DOI: 10.1109/ICCUBEA61740.2024.10775258

Jayavadivel, R., Arunachalam, M., Nagarajan, G., Shankar, B. P., Viji, C., & Rajkumar, N., (2024). Historical overview of AI adoption in libraries. In *AI-Assisted Library Reconstruction* (pp. 267–289). IGI Global., DOI: 10.4018/979-8-3693-2782-1.ch015

Joel, M. R., Ebenezer, V., Jeyaraj, K. A., Navaneethakrishnan, M., Arunadevi, R., & Jenifa, D. R. (2023). Decoding and analysing consumer feedback for companies and goods using machine learning. In *2023 Third International Conference on Artificial Intelligence and Smart Energy (ICAIS)* (pp. 1085-1091). IEEE. DOI: 10.1109/ICAIS56108.2023.10073801

Jose Diaz Rivera, J., Muhammad, A., & Song, W.-C. (2024). Securing digital identity in the zero trust architecture: A blockchain approach to privacy-focused multi-factor authentication. *IEEE Open Journal of the Communications Society*, 5, 2792–2814. DOI: 10.1109/OJCOMS.2024.3391728

Judge, C. S., Krewer, F., O'Donnell, M. J., Kiely, L., Sexton, D., Taylor, G. W., Skorburg, J. A., & Tripp, B. (2024). Multimodal artificial intelligence in medicine. *Kidney360*, 5(11), 1771–1779. DOI: 10.34067/KID.0000000000000556 PMID: 39167446

Kalra, S., Bansal, Y., Sharma, Y., & Chauhan, G. S. (2023). FakeSpotter: A blockchain-based trustworthy idea for fake news detection in social media. *J. Inf. Optimiz. Sci.*, 44(3), 515–527. DOI: 10.47974/JIOS-1411

Kamalov, F., Calonge, D. S., & Gurrib, I. (2023). *New Era of Artificial Intelligence in Education: Towards a Sustainable Multifaceted Revolution*. arXiv preprint arXiv:2305.18303.

Katsaridou, M. I., & Kostopoulou, L. (2023). The semiotics of animation: From traditional forms to contemporary innovations. *Punctum International Journal of Semiotics*, 9(2), 121–143. DOI: 10.18680/HSS.2024.0000

Kim, E., Isozaki, I., Sirkin, N., & Robson, M. (2023). Generative Artificial Intelligence Consensus in a Trustless Network. *arXiv preprint arXiv:2307.01898*.

Kingma, D. P., & Welling, M. (2013). Auto-encoding variational Bayes. *arXiv*. https://arxiv.org/abs/1312.6114

Krishna Jyothi, K., & Chaudhari, S. (2022). A novel block chain based cluster head authentication protocol for machine-type communication in LTE network: Statistical analysis on attack detection. *Journal of King Saud University. Computer and Information Sciences*, *34*(6), 3713–3721. DOI: 10.1016/j.jksuci.2020.08.014

Kshetri, N., Hutson, J., & Revathy, G. (2023, December). healthAIChain: Improving security and safety using Blockchain Technology applications in AI-based healthcare systems. In *2023 3rd International Conference on Innovative Mechanisms for Industry Applications (ICIMIA)* (pp. 159-164). IEEE.

Kulothungan, V. (2025). Using blockchain ledgers to record the AI decisions in IoT. In *Preprints*.

Ku, M., Jiang, D., Wei, C., Yue, X., & Chen, W. (2023). Viescore: Towards explainable metrics for conditional image synthesis evaluation. arXiv. https://arxiv.org/abs/2312.14867

Kumar, V., (2024). *Generative AI and blockchain synergy for healthcare applications: privacy and trust at scale*. Health Inform J.

Lalitha, B., Ramalakshmi, K., Gunasekaran, H., Murugesan, P., Saminasri, P., & Rajkumar, N. (2024). Anticipating AI impact on library services: future opportunities and evolutionary prospects. In *Improving Library Systems with AI: Applications, Approaches, and Bibliometric Insights* (pp. 195–213). IGI Global., DOI: 10.4018/979-8-3693-5593-0.ch014

Lamothe-Fernández, P., Alaminos, D., Lamothe-López, P., & Fernández-Gámez, M. A. (2020). Deep Learning Methods for Modeling Bitcoin Price. *Mathematics*, *8*(8), 1245. DOI: 10.3390/math8081245

Liu, R., Garrette, D. H., Saharia, C., Chan, W., Roberts, A., Narang, S., Blok, I., Mical, R. J., Norouzi, M., & Constant, N. (2022). Character-aware models improve visual text rendering. In *Proceedings of the 60th Annual Meeting of the Association for Computational Linguistics* (pp. 7143–7157). Association for Computational Linguistics. DOI: 10.48550/arXiv.2212.10562

Liu, Y., (2023). Blockchain-empowered lifecycle management for AI-generated content (AIGC) products in edge networks. *ACM Transactions on Internet Technology*, DOI: 10.1109/MWC.003.2300053

Lu, H., Wang, S., Zhang, D., Huang, B., Chen, E., & Sui, Y. (2024). Toward accurate quality assessment of machine-generated infrared video using Fréchet Video Distance. *IEEE Access: Practical Innovations, Open Solutions*, *12*, 168837–168852. DOI: 10.1109/ACCESS.2024.3453406

Luo, Z., Chen, D., Zhang, Y., Huang, Y., Wang, L., Shen, Y., Zhao, D., Zhou, J., & Tan, T. (2023). VideoFusion: Decomposed diffusion models for high-quality video generation. arXiv. https://arxiv.org/abs/2303.08320

Maaz, M., Rasheed, H., Khan, S., & Khan, F. (2024). Videogpt+: Integrating image and video encoders for enhanced video understanding. arXiv. https://arxiv.org/abs/2406.09418

Mahadevappa, P., Muzammal, S. M., & Tayyab, M. (2024). Introduction to generative AI in web engineering. In *Advances in web technologies and engineering* (pp. 297–330). IGI Global. DOI: 10.4018/979-8-3693-3703-5.ch015

Mala, C. S. (2023). Revolutionizing industries with blockchain and AI: A journey into decentralized intelligence. In 3rd International Conference on AI ML, Data Science and Robotics. United Research Forum. DOI: 10.51219/URForum.2023. Chandana-Sree-Mala

Mandych, O., Staverska, T., & Maliy, O. (2023). Integration of artificial intelligence into the blockchain and cryptocurrency market. *MODELING THE DEVELOPMENT OF THE ECONOMIC SYSTEMS*, *4*(4), 61–66. DOI: 10.31891/mdes/2023-10-8

Mazhar, T., Khan, S., Shahzad, T., Khan, M. A., Saeed, M. M., Awotunde, J. B., & Hamam, H. (2025, January 13). Generative AI, IoT, and blockchain in healthcare: Application, issues, and solutions. *Discov Internet Things.*, *5*(1), 5. DOI: 10.1007/s43926-025-00095-8

Mazurczyk, W., Wendzel, S., & Zander, S. (2016). Unified description for network information hiding methods. *Journal of Universal Computer Science*, *22*(11), 1456–1486. DOI: 10.3217/jucs-022-11-1456

Meng, C., He, Y., Song, Y., Song, J., Wu, J., Zhu, J.-Y., & Ermon, S. (2021). SDEdit: Guided image synthesis and editing with stochastic differential equations. In *International Conference on Learning Representations*. DOI: 10.48550/arXiv.2108.01073

Mikolov, T., Sutskever, I., Chen, K., Corrado, G. S., & Dean, J. (2013). Distributed representations of words and phrases and their compositionality. In *Advances in Neural Information Processing Systems* (Vol. 26). https://papers.nips.cc/paper/5021-distributed-representations-of-words-and-phrases-and-their-compositionality

Mileva, A., Velinov, A., Hartmann, L., Wendzel, S., & Mazurczyk, W. (2021). Comprehensive analysis of MQTT 5.0 susceptibility to network covert channels. *Computers & Security*, *104*, 102207. Advance online publication. DOI: 10.1016/j. cose.2021.102207

Minkin, I. (2020). *Applications of the Compacted de Bruijn Graph in Comparative Genomics* (Doctoral dissertation, The Pennsylvania State University).

Mishra, S. (2024). Exploring the transformative potential and generative AI's multifaceted impact on diverse sectors. In Ara, A., & Ara, A. (Eds.), *Exploring the ethical implications of generative AI* (pp. 88–103). IGI Global. DOI: 10.4018/979-8-3693-1565-1.ch006

Moerel, L. (2018). Blockchain & data protection … and why they are not on a collision course. *Eur. Rev. Priv. Law*, *26*(6), 825–851. DOI: 10.54648/ERPL2018057

Mukhopadhyay, M. (2025). Golden brush and evolving canvas—Navigating the digital art and Non-fungible tokens. *J. Inf. Technol. Teach. Cases*, *15*(1), 123–132. DOI: 10.1177/20438869231215085

Nachiappan, B., Rajkumar, N., Jagannathan, J., Mohanraj, A., Karthikeyan, N., & Viji, C. (2025). Synergizing blockchain and collaborative networks. In *Leveraging Blockchain for Future-Ready Libraries* (pp. 285–318). IGI Global Scientific Publishing., DOI: 10.4018/979-8-3693-7783-3.ch013

Nachiappan, B., Viji, C., Mohanraj, A., Moorthi, I., Mir, M. H., & Rajkumar, N. (2025). Enhancing data security and accessibility in libraries through blockchain technology. In *Enhancing Security and Regulations in Libraries With Blockchain Technology* (pp. 87–116). IGI Global., DOI: 10.4018/979-8-3693-9616-2.ch005

Narayanan, C. A., Bharath, E., & Vijayakumar, R. (2024). Implications of virtual reality on environmental sustainability in restaurants based on AI. In *2024 10th International Conference on Communication and Signal Processing (ICCSP)* (pp. 1488–1493). IEEE. http://dx.doi.org/DOI: 10.1109/ICCSP60870.2024.10544119

Nash, A. (2024). Decentralized intelligence network (din). *arXiv preprint arXiv:2407.02461*.

Nassar, M., Salah, K., Ur Rehman, M. H., & Svetinovic, D. (2020). Blockchain for explainable and trustworthy artificial intelligence. *Wiley Interdisciplinary Reviews. Data Mining and Knowledge Discovery*, *10*(1), e1340.

Navidan, H., Moshiri, P. F., Nabati, M., Shahbazian, R., Ghorashi, S. A., Shah-Mansouri, V., & Windridge, D. (2021). Generative Adversarial Networks (GANs) in networking: A comprehensive survey & evaluation. *Computer Networks, 194,* 108149. DOI: 10.1016/j.comnet.2021.108149

Nayomi, B. D. D., Mallika, S. S., & Bhavsingh, M. (n.d.). A Cloud-Assisted Framework Utilizing Blockchain, Machine Learning, and Artificial Intelligence to Countermeasure Phishing Attacks in Smart Cities. *International Journal of Intelligent Systems and Applications in Engineering.*

Nguyen, C. T., Liu, Y., Du, H., Hoang, D. T., Niyato, D., Nguyen, D. N., & Mao, S. (2024, June 11). Generative AI-enabled blockchain networks: Fundamentals, applications, and case study. *IEEE Network, 39*(2), 232–241. DOI: 10.1109/MNET.2024.3412161

Nieminen, M. (2023). *The Transformer Model and Its Impact on the Field of Natural Language Processing.*

Nieto García, J. M., & Wyss, L. (2022). Jordan blocks and the Bethe Ansatz I: The eclectic spin chain as a limit. *Nuclear Physics B, 981,* 115860. DOI: 10.1016/j.nuclphysb.2022.115860

Nurudeen, M. O., Latilo, A., Imosemi, H. O., & Imosemi, Q. A. (2024). Integrative legal operating model design: Incorporating ai and blockchain in legal practice. *Global J. Res. Multidiscip. Studies, 2*(1), 1–16. DOI: 10.58175/gjrms.2024.2.1.0036

Okatani, N., Shioya, R., & Nakabayashi, Y. (2025). Effects of AI-generated motion pictograms on comprehension and user experience. *International Journal of Computer Science & Network Security, 25*(5), 159–171. DOI: 10.2139/ssrn.5107189

Omowole, B. M., Omokhoa, H. E., Ogundeji, I. A., & Achumie, G. O. (2022). Blockchain-enhanced financial transparency: A conceptual approach to reporting and compliance. *International Journal of Social Science Exceptional Research, 2*(5), 141–157. DOI: 10.54660/IJSSER.2022.1.1.141-157

Onyejelem, T. E., & Aondover, E. M. (2024). Digital generative multimedia tool theory (DGMTT): A theoretical postulation in the era of artificial intelligence. *Advances in Machine Learning and Artificial Intelligence, 5*(2), 1–9. DOI: 10.13140/RG.2.2.20175.70563

Oshani, S. (2022). Blockchain for Social Good: Combating Misinformation on the Web with AI and Blockchain. .DOI: 10.1145/3501247.3539016

P., U., S., A., M., K., & P., D. (2022). Potential Market-Predictive Features Based Bitcoin Price Prediction Using Machine Learning Algorithms: In A. Srinivasan (Ed.), *Advances in Computational Intelligence and Robotics* (pp. 233–245). IGI Global. DOI: 10.4018/978-1-7998-8892-5.ch014

Pal, A., Mitra, S., & Lakshmi, D. (2025). Illuminating the path from script to screen using lights, camera, and AI. In *Transforming cinema with artificial intelligence* (pp. 97–142). IGI Global. DOI: 10.4018/979-8-3693-3916-9.ch006

Park, C., Yang, Y., Park, K., & Lim, H. (2020). Decoding strategies for improving low-resource machine translation. *Electronics (Basel)*, 9(10), 1562. DOI: 10.3390/electronics9101562

Pasupuleti, M. K. (2025a). *Decentralized creativity: AI-infused blockchain for secure and transparent digital innovation.* National Education Services. DOI: 10.62311/nesx/rrvi125

Pecheranskyi, I., Oliinyk, O., Medvedieva, A., Danyliuk, V., & Hubernator, O. (2024). Perspectives of generative AI in the context of digital transformation of society, audio-visual media and mass communication: Instrumentalism, ethics and freedom. *Indian Journal of Information Sources and Services*, 14(4), 48–53. Advance online publication. DOI: 10.51983/ijiss-2024.14.4.08

Picha Edwardsson, M., & Al-Saqaf, W. (2024). Blockchain solutions for generative AI challenges in journalism. Front. Blockchain, 7.

Piller, F. T., Srour, M., & Marion, T. J. (2024). Generative AI, innovation, and trust. *The Journal of Applied Behavioral Science*, 60(4), 613–622.

Poonkuzhali, S., Shobana, M., & Jeyalakshm, J. (2023). A deep transfer learning approach for IoT/IIoT cyber attack detection using telemetry data. *Neural Network World*, 33(4), 205–224. DOI: 10.14311/NNW.2023.33.014

Poposki, Z. (2024). Critique of reification of art and creativity in the digital age: A Lukácsian approach to AI and NFT art. *Open Philosophy*, 7(1), 20240027. DOI: 10.1515/opphil-2024-0027

Pour, E. S., Jafari, H., Lashgari, A., Rabiee, E., & Ahmadisharaf, A. (2022a). Cryptocurrency Price Prediction with Neural Networks of LSTM and Bayesian Optimization. *European Journal of Business and Management Research*, 7(2), 20–27. DOI: 10.24018/ejbmr.2022.7.2.1307

Prajapati, C. (2025). AI and blockchain integration in finance. [IJISRT]. *International Journal of Innovation and Scientific Research*, 2537–2538.

Prasad, S. N., & Rekha, C. (2023). Block chain based IAS protocol to enhance security and privacy in cloud computing. *Measurement. Sensors, 28*, 100813. DOI: 10.1016/j.measen.2023.100813

Prather, J., Leinonen, J., Kiesler, N., Gorson Benario, J., Lau, S., MacNeil, S., & Zingaro, D. (2025). *Beyond the hype: A comprehensive review of current trends in generative AI research, teaching practices, and tools. In 2024 Working Group Reports on Innovation and Technology in Computer Science Education.* Association for Computing Machinery.

Priya, V., & Sofia, A. S. (2025). An efficient deep learning framework for malware image classification using gray-level co-occurrence matrix and sparse convolution. *Iranian Journal of Science and Technology. Transaction of Electrical Engineering, 49*(1), 65–88. DOI: 10.1007/s40998-024-00757-3

Puppala, S., Hossain, I., Alam, M. J., Talukder, S., Ferdaus, J., Hasan, M., . . . Mathukumilli, S. (2024). Generative AI like ChatGPT in Blockchain Federated Learning: use cases, opportunities and future. *arXiv preprint arXiv:2407.18358.*

Radford, A. (2021). Learning transferable visual models from natural language supervision. arXiv. https://arxiv.org/abs/2103.00020

Radford, A., Metz, L., & Chintala, S. (2015). Unsupervised representation learning with deep convolutional generative adversarial networks. *arXiv.* https://arxiv.org/abs/1511.06434

Raffel, C., Shazeer, N., Roberts, A., Lee, K., Narang, S., Matena, M., Zhou, Y., Li, W., & Liu, P. J. (2020). Exploring the limits of transfer learning with a unified text-to-text transformer. *Journal of Machine Learning Research, 21*(1), 5485–5551.

Raj, Y. A., Kumar, A., Kumar, V. D. A., Kumar, A., & Kumar, V. D. (2023). Prediction of cardiovascular disease using deep learning algorithms to prevent COVID-19. *Journal of Experimental & Theoretical Artificial Intelligence, 35*(6), 959–977. https://ui.adsabs.harvard.edu/link_gateway/2023JETAI.35.791S/doi:10.1080/0952813X.2021.1966842

Ramesh, A., Pavlov, M., Goh, G., Gray, S., Voss, C., Radford, A., Chen, M., & Sutskever, I. (2021). Zero-shot text-to-image generation. arXiv. https://arxiv.org/abs/2102.12092

Rane, N., Choudhary, S., & Rane, J. Blockchain and Artificial Intelligence (AI) integration for revolutionizing security and transparency in finance. *SSRN.* 2023 Nov 17. DOI: 10.2139/ssrn.4644253

Reuel, A., & Undheim, T. A. (2024). Generative AI needs adaptive governance. *arXiv preprint arXiv:2406.04554.*

Ria, J. (2023). Blockchain Technology and Its Synergy with Bitcoin, Information Technology Psychology, and AI: A Comprehensive Review. doi: DOI: 10.31234/osf.io/v23k9

Rombach, R., Blattmann, A., Lorenz, D., Esser, P., & Ommer, B. (2022). High-resolution image synthesis with latent diffusion models. arXiv. DOI: 10.1109/CVPR52688.2022.01042

RoselinKiruba, R., & et al. (2024). Text summarization based on feature extraction using GloVe and B-GRU. In *2024 2nd International Conference on Sustainable Computing and Smart Systems (ICSCSS)* (pp. 1–6). IEEE. DOI: 10.1109/ICSCSS60660.2024.10625311

Rzayev, K., Sakkas, A., & Urquhart, A. (2024). An adoption model of cryptocurrencies. *European Journal of Operational Research.* Advance online publication. DOI: 10.1016/j.ejor.2024.11.024

Sağlam, M. H., & Kirçova, I. (2025). The role of artificial intelligence in ad fraud detection in the blockchain and programmatic advertising ecosystem. In Advances in Marketing, Customer Relationship Management, and E-Services (pp. 43–82). IGI Global.

Saharia, C., Chan, W., Saxena, S., Li, L., Whang, J., Denton, E. L., Ghasemipour, K., Lopes, R. G., Ayan, B. K., Salimans, T., & Ho, J. (2022). Photorealistic text-to-image diffusion models with deep language understanding. *Advances in Neural Information Processing Systems, 35,* 36479–36494. DOI: 10.48550/arXiv.2205.11487

Salem, F. M., & Salem, F. M. (2022). Gated RNN: the gated recurrent unit (GRU) RNN. In *Recurrent neural networks: from simple to gated architectures* (pp. 85-100). DOI: 10.1007/978-3-030-89929-5_5

Salimans, T., Goodfellow, I., Zaremba, W., Cheung, V., Radford, A., & Chen, X. (2016). Improved techniques for training GANs. In *Advances in Neural Information Processing Systems* (Vol. 29). https://papers.nips.cc/paper/6125-improved-techniques-for-training-gans

Samad, A., Izani, M., Abdulla, D., Faiz, M., Wadood, R., & Hamdan, A. (2024). Innovative Workflow for AI-Generated Video: Addressing Limitations, Impact and Implications/ *2024 IEEE Symposium on Industrial Electronics & Applications (ISIEA),* 1-7. DOI: 10.1109/ISIEA61920.2024.10607369

Saranya, M., & Amutha, B. (2025). Comparative Analysis of Several Different Multimodal Methods for the Development of Generative Artificial Intelligence. In *Generative Artificial Intelligence and Ethics: Standards, Guidelines, and Best Practices* (pp. 109-126). IGI Global.

Sardana, A., Sethuraman, S., & Kalyanasundaram, P. D. (2024). Compliance-as-code 2.0: Orchestrating regulatory operations with agentic AI. Journal of Artificial Intelligence General Science (JAIGS), 5(1), 546–563.

Sarra, C. (2025). Artificial Intelligence in decision-making: A test of consistency between the "EU AI Act" and the "General Data Protection Regulation". *Athens J. Law*, *11*(1), 45–62. DOI: 10.30958/ajl.11-1-3

Sengar, S. S., Hasan, A. B., Kumar, S., & Carroll, F. (2024). Generative artificial intelligence: A systematic review and applications. *Multimedia Tools and Applications*, *84*(21), 23661–23700. Advance online publication. DOI: 10.1007/s11042-024-20016-1

Shamshad, H., Ullah, F., Ullah, A., Kebande, V. R., Ullah, S., & Al-Dhaqm, A. (2023). Forecasting and Trading of the Stable Cryptocurrencies With Machine Learning and Deep Learning Algorithms for Market Conditions. *IEEE Access : Practical Innovations, Open Solutions*, *11*, 122205–122220. DOI: 10.1109/AC-CESS.2023.3327440

Sharma, K. V., Sarada, Ch., Vasavi, M., & Ambika, K. (2024). Securing IoT Devices from DDoS Attacks through Blockchain and Multi-Code Trust Framework. *E3S Web of Conferences, 472*, 03001. DOI: 10.1051/e3sconf/202447203001

Shrestha, M., Ravichandran, Y., & Kim, E. (2024). Secure Multiparty Generative AI. *arXiv preprint arXiv:2409.19120*.

Singer, U., Polyak, A., Hayes, T., Yin, X., An, J., Zhang, S., Hu, Q., Yang, H., Ashual, O., Gafni, O., Kronrod, Y., & Lischinski, D. (2022). Make-a-video: Text-to-video generation without text-video data. arXiv. https://arxiv.org/abs/2209.14792

Singh, B., Wongmahesak, K., & Chandra, S. (2025). Transforming Digital Ownership and assessing role of blockchain technology and NFTs in future economy. In *Practical Strategies and Case Studies for Online Marketing 6.0* (pp. 343–368). IGI Global. DOI: 10.4018/979-8-3373-2058-8.ch015

Singh, R., Kim, J. Y., Glassy, E. F., Dash, R. C., Brodsky, V., Seheult, J., de Baca, M. E., Gu, Q., Hoekstra, S., & Pritt, B. S. (2025). Introduction to generative artificial intelligence: Contextualizing the future. *Archives of Pathology & Laboratory Medicine*, *149*(2), 112–122. DOI: 10.5858/arpa.2024-0221-RA PMID: 39631430

Sohl-Dickstein, J., Weiss, E., Maheswaranathan, N., & Ganguli, S. (2015). Deep unsupervised learning using nonequilibrium thermodynamics. In *International Conference on Machine Learning* (pp. 2256–2265). PMLR.

Sorna Shanthi, D., Vijay, P., Sam Blesswin, S., Sahithya, S., & Sreevarshini, R. (2023). RATSEL: A game-based evaluating tool for the dyslexic using augmented reality gamification. In Joshi, A., Mahmud, M., & Ragel, R. G. (Eds.), *Information and communication technology for competitive strategies (ICTCS 2021)* (pp. 703–713). Springer. DOI: 10.1007/978-981-19-0095-2_69

Sorna, S. D., Bhuvaneswaran, B., Manoj, A. R., & Pooja, S. (2023). MonuAR: M.A.R application for visualising 3D monuments. In *2023 International Conference on Networking and Communications (ICNWC)* (pp. 1–10). IEEE. DOI: 10.1109/ICNWC57852.2023.10127425

Sriram, K. P., Sujatha, P. K., Athinarayanan, S., Kanimozhi, G., & Joel, M. R. (2024, July). Transforming Agriculture: A Synergistic Approach Integrating Topology with Artificial Intelligence and Machine Learning for Sustainable and Data-Driven Practice. In *2024 2nd International Conference on Sustainable Computing and Smart Systems (ICSCSS)* (pp. 1350-1354). IEEE. DOI: 10.1109/ICSCSS60660.2024.10625446

Stone, D., Heinrichs, D., Angus, P., Gadd, M., Goda, J., Grove, T., Hall, R., Hamilton, C., Hays, S., Howard, B., Hulsey, S., Ianakiev, A., Jessop, N., Johnson, R., Jones, T., Keffer, M., Kouzes, R., LeBrun, T., Lewis, B., . . . Stephens, J. (2022). *Experiment Logistics for an International Blind Intercomparison Exercise for Nuclear Accident Dosimetry at Godiva-IV* (No. LLNL-TR-824087). Lawrence Livermore National Laboratory (LLNL), Livermore, CA (United States).

Su, J., Lu, Y., Pan, S., Murtadha, A., Wen, B., & Liu, Y. (2021). RoFormer: Enhanced transformer with rotary position embedding. arXiv. https://arxiv.org/abs/2104.09864

Sundar, K., Ravikumar, S., Jeyalakshmi, J., Berna, E., & Samuel, P. (2024). Streamlining attendance with fast face recognition model. In *2024 8th International Conference on I-SMAC (IoT in Social, Mobile, Analytics and Cloud)(I-SMAC)* (pp. 811–816). IEEE. DOI: 10.1109/I-SMAC61858.2024.10714689

Suripeddi, M. K. S., & Purandare, P. (2021). Blockchain and GDPR – A study on compatibility issues of the distributed ledger technology with GDPR data processing. *Journal of Physics: Conference Series*, *1964*(4), 42005. DOI: 10.1088/1742-6596/1964/4/042005

Szegedy, C., Liu, W., Jia, Y., Sermanet, P., Reed, S., Anguelov, D., & Rabinovich, A. (2015). Going deeper with convolutions. In *2015 IEEE Conference on Computer Vision and Pattern Recognition (CVPR)* (pp. 1–9). IEEE. DOI: 10.1109/CVPR.2015.7298594

Tang, Y., Guo, J., Liu, P., Wang, Z., Hua, H., Zhong, J.-X., & Yang, H. (2025). Generative AI for cel-animation: A survey. *arXiv*. https://arxiv.org/abs/2501.06250

Tang, Y., Wang, S., & Munos, R. (2025). Learning to chain-of-thought with Jensen's evidence lower bound. arXiv. https://arxiv.org/abs/2503.19618

Thin, A., Kotelevskii, N., Doucet, A., Durmus, A., Moulines, E., & Panov, M. (2021). Monte Carlo variational auto-encoders. In *International Conference on Machine Learning* (pp. 10247–10257). PMLR.

Tian, R., Kong, L., Min, X., & Qu, Y. (2022, May). Blockchain for ai: A disruptive integration. In *2022 IEEE 25th International Conference on Computer Supported Cooperative Work in Design (CSCWD)* (pp. 938-943). IEEE.

Tian, J., Xiong, G., Li, Z., & Gou, G. (2020). A survey of key technologies for constructing network covert channels. *Security and Communication Networks, 2020. Security and Communication Networks, 8892896*, 1–20. DOI: 10.1155/2020/8892896

Tian, Y., Yang, L., Yang, H., Gao, Y., Deng, Y., Wang, X., Wang, Y., Yu, Z., Tao, X., Wan, P., Zhang, D., & Cui, B. (2024). Videotetris: Towards compositional text-to-video generation. *Advances in Neural Information Processing Systems, 37*, 29489–29513.

Turner, R. E., Diaconu, C. D., Markou, S., Shysheya, A., Foong, A. Y., & Mlodozeniec, B. (2024). Denoising diffusion probabilistic models in six simple steps. arXiv. https://arxiv.org/abs/2402.04384

Vaccari, I., Narteni, S., Aiello, M., Mongelli, M., & Cambiaso, E. (2021). Exploiting Internet of Things protocols for malicious data exfiltration activities. *IEEE Access : Practical Innovations, Open Solutions, 9*, 104261–104280. DOI: 10.1109/ACCESS.2021.3099642

Vallis, C., Wilson, S., & Casey, A. (2024). Generative AI. In *ASCILITE 2024 Conference Proceedings* (pp. 590–595). Australasian Society for Computers in Learning in Tertiary Education. DOI: 10.14742/apubs.2024.1408

Van den Oord, A., Kalchbrenner, N., & Kavukcuoglu, K. (2016). Pixel recurrent neural networks. In *Proceedings of the 33rd International Conference on Machine Learning* (Vol. 48, pp. 1747–1756). PMLR. http://proceedings.mlr.press/v48/oord16.html

Vanderhallen, S., Van Bulck, J., Piessens, F., & Mühlberg, J. T. (2021). Robust authentication for automotive control networks through covert channels. *Computer Networks, 193*, 108079. Advance online publication. DOI: 10.1016/j.comnet.2021.108079

Varadarajan, M. N., Rajkumar, N., Viji, C., & Mohanraj, A. (2024). AI-powered financial operation strategy for cloud computing cost optimization for the future. Salud. *Ciencia y Tecnología-Serie de Conferencias.*, *3*, 694. DOI: 10.56294/sct-conf2024694

Vaswani, A., Shazeer, N., Parmar, N., Uszkoreit, J., Jones, L., Gomez, A. N., . . . Polosukhin, I. (2017). Attention is all you need. In *Advances in Neural Information Processing Systems* (Vol. 30). https://papers.nips.cc/paper/7181-attention-is-all-you-need

Vayadande, K. (2024). Generative AI-powered framework. In *Deep learning model optimization, deployment and improvement techniques for edge-native applications* (p. 311).

Vundela, S. R., & Kathiravan, M. (2025). Virtual reality technology and artificial intelligence for television and film animation. *Journal of Advanced Research in Applied Sciences and Engineering Technology*, *43*(1), 263–273. DOI: 10.37934/araset.43.1.263273

Wang, F.-Y., Yang, J., Wang, X., Li, J., & Han, Q.-L. (2023). Chat with ChatGPT on Industry 5.0: Learning and decision-making for intelligent industries. *IEEE/CAA Journal of Automatica Sinica, 10*(4), 831–834.

Wang, Y., Chen, X., Ma, X., Zhou, S., Huang, Z., Wang, Y., Yang, C., He, Y., Yu, J., Yang, P., Guo, Y., Wu, T., Si, C., Jiang, Y., Chen, C., Loy, C. C., Dai, B., Lin, D., Qiao, Y., & Liu, Z. (2023). *LaVie: High-Quality Video Generation with Cascaded Latent Diffusion Models.* arXiv preprint arXiv:2309.15103. https://arxiv.org/abs/2309.15103

Wang, H., Zhou, M., Jia, X., Wei, H., Hu, Z., Li, W., Chen, Q., & Wang, L. (2025). Recent progress on artificial intelligence-enhanced multimodal sensors integrated devices and systems. *Journal of Semiconductors*, *46*(1), 11610. DOI: 10.1088/1674-4926/24090041

Wang, X., Yu, Z., Tao, X., Wan, P., Zhang, D., & Cui, B. (2024). VideoTetris: Towards compositional text-to-video generation. arXiv. https://arxiv.org/abs/2406.04277

Wang, Y., Bilinski, P., Bremond, F., & Dantcheva, A. (2020). Imaginator: Conditional spatio-temporal GAN for video generation. In *Proceedings of the IEEE/CVF Winter Conference on Applications of Computer Vision* (pp. 1160–1169). DOI: 10.1109/WACV45572.2020.9093492

Wang, Y., Chen, X., Ma, X., Zhou, S., Huang, Z., Wang, Y., Zhang, L., Zhang, Y., Cao, Y., Li, H., Qiao, Y., & Liu, Z. (2025). Lavie: High-quality video generation with cascaded latent diffusion models. *International Journal of Computer Vision, 133*(5), 3059–3078. DOI: 10.1007/s11263-024-02295-1

Wee, J. (2018). *Tee., Raja, Kumar, Murugesan.* Trust Network, Blockchain and Evolution in Social Media to Build Trust and Prevent Fake News., DOI: 10.1109/ICACCAF.2018.8776822

Wei, Y., Zhang, S., Qing, Z., Yuan, H., Liu, Z., Liu, Y., Wang, J., Zhang, W., & Shan, H. (2024). Dreamvideo: Composing your dream videos with customized subject and motion. In *Proceedings of the IEEE/CVF Conference on Computer Vision and Pattern Recognition* (pp. 6537-6549).

Wu, T., He, S., Liu, J., Sun, S., Liu, K., Han, Q.-L., & Tang, Y. (2023). A brief overview of ChatGPT: The history, status quo and potential future development. *IEEE/CAA Journal of Automatica Sinica, 10*(5), 1122–1136. DOI: 10.1109/JAS.2023.123618

Wu, C., Huang, L., Zhang, Q., Li, B., Ji, L., Yang, F., Sapiro, G., & Duan, N. (2021). GODIVA: Generating open-domain videos from natural descriptions. arXiv. https://arxiv.org/abs/2104.14806

Wu, C., Liang, J., Ji, L., Yang, F., Fang, Y., Jiang, D., & Duan, N. (2021). NÜWA: Visual synthesis pre-training for neural visual world creation. arXiv. https://arxiv.org/abs/2111.12417

Wu, Z., Wang, Y., Shen, X., Xiong, Q., & Liu, G. (2021). A review of steganography and steganalysis in Voice over IP. *Sensors (Basel), 21*(4), 1032. DOI: 10.3390/s21041032 PMID: 33546240

Xue, L., Barua, A., Constant, N., Al-Rfou, R., Narang, S., Kale, M., Roberts, A., & Raffel, C. (2022). ByT5: Towards a token-free future with pre-trained byte-to-byte models. *Transactions of the Association for Computational Linguistics, 10*, 291–306. DOI: 10.1162/tacl_a_00461

Xu, P., Zhu, X., & Clifton, D. A. (2023). Multimodal learning with Transformers: A survey. *IEEE Transactions on Pattern Analysis and Machine Intelligence, 45*(10), 12113–12132. DOI: 10.1109/TPAMI.2023.3275156 PMID: 37167049

Yadav, P., Rathwad, G., & Jain, J. (2024). Generative AI: Shaping the future while disrupting the present. *International Journal for Multidisciplinary Research, 6*(5), 28085. Advance online publication. DOI: 10.36948/ijfmr.2024.v06i05.28085

Yang, Z., Teng, J., Zheng, W., Ding, M., Huang, S., Xu, J., Zhang, L., Wang, W., & Tang, J. (2024). Cogvideox: Text-to-video diffusion models with an expert trans-former. arXiv. https://arxiv.org/abs/2408.06072

Yenduri, G., Ramalingam, M., Selvi, G. C., Supriya, Y., Srivastava, G., Maddikunta, P. K. R., Raj, G. D., Jhaveri, R. H., Prabadevi, B., Wang, W., Vasilakos, A. V., & Gadekallu, T. R. (2024). GPT (Generative Pre-trained Transformer)—A comprehensive review on enabling technologies, potential applications, emerging challenges, and future directions. *IEEE Access : Practical Innovations, Open Solutions*, *12*, 54608–54649. DOI: 10.1109/ACCESS.2024.3389497

Ye, Z., Wu, Y., Chen, H., Pan, Y., & Jiang, Q. (2022). A Stacking Ensemble Deep Learning Model for Bitcoin Price Prediction Using Twitter Comments on Bitcoin. *Mathematics*, *10*(8), 1307. DOI: 10.3390/math10081307

Yin, L. (2024). A review of text-to-image synthesis methods. In *2024 5th International Conference on Computer Vision, Image and Deep Learning (CVIDL)* (pp. 858–861). IEEE. DOI: 10.1109/CVIDL62147.2024.10603609

Yli-Huumo, J., Ko, D., Choi, S., Park, S., & Smolander, K. (2016). Where Is Current Research on Blockchain Technology?—A Systematic Review. *PLoS One*, *11*(10), e0163477. DOI: 10.1371/journal.pone.0163477 PMID: 27695049

Zafar, A. (2025). Reconciling blockchain technology and data protection laws: Regulatory challenges, technical solutions, and practical pathways. *Journal of Cybersecurity*, *11*(1), tyaf002. DOI: 10.1093/cybsec/tyaf002

Zhang, H., Goodfellow, I., Metaxas, D., & Odena, A. (2019). Self-attention generative adversarial networks. In *Proceedings of the 36th International Conference on Machine Learning* (Vol. 97, pp. 7354–7363). PMLR. http://proceedings.mlr.press/v97/zhang19d.html

Zhang, Z., Rao, Y., Xiao, H., Xiao, X., & Yang, Y. (2024). Proof of quality: A costless paradigm for trustless generative ai model inference on blockchains. *arXiv preprint arXiv:2405.17934*.

Zhang, L., Huang, T., Rasheed, W., Hu, X., & Zhu, T. (2019). An enlarging-the-capacity packet sorting covert channel. *IEEE Access : Practical Innovations, Open Solutions*, *7*, 145634–145640. DOI: 10.1109/ACCESS.2019.2945320

Zhang, L., Rao, A., & Agrawala, M. (2023). Adding conditional control to text-to-image diffusion models. In *Proceedings of the IEEE/CVF International Conference on Computer Vision* (pp. 3836–384). IEEE. DOI: 10.1109/ICCV51070.2023.00355

Zhang, Z., Rao, Y., Xiao, H., Xiao, X., & Yang, Y. (2024)Proof of quality: A costless paradigm for trustless generative AI model inference on blockchains.

Zhuk, A. (2025). Beyond the blockchain hype: Addressing legal and regulatory challenges. *SN Social Sciences*, *5*(2), 11. DOI: 10.1007/s43545-024-01044-y

Zon-Yin, S. (2019). *Jeffrey, J., P., Tsai*. AI Blockchain Platform for Trusting News., DOI: 10.1109/ICDCS.2019.00160

About the Contributors

G. Revathy has been working as a academic professional for past 15 years. She has numerous publications in the field of Artificial intelligence and wireless mesh networks. She has also been an editor for the book "Advanced Applications of Osmotic Computing" by IGI Publishers.

Arul Kumar Natarajan currently serves as an Assistant Professor in the Department of Computer Science at the Samarkand International University of Technology in Uzbekistan. He earned his Doctor of Philosophy degree in Computer Science from Bharathidasan University, India, in 2017. Concurrently, he is engaged in postdoctoral research in Generative AI for Cybersecurity at the Singapore Institute of Technology, Singapore. Throughout his 14-year teaching career, Dr. Arul has held esteemed positions at various institutions, including Christ University, Bishop Heber College in India, and Debre Berhan University in Ethiopia. Dr. Arul has made significant contributions to academia, specializing in cybersecurity and artificial intelligence, as evidenced by his portfolio of scholarly works. He has authored 52 peer-reviewed and internationally indexed publications and delivered 35 conference presentations. Additionally, he has edited and published 04 books with IGI Global, USA, which are indexed in Scopus and focus on Artificial Intelligence and Cybersecurity. He also has 04 more books in the processing stage with IGI Global, Wiley, and Springer. In addition to his academic pursuits, Dr. Arul is a prolific innovator. He has 17 patents granted in India and 1 granted in the United Kingdom, spanning diverse fields such as communication and computer science. His latest work involves 1 copyrighted research (Govt. of India) in Artificial Intelligence and Machine Learning, specifically focused on segmenting, classifying, and tracking issue nuclei in images. Dr. Arul also exhibits notable proficiency in networking and cybersecurity, having completed the CCNA Routing and Switching Exam from CISCO and the Networking Fundamentals exam from Microsoft. He continues to demonstrate a strong interest in Generative AI for Cybersecurity.

Naresh Kshetri is an excellent academician working in USA. His area of interest are block chain and cyber defense.

***

Kiran A. is currently pursuing his Bachelor of Technology degree in Computer Science and Business Systems at K.S. Rangasamy College of Technology, Tiruchengode, Tamil Nadu, India. He has developed a keen interest in areas such as data analytics, machine learning, and software development. Throughout his academic journey, he has actively participated in technical projects and research activities aimed at integrating computational technologies with business processes. His research interests include artificial intelligence, cloud computing, and business intelligence systems. Mr. Kiran aspires to apply his knowledge and skills towards innovative solutions that address real-world business challenges through technology.

Maragatham G. is working as Associate Professor, School of Computing, SRM Institute of Science and Technology. She has more than fifteen years of interdisciplinary academic teaching and research experience. She is a member of the Artificial Intelligence and Machine Learning research group. Her research interests span various areas in cyber-security of cloud computing, Data Mining Techniques, the Internet of Things, 5G wireless networks, and big data systems. She has received several recognitions, three patents and published of her research papers with international journals.

Nagarajan G. is currently working as Professor in the Department of Computer Science & Engineering in Saveetha of Engineering at SIMATS, Chennai - TamilNadu, India. He received his Ph.D. in Galgotias University, Utta Praddesh, India. His current research interests Cloud Computing, Big Data, Security, Data Analytics and AI. He published more then 14-research article also attended various conference and he has Indian patent also. He is member of International Association of Engineers (IAENG), The Institute of Research Engineers and Doctors (IRED), and International Association of Computer Science and Information Technology (IACSIT).

Eugene Berna I. is currently working as an Assistant Professor in the Department of Artificial Intelligence and Machine Learning, Bannari Amman Institute of Technology, Sathyamangalam. She completed her M.E in Computer Science and Engineering from Dhanalakshmi Srinivasan Engineering College, Anna University. She is pursuing her PhD from Anna University in Information and Communication Engineering and presently working in Machine Learning, Natural

Language Processing and Deep Learning Projects. She has teaching experience of more than 10 years.

Jude Moses Anto Devakanth J. is an Assistant Professor in the Department of Computer Applications, Madanapalle Institute of Technology & Science, Madanapalle, Andhra Pradesh, India. He was awarded with Doctorate in Computer Applications from Manonmaniam Sundaranar University in the year of 2024, Tirunelveli. He received his Mphil in Computer Science from Manonmaniam Sundaranar University, Tirunelveli in 2016 and MCA in Computer Applications from Manonmaniam Sundaranar University, Tirunelveli in 2015. He has published 6 research articles in International and National Journals and 1 in Web of Science. His areas of interest are Artificial Intelligence & Machine Learning, Deep Learning, Image Compression, Big Data Analytics and Network Security.

Obuli Prasad J. is currently pursuing his Bachelor of Technology degree in Computer Science and Business Systems at K.S. Rangasamy College of Technology, Tiruchengode, Tamil Nadu, India. He has demonstrated strong academic performance and actively engages in research activities within the fields of data science, machine learning, and business systems. His academic journey has been marked by several honors and recognitions, reflecting his dedication to excellence in the computing domain. His research interests include artificial intelligence, software engineering, and modern business technologies. Mr. Prasad aims to contribute to cutting-edge innovations that bridge the gap between computer science theory and practical business applications.

M. Robinson Joel received the Doctorate Ph.D degree in Computer and Information Technology from the Manonmaniam Sundaranar University, Tirunelveli in March 2019. He completed his M.Tech and MCA from the same university year 2008 and 2002 respectively. He is currently working as an Associate Professor in the Department of Computer Science and Engineering at KCG College of Technology, Chennai. He has 16 years of teaching experience.

Vijay K. is working as Assistant Professor (SG) in the Department of Artificial Intelligence and Machine Learning Rajalakshmi Engineering College, Chennai, Tamilnadu, India. He is B.Tech., M.E., graduate and pursuing PhD in Anna University, Chennai in the area of Cloud Computing. Having 17 years of experience in teaching. Received the award, "Active Participation Youth", under CSI Service Award at the CSI Annual Convention 2016. He was awarded with "Inspire Faculty Partnership Level award" in 2017 (Bronze Level) by Infosys. He is a life time member of Computer Society of India, IEI-India. He received the Best Faculty Award many times. Presented / Published more than 100+ papers in various Conferences,

Book Chapters and Reputed Journals. His areas of interest include Cloud Computing, Image Processing, IOT and Machine Learning.

Sharmila L. is working as a Professor in the Department of Computer Science & Engineering at Vel Tech Rangarajan Dr. Sagunthala R&D Institute of Science and Technology, Chennai, India. She received her M.E., and Ph.D. degrees in Computer Science and Engineering from Anna University and Sathyabama University. She has secured distinction in both B.E., and M.E. She is an Anna University Rank Holder in PG degree. She has 19 years of Teaching Experience with 6 years of research experience. She is a reviewer for many SCI Indexed Journals like Ambient Intelligence and Humanized Computing (Springer), Journal of Supercomputing, Computer Communications (Elsevier), Microprocessor and Microsystems, Wiley and so on. Her main area of research activity is Data Mining, Medical Image processing, Wireless Networks, Network security, Big data analytics. She has published many research articles in refereed journals like Elsevier and Springer. She has been serving as an Organizing Chair and Program Chair of several International conferences and in the Program Committees of several National / International conferences.

Santhosh Kumar M. is an Assistant Professor in the Department of Computer Science and Engineering (Cyber Security) at Nandha Engineering College, Erode. With a strong academic background and a keen interest in the field of cyber security, he contributes to the development of knowledge and skills among students. Through his teaching, research, and dedication to fostering a deeper understanding of the ever-evolving cybersecurity landscape, he plays a key role in preparing the next generation of professionals to address modern technological challenges.

Balusamy Nachiappan is an experienced IT professional with a strong background in object-oriented Software Development, Design, and Architecture. Certified as a Salesforce System Architect and Salesforce Application Architect. Specialized in Banking, including Investment Banking and Core Banking, with international exposure. Extensive experience in the Travel Domain encompassing Airlines, Ship & Cargo industries, along with proficiency in Supply Chain Management and Real Estate. A solid track record of over a decade in Product Development across various sectors. Proficient in Waterfall, V Model, and Agile-Scrum methodologies. Holds extensive onsite exposure in the US, Japan, the UK, and Qatar.

Umamaheswari P. holds a B.E. in Information Technology from Periyar Maniammai College of Engineering and Technology (2003), an M.B.A. from Alagappa University, Karaikudi, Tamil Nadu (2006), and an M.Tech in Computer

Science from SASTRA Deemed University, Thanjavur, Tamil Nadu (2011). She earned her Ph.D. in Computer Science and Engineering from SASTRA Deemed University. With two decades of experience, she has taught both undergraduate and postgraduate courses in Computer Science. She is currently an Assistant Professor in the Department of Computer Science and Engineering at SRC Campus, SASTRA University, Kumbakonam. Her research interests focus on Data Mining, Machine Learning, and Deep Learning. She has published numerous research papers in international conferences, SCI-indexed journals, Scopus, and book chapters.

Jamshid Pardaev is working as an associate professor in the Department of Finance and Tourism at Termez University of Economics and Service, Termez, Uzbekistan.

Albert Paulin Michael is an Assistant Professor of Computer Applications in Erode Sengunthar Engineering College (Autonomous), Erode. He has 11 years of experience in teaching. He has secured his MCA Degree from Madurai Kamaraj University and MPhil degree from Bharathidasan university. He has published Three research paper in various peer reviewed national/international journals and also presented over eight papers in various international/national conferences. His areas of interest includes computer networks, image processing, web technology, big data analytics.

Karthik R. is currently serving as an Assistant Professor in the Department of Computer Science and Business Systems at K.S. Rangasamy College of Technology, Tiruchengode, Tamil Nadu, India. He holds a postgraduate degree in computer science and has several years of experience in academia, specializing in teaching and research. His areas of expertise include data structures, machine learning, and business analytics. He has guided numerous undergraduate research projects and has actively contributed to scholarly publications in national and international journals. His research interests encompass artificial intelligence, big data technologies, and business system integration. Mr. Karthik is dedicated to fostering innovation and bridging the gap between academic theory and practical application in the field of computer science.

Menaha R. received B.E Computer Science engineering degree from Bharadhidhasan University, Trichy, in 2003. She completed M.E computer science engineering degree from Anna University, Chennai, India in 2012 and awarded doctoral degree from Anna University, Chennai, India, in 2021. She has 2 years' industry experience and 19 years teaching experience. Now, she is currently working as Associate professor in Sri Eshwar College of Engineering, Coimbatore. She published 12 articles in journals, 3 articles in book chapter, 9 papers in reputed international conferences. She has Published 6 patents including 1 design patent. Her research interest includes Machine learning, Natural Language Processing, Data Mining, Data Analysis. She has reviewed multiple journal papers. She has membership in ISTE, IAENG, IETE, IENG.

Ravikumar R. N. is an experienced educator with 11+ years of teaching in Computer Science across India and overseas. Currently an Assistant Professor at Marwadi University, Rajkot, he specializes in Advanced Java, Machine Learning, Data Science, and AI. He holds a Mini MBA from the Swiss eLearning Institute (2015), an M.E. in Computer Science Engineering from VMRF University (2013), and a B.E. from Anna University (2010). Completed PhD at Amity University, Jaipur, he is dedicated to research, professional development, and advancing education through technology.

Balaji Ragunathan is currently pursuing his Bachelor of Technology degree in Computer Science and Business Systems at K.S. Rangasamy College of Technology, Tiruchengode, Tamil Nadu, India. He has actively engaged in research and technical projects focused on machine learning, cybersecurity, and full-stack development. He has completed internships at reputed organizations including the Indian Space Research Organisation (ISRO) and Salesforce, enhancing his practical skills in software development and data analytics. His research interests include artificial intelligence, covert timing channel detection, and secure computing systems. Balaji R is committed to contributing to innovative solutions at the intersection of computer science and business technologies.

Vinston Raja R. is an Assistant Professor in the Department of Computational Intelligence in SRM Institute of Science and Technology, SRM Nagar, Kattankulathur with 15 years of teaching experience. He has completed his PhD in the area of Deep Learning at Sathyabama Institute of Science and Technology. He also completed his M.Tech IT at Sathyabama University in 2012. Before becoming a professor, he worked as a Software Developer at Dexter Matrix Solution from 2007 to 2009. Dr. Raja's areas of interest are IOT with Wireless Sensor Networks, Robotics and Artificial Intelligence. He was awarded the Best Teacher Award in the academic year 2017-2018. He has experience in guiding student development projects and has presented many research papers at International and National Conferences. Additionally, he has published ten papers in International and National Journals and ten Anna University Curriculum textbooks.

N.Rajkumar is an Associate Professor in the Department of Computer Science and Engineering. He earned his Ph.D. in Information and Communication Engineering from Anna University, Chennai. With a rich experience of 15 years in the realm of technical education, he has made substantial contributions to the academic arena. His research background is highly commendable, encompassing over 20 publications in esteemed international journals, coupled with numerous presentations at both international and national conferences. Moreover, he actively engages as a member of prestigious professional societies such as ISTE, IAENG, and CSTA. His primary areas of interest comprise Software Engineering, Computer Networks, Internet of Things, and Machine Learning.

C. Viji holds the position of Associate Professor in the Department of Computer Science and Engineering. She accomplished her Ph.D. in Information and Communication Engineering from Anna University, Chennai. Dr. C. Viji's expertise in the realm of technical education has resulted in noteworthy contributions to the academic sphere. Her research background is indeed impressive, encompassing over 10 publications in esteemed international journals, along with numerous presentations at both international and national conferences. Furthermore, she actively engages as a member of renowned professional societies such as IAENG and CSTA.

Arockia Raj Y. is presently working as an Assistant Professor of Computer Science and Engineering department in PSNA College of Engineering and Technology, Dindigul, Tamilnadu, India. Affiliated to Anna University- Chennai, Tamilnadu, India. He has received Ph.D. Degree from Anna University, Chennai in the year 2019. He has completed B.Tech Information Technology in the year 2006 and M.E Computer Science and Engineering in the year 2009 at Anna University, Chennai. He had published and presented more than 20 research papers in National, International Journals and Conferences. His research interest focuses on Image processing. He is an active life time member of ISTE and IFERP.

Index

S

T

V

www.ingramcontent.com/pod-product-compliance
Lightning Source LLC
Chambersburg PA
CBHW080908220326
41598CB00034B/5511